CHRISTIAN ACTION
AND
OPENNESS TO THE WORLD

CHRISTIAN ACTION

AND

OPENNESS TO THE WORLD

Edited by Joseph Papin

The Villanova University Press

03021

Volume II
Library of Congress Catalog Number 72-155-102
Complete Series SBN—87723-007-2
Volume II—SBN 87723-009-9

Volume III
Library of Congress Catalog Number 76-155-103
Complete Series SBN 87723-007-2
Volume III SBN 87723-010-2

Printed in the United States of America by
Abbey Press
Saint Meinrad, Indiana 47577

First printing: 1000 copies
1-100 are numbered

7.65   6-12-73

Gratefully dedicated to the serene memory of my mother, Mrs. Helen Papin, who, on the 12th of September, 1970, in her native Slovakia passed from the Hands of God into His Heart during the preparation of these volumes.

Editor

Contents

*God had anointed him with the Holy Spirit and
with power, and because God was with him, Jesus
went about doing good and curing all* ... The Jerusalem Bible, *Ac 10:38* †

*Apart from Christ, we know neither what our life
nor our death is; we do not know what God is nor
what we ourselves are.*

Pascal, Pensées

*That calm and joy in thy soul
is the first fruit to thee of recompense
And heaven begun*

Cardinal Newman, Dream of Gerontius

*And God, being at once transcendental in Himself
(abiding beyond the limits of the world),
at the same time in relation to the world
appears as the active creative force
which becomes incarnate
in order to communicate to the world-soul
what it seeks and yearns namely for fullness of being
in the form of all—unity.*

Vl. S. Soloviev, Lectures on Godmanhood

*The age of nations is past
The task before us now,
if we would not perish,
is to build the earth*

Teilhard de Chardin

*Le nom de Dieu était chéri
Plus que la vie*

Lena Allen-Shore, Le Dieu Qui Chante

ix

Yahweh, I am your servant,
Your servant, son of a pious mother

The Jerusalem Bible, *Ps* 116:16

CHRISTIAN ACTION

Edited by Joseph Papin

Volume II

The Villanova University Press

Second Sight: From Aggiornamento to Approfondimento

Joseph Papin

WITH aggiornamento (keeping abreast of the times) action started, but with approfondimento, (deepening of theological thought, adopted from the Second Vatican Council)[1] strong action was taken to amend the occurrence of superficiality in updatedness.

With aggiornamento we have started a new beginning, a new milestone in man's "savoir vivre" and "savoir faire." But this brought in also two inevitable dangers facing Christian religious thought: first a reduction of Christianity to the status of a precious relic of a previous era, considered irrelevant to modern times; second, a tendency to reject the Bible as a mythology.[2] The honeymoon with the Bible (to use Krister Stendahl's expression) so noticeable among biblical scholars in the last few decades is over.

Christianity accepted the "Old" Testament as its adopted child in harmony with its natural child, which is the "New" Testament. With this written charter[3] (guaranteed by the Spirit of God) crystallized in antiquity, the Christian faith has been able without betrayal to adjust itself to the needs of succeeding centuries to ensure complete conformity of man's insight with the will of Yahweh, revealed in the "Old" Testament[4] and sealed in Christ.

This crystallization must not be confused with fossilization as may be stridulously proclaimed by some in the last scurrying decades of the twentieth century.

The Bible must be read today in context with today's problems of man facing the realities of a changing world, problems which in contrast with the problems of two thousand years ago seem to be altogether new.

But life-death, love-hate encompassing the whole of man's prob-

1

lems are not changeable; the guidelines given by Christ simply assume different proportions.

Our culture, philosophy, theology, and human sciences in general experience crisis because man has experienced it first.

The long-familiar horizons fade away. The magnitude of the cosmos confronts man. Today's man is prone to descend into mythology. Contemporary secularism is less inhibited in relation to earthly realities. In the Marxist's Weltanschauung (view), a Christian is helpless in facing the future of the world. I want to present here briefly that the relationship between faith and the world of today is not arbitrary any more. Man today is threatened by loss of his understanding of history in connection with eschatological history. Is our faith able to face calmly these new trends towards secularity within the framework of Christ's redeeming liberation of man? Common human destiny cannot be isolated from the reaction to modern life. It would be equally one-sided to view the violent reaction to the new re-examination as a decay of the traditional values of faith in a faithless, secularistic world. We must admit that present-day revolutionary thinking brings something positive and theologically meaningful. It is not just a new form of escapism from traditional values. The new development of Christian doctrine started by Newman, Soloviev, Baur, Kierkegaard, Franzelin, Scheeben and Harnack paved a new way for advancement in Christian theology and penetrated gradually all dimensions of today's man. Emergence of the third world, the world of non-Christians, until now culpably neglected, is in our midst and we have to take the challenge today.

I do not intend to say that theology or the pluralities of theologies will solve all problems of Christians in secular polities, but pluralities of theologies will definitely contribute to the new vision of man in his continuous search for God.

The guidelines of tradition or traditions and the new insights presented in "The Villanova University Series" indicate a "raison d'être" for the emergence of the pluralities of theologies which presumably will shape the theology of the future.

The demands of today's man have changed, at least partially, the structure of institutionalized religion. This cannot be ignored.

The conditions of the modern world make it difficult for a speculative theologian to ignore these new demands of the modern man. A speculative theology must give renewed attention to the issues and not circumvent the validity of these newly arisen speculative, practical, and ethical issues.

Growth has to happen, otherwise there is no life.

Action, progress, development are necessary, but the wings of man are thoughts. Therefore, *The Dynamic In Christian Thought*[5] preceded *The Dynamic In Christian Action*,[6] as a preamble to *Openness To The World*[7] of *The Pilgrim People*[8] who walked through the darkness with only light in their soul: one man's death became pilgrim man's life. The pilgrim entering the road of life entered in the past with a vision of God's salvific work of presence. Thoughts and action are not just parure in a sense of matching sets of jewels. The thinker is not a parvenu acquiring importance without qualifications and his thought is not a pinafore for action. Renewal of human society is on its way. The Church after the Council will not be the same anymore. Action underwent radical changes.[9] To see the changes and to try to employ only paronomasia would defeat the purpose of the Council and reduce the strong voices of leading scholars to a parochialized action.

After more than a decade of effort (which was not present for many decades before) to preserve the basic truth and make thought relevant, today's serious action for a change in the world is in some way gratifying to the pilgrim man.[10]

Whether we will move forward[11] or relapse into unproductive thought depends on whether we will allow ourselves to fall behind again, forfeiting the entire purpose of the incentive given us by Vatican II. The dream of Vatican II should not die, but get better if we do not intend to cast a new shadow over the last years of the twentieth century at the threshold of the third millennium.

The angry times caused a way of life incompatible with the message of God. The change is here, but it is up to us to make it a viable way of life in today's thought. Who wants to build the world of tomorrow must overcome the weakness of non-discipline because discipline is an integral part of greatness in engineering the future.

The extraordinary possibilities[12] of a new time (era) will bury our unessential differences in man's religious quest for truth.[13]

Search for truth without adherence to the Reason ruling man's unreasonableness is unthinkable. God is not distant from us. He is not only transcendental but also immanent and so every heteronomy of God is also man's autonomy. The Kingdom of God is in us. God did not forget us in this virulent age. He comes to us with the sunrise and with the sunset of our lives. He comes to us every moment of our lives. He comes to us in Jesus Christ. He comes to us in life and death when He tells us eschatologically: Come home. And man's answer is Maranatha.

Divorce from God and His cross caused discouragement and despair. A great divorce among the believers in the world, especially between Christians of the West and East, caused irreparable damage in the annals of Christianity.[14]

Division among Christians is based on orientation towards eternity and history. On one hand, there is a strong warning against the Church using inept means to affect history; on the other hand, evangelism is considered the only proper means to affect history. The problem arises from the Church's conclusions which contradict cultural and ideological positions of non-Christian views with regard to world community.

To form a new course of implementation of Vatican II will help the leaders of the Church to decide the future course of the Church in the world and to bring the tranquillity which is not present. Theologians must go beyond the Council because the Council did not speak of everything. If this is true for theologians today; it is even more valid for the International Papal Theological Commission.

If we look at these problems only from one angle of vision, even if it is an American angle of vision, the truth of the world community will elude us. Looking at the odds against tomorrow will terminate the action of today and life will threaten to pass us by or destroy us in a slow process. Life is a journey of a pilgrim, not a destination. A proclivity for a partial solution is very dispensable. A vision for a solution of the global village for a thinker of promise is indispensable.

There are many indications that the Villanova Institute is effectively reaching many in the United States and abroad. The dynamic contemplation of the leading scholars could give the reader a deep personal enrichment and safe orientation. A specially valuable service consists in presenting the question of Christ in Schoonenberg's study: "From A Two-Nature Christology To A Christology of Presence"[15] written with dedication for our readers.

The impact of these volumes is designed for the maturing in Christ and to bring the modern man the significant achievement of today's leading scholars in the world.

Villanova University presenting here the theologians of Intellectual Renewal believes that the new dimensions of the Church's quest are viable because of the presence of the Holy Spirit in the Church.

The Council and the Popes, John and Paul, surprised the world. They took us aback.

God's love for man is inexhaustible.

"If the characteristic of wisdom is knowledge of realities, no one can be called wise if he does not embrace also the things to come."[16]

"The Villanova Series" under the guidance of the theologians and the Administration presents these volumes as a humble contribution to today's new demands, probing the new frontiers of modern thoughts with an intention to contribute to the theological scene in the United States and hopefully to the world.

I am very much indebted to John Cardinal Krol for his continuous interest in the Institute and to Harry A. Cassel, who, the preoccupations of his highest office in the Province of the Augustinian Order notwithstanding, on the eve of the Symposium: "The Pilgrim People: A Vision With Hope," took the time to write me a personal letter of encouragement and his high appreciation of the "exhausting work ... of the Theology Institute and its contribution to the development of theology and of a deeper awareness in so many ..."

I wish to express my cordial thanks also to Bishop Andrew G. Grutka, whose initial assistance, so kindly given, helped me to dedicate myself to such an expanded scholarly activity.

Here on that note I will close my lines with a thought of Gregory of Nyssa: "The only thing that is really worthwhile is to become God's friend."

NOTES

[1] Joseph Papin, "Post-Vatican Perspectives," in *The Dynamic in Christian Thought*, The Villanova Series, Vol. I, 1970, p. 1 ff.

[2] Eugene Maly, *ibid.*, p. 166.

[3] Krister Stendahl, *ibid.*, p. 45.

[4] Avery Dulles, *ibid.*, p. 69.

[5] The Villanova University Series, Vol. I.

[6] The Villanova University Series, Vol. II.

[7] The Villanova University Series, Vol. III.

[8] The Villanova University Series, Vol. IV.

[9] Jürgen Moltmann, *Religion, Revolution, and the Future*, translated by M. Douglas Meeks, (Charles Scribner's Sons, New York, 1969) p. 129.

[10] Paul Evdokimov, *The Struggle With God*, translated by Sister Gertrude, S.J., (Paulist Press [Paulist Fathers], Glen Rock, New Jersey, 1966) p. 161; Bernard Lonergan, *The Subject*, (Marquette University Press, Milwaukee, 1968) p. 3.

[11] Eulalio R. Baltazar, *God Within Process*, (Newman Press, Paramus, New Jersey/New York, N.Y./Toronto/London, 1970) p. 108.

[12] Eugene Fontinell, *Toward a Reconstruction of Religion: A Philosophical Probe* (Doubleday and Company, Inc., Garden City, N.Y., 1970) p. 173.

[13] Bernard Lonergan, *The Subject*, (Marquette University Press, Milwaukee, 1968), pp. 4-5.

[14] Joannes Mastylak, *Fuitne Vladimirus Soloviev Catholicus?* (Sant' Alfonso, Roma, 1942), p. 14.

[15] The Villanova University Series, Vols. II-III.

[16] Gregory of Nyssa, P.G. 45, 580 C.

Acknowledgments

Besides those mentioned in Volume I, I wish to acknowledge at this time the invaluable service contributed by our panelists to the success of the Institute: Ronald E. Murphy, Abraham I. Katsh, Terrence J. Toland, Edward F. Jenkins, Donald A. Giannella, John O'Rourke, Donald W. Dowd, W. James Walsh, Thomas H. Doyne, Wilson L. Frescoln, Victor Krupitsch, Michael F. Glessner, Donald B. Kelley, Charles J. O'Neil, Robert W. Langran, Robert Francoeur, Ralph C. Shurer, Anthony J. Mullen, Sr. George O'Reilly, Sr. Luella, Edward Davis, George P. Lawless, Larry Hjelle, Edward Gannon, Amadeo Giorgi, Bernard L. Bonniwell, John Walsh, Hugh Nolan, Barry S. Young, Lawrence J. McGarry, Joseph H. Fichter, Michael J. Scanlon and Charles Bruderle.

I wish to express my thanks to Edward C. Doherty and Edward L. Hamel for their correspondence with the participants of the Institute, Bernard Shanley and John L. Hemmer for recording the lectures and panel discussions, James L. Holstein for the promotion of the book and Albert H. Buford, Bernard J. Downey, and Henry F. Weeks for their encouragement, and to James McGrath for his kindness in reading the proofs. Among many of my students participating, special mention must be made of Rose Picardi, Glenn I. Scott, Mary Murphy, Janet Hinckle, Richard Salvucci, and Thomas A. Nemeth.

J. P.
DIRECTOR of the INSTITUTE

The Pauline Spirit - An Inspiration For Action

Barnabas M. Ahern

SOME readers may find an anomaly in the following pages. Though this paper is part of a symposium on the dynamics of Christian action it contains no reference to the teeming activities of our day or to contemporary forms of service. This seeming irrelevance may occasion the criticism which has often been leveled against the writings of Karl Barth, who likewise seems to pay little heed to the word of God speaking in the historical present.

At times, however, it is a benefit for modern man to listen attentively to a voice from the past, especially when he who speaks utters the word of God which endures forever. Times pass and men change; but humanity itself, made by God and for God, is rooted in Him at the deepest dimension of its being. The cry of Augustine is as old and new as the human heart itself: "You have made us for yourself, O God, and our hearts are restless until they rest in Thee!" When, therefore, a man speaks who knows God and man's centeredness in Him, he becomes an ageless prophet, a "man of the Spirit" for all seasons, revealing to every age the depths of God's Spirit and evoking response from the depths of the human spirit. In the eternal "today" of God's world, this man's word is "something alive and active; it cuts like any double-edged sword but more finely; it can slip through the places where the soul is divided from the spirit, or joints from the marrow; it judges secret emotions and thoughts" (Heb. 4:12).

Paul the Apostle was this kind of man, a prophet for all ages. Ours is an entirely different world from that in which he lived. We view life from the perspectives of a philosophy which he never shared. Our creative thinkers unfold their insights in language more familiar to us and more relevant to our needs; but Paul is still a man to conjure with. Because his words bear authentic divine credentials this prophet deserves a hearing. If he fails to accord with present ways of thinking and acting, the very contrast of his message to modern attitudes spells out a claim for radical reform and adjustment.

7

Paul's seeming irrelevance to present modes may be the most striking feature of his true relevance to the needs of our age. Like the words of every prophet, his words come from above to illumine our times with the perennial thoughts of God. Whatever may be the inspired word of today's prophets (for God still speaks through persons, events and situations), this divine voice is always resonant with the enduring thoughts once uttered through Paul. As the spokesman of divine truth Paul, Teacher of the Nations, is relevant to every age.

1—THE APOSTLE'S DEBT TO THE FAITH OF ISRAEL

UNDERSTANDING Paul's message involves awareness of his background in Judaism. Each time the Christian apostle refers to his Jewish heritage he speaks of it with obvious pride (cf. Rom. 9:1-5; Phil. 3:4-7). Even in the full flowering of his Christian faith he remained deeply indebted to Judaism for those insights which bind together the revelation of the Old and New Covenants. The heart of Saul the Jew and of Paul the Christian would have thrilled to the words in which, centuries later, Pascal summed up the soul-stirring experience of his night of ecstatic prayer: "Now I know that the God of Abraham, Isaac and Jacob is my God!"

From his earliest years as a Jew the whole cast of Paul's mind was seared with a sense of creaturehood before the almighty and supreme Yahweh who rules heaven and earth and who fills the universe with the radiance of His glory. Israel's daily prayer, "Hear, O Israel, the Lord thy God is one God," marked Paul's life with the rhythm of adoring dependence. Like every devout Israelite he saw God as ever present in the world and ever active to save. For Israel every activity of God's immanence was revelatory of His transcendence. No one but God alone could be so much at the heart of things as to be able "to tear up and to knock down, to destroy and to overthrow, to build and to plant" (cf. Jer. 1:10).

For Saul the Jew, God was the beginning and the end of all life. In the days of his Judaism he who has been called the Isaia of the New Testament was heir to Isaia's abiding awareness of God's universal presence, His supreme and ever operative power, His devoted and tender love for those whom He has chosen. The dynamism for good to be found in every life is always the personal and powerful work of God. Like every devout Jew, Paul saw the sweep of human history not as the cyclic movement of natural power passing through phases, nor as the creation of men fumbling to build a new tower of Babel, but as the unfolding of a plan which God conceived from the beginning and is ever working to bring to consummation (cf. Is. 40-41).

Paul, therefore, shared Israel's faith in and reverence for the Torah, the teaching which reveals God and charts the way of life leading to Him; inspired and inspiring, the Law was for Saul the Jew God's perfect gift. If the Prophets of Israel apotheosized this word of God, it was because they knew that this word is not a mere noetic expression of what men think but a dynamic power bearing the very thoughts of God which are powerful to transform all creation like rain and seed coming from heaven (cf. Is. 55:10-11). On the one hand, God bound Himself with mercy and rock-like fidelity to fulfill His word. For his part, man was to match this divine fidelity with total conformity to the ways which God had charted. Through mutual faithfulness God would accomplish His best work in man; and man, made righteous through observance of the Torah, would find acceptance before God and would live with His life. No matter what may have been Isarel's faulty attitudes in the observance of the divine Law, no matter how its spirit was blighted by self-centered Pelagianism and legalistic formalism, the truth is to be found in Paul's own appraisal: "The Law is sacred, and what it commands is sacred, just and good" (Rom. 7:12).

Saul the Jew, therefore, was not a beginner in the ways of God; in the words of his own confession he was rich with the patrimony of Israel's faith: "As far as the Law can make you perfect, I was faultless" (Phil. 3:6). To him God was truly God—transcendent yet immanent, personal yet eminently mysterious, sole ruler of men and creator of all history, source of every power for good and operative in every saving action, inseparably bound to the fulfillment of His word with an unfailing love that was elective, dynamic, tender and compassionate. A sharer in the revelation given by God to the Prophets, Paul received from Judaism perspectives and attitudes which God claimed as His own and not man's, as heavenly and not of earth: "Yes, the heavens are as high above earth as my ways are above your ways, my thoughts above your thoughts" (Is. 55:9). Because God's word to Israel presented His point of view, this word which endures forever continued to form Paul's perspective as a Christian and constantly illumined his tireless search into the mystery of Christ.

2—PAUL'S DEBT TO HIS INAUGURAL VISION

THE day of the Damascus revelation is best understood as the great water-shed in Paul's life. With the heightened language of grateful appreciation for the fullness of God's gift, the Apostle speaks of this turning-point in his life as a new beginning and a veritable creation; in the light of this revelation he professes to reject his whole Jewish past "as so much rubbish" (Phil. 3:8). "When the kindness and love of God our savior for mankind were revealed" in Christ (cf. Tit. 3:4), Paul saw only ignorance and sin in his own and in mankind's previous history (cf. Tit. 3:3). All this, however, is the language of rhetoric welling up from the heart of a man enraptured by the gift of God which surpasses all previous revelation and overwhelms every human thought and dream.

The simple truth is that at the gates of Damascus the perennial
stream of Old Testament theodicy flowed into the flood-tide of New
Testament Christology. Between the two revelations there is both
continuity and change as between an inflowing stream and the vast,
mighty ocean. "The waters of Shiloah which flowed gently" to give
life to Israel (cf. Is. 8:6) became now, in Christ Jesus, "a fountain
of living water, welling up to eternal life" for the whole world (cf.
Jn. 4:14). And yet the thoughts and the ways of God remained the
same. All that God had said and done for His people Israel now became an incarnate Word in the human flesh of His Son who is "the
image of the unseen God" (Col. 1:15) and "the perfect copy of His
nature" (Heb. 1:3).

The thoughts and the ways of God are the thoughts and the ways
of the Son. Between the Old Covenant and the New there is the
continuity of the invisible becoming visible: "The Father goes on
working, and so do I" (Jn. 5:17). This word of Jesus in the fourth
gospel formed a fundamental conviction in the mind of Paul. Whatever he has written of Christ or of Christ's life in men is always
illumined by the revelation which he had received from Israel's prophets
on the thoughts and ways of God.

To unfold the mystery of Christ in the light of this conviction was
Paul's mission. The revelation given to him at Damascus consecrated
and empowered him as the New Testament "Servant of Yahweh," the
prophet-teacher of the nations. Because his tongue is that of a disciple
(cf. Is. 50:4), he says of Christ and of His saving mission all and
only those things which he has learned from God. Today men celebrate Paul's creativeness and hail him as an archetype of the rugged
individualist so dear to our age. Yet the fact is that Paul's thoughts
about Christ and our life in Him follow faithfully the pattern of the
thoughts and ways of God revealed in the Old Testament.

Like The Isaian Servant, Paul could truly say, "He made my mouth
a sharp sword" (Is. 49:2); but all the thoughts he uttered, he himself,
as a disciple, had first received. His insights and convictions, his teaching and directives—these he owed to the daily fidelity which the Isaian
Servant describes as the source of all his teaching: "Each morning
he wakes me to hear, to listen like a disciple. The Lord Yahweh has
opened my ear" (Is. 50:4-5). Because he had learned the ways and
the thoughts of God and because he ceaselessly studied the mystery
of Christ under the light of these principles, Paul was able to boast,
"I, who am less than the least of all the saints, have been entrusted
with this special grace, not only of proclaiming to the pagans the infinite treasure of Christ, but also of explaining how the mystery is
to be dispensed" (Eph. 3:8-9).

As a human phenomenon Paul's activity in fulfilling his mission has
never been equalled save in the surpassing human life of Jesus. Both
by temperament and by grace Paul was an activist to his finger-tips.

The richness of his gifts, the variety and abundance of his confrontations, the limitless spectrum of his kaleidoscopic emotional responses, the consistency of his faith commitment and the constancy of his abiding hope amid the ups and downs of a gruelling apostolate—all these aspects of his life as a minister of Christ lifted his ever shifting experiences beyond the pale of prediction or description. When one reads the quixotic story of this apostle there comes to mind a sentence from the song of the Prioress in *The Sound of Music;* "Can you hold a moonbeam in your hand?"

Mere men will never really understand Paul's life, much less encompass it with a pattern of unity. There are too many contradictions in the Pauline letters and too many antinomies in Paul's life to fit neatly into an acceptable form of human consistency. The truth is that no one can ever hope to understand Paul unless he has accepted fully the contents of St. John Chrysostom's summation of the apostle's life and character: "The heart of Paul was the heart of Christ." It is Paul himself who makes clear that this is the explanatory and unifying secret of his life and activity. In his apologia to the Corinthians for the embarrassing shifts in his way of acting, he gives as the compelling reason for his unreasonable conduct: "It is the love that was in Christ which urges us on" (2 Cor. 5:14).

For the Apostle, "God was in Christ, reconciling the world to Himself" (2 Cor. 5:14). The whole activity of Christ's life was for Paul the activity of God: In and through His Son God fulfilled His thoughts and worked out His ways. Far from sharing the fantastic nightmare of some moderns who speak of the death of God at the incarnation of His Son, Paul sees God alive and working as never before in Christ. With one solitary exception in the midst of multitudinous affirmations, (I Thes. 4:14), Paul constantly attributes the supreme triumph of Christ's life, the resurrection, to the activity of the Father's power. Whatever salvation has come to the world in and through Christ is for Paul the thought and the ways of God made manifest and operative in human flesh.

The Apostle would have shouted with joy to hear the word once uttered by St. Catherine of Genoa. During one of her ecstasies this holy woman was given to see the soul of Christ. Later, when her confessor asked her to describe what she had seen, the saint answered simply, "Only one word will describe it—*nettezza* (limpidity)!" Like a limpid pool Christ's whole being reflected perfectly the master-plan of God's saving love for men.

If Paul has unfolded the saving work of Christ with a fullness which has no parallel, this is because he constantly saw the thoughts and the ways of God operating in Him. Pauline Christology, therefore, is simply Old Testament theodicy at work in Christ Jesus. The fourth gospel, it is true, is far more explicit than Paul in affirming and explicating the bond of union between Father and Son in the work of

salvation. Nascent error at the end of the first century made it imperative that the author of the gospel of John should clearly affirm the
divinity of Jesus and should stress the bond between Him and His
Father. In the earlier days of Paul's letters the need for such explicit-
ness was not present; the Church was in calm possession of the truth
that Christ is God's Son and that the Father works in and through
Him. Accordingly, Paul was free to center all his attention on the work
of Christ, utilizing his theodicy to interpret this work and taking it for
granted that the well-instructed converts to whom he writes will recognize in his portrait of Christ a faithful tracing of God's thoughts and
ways.

3—THE PAULINE THEOLOGY OF LIFE AND ACTION

THE conviction that God was at work in and through Christ is the
basic analogue that gives form and unity to Paul's total concept
of Christian life and activity. Before explaining what this means, it is
necessary to reject two fundamental misconceptions: (a) Though no
writer can equal Paul in his esteem for the human person and in his
insistence on its liberty, the Apostle is totally opposed to anthropocen-
trism. For him the most radical and all embracing dimension of man's
personality is its total dependence upon God and His Christ. (b)
Though no writer can equal Paul in affirming the dynamism of Christian life and the limitless potentialities of Christian service, the Apostle
is adamant in affirming that God's power is the only source of fruitful-
ness and, to be truly operative, this power must be conjoined with
humble recognition of our dependence and with readiness to accept
peacefully and joyously control by God's will and the checks of frustration and suffering which the bearer of God's power always encounters
in his work with blighted human nature.

This rejection of faulty notions and this clarification of Paul's authentic thoughts on Christian life and activity flow from the underlying principles of his theocentric Christology. For Paul God is the
source, the support, and the end of all Christian action. To say this is
to place Paul in the ranks of the Old Testament prophets. For them,
too, God was the alpha and omega of His people's destiny. Strange
as it may sound, it is necessary to keep in mind this prophetic character of Paul if we are to understand the intransigent theocentrism of
his doctrine. Vicariously his soul had been burned with the seraphim
tongs which cleansed the heart of Isaia. He, too, had heard the hymn
to God's transcendence and immanence, "Holy, Holy, Holy is Yahweh
Sabaoth. His glory fills the whole earth" (Is. 6:3). All his life long,
both as Jew and Christian, Paul's heart beat with the humble response
of his own felt creaturehood.

Now in one way and again in another way he reiterates over and
over that man receives all that he is and all that he has from God. A

man becomes a Christian only because God has foreknown and called him (Rom. 8:28-30; Eph. 1-3-12). Every manner of living Christian life is for Paul a *charisma* (God's gift) (cf. 1 Cor. 7:7; 12:1-11). In every decision and in every action man must fearfully take into account the ways, the thoughts and the commands of God: "Work out your salvation with fear and trembling, for it is God who, for His own loving purpose, puts both the will and the action into you" (Phil. 2:13). All claim to self-sufficiency and to God-forgetful autonomy Paul batters down with the challenging cry of a man who really knows God and who really knows himself: "What do you have that was not given to you? And if it was given, how can you boast as though it were not?" (1 Cor. 4:7). The more a man is involved in God's work, the more obvious is his need for God; this is why Paul confesses, "We are not qualified in ourselves to claim anything as our own work: all of our qualifications come from God. He is the one who has given us the qualifications to be the administrators of this new covenant" (2 Cor. 3:4-6).

The deepest conviction of Paul's heart is that "God is not far from any of us, since it is in Him that we live, and move, and have our being" (Acts 17:27-28). If any may, therefore, is to be God's man in life and in activity, he must live out every hour of his waking day the pattern of complete dependence upon God which the perfect Son of God traced in His earthly life: "During His life on earth, He offered up prayer and entreaty, aloud and in silent tears, to the one who had power to save Him out of death, and He submitted so humbly that His prayer was heard" (Heb. 5:7).

Whether it is a Prophet of the Old Testament who speaks or whether it is Paul, the first rule they give for dynamic activity on the part of God's people is to think right thoughts about God and about themselves, to live always in His presence with abiding awareness of their total dependence on Him, with hearts open to receive the power which He alone can give, and with sincere readiness to make His thoughts their thoughts, His ways their ways, and His commands the inflexible pattern of their life.

It is obvious that, though this message is essential to Christian life and activity, there is nothing distinctively Christian about it. As a son of the Prophets, Paul cherished and lived it even as a Jew. But at the gates of Damascus something tremendous happened to Saul the Jew. The word that had previously spoken from afar of God's love and power now came near clothed in human flesh. The vision was so full of newness that all his life long Paul would cry out, "The old creation has gone, and now the new one is here" (2 Cor. 5:17).

Faith in God now became for Paul a matter of believing and confiding in a God-man whom he could see and hear and touch. Union with God now meant clinging to a man who "openly calls us brothers" (Heb. 2:11). Dependence on God now implied reliance on an older

Brother who "upholds the whole universe by His powerful word" (Heb. 1:3). To think the thoughts of God and to follow His ways were now identical with becoming like Him who is the way of our going, the truth of our groping, and the life of our ephemeral passing. To be totally acceptable to God now meant simply to live before Him in Christ Jesus; for in God's beloved Son man the creature is beloved.

In all this Paul saw that "for anyone who is in Christ, there is a new creation" (2 Cor. 5:17). Through the gift of His Son, God, as it were, exhausted His boundless power. In His will to perfect the creative potentialities of human life, even the infinite God had nothing more or better to give of His boundless resources than the gift of His own Son in human flesh. Paul, therefore, sums up and places the final seal on the good news of his gospel when he writes, "He who spared not His own Son but gave Him up for us all, how could He fail to grant us with Him all things?" (Rom. 8:32).

Christ, the supreme gift of God, and "all the things" which came through Him to create the newness of Christian life provide the unifying theme of all that Paul has written on Christian life and Christian activity. True to the fundamental principle of his theodicy Paul sees Christ as the eminent source, the constant support, the perfect pattern, and the final end of all creation. Time and changing event, meditation and conflict were all needful to press Paul's faith in Christ to ultimate conclusions which would reach out to the height and depth, the length and breadth of the whole universe and of all human existence. The Paul of Thessalonians with his clear faith in the allness of Christ was still a long way from the Paul of Colossians with his clear faith in the allness of Christ in all things. To trace the development of his doctrine and to mark its advance from crisis to crisis is not the purpose of this paper. Our concern here is to single out the three principles in his total corpus which inspire, energize and direct Christian action.

a)—First Principle: Life in Christ

Paul's underlying conviction of man's total dependence upon God leads him to emphasize dependence upon Christ as a dominant characteristic of all Christian life. Summing up his thought on the operative causality of Christ, he affirms that the life-giving power of the Son of God extends universally to the whole world and to the whole Church: "All things were created through Him and for Him . . . and He holds all things in unity. And the Church is His Body, He is its head; . . . for God wanted all perfection to be found in Him and all things to be reconciled through Him and for Him, everything in heaven and on earth" (Col. 1:15-20).

This universal operative role of Christ in the world and in the Church calls for a concomitant response on the part of the Christian. A special mentality is asked of believers which Paul refers to repeatedly when he reminds his readers that they are "in Christ Jesus." This phrase is multifaceted in its meaning and all-extensive in its application.

First of all, it means that Christian life, from start to finish, is a gift which God has given through His Son. Because Christ can truly say, "Without me you can do nothing" (Jn 15:5), the Christian must look to Him and depend upon Him for everything. Paul has spelled out what this attitude means in an assertion which Dr. Knox regards as one of the most significant texts in the Pauline corpus: "The human race has nothing to boast about to God; but by God's doing you are in Christ Jesus who through God has become our wisdom, our justice, our holiness, and our redemption so that, as it is written, 'If anyone wants to boast, let him boast of the Lord' " (1 Cor. 1:30-31).

Secondly, because Christ is the source of all things both in the world and in the Church, human nature itself bears a resemblance to His person, and, above all, Christian life is marked with the impress of His redemptive mysteries. In a certain sense, all things have been "Christed." As for the world, Joseph Mary Plunkett, with the intuitive vision of the poet, has expressed this truth in the words, "I see His blood upon the rose." As for Christian existence, St. Francis of Assisi, with the intuitive vision of the mystic, cried out to his little brothers as he extended his arms to them, "Look, we are even made in the sign of the cross." For Paul the best thing to be said of a man is that he is "in Christ Jesus." For him the phrase is pregnant with the saving work of God already begun and is full of limitless possibilities for the perfecting of this work.

Thirdly, the very operativeness of Christ in human life means a fixed pattern of conduct to be radicated ever more deeply in human existence. Each gift of God through Christ brings with it a radical exigency for ever greater conformity to Christ. To receive from Him creates the real need to live out Paul's injunction, "Let this mind be in you which was also in Christ Jesus (Phil. 2:5). Hence, there is a law of uniform acceleration in Christian living. Long before Newton discovered the law of physical gravity Paul affirmed the law of spiritual gravity in his oft-recurring phrase, "more and more." The nearer a Christian approaches God, the very center of his being, more and more must he move with the pace of Christ.

This truth of total dependence on Christ led the Apostle to make daring expressions of identity between Christ and the Christian. Since all that we are and all that we have come from Him, the Christian is one who can truly say, "I live, now no longer I, but Christ lives in me" (Gal. 2:20). Baptism itself, the initial step of Christian life, is for Paul a "putting on" of Christ, so that all those who live the Christian life are really only "one person in Christ" (Gal. 3:27-28). Growth in Christian life is a rich experiential process of "putting on Christ" (Rom. 14.14), an ever deeper radication of His life in ours.

Throughout his epistles Paul emphasizes this truth that dependence on Christ brings identity with Him. The way in which a woman who loves and is loved becomes one body-person with a man is for Paul a faithful image of the intimate union which binds the Christian to Christ (cf. 1 Cor. 6:15-17). Paul's doctrine on the Body of Christ (no matter what may be the source of the figure he uses) flows from his conviction that, because each Christian owes all that he is and has to Christ, all Christians together are a vital extension in the world of the life and activities of the Body-Person of Christ. Christian dependence upon the Lord creates another "self" for Him in the world where He is not visible: "The fact that there is only one loaf means that, though there are many of us, we form a single body because we all have a share in this one loaf" (1 Cor. 10:17). For Paul it is not mere community or togetherness which makes Christ present; rather, it is Christ, present and operative in each Christian, who integrates all into a *koinonia* (fellowship) with His Body-Person and with one another.

There is nothing static or merely passive in the dependence of the Christian on Christ. Because Christ shares His own life with the man who believes in Him, authentic Christian existence must be vital with living conformity to Him. Paul's insistence on the need to live the virtues of Christ. His urgent recommendations to serve devotedly both God and man, His constant emphasis on the need for a recurring share in the death and resurrection of Jesus, his explanation of the sacraments as a renewal in Christian life of the Paschal mysteries, his concept of the apostolate as a re-living of Christ's zeal and as a death to self that others may live—all of this doctrine rests squarely on the Apostle's fundamental conviction that the life we live and the activity we exercise are not our own creation but are, instead, God's gift to us of the life and love of Christ.

All that has been said of this gift is unfolded at great length in Paul's letters. We have merely summarized the chief points of his doctrine on what it means to live in Christ.

b)—SECOND PRINCIPLE: LIFE IN THE SPIRIT

There is a second essential aspect of Paul's teaching which we have not yet touched upon. Without it the Apostle's words might be dismissed as mere rhetoric lacking in substance. For Paul's urgent recommendations to dependence on Christ and his pointed directives on living Christian life will have little practical impact if they are the only teaching he offers to men who know by faith and who feel in daily experience their own helplessness. In Chapter Seven of Romans Paul himself bears eloquent witness to the inherent weakness which besets all men: "The fact is that I know of nothing good living in me. . . . For though the will to do what is good is in me, the performance is not, with the result that instead of doing the good things I want to do, I carry out the sinful things I do not want" (Rom. 7:18-19).

If there is to be substance, then, in Paul's teaching on life in Christ, full account must be taken of his concomitant doctrine on life in the Spirit. So intimately are these two aspects of Christian life combined in the Apostle's thought that, time and again, he uses the two phrases with perfect equivalence. Their inter-relation calls for explanation.

From the Pentecostal community of Jerusalem Paul received corroboration of his faith in Jesus as the God-appointed agent of salvation. Judaism had looked forward to the Messiah as a man who would come from God endowed with His spirit and empowered to share this spirit with others. The life, death and resurrection of Jesus made clear that He Himself had been "anointed by the Spirit" (Acts 10:38). The inspiring and guiding influence of the Spirit of God in His earthly life was to become a dominant theme in the record of that life written by Luke. More than this, the events of Pentecost and the days which followed made clear that the risen Christ, as Messiah and Lord, was present in the midst of His followers to fill them with the personal Spirit of God who had ruled His own life. For, in its early days, the Church constantly experienced in a phenomenally tangible way not only the invisible presence of the Spirit but also the compelling impetus of His inspiration, strength and guidance. Once Paul became a Christian, he, too, experienced the Spirit's activity both in his personal life and in the lives of his converts. Every letter he writes is eloquent of the fact that Paul is vitally conscious of living in a Spirit-charged world. For him, therefore, Christ's perfect response to the faith of men who depended upon Him was the gift of His own Spirit to fill them with His life and to transform them into His likeness.

Life in Christ is substantial and real precisely because it includes also life in the Spirit. To stand before God as another Christ is not just an idle dream but a reality through the work of Christ's Spirit. When Paul writes, "God has sent the Spirit of His Son into our hearts . . . and it is this that makes you a son" (Gal. 4:6-7), he singles out the basic fact which makes life in Christ a reality. All that the Apostle has written in the Sixth Chapter of Romans of the union of the Christian with Christ derives its truth and power from the reality of life in the Spirit which he describes in Chapter Eight of the same Epistle. There he affirms that the Spirit is the very source of the Christian's divine sonship (Rom. 8:14), the guarantee of his hope for heaven (Rom. 8:23-25), the support of his weakness (Rom. 8:26-27), the mentor and uplifter of all his attitudes (Rom. 8:9).

The very vocabulary of the Pauline letters is indicative of the fact that all strength for Christian living and activity comes from the Spirit of Jesus who makes His home in each believer. Humanness without the Spirit *(sarx)* is synonymous with weakness *(astheineia)* even after Christ accomplished His redemptive work. Only the activity of the Spirit in redeemed man *(pneuma)* brings the power *(dynamis)* to live and to act in Christ.

Today power is most often thought of in terms of impersonality and anonymous force. The "power" *(dynamis)* of which Paul speaks is just the opposite. It always involves persons who love—the Father, Son, and Spirit—and persons who are loved. The "power" is love itself with all the drives and fidelity, the clinging and rejections, the approvals and hatred, the strategies and evasions, the pleas and commands which are essential to the multifaceted activity of true love. When Paul writes of the love of God "poured into our hearts by the Holy Spirit which has been given to us" (Rom. 5:5), he brings to the fore the essential dynamism of Christian life. The love with which the Spirit filled the heart of Christ to drive Him on in His life of devotedness to God and to man is the very same love with which He fills the heart of the Christian. This is the secret of all life in Christ; this is the power which inevitably conforms men to Him.

When the Christian surrenders to the Spirit and faithfully follows the drive of Spirit-given love, he becomes a mature and perfect Christian with all the freedom of a true son of God. Speaking to men like this, Augustine cries out, "Love, and do what you will." In this directive he echoes the bold affirmation of Paul: "A spiritual man is able to judge the value of everything, and his own value is not to be judged by other men" (1 Cor. 2:15).

The Apostle is not speaking here of mere men with their idiosyncratic judgments and spontaneous drives. He is too aware of man's dependence upon God in Christ to endorse any form of God-forgetting autonomy and antinomianism. If he claims liberty for the mature Christian, it is precisely because of the maturity of Spirit-given love in such a man. This love conforms the Christian to Christ who, out of love, fulfilled the will of the Father perfectly in all things. With the spontaneity of a lover the perfect Christian follows the intransigent will of the Father not as an adventitious law coming from without, but as the only course he desires to follow. For such a man the law of God is no longer merely a compelling command written on stone; it is rather the consuming desire of his whole being—as Paul puts it, the very drive of love "written on the tablets of your living hearts" (2 Cor. 3:3).

The mature Christian, therefore, knows instinctively that there is a time for speech and a time for silence, a time to be assertive and a time to obey, a time to stand on the pedestal of prestige and a time to live in the shadow of humility. He sees life as involving moments of sharing in Christ's Passion and Death and moments of living in the light and joy of the resurrection. He meets each event and situation with a full-hearted embracing of God's will, equally ready to accept the cross or the glory which follows upon it. If this kind of life is marked by antinomies, its very contrasts are but the variant responses of love to the simple will of God in its variant manifestations. Paul himself offers the best example of what it means to live in the Spirit and to be mature with the love of Christ. His life as a Christian was perfectly simple in its whole-hearted clinging to God's will amidst the most diverse situations and experiences (1 Cor. 4:9-13; 2 Cor. 1:3-7; 5:3-10). God's will in the pattern of Christ's own life and love, on the one hand, and, on the other, the totality of Paul's sincere and loving conformity—these are the two factors which account for the sublime unity of Paul's life and provide the secret of its liberty.

In a single word, the mature Christian, like Paul, is a wise man. From the very beginning "wisdom" in Israel meant something more than mere knowledge; it always involved an experiential flavor which adds sureness and intensity to knowledge, for wisdom implied a special ability and a special flare for applying knowledge. Transferred into Paul's own vocabulary, wisdom always implies that special kind of knowledge which is inspirited and empowered by love. Hence, for the Apostle, the "wise man" is one who, possessing the knowledge of God's will and word, loves that will so perfectly that he fulfills it with spontaneous instinctiveness. Paul's wise man always knows what to do and how to do it, for love gives him reasons and shows him the way which mere knowledge never glimpses. The wise man, therefore, fulfills the will of God perfectly, for not only does he know God's word, he loves it. Far from following the dictates of mere reason and far from modelling his life on merely human patterns, such a one—in Paul's words—has "the mind of Christ" (1 Cor. 2:16). Through the perfect work of the Spirit in him, the mature Christian is totally conformed to the character profile of Christ which Paul has delineated: "What the Spirit brings is love, joy, peace, patience, kindness, goodness, trustfulness, gentleness and self-control" (Gal. 5:22-23).

c)—CHRISTIAN ACTIVITY, A SHARE IN GOD'S ESCHATOLOGICAL WORK

Because the Christian lives in Christ through the power of His Spirit, he shares inevitably in God's work of bringing all creation to the final consummation of His glory. From the time when he wrote his first letter to the Thessalonians until the eve of his death, Paul was preoccupied with the perfecting of God's saving work in the Parousia. Though his thought on eschatology went through successive developments he never lost sight of the moment when the full riches of Christ's saving work would penetrate the world of God's creation.

For many, Paul's expectancy of an imminent Parousia weakens the impact of his directives urging certain attitudes and ways of conduct. His estimate of virginity, for instance, and his censure of too great preoccupation with the world that passes (cf. 1 Cor. 7) seem to many to have lost all meaning in view of the more enlightened knowledge of our day. This dilution of Pauline doctrine, however, fails to take into account the real meaning of Paul's eschatology. For him the quantitative measure of time between now and the last day bears no comparison to the qualitative impact of the last day upon the present.

For Paul eschatology is a reality which is always being realized. Like his Master he knows that "The kingdom of heaven is at hand"—always breaking through into the here and now to enrich the lives of men presently with a salvation which anticipates God's full glory at the end-time. Whatever may have been the preoccupation of Paul's letters to the Thessalonians, he makes crystal clear in the letters written during his captivity that the riches of the last day already impinge upon Christian life in the present.

The Christian workman, therefore, must be like his Master a "man in a hurry;" he has divine riches to bring and a work to do for his own generation. The men with whom he rubs elbows are men who must be saved with the abundant riches of the last day which are already present. If Christian life knows its "*Jetztnoch*" (the now-still of hope for riches to come) it also knows its "*jetztschon*" (the now-already of riches at hand). Hence, Christian life must always be trim in its spartan detachment from the cloying molasses of a world that is passing (cf. 1 Cor. 7:31), just as it must be preoccupied with the need to spend and to be spent for the salvation of men (2 Cor. 12:15). Christ Himself had spoken of the need for "girt loins and a traveler's lamp in the hand" (Lk. 12:35-36). Paul is just as insistent on full cooperation with the saving activity of Christ in the here and now. For every Christian the present moment is alive with opportunity. In a special way the apostolic minister of Christ must be ready to yield all and to do all that a door may be opened in his own generation for the inflow of Christ's eschatological riches.

For Paul, therefore, "life is real, life is earnest." If in the end-time Christ will present His followers to the Father to form the eternal kingdom, now already He is at work through His Church to do the same. Christian activity, therefore, means a whole-hearted commitment to the saving work of Christ, with all it involves in self-giving and in devoted love, in renunciation and in commitment, in prayer and in action, in sharing Jesus' death and resurrection.

CONCLUSION

I T IS Paul himself who sums up all he has written on Christian life and action. Fully aware of his total dependence on Christ he describes himself as "an earthenware jar" (2 Cor. 4:7), fragile and empty. The Christian of himself has nothing; he is simply a great emptiness which needs to be filled. His whole life long he lives as a beggar with arms wide-open to receive. But Paul insists that, through the goodness of Christ and the work of His Spirit, God fills the believer with a "treasure"—the power of the Spirit in man's earthenware jar "to make it clear that such an overwhelming power comes from God and not from us" (2 Cor. 4:7). This treasure is the very life of God's Son operative in the Christian through the power of the Spirit. Because of this gift the Christian lives a vital life for God and sanctifies others with a dynamic activity. Therefore he is able to say with Paul: "Always, wherever we may be, we carry with us in our body the death of Jesus, so that the life of Jesus also may always be seen in our body . . . So death is at work in us, but life in you" (2 Cor. 4: 10-12).

BIBLIOGRAPHY

Ahern, B. M. "The Christian's Union with the Body of Christ in Cor. Gal. and Rom." *Catholic Biblical Quarterly*, 23 (1961), 199-209.
———. "The Fellowship of His Sufferings," *CBQ*, 22 (1960), 1-32.
———. "The Spirit and the Law," *The Way*, 6 (1966), 219-229.
Cerfaux, L. *Christ in the Theology of St. Paul*. St. Louis: B. Herder 1958.
———. *The Church in the Theology of St. Paul*. St. Louis: B. Herder, 1959.
———. *The Christian in the Theology of St. Paul*. New York: Herder and Herder, 1967.
———. *The Scriptural Journey of St. Paul*. New York: Sheed and Ward, 1968.
Danielou, J. *History of Early Christian Doctrine*. London: Darton, Longman and Todd, 1969.
———. *The Theology of Jewish Christianity*. Chicago: H. Regnery, 1964.
Davies, W. D. *Paul and Rabbinic Judaism*. London: S.P.C.K., 1958.
Durrwell, F. X. *In the Redeeming Christ: Towards a Theology of Spirituality*. Trans. R. Sheed. New York: Sheed and Ward, 1963.
———. *The Resurrection, A Biblical Study*. Trans. R. Sheed. New York: Sheed and Ward, 1960.
Fitzmyer, J. *Pauline Theology*. Princeton: Prentice-Hall, 1967.
Hunter, A. M. *The Gospel of Paul*. London: SCM Press, 1963.
Lyonnet, S. "St. Paul: Liberty and Law," *The Bridge*, 4 (1961), 229-251.
Montague, G. *Growth in Christ*. Kirkwood, Mo.: Maryhurst Press, 1961.
Moore, G. F. *Judaism in the First Centuries of the Christian Era; The Age of Tannaim*, 3 vols., Cambridge, Harvard University Press, 1970.
Schillebeeckx, E. *Christ the Sacrament of the Encounter with God*. New York: Sheed and Ward, 1963.
Schnackenburg, R. "Christian Adulthood according to the Apostle Paul," *CBQ*, 25 (1963), 354-370.
Spicq, C. "L'Esprit-Saint, vie et force de l'église primitive," *Lumiere et Vie*, 10 (1953), 9-28.
———. *Agape in the New Testament*, 3 vols. St. Louis: B. Herder, 1970.
———. *Charity and Liberty in the New Testament*. New York: Alba House, 1965.
Stanley, D. M. *Christ's Resurrection in Pauline Soteriology*. Rome: Pontifical Biblical Institute, 1961.
Wikenhauser, A. *Pauline Mysticism*. New York: Herder and Herder, 1960.

Liturgy: Shaped by and the Shaper of the Ongoing Christian Community

Godfrey L. Diekmann*

THERE are two extreme views about the liturgical renewal of today. It is needless to cite the traditionalists; their shrill statements almost succeed in disproving themselves. But there is a rather good representative of the moderate party, Aelred Graham, who wrote in the *London Tablet* on March 1, 1969:

> Where the faithful may have been unintentionally misled is by the changes in the manner of public worship. Let full recognition be given to the merits of the liturgical renewal; the fact remains, as Confucius pointed out long ago, that to interfere with the public rites is to touch the very fabric of government. Future historians may well conclude that the Church brought upon herself her present unsettled state, not in the first place by any insistence on traditional morality, but by embarking without sufficient consideration on a whole series of relatively superficial, though to many sensibilities drastic, changes in the conduct of public worship.[1]

The other extreme is perhaps best represented by Andrew Greeley, writing in general about the changes in the Church. Certainly what he says applies also to liturgical renewal. He believes that the forces of renewal unleashed by John XXIII at the Vatican Council have gained momentum. Consequently, the type of reform that would have satisfied

* Transcribed and edited by Francis A. Eigo.

all but the most extreme in the early 1960s is rapidly becoming commonplace today. Therefore, only the most creative guidance can maintain balance at the present time.[2]

And, in between there is the vast majority who in fact, if not in
words, say: "So what?" It is a curious thing that so many of us who
had attached our hopes to the liturgical movement now see those treas-
ured things that we had thought so important seem quite irrelevant
to a younger generation. The history of the Council will tell us
that it was, humanly speaking at least, rather providential that we have
the document on the Liturgy first. This was the only one of the documents acceptable to the Church Fathers as a basis of discussion, and it
was satisfactory because it was the result of fifty years of the Church's
experiencing herself in a new way. As you know, this document was
prepared, not by men of the Curia, but by men who had been in the
field of the liturgical-pastoral apostolate for fifty years. Above all, this
document laid the foundation for the most important document doc-
trinally, *Lumen Gentium (Dogmatic Constitution on the Church)*.

In the Council's debate on "The Church," it was Archbishop Martin
of Rouen who, in the name of the French hierarchy, pointed out that
the proposed doctrine on the Church was unacceptable because it contradicted the ecclesiology already accepted in the document on the Liturgy. In the document on the Liturgy is an ecclesiology that simply became commonplace in the subsequent documents: personalizing the
Church; emphasis on the role of the people of God (the priesthood
of the laity); emphasis on the local Church (the most important self-
manifestation of the Church); the need for adaptation and, hence, the
necessity of having territorial groups of bishops, demanded by this
document before the Council even discussed the problem; and lastly
and perhaps most important, the new discovery of Christ, that is, the
presences of Christ.

The Constitution on the Liturgy was quoted fifteen times in the
Constitution on the Church, and it is simply the foundation of that
theology. There are more than a hundred references to it in the other
documents. Certain statements of the Constitution have become part
and parcel of Vatican II: "The Eucharistic sacrifice ... is the fount
and apex of the whole Christian life ..."[3] "No Christian community,
however, can be built up unless it has its basis and center in the celebration of the most Holy Eucharist. Here, therefore, all education in
the spirit of community must originate."[4]

In intervening years some changes have taken place. Seen at the
pace of history, they have occurred at a revolutionary speed: the introduction of the vernacular, the three new Eucharistic prayers, con-
gregational singing and praying, et cetera. But, what happened to
those beautiful statements of the Constitution? To very many, certainly in terms of any effective renewal, the results seem miniscule. We
may perhaps distinguish two groups: first of all, those who are still

attaching expectation to the power of the liturgy, even though the pace is too slow. These sometimes find expression in the so called underground churches and celebrate their own creations of liturgy. Then, there are those who are turning against the very principle of liturgy and the dynamics of renewal. You remember Dan Callahan's famous article in the *National Catholic Reporter* to the effect that we have allowed the Christ of the Eucharist to obscure our view of Christ and our neighbor of the street. Perhaps the same sort of reaction is discoverable in the present identity crisis on the part of many priests— a strong reaction against a cultic priesthood.

The new *Ordo Missae*, published a few weeks ago and being put into effect by the first sunday of Advent, gives us a long awaited reform of the structure of the Mass. As far as I can judge, it is meeting with widespread indifference or even skepticism. Perhaps we naively expected too much. Even though we have been criticizing the rather automatic understanding of the principle *ex opere operato*, we ourselves unwittingly, unknowingly applied it, thinking that merely having changes—a guitar Mass, for example—would solve things.

In this whole context let us remember something that the recent (about two years ago) instruction on the Eucharist underlined—the Eucharist is the memorial of the Lord.[5] That aspect of the Eucharist was not underscored at Vatican II, but it has been emphasized in subsequent documents. The Eucharist is the memorial of Christ, of the Paschal mysteries, but it is not just a recalling of past events. It is like the Old Testament. In the Old Testament the Jews were told that at the Paschal meal the saving event was not happening merely to their forefathers; this was happening to them, now. The Exodus was a saving event, not merely hundreds of years ago, but in the present, for this people on the present stage of their pilgrimage. There was continuity on the part of God; the reactivation of these saving events took place in the present, for the present needs of this community. Thus, the Mishnah says that in every generation man must so regard himself as if he himself came forth out of Egypt.

Personally, I am inclined to agree that the new *Ordo Missae* is too little and too late. I hope that the announcement that its introduction will mean a cerain lull, a period of rest in the reform, will not be realized, that it will not be allowed to be realized, because I think it would be tragic. Rather, I consider this *Ordo Missae* the first small step in an immense journey of liturgical reform to be accomplished if the brave words of the Liturgy Constitution about the Eucharist's being the apex and the source of all Christian life, the foundation of all Christian community, can ever be realized. Of course, I hardly need point out to a group like this the essential need of human collaboration. I think the best way to bring this home to ourselves and to others is to remind ourselves that two of the evangelists dared to speak of Christ's going back to Nazareth, his home town, and not being able to work miracles there because of the lack of faith of the Nazarenes. It is the same Christ working today. If he cannot work miracles with us, perhaps this human collaboration has not been sufficiently stressed.

We are on a journey; we are a pilgrim Church. Just as in the former journey in the desert the manna was not merely calories for the people, but was the food that united them as a people and welded them together, so this certainly is the purpose of the Eucharist, to make us into a people of God. That is the reason Saint Augustine could say that not only does the Church make the Eucharist, but the Eucharist makes the Church. This demands on our part a rethinking of the interpretation of the principle of change as given in the Constitution on the Liturgy. There, the document rather naively says that there are changing and unchangeable elements in the liturgy; those that come from Christ are unchangeable, and those that come from the Church can be changed.[6] Well, it is not so simple as that. I think we are beginning to realize that even the things from Christ are not necessarily unchangeable. I think we learned that lesson when we began to think about the institution of the Sacraments. As you know, it is difficult to prove the institution of some of the Sacraments from the Scriptures themselves. We speak, therefore, of the institution of the Church. In the course of centuries the Church became aware of what is necessary to a way of life, and, so, the Sacraments arose. Instituted by Christ? Yes.

Sometimes I allow myself to speculate whether, in this very, very new situation, the Church could not perhaps even discover new needs. Is it entirely out of the question that perhaps new Sacraments might arise? Has Trent definitely shut the door to that? Have you ever asked yourself why the reading of Scripture in public is not a Sacrament in the strict sense of the word? It seems to fulfill all the requirements. Anyway, Trent did speak of the Sacraments and said that the Church may change anything, *salva substantia*—the substance must remain the same. Now, the rule of substance does not merely mean the matter and form, but rather Christ's intention, and the Church has been interpreting Christ's intention. Thus, we have some very radical changes in regard to some of the sacraments—for instance, in the area of Penance: first, only once in a lifetime for major crimes; in our own time, devotional confession. There are the changes in regard to Extreme Unction: it was a rite for the sick, and it became a rite for the dying; now we are rediscovering the Sacrament as a rite for the sick.

Consider especially the Eucharist. The sign undoubtedly was first understood as a meal, with sacrificial connotations, of course. Its exact significance was not unknown, but it was the form of a meal. Then, it gradually became a sacrificial, rather ceremonious, celebration, and the meal was almost entirely forgotten; it was requisite merely that the celebrant eat. I remember the great Assisi pastoral-liturgical conference in 1956—the first time in the world that a liturgical movement dared to flex its muscles in public. Even there, in the program for each day, it was printed that no one was to receive Holy Communion at the Pontifical Mass. Well, we are again stressing the meal aspect, not, of course, in any which way minimizing or forgetting the theological deduction concerning the sacrificial nature of this meal. But, if we take this seriously, recovering the meal aspect of the Eucharist without diminishing the sacrificial must necessarily bring with it a considerable change in our method of celebration. A few years ago, Guardini startled the liturgical world by asking whether modern man is still able to understand symbols; he himself was rather skeptical. Perhaps we have lost the power, but there are certain basic rites which we still accept, and among them is the eating of the meal. Therefore, this is not a minor matter for us, to cling to something which is so natural to us as a sign, as a rite which Christ has taken over and given deeper dimensions. If we take the Eucharist seriously as a meal, I think it will necessarily come about that adults who wish may receive it in their own hand. This will mean the possibility of gathering around the table, and I am wondering whether in the future the pews that immobilize people, that make it impossible for them to understand themselves as a pilgrim Church, will be a normal part of every parish. I wonder whether this emphasis will not necessarily bring with it quite a radical change in regard to the discipline of Penance. If we expect our people to come together for a common meal every Sunday, they should be allowed to partake of that meal. If there is a hindrance, provision should be made. Therefore, I would say that there should be such a thing as an absolution which is sacramental, perhaps with the obligation to submit their sins to the keys later, but normally all present should participate in that meal to which they have been invited. Furthermore, if duty brings one to another participation in the same day, I think it should be participation, that one really receives the Eucharist also on that occasion.

There is another application about Christ's intention in regard to the Liturgy of the Word. Christ did institute ministers of His liturgy, and they also have been instituted as teachers; they are to preside at the Liturgy of the Word. I suppose that this could be considered as something unchanging, something coming from Christ and intended by Christ. But, there is another element that comes from Christ, and we have not given attention to it: Christ Himself adapted His teaching to His audience by the use of the parables and so on. Christ said nothing about the method of teaching. There is a present danger of clinging to customary methods, even though this means defeating the purpose itself of teaching. Let us not forget the liturgy is for man, not man for the liturgy. It is normal for people to wish to participate, and this is a way of learning—a better way of learning. That is the reason I think that for certain circumstances the dialogue homily is necessary, especially for some groups. This presupposes however that we should not tempt the Holy Spirit. If the priest has no right to go into the pulpit and preach without preparation, I think it is really tempting the Holy Spirit to have a good dialogue properly unless all the people present have been told well in advance what the readings are and they are asked to pray or fully think about them, so they really come together and share their insights. Regarding this, Urs von Balthasar says:

> The essential and necessary complement of preaching, by which the word of God is expounded, is the spiritual exchange of ideas, where different Christians communicate the insights obtained in prayer, to their mutual profit ... whereby "the members are mutually careful one for another" (I Cor. XII, 25).[7]

Furthermore, I think most people do not particularly care for so called children's Masses on Sunday. We think that children should come with their parents, but, then, we subject them to listening to a sermon which has no possible relevance whatsoever for them. Could not some young girl who knows how to get along with children take them to a side room and read a little story to them, followed by a Gospel story, perhaps even a fairy story, and try to tell them what it is all about? Then, all would come together again for the Eucharist, gathering around the altar. I think it must come as our normal Sunday celebration that we adapt ourselves to the capacity of our listeners. What does Saint Paul ever mean to small children? A little Gospel story or a story from daily life, climaxed by a Gospel story, would certainly be sufficient.

There is another aspect to the same problem of the Liturgy of the Word. We are living in an age of the science of communication, and it is one of the tragedies of Vatican II that the worst document by far is that on communications. As somebody said, it is like a third rate pastoral by a second rate bishop on a first rate subject. I think we must apply here what John XXIII said about doctrine itself; he said that the substance of the ancient doctrine of the deposit of faith is one thing, and the way it is presented is another. That famous statement has been picked up, cited, and made its own by the Council in the document of the Church in the Modern World.[8] We are living in an age of the science of communication. Even though I am not competent to judge, I have been very much impressed by some of the things that McLuhan has been telling us. At least in his sketching of the eras of human learning there may be some validity. He speaks of an era of hearing, that all knowledge was through the ear. Well, I wonder whether we have not fallen victim to that. We have a little phrase which we picked up from Saint Paul, "Fides ex auditu—Faith from hearing." Instead of realizing this is the only thing Paul could have said at that time, since there was no reading, we have sort of absolutized that—"faith from hearing"—as if we had no other senses. Then, of course, there came the period of reading, of the printing press. We caught up with that centuries later when we had our hand missals, and each one buried himself in his little missal and was quite absorbed in himself.

The varied changes indicate that we are no longer in this period of reading. The priest is facing the congregation; face to face they are seeing him. Therefore, what he does and how he does it are important. That is the reason the Council did not hesitate to state in article 59 that the very manner of celebrating is the most important means of stirring the faith.[9] The priest is a man of signs, and his very celebration is a sign. So, I say we are in an era of seeing also. Yet, we have hesitated to keep up with the times; we still have not used the various audio-visual aids, as if in some way or another they were not quite human. After all, who invented them? We have not yet caught up in that respect, and now we are already in the wrap around era of sense images, especially in the case of our youngsters. Two years ago we had a meeting of our Institute of Spiritual Life, and we invited Sister Corita Kent to give us a slide lecture; we have never been the same since. We were bombarded with all sorts of sense images, with all sorts of noises. Then, when it was all finished, she said: "All right—your whole discussion has been about prayer, and you talk about recollection and silence. What you have just seen and heard is what our children live in, that sort of world. They, also, must be taken into account." Again, this is an example of adaptability in the way of Christ's getting His message across.

I am all for flexibility and for the most basic principles the Council has given us. Let us cling to flexibility and never betray it; it is one of the most precious things that we have—the principle of adaptability, of flexibility. In the light of that, therefore, I plead for mothers, especially. Some women welcome pregnancy because it gives them five days of quiet in the hospital. They look forward to the Sunday Mass as the only time they will have some peace and quiet. I think it might be good to have it more quiet at Mass for some of those people who really need it for their spiritual life—again, flexibility.

There is a real need for rethinking more courageously the principle of adaptation of which I just spoke. This is in Articles 37 to 40.[10] These articles are revolutionary, the most revolutionary things the Council has given us, once and for all breaking with the principle of the monolithic Church. What we have in Articles 37 to 40 is a good statement, but the world has moved fast since then. We have already taken for granted that cultural and intellectual and even doctrinal pluralism is a good thing. We have not yet arrived at the acceptance of the principle that cultural pluralism is not only a good thing, but is necessary for the welfare of souls. Therefore, I beg to submit that one *Ordo Missae* which has been promised us will be far less than satisfactory, particularly if its unicity is maintained. I would say that then the results might even be disastrous. The Mass that we are being given, even the new *Ordo Missae,* is in some way the sixth century papal Mass. However much it is whittled down, it is hardly adequate for quite other circumstances than those then envisioned. Therefore, I would plead for at least several such basic forms, still allowing flexibility for each one, according to local circumstances and need. After all, what I am asking is not so revolutionary because we did have four forms of the Mass. Do you remember? There was the low Mass; there was the sung Mass; there was a solemn Mass; there was a Pontifical Mass. The basis of differentiation was the number of ministers in the sanctuary and the extent of the ceremoniousness of their behavior, with no account whatsoever taken of the People of God for whom this was being celebrated. They could be entirely absent, and still there could be a Pontifical Mass. I think, therefore, we must plead and continue to push for greater variety of basic forms, *Ordines Missae,* not in terms of the minister, but in terms of the People of God. Unless and until we get such multiple forms, I think that Church authorities may never be able again to regain the initiative of liturgical renewal.

My own hope is rather a footnote to this. Not only do we have four Eucharistic Prayers now, but, if we compare those four prayers with the best of the so-called Dutch Canons, we will see quite a difference. The four prayers that we have are mosaics from medieval manuscripts, medieval sacramentaries. They are hardly vital in terms of our own experience of life and our own experience of God. There are promised 75 to 80 new Prefaces. I think even those will hardly begin to touch the real need if they are taken from medieval sacramentaries. My own opinion of this matter is as follows: I think the Eucharistic Prayer is far too important to expose it to general experimentation. In its own way it has been historically, and is meant to be, a more important doctrinal statement than any declaration of any General Council that I know of. It is the entire Church proclaiming her faith. Therefore, it is too important to allow it to be tampered with at the whim of each one who feels the need. But, I do think there is a need, and my own suggestion is that the Preface, which technically belongs to the Eucharistic Prayer and is still distinct from it, could be more or less open to such individual, not spontaneous, but studied, composition. Thus, a Preface could be created to conform to a local situation, to the present need, to the present congregation, and so on. In that way there would be a certain combination of spontaneity together with the inherited form.

Not only do we need several new *Ordines Missae* and such basic forms, but the principle that we now apply to the other sacraments we must also come to apply to the Mass. Regarding the other Sacraments, you know that, even though Rome gives us a basic form, nations can adapt this according to their need. This has been taken for granted for centuries: as far as the other Sacraments are concerned, there may be local adaptation under the direction of the respective hierarchies of the Churches. As you know, there are quite a few different ways of celebrating Matrimony. Regarding Baptism, we have a Baptism for adults and a Baptism for infants; it is up to the local Churches to adapt those, if they see the need. Thus, I think this same principle must be applied also to *the* Sacrament, the Eucharist. Some years ago I happened to have made some studies and discovered to my surprise that until about the twelfth century in the West, the Church gloried in that little phrase (I thing it is from the Canticle of Canticles) which describes the bride, *circumdata varietate*. How would you translate that —"garbed in variety"? She gloried in that for twelve centuries, and then began the emphasis on uniformity. We ourselves are still glorying in the variety in the East and West, that the Church was big enough to correspond to the different mentalities in East and West. Well, I have wondered whether the mentality between a man forty years old and his twelve year old son is not a far greater difference than between East and West in the sixth century, because, in a different way, both East and West derived from the Hellenistic civilization. We have greater variety now because of the generation gap; we have greater variety between the peoples, and, therefore, there is the greater need for such adaptation.

I spoke earlier of the fact that the Church is a pilgrim Church. One of our problems has been that we did not take a step until we had a blue print for it, and I think we still more or less expect that. That is the one thing we should have learned not to expect of the Holy Spirit; He does things in strange ways. We have no right to make a blueprint for Him; we have to have a little more faith in His guiding spirit. That is part and parcel of our pilgrimage. Since the Eucharist is the memorial of the saving events, what are we memorializing? We are an historical Church, and, yet, it was not until I began to prepare for this paper that what we have been memorializing suddenly struck me. We have been celebrating the events in the Old Testament. We have been celebrating events in the life of Christ; then, we jump two thousand years and get to His Parousia—as if the Church had no history. We have not been celebrating the saving events in time, but as if the Church merely looked back and looked forward to a distant future and not to the present. There has been a failure to recognize the notion of memorial—Christ's saving events in the present for the Church in her present need. Why are we afraid of introducing such things that really have manifested God's presence? I was present in Washington at the March of 1963; I carried a banner. And, I will never forget that speech of Martin Luther King, "I Had a Dream." I think this was one of the great Christian events of our time. I lived under Mussolini for four years and under Hitler for one year; I know what a demagogue is. When I first heard Martin Luther King, I trembled because he had that power. Yet I think I have never heard a more Christian speech; I think this was a manifestation of God in our midst. There are many things we can celebrate; we can celebrate

Gandhi, his teaching us a Christian lesson; we can celebrate John XXIII more than we have been doing. But this suggests further application. Since the Eucharist is the most important self-manifestation of the Church, it should also be the greatest and best self-realization. Our talk of the four notes of the Church does not mean something happened in the past. This is a process of becoming; we are constantly becoming more one, holy, catholic, and apostolic; we are becoming a Church. It is in the Eucharist that the Church is an event, that the Death and Resurrection become a reality for the present dying and rising of the Church.

After the document on the Liturgy had been published, the Council developed its ecclesiology. I think our great problem is that the reforms correspond to the ecclesiology we find in the document on the Liturgy and not sufficiently to the ecclesiology which developed since that time, even though it was sparked by that document. Thus, it is only subsequently that we discovered that the Protestant bodies also are Churches, that the Holy Spirit is working in them as Churches, as means of salvation. We should have learned that we in our own day are learning much from the Holy Spirit's working in these Protestant Churches: the building for renewal, the common priesthood of the faithful, authority as *diakonia,* the sense of personal commitment of faith, religious liberty, *ecclesia semper reformanda*—all these things. We used to think that the liturgy especially was the one area where we had nothing to learn from our Protestand friends; we are beginning to understand that this is one area in which we have not only much, but perhaps most, to learn. In the document on Ecumenism we read that we should search "together with separated brethren into the divine mysteries. . . ."[11] The Divine Mystery, *Mysterium fidei,* is the Eucharist. This is a question not merely of the historical Protestant Churches, but also of the Pentecostal Churches. It is very embarrassing to read Paul's first letter to the Corinthians and to find that one of the characteristics of the Holy Spirit is to have diversity expressed in various ways. Saint Paul did not seem to be afraid of the manifestations of the Spirit, but those who led them must see to it that everything was done decently and orderly, that the charismatic gifts and everything be used for the Church. From some of our Pentecostal friends perhaps we can learn a certain spirit of spontaneity. We talk about the hierarchical and prophetic Church, but I think we can learn some of the prophetic office from our Pentecostal friends. I think when all is said and done, this is what the liturgical renewal is about: how to balance the hierarchical-institutional with the more spontaneous, with the prophetic, the leader's always seeing to it that all things are done in decency and order.

I think the Spirit has been speaking through men like Luther, through the World Council of Churches. I think we have a great Jewish prophet in our midst—Abraham Heschel. There is a great Quaker prophet here at Haverford—Douglas Steere; I know of no one who can really give one a sense of prayer better than he. I think Malcolm X as a Muslim has a Christian message for us; his autobiography is a real discovery. In addition, there are Martin Luther King, perhaps Eldridge Cleaver and some of the agony of what he is asking for. Since we are celebrating the modern Church, we are celebrating the present Church and her present obligations to the modern world. I think one of the best preparations for celebrating Mass would be to read the headlines of the day's paper. It would not be a distraction because we would realize what sort of world God is trying to save at the present time.

Vatican II went to some pains to get a good title for that final big document which, I think, will prove the most important: *The Church in the Modern World—in the modern world.* It was Paul VI who finally rescued us from a little slogan which did a lot of damage: the Church is in this world, but not of it. He concluded that with another nice little prepositional phrase: the Church is not in the world, not of the world, but for the world. I think it is magnificent. The days when we listened to the advice of the author of the *Imitation of Christ* without question, as if he were infallible, are gone. He has good things, but consider the statement about going out into the world and coming back less a man. As far as I understand, the Council has said the exact opposite by talking about salvation opportunities. The spiritual life is not something whereby we fill ourselves during Mass and prayer, and, during the rest of the day, have it leak out of us, after which we go back again to the filling station. These daily encounters with others are meeting Christ—Christ on location. The Church is a mystery to the world—the sacrament, the sign, not to herself, but to the world, that must be recognized as such by the world. That includes also the language that is used. It is curious how blind a person can be; I did not fully realize this until I read Ray Brown a few years ago. He reminded us that when John says that God is love, God is light, God is life, this is not a definition of God. What John means to say is that God gives love, God gives life, God gives light. This makes all the difference in the world.

God reveals Himself in saving acts, and the Church is the saving act. The Church today in the modern world, above all the Church celebrating the liturgy, should be the saving act for us. Hence, we need new ways for talking about God; this is especially true of the Collects. I think that every one here will realize that merely translating the Collects almost compounded the problem; they are not satisfactory; they are very abstract. It is not enough merely to pray for an increase of faith, hope, and charity. That does include all, and if you meditate about it for half an hour, perhaps then you put a meaning into it in terms of your own concrete situation. But, for most people this is hardly enough as a real prayer. That is the reason it is good that we have men who are experimenting with prayer. It is possible to have general prayers and to be concrete in terms of our own need.

The Eucharist is for the world; it is not, therefore, only for the members of the one, holy, Roman Catholic, and apostolic Church. Christ is the head of all creation, not merely the members of the Holy Roman Catholic Church. The liturgy must reflect this. Since the liturgy is a celebration of Christ's saving acts, the liturgy must reflect not just what happens in the Holy Roman Catholic Church. For sixteen hundred years we have sinned—by being selfish in the prayers of the liturgy, not sufficiently reflecting our real obligation to the world which Christ came to redeem. The prayers were not general enough. Only on Good Friday did we pray for some of those intentions. The three new Eucharistic prayers mention all others, at least very modestly, but much more has to be done in that way.

We are a pilgrim Church, and that means we are an eschatological Church. We are looking to the future which we are helping to create through the Holy Spirit. I would like to give a good plug here for the Dutch catechism. The one wonderful thing it reminds us of is that creation is not something of the past; it is a continuing process. We are called upon to help create, therefore, we are a people of the future, living in the present; the Holy Spirit is still brooding over the water of the present. The documents of Vatican II talk about the Church as being the community of faith and love. I do not recall a single statement in which it is said in so many words that it is a community of hope. Yet, I think that is precisely what we need to stress now more than anything else. Surely it is a community of faith and of love, but also a community of hope. We have only the beginning of a theology of hope; what we need is a liturgy of hope. It is rather ominous that we have a theology of hope before we have a liturgy of hope; this is not the way things should happen.

There is one final thought, and it is about the priest. He faces the people; that means he must see them, he must recognize them as persons. Obedience comes from the Latin word *ob audire,* which means "to listen to." Therefore, the bishop must be obedient to his people. The priest must be obedient to his people. The only pronoun that really counts is *we*—the Holy Spirit, the priest, and his people. The liturgy will lead us from the altar to the streets of the city. Liturgical reforms must be a continuation of the difficult but critically necessary process of the Church's self-discovery—in itself, in relation to the non-Catholics, in relation to the world.

NOTES

[1] Aelred Graham, O.S.B., "The Larger Ecumenism," *The Tablet* (London), March 1, 1969, pp. 204-05.

[2] Cf. Andrew M. Greeley, *The Hesitant Pilgrim* (New York: Sheed and Ward, 1966); *The Crucible of Change* (New York: Sheed and Ward, 1969).

[3] Walter M. Abbott, S.J., ed., *The Documents of Vatican II* (New York: Guild Press, 1966), p. 28.

[4] *Ibid.*, p. 545.

[5] Sacred Congregation of Rites, *Instruction on Eucharistic Worship* (Washington, D.C.: United States Catholic Conference, 1967).

[6] Abbott, *op. cit.*, p. 146.

[7] Hans Urs von Balthasar, *Prayer*, trans. by A. V. Littledale (New York: Paulist Press Deus Books, 1967), p. 169.

[8] Abbott, *op. cit.*, pp. 201-02.

[9] *Ibid.*, p. 158.

[10] *Ibid.*, pp. 151-2.

[11] *Ibid.*, p. 354.

The Future of the Dialogue: Pluralism or an Eventual Synthesis of Doctrine?

George A. Lindbeck

I—INTRODUCTORY

IN this paper I shall try to pull together my reflections on the current status and possible future of that portion of the ecumenical dialogue which centers on the doctrinal issues dividing the major Christian traditions. The first phase of that dialogue has been completed and a second set of questions now looms large, yet in the meantime the whole enterprise has come to seem irrelevant. These are the three themes I would like us to consider, but first it is necessary to explain in more detail what they involve.

Doctrinal pluralism has been the concern of the first stage. Its legitimacy has now been established. Even the Roman Catholic Church speaking through the Second Vatican Council has affirmed, in reference to the differences between East and West, that there can be an irreducible yet enriching diversity of doctrinal systems. This makes it possible to envision a situation in which Orthodox, Catholic and Protestant could, without capitulation or compromise, recognize each other's positions as authentically Christian, as not church-dividing. In order to do this, it is not necessary to have a synthesis in which the competing formulations are integrated from a new and common perspective into a larger and universally accepted whole. No, as in the case of what the biblical scholars tell us about New Testament theologies, the differences are irreducible. Each tradition retains its distinctiveness. Yet we now see that they might still be able to acknowledge each other as fully legitimate and highly valuable explications of Christian truth and faith.

This achievement, however, means that the dialogue has reached the end of one line of inquiry and must, if it is to advance, change direction. The next problem is that of unity rather than diversity. How can we identify the unity of faith which embraces an irreducible doctrinal pluralism? The criteria for identifying this unity canot themselves be doctrines. They must be infra-doctrinal or meta-doctrinal, either given before or found beyond dogmatic formulations. Yet they must be capable of articulation, they must be objectively specifiable, for otherwise unity in the faith turns into something wholly invisible and the oneness of the Christian community becomes intangible.

As far as I can see, the ecumenical specialists are so far doing little with this problem. They continue to concentrate on pluralism even though all that here remains is to apply generally recognized principles and procedures to concrete cases, of which, to be sure, there is a never-ending supply. The result, however, is that the dialogue is drained of intellectual excitement. It now arouses much less interest even among ecumenically-inclined theologians than it did three or four years ago.

There is also another reason for the dialogical doldrums: it no longer seems relevant. External developments in world, church and theology have appeared to be passing beyond it. The historic dogmatic divisions and, indeed, official doctrine in general are said to be hopelessly outmoded. Some claim that doctrine as traditionally understood will never again be important. It will never again be necessary or desirable officially to establish standards of belief, norms of orthodoxy and criteria of heresy. If this is true, then the doctrinal dialogue is at best a harmless diversion, at worst a dangerous distraction.

II—RELEVANCE

IT is with these external difficulties, with this question of practical relevance, that I would like to start our discussion. The way we deal with the internal problems of the dialogue, with the questions of pluralism and unity, will be largely determined by what we think is their concrete importance.

More and more I find myself agreeing that the dialogue is of little current significance either to the organized churches or to movements of renewal. The churches are interested only to the degree that it provides theological justification for doing what they wish to do on other grounds. Ecumenism is largely the product of non-theological forces, but as some of the obstacles it confronted were theological, it was necessary to appeal to ecumenical experts. They, however, have opened up more possibilities than the churches are willing or able to exploit. It will be a long time before the Protestant, Orthodox and

Catholic establishments will seriously seek to implement either in word or deed that full mutual recognition which is now in principle possible; and it will be even longer before they undertake to develop new ways, appropriate to the pluralistic situation, of distinguishing between Christian truth and falsity in a contemporaneously relevant fashion. They will, of course, continue to sponsor inter-confessional discussions, but with declining interest in their results.

The *avant garde* activists and theological progressives are even less concerned. As little as four years ago, the dialogue was the rage, but now the situation has in one respect reverted to what it was before John XXIII opened wide the ecumenical windows. Many of my students, both Catholic and Protestant, are once again unwilling seriously to discuss the dogmatic differences of their churches. Their reason, to be sure, is entirely different from the old one. A decade or more ago, discussion was stifled by the supposed immensity of the dogmatic disagreements, while now these are thought to be too trivial to be worth talking about. Who among those in tune with the modern world could possibly care about the *filioque,* which divided Greeks and Latins in the eleventh century, or justification *sola fida,* which split the West in the sixteenth, or the old arguments over transubstantiation, or even discussions of episcopacy and papacy? What counts is Christian participation in revolutionary action or, if one insists on being theological, how to talk about God in a secular age. To be sure, secular ecumenism evokes growing enthusiasm, but the doctrinal variety is even less important to the younger generation and the anti-institutionalists than it is to the church bureaucrats.

If, then, there is any practical significance to the dialogue, it must be found in the future. Doctrine, I shall argue, will once again become a burning issue. The problem of how to embrace radical pluralism within identifiable unity will be crucial to the health of the church. Thus for those who are genuinely forward-looking and capable of discerning deeper currents beneath the surface tempests, the dialogue is even now important. It has a vital role to play in influencing those underlying trends which will eventually emerge as dominating forces.

Those who think otherwise usually make the elementary mistake, it seems to me, of envisioning the future in terms of the uniform extrapolation of present tendencies. Because activism, theological pluralism and the speed of change are now increasing, they assume that it will always be so. But most processes, whether physical, psychological or social, are incapable of infinite extension. At some point they must stop or reverse themselves.

Anti-doctrinalism will reverse itself, I suspect, when Constantinian mass Christianity finally collapses and is replaced by a Christian diaspora. Once Christians are again a small minority everywhere in the world, even in traditionally Christian countries, they will be at least

as much concerned about dogmatic questions as were their predecessors
of the first three centuries.

The case for expecting a drastically diminished church is of course
not conclusive, but it is familiar, and so here I shall assume it and
simply explain why shrinkage will, from the viewpoint of the sociology
of knowledge, lead to renewed stress on orthodoxy and heresy.

In the first place, the present irrelevance of doctrine in the church,
or of ideology in society at large, is anomolous. It is not likely to continue, but is characteristic of an age of transition when socially inte-
grating belief systems are dissolving and new ones have not yet
coalesced. In the case of the church this problem is intensified by the
fact that ecclesiastical Constantinianism is dying, but not yet dead.
Most people in the West continue to identify themselves as Christian,
not out of personal commitment, but for social and traditional reasons.
Even these reasons for being religious play a smaller and smaller part
in their lives. This reduces the organized churches to doctrinal im-
potence. They are preoccupied with the effort to retain their increasingly unengaged membership, and so their natural tendency is to be
as tolerant as possible of all kinds of opinions and practices whether
on the right or the left. Sometimes they act, but except in the case
of charismatic explosions such as those which influenced the Second
Vatican Council, this is likely to be in a conservative direction. Doctrine is thereby further discredited, for the conservatives are generally
not interested in the preservation and effective restatement of the substance of past dogmas, but are simply nostalgically attached to eviscer-
ated formulas. The progressives, of course, are alienated and become
increasingly anti-institutional. In a sense they are right, for the religious
institutions are captive to constituencies for whom religion is a conventional matter of declining importance. Under these circumstances,
the system is necessarily stifling. Even good men are doomed to futility
when they try to operate within it.

Such accommodation to culture cannot, however, go on forever.
Any social grouping whose distinctiveness is imperiled by compromise
with alien forces must ultimately become sectarian in the sociologcal
sense of the term in order to preserve its identity. This is as true of
political parties or ethnic communities as it is of religious ones. Thus
as the de-christianization of the West progresses, the major churches
will in the long run survive only to the extent that they lose the structures they have had for fifteen hundred years. They must reconcile
themselves to the loss of mass membership. They must strive to become
close-knit fellowships of the personally committed who mutually support and encourage each other in the difficult task of maintaining
what in the eyes of society as a whole are increasingly odd and strange
ways of thinking and acting. This will require vast transformations
in the organization of parishes, bureaucracies and hierarchies, for at
the center will not be passive multitudes of customers who are mildly

interested in some of the churches' wares, but rather face-to-face cell groups whose chief interest is God and his will for themselves and the world.

Doctrine will be important to these groups. Their distinctiveness cannot reside only in personal morality, communal liturgies and social action, but these must be legitimated by what outsiders will consider fantastic beliefs and impossible definitions of reality. Without definite and peculiarly Christian convictions regarding God, man, Jesus and the world they could not in the long-run resist the pressures of a society which, we are assuming, will more and more regard Christian behavior and values as foolish or perhaps even dangerous.

Ecumenism will also be vital, far more so than in the days of Christian majorities. Small groups are particularly susceptible to all kinds of distortions. They need to be linked together in local and regional bodies. But these bodies, if they themselves are small minorities without special cultural prestige, are also particularly vulnerable to alien pressures. Nevertheless, they can survive and even prosper in extraordinarily adverse environments if sustained by being part of a unified net-work, a world-wide movement. This has been partially illustrated in our day by Communism, but the most pertinent example comes, of course, from the early history of the church. The victorious portion of the Christian movement was the part which remained united in the confrontation with Roman power and pagan culture. The many Christian groups in the Empire which did not emphasize unity, which were isolated and fragmented, tended to disappear one by one even in the early centuries before the power of the state was brought to bear against them. Only the catholic or ecumenical Christians—i.e., those who stressed universality and unity—persisted and prevailed.

It is a real question, however, whether the future diaspora will in fact be ecumenical. Both inside and outside the major churches, the groups which have the most sectarian intensity and therefore the greatest potential for survival in unpleasantly minority situations are in our day generally anti-ecumenical. They are backward-looking, fundamentalist and divisive, and thus quite different from the early Christian sectarianism which succeeded in embracing a remarkable variety of social classes, races and theologies in an ecumenical and catholic unity. They are extraordinarily poor building blocks for an ecumenical church. Yet without the doctrinal and religious intensity which they exemplify, there will be no identifiably Christian communities in coming centuries.

Doctrinal dialogue is therefore crucial. To be sure, it is of little significance to the large organized churches as they are at present constituted, and it is irrelevant to religionless Christianity and Christian secularism. But the future does not belong to them. It belongs to those groups, however small or unfashionable they may be at the moment, which take doctrine seriously. And it is only by breaking down the dogmatic barriers between them in a way which does not destroy their concern with correct belief that the future will be ecumenical.

This, then, is the historical and sociological perspective within which I view the practical import of the dialogue. This provides the setting within which we shall now treat the twin problems of doctrinal pluralism and identifiable unity in the faith.

III—PLURALISM

YOU will recall that my own view is that the problem of pluralism has in principle already been settled. It is possible to envision a situation in which the major Christian traditions mutually recognize each other's positions without denying their respective doctrinal heritages. There are responsible Catholic, Protestant and Orthodox theologians, men recognized as loyal sons of their churches, who interpret all the major controversies of the past in such a way that the opposing dogmas are understood as complementary rather than contradictory.

This is common knowledge, I would suppose, in reference to the doctrine of justification as understood, for example, by Hans Küng and Karl Barth, or in reference to transubstantiation and the sacrifice of the mass as they were recently expounded, to cite a collective work, in the American Catholic-Lutheran conversations sponsored by the respective churches. It is also true of the Marian dogmas as these are interpreted, to mention just one theologian, by Karl Rahner. Even from a thoroughly Reformation perspective, his interpretations of the Assumption and Immaculate Conception are legitimate theological opinions. The Protestant is not likely to accept these opinions as his own and he would almost certainly object to their being made into dogmas binding on the whole church, but he can admit that they are not in themselves heretical, that they do not contradict the Gospel, that they need not divide the church.

The same situation prevails, I would argue, even in the most difficult questions of scripture and tradition, doctrine of the church, episcopacy and papacy. There are genuinely Catholic versions of these dogmas now available which good Protestant and Orthodox theologians, thoroughly faithful to their own traditions, see no reason to reject as heretical so long as they are not made obligatory for all Christians.

Some Catholics on their side are now wondering whether it is necessary for the unity of the church to insist on the acceptance by other Christians of all the Roman dogmas. The Decree on Ecumenism says that Roman Catholic theologians "When comparing doctrines ... should remember that in Catholic teaching there exists an order or 'hierarchy' of truths, since they vary in their relationship to the foundation of the Christian faith" (art. 11). The drafters of this document, in explaining the reasons for this recommendation, state that "It seems to be of the greatest importance for the ecumenical dialogue that both the truths in which Christians agree and those in which they differ should be weighed rather than counted. Although all revealed truths are undoubtedly to be held by divine faith, their importance and 'weight' differ according to their connection with the history of salvation and the mystery of Christ."

Is it then possible that the Roman Catholic Church could eventually come to rate the papal and Marian dogmas which are peculiar to it as low enough in the hierarchy of truths, as sufficiently remote from the central Christological affirmations, that it would ask other churches simply not to deny them, simply to accept them as legitimate optional theological opinions? Is it possible that this might someday be considered a sufficient doctrinal consensus for the re-establishment of full ecclesiastical communion? The Roman Catholics presumably would in addition insist on arrangements for governing and preserving the unity of the church which would include a perhaps vastly modified "practical" primacy of the Petrine See, but it is an open question whether they need to require that the Orthodox and Protestants accept this primacy as part of revealed truth, as *de iure divino* in the sense implied by Vatican I.

As a number of Catholic authors have pointed out, there is an at least partial precedent for this in the Council of Florence (1438-1439), which agreed to a union between East and West without demanding that the Greeks insert the *filioque* in the Creed. In historical retrospect, it seems evident that this was a case of the official mutual recognition of irreducibly diverse dogmatic systems. It opens up the at least theoretical possibility of future union between the major Christian traditions in which real dogmatic differences remain and yet there is full mutual acceptance of each other as authentically Christian.

These possibilities seem fantastic from the viewpoint of even a few years ago, but given contemporary awareness of historical and linguistic relativity, they are almost commonplace. The first lesson we have learned is that any doctrinal statement depends for its meaning on the practical and intellectual situation within which it is uttered. Thus, to give a familiar example, the central affirmation of the early church, "Jesus is the Messiah, the Anointed one," was an enormously rich concept in the Jewish environment. It meant, however, much less to the Greeks, and quickly in their mouths become simply a proper name, *Xristos.* It therefore was in effect largely replaced by another way of professing basically the same faith, "Jesus is Lord," *kyrios,* which introduced new ways of thinking about the supreme importance of Jesus, and also resulted in the neglect of some old ones which the current theology of hope is now seeking to recover.

It can be seen from this that dogmatic affirmations are susceptible of an indefinite number of re-interpretations depending on the new concrete circumstances and intellectual frameworks within which they are of necessity inserted in the course of history. This process of re-interpretation and re-formulation is not simply an unfortunate necessity, even though it can result in loss as well as gain, but is positively desirable. In radically changed circumstances, old formulas may no longer express what was originally intended. Often the only way to be faithful to the substance of the tradition is to state the old truths in new words and concepts. In some cases, as we have already illustrated at length, this new, faithful and necessary re-interpretation of old formulas may make possible the overcoming of historic dogmatic oppositions.

A second lesson, it seems to me, is that dogma is essentially defensive. I am inclined to emphasize this more than many of those who are engaged in the ecumenical dialogue, but this is in part, perhaps, because I am influenced by Anglo-Saxon empiricism, especially in its current linguistic-analytic phase. It is important to observe, I believe, that dogma is not primary religious language. It is twice removed from the basic articulations of the faith. The first strata consists of the non-technical language of prayer and worship and especially, for the Christian, of the biblical stories about Jesus, Israel and the church. On the second level are the interpretations of these stories, not only in theology, but also in individual and communal practice, piety and structure. Through these interpretations, believers and the believing community relate the biblical stories they profess to accept as permanently revelatory to the ever-changing realities of their life and thought. Thirdly, comes doctrine which consists of the community's official guides, norms or rules of interpretation. Doctrinal formulations may also function as doxologies, confessions of faith or premises in theological constructions, but in their specifically doctrinal role, their import is essentially negative. In that role, they do not determine positively how the stories are to be interpreted, but rather indicate how they should not be interpreted. No interpretation should contradict them. Theologians are free to seek for entirely fresh ways of explaining and applying the stories, and these fresh explanations and applications may, in fact, entirely replace the old ones as more relevant or intrinsically more adequate. But even if a formula is no longer repeated, it retains its dogmatic status as long as there is a recognized obligation not to deny it.

The consequence of thus viewing dogmas as historically conditioned, partial and defensive rules of interpretation is, of course, to admit, not only the possibility but the necessity and desirability of radical pluralism. In a way we have come full circle. The ecumenical dialogue started with the problem of how it is possible for staunch adherents of separated traditions to admit doctrinal diversity. Now we find ourselves asking whether there is such a thing as an identifiable unity and continuity in the faith which spans the centuries and embraces vast differences. I have already argued that some kind of specifiable unity is necessary, if not for the churches of today, then for the diaspora of tomorrow. Non-contradiction is not enough for mutual recognition. There must be the acknowledgment of something in common, of a shared faith. By what objective means, if any, can we discern a non-doctrinal identity in the midst of an irreducible pluralism?

IV—UNITY

THERE is nothing conclusive or definitive in what I am going to say about this problem of unity. This is simply a groping attempt to explain how it is possible to have an at least somewhat objective apprehension of full Christian brotherhood within the most immense dissimilarities. I personally think that such an apprehension exists. It was operative, it seems to me, in the early days of the church between the adherents of the very different theologies which we now find side by side in the New Testament. It also functions when we sense in reading an Augustine or Origen that we are fully a part of the same Christian family despite drastic differences in sensibility, conceptuality and theology.

Let us start by trying to be concrete and imaginative rather than abstract and technical. Let us try to envision a Christianity as remote as possible from anything which we know and then ask what it would have in common with the church of all ages.

This Christianity would, of course, be in the far future, perhaps a few million years from now. Christian orthodoxy is committed to believing that even then there would be a community, a church, which would be identifiably Christian. It would exist in a situation unimaginably different from the present. The planet on which we live might have vanished. Men might be living in immeasurably distant stellar systems or galaxies. Their physical setting, their flora and fauna, might have no resemblance to the seascape and landscape, the plants and animals, of old mother earth. Intellectual culture, the social environment and perhaps even the genetic constitution of these distant descendants of ours might be far more different from our own than we are different from the first muttering ape men. Perhaps, as Huxley predicted, embryos will then grow in artificial wombs, not in their mothers' bodies. Perhaps individuals will live for hundreds or even thousands of years. Maybe telepathy will be a tool of concretely controllable communication so that humanity will be knit together with unimaginable intensity and extensity. Or, on the other hand, perhaps mankind will have split into various branches which have lost touch with each other in the vastness of stellar space.

And yet, so the Christian asserts, there will be at least some among these supermen who repeat and believe certain archaic stories of a man in the mists of their pre-history who lived, died on a cross and rose again. They may no longer know where in space his planet was located.

He may seem to them almost inconceivably primitive, practically indistinguishable from the ape men. Yet they will think of him as incomparably significant, as the greatest of all realities, of all events, in the space-time world of human experiences. The stories about him will mold their thinking about the nameless mystery which surrounds their beginning and end as it does ours. They may not conceptualize this mystery in the ways we now think of God. Yet, for them, as for Christians today, the climatic clues to why we are here and where we are going, the beginning and the end, the Alpha and the Omega, will be found in these tales of life, death, resurrection and the promise of Christ's coming again.

If one grants that such memories and such hopes will survive, then it is easy to predict more. The Christian denizens of this unimaginable future will engage in certain startlingly primitivistic rites recognizably similar to our baptism and eucharist. Further, no matter how completely Greek and Hebrew may have been forgotten and the Bible translated and retranslated, fragmented and paraphrased, still there will be a scripture, there will be some kind of account of the basic outlines of the story of Jesus and of the way this was understood by those who first received the revelation.

Roman Catholics may wish to add to this list of enduring elements. They believe, for example, that the papacy and the episcopacy will continue. But, as Karl Rahner and others have pointed out, the concrete organizational forms of these institutions may be vastly different. Perhaps the secretary of a Quaker meeting may be a better analogue of the future papacy than is the monarchical pattern of recent centuries. Or conversely, and one suspects unhappily, humanity may then be involved in a hyper-Constantinian era in which the pope serves as the chief executive of an Intergalactic League of Planets.

Is there anything else of which the Christian can be so bold as to assert that it will endure to the end of time? More particularly, can this be said of any of the church's post-biblical doctrinal formulations and decisions?

I wonder if this question can't be answered negatively with perfect orthodoxy, even from a Roman Catholic point of view, as long as one makes a distinction between denying a dogma and positively affirming it, and between a dogmatic formulation and the reality to which it points. Thus the Catholic believes *de fide,* and the Protestant hopes and trusts, that no matter how long the world continues, the church as a whole will not repudiate the realities, the truths, to which the dogmas point. There will always be at least a faithful remnant which does not deny the Trinity and the Incarnation.

But to say that the church will not repeal these dogmatic formulations is not at all the same thing as to assert that it will continue to remember them. It seems both unnecessary and rash to insist that these truths will continue to be positively affirmed in terms and concepts recognizably similar to those which we use. There seems to be no vital reason for supposing that any word or concept translatable into Nicea's *homousion* will be part of theological equipment of this hypothetical church of a million years from now. The Trinitarian conceptuality of the post-biblical period could be entirely forgotten and the realities this is meant to express be dealt with in other terms—terms perhaps totally unintelligible from our perspective. If this is granted about so central a dogmatic development as the Trinitarian, then it would appear that none of our present dogmatic formulations can be declared exempt from this process of possible obsolescence and forgetfulness. To mention only some doctrines disputed between Protestants and Catholics, the *sola fide* and the Marian dogmas might pass into the limbo of forgotten things and only the most erudite scholarship would be capable of showing that the church still believed, or at least did not disbelieve, the truths inadequately pointed to by these formulations.

I may be mistaken, but it seems to me that most Christian thinkers who concern themselves with problems of diversity and unity would find this imaginative projection not too unacceptable. It strongly emphasizes both the constants and the relativities of Christian belief and therefore meets the major concerns of both parties.

But it does this, you will observe, by finding the objective constants of Christianity, not on the level of such technical theological concepts as the *homousion* and the hypostatic union, but in concrete particularities and events, the stories which tell of them, the rites which celebrate them, and the non-technical ordinary language statements such as "Jesus Christ died for us" or "Christ will return," which explain their significance. This supports the thesis of the ordinary language philosophers that the constants in human thought are to be found on the common sense level. Reflective analysis, whether theological or non-theological, instead of penetrating to the permanent essence of things is, at least usually, an especially susceptible victim of cultural and historical relativity. The fundamental human import of a man dying to save another need not vary from the cave, to the twentieth century, to a million years from now, but the explanations of why and how this is so may vary enormously. Similarly, fundamental physical concepts, such as that of the rising sun, will remain unchanged as long as man has anything remotely resembling his present biological constitution, but the explanations of exactly what happens have already passed through the mythic, Ptolemaic, Newtonian and Einsteinian phases and may well be revolutionized again and again in the future. Theological explanations of the saving power of Jesus' death, while logically quite different from scientific hypothesis, are capable of a similar diversity as is evident when we compare St. Anselm's judicial satisfaction theory of the atonement with the Greek "Christus Victor" view.

It should not be supposed that this makes reflective theological analysis and technical doctrinal formulations superfluous. It is precisely through them that the gospel stories are protected from abuse in particular circumstances or become incarnate and effective in a given intellectual and cultural milieu. It is perhaps only through something like the Anselmic theory that Jesus' death could have been vividly expressed and apprehended in the medieval feudal context. Yet this does not mean that it is permanently or universally indispensable, and the same can perhaps be said of all other doctrines including the *homousion*.

These considerations reinforce our earlier conclusion that unity and continuity cannot be identified by means of theological or doctrinal formulations. This, however, is liberating. It frees us to look for unity in simple and unsophisticated places, in infra- and meta-doctrinal factors.

The infra-doctrinal unity is obvious, so obvious that it is easily overlooked and is almost embarrassing to mention. It consists of the stories about Jesus Christ and of their celebration in worship and conduct. There is no objectively specifiable deeper unity or abiding essence behind them. All metaphysical and existentialist efforts to penetrate to universal constants are illusory because they are themselves simply abstract and secondary commentaries on the richer and fuller meaning intrinsic to the narratives. What unifies the various interpretations of Hamlet is the play itself, and similarly what unifies theological and doctrinal systems is simply the revelatory events as witnessed to in Scripture.

This insight, however, does not help us to distinguish between good and bad interpretations. It enables us to identify those which can plausibly claim to be Christian, but it does not differentiate between orthodoxy and heterodoxy. A meta-doctrinal criterion is necessary. The most obvious one, as it happens, is extensively used in the New Testament, and it is also the most useful one. The New Testament literature, we recall, reflects a theological situation which was in some ways even more chaotic and variable than our own. The early Christians interpreted and reinterpreted the Gospel in radically diverse ways in order to make it intelligible, relevant and persuasive to different kinds of people. Yet there were limits, and the limits of allowable diversity were set by the confession "Jesus is Lord." Roughly paraphrased, this affirms that the specific, concrete, historical man Jesus who lived and died and rose again is for all times and places the most important event, the crucial reality, within the universe of human experience and knowledge.

What is invariant about this confession, let it be noted, is not the words or conceptuality in which it is expressed. Rather it is a confession of faith, an expression of ultimate concern, a judgment of unsurpassable significance. It is meta-doctrinal rather than doctrinal because it defines the rules by which all Christian games of interpretation should be played rather than being itself part of a game.

The result is that it superbly unifies diversity, and it does so with sectarian intensity. That is why it was so useful a criterion in the first centuries, and why it may become so again in a future diaspora. As far as diversity is concerned, there are as many different ways of asserting that Jesus is Lord as there are different patterns of attitudes, behavior and concepts. An early apologist like Justin Martyr, for example, knew of no better way of explaining the supreme importance of Jesus than to say that he was the promulgator of the true philosophy. For Justin Martyr, philosophy and the philosophers were at the pinnacle of that which is significant, and consequently, "Jesus is Lord" necessarily meant for him, in effect, that Jesus was in the line of Socrates and Plato although incomparably greater. For the most part, the Christian tradition has not questioned Justin Martyr's orthodoxy because he was so obviously devoted to affirming this supreme importance of Jesus; yet when others have talked in rather similar terms of Jesus as a philosopher or wise man, they have been rejected because they used this language, not to emphasize, but to minimize his universal and total cruciality and centrality. Other examples could be cited. For some, the supremely important reality has been Jesus as the one through whom sins are forgiven, or Jesus as the sum and center of the cosmos, or Jesus the God-Man, or Jesus as the source and norm of full humanity, or authentic existence or true secularity. Each one of these formulations and innumerable others could conceivably be orthodox —that is, explanations and persuasions which do not water down and betray the faith—and each of them, including "Jesus the God-Man," and "Jesus the Forgiver," if used to assert something less than that Jesus is Lord in the sense of being supremely important for the whole of your life and the whole of my life and for all humanity, can be heterodox. Clearly this criterion allows for extreme doctrinal pluralism while still unmistakably pointing to a common center of faith, of personal and communal commitment and loyalty.

More than this, however. The unity indicated by this criterion is not only to be seen in the loyalty and commitment of persons and communities, but also in doctrinal or theological systems. Certain positions are clearly disqualified, while others are not. For example, cultural Christianity, whether of the modernist or conservative varieties, is ruled out. A modernist, as I am using the term, is one who unabashedly makes the attitudes and convictions of his milieu into a kind of Procrustean bed into which he tries to fit as much of the tradition as he finds convenient. He quite openly takes his canons of what is reasonable and good from non-Christian sources, and then cheerfully stretches, compresses and chops off whatever cannot be accommodated. The most glaring examples of this are early gnostics, medieval Averroists, some Renaissance humanists, extreme nineteenth and twentieth century liberals, and the *Deutsche Christen* of the Nazi period. Obviously, however, the conservative who capitulates to a traditionalist culture makes

the same error. Most mainstream theologians stand in sharp contrast
to this. They tend to resemble the modernists in their concern for the
contemporaneous, but they shape their world by the faith rather than
the other way around. The Greek and Latin Fathers, Augustine,
Aquinas, Luther, Calvin, Karl Barth and Teilhard de Chardin tried
to reshape whatever convictions they may have had about the world,
whether Platonist, Aristotelian, nominalist, German idealist or modern
evolutionary, in the light of their primary commitment to the reality
and truth which is in Jesus Christ. They certainly were not always
successful, but their conscious intention obviously was "to make every
thought captive to him." Looked at statically, both the modernists and
the main-line theologians synthesized the traditional with whatever was
current wisdom, but the rules by which they played were actually entirely
different. One group re-interpreted the tradition in order to make it
more credible or attractive in terms of the currently popular norms of
reasonablenesss or goodness. The other group, one might say, re-interpreted the world in terms of the Gospel, in terms of the Lordship of
Christ, so that a given period would see what that Lordship means in
terms of what to it is the real, the true and the good.

There is, it would seem, a certain consonance between this latter procedure and sectarian intensity. While the theologians of the great
tradition were devoted to making the faith relevant and meaningful,
they were not in the least concerned about whether this made it more
palatable. Often, indeed, they sharpened the offense of the cross by
transforming Christian claims from peripheral archaisms into contemporary realities. They insisted that Christ is the Lord of all and therefore
cannot be confined to the sphere of private piety and explicitly religious
practices. He is also, as we would say in our day, Lord and Judge of
the civil rights movement and of the war in Vietnam. On the other
side, however, it is also true that one does not effectively acknowledge
Christ as Lord if one is unconcerned about the church and its worship
and structures, or if one is indifferent to the personal relation of the individual to God and neighbor. This was clearly recognized by the
theologians we have mentioned. For them, religion was both intense
and all-embracing, and therefore highly suitable for a minority diaspora.

I hope that I have now said enough to make plausible, even if not
wholly convincing, the claim that a sectarian church of the future could
be genuinely unified even in the midst of a radical doctrinal pluralism
unmitigated by synthesis. The first requirement, of course, is non-
contradiction, but that, we have suggested, is not enough. Both our
historical awareness and logical considerations make us keenly aware
that non-contradiction is a rather cheap commodity. It is easy for
positions to be wildly different without actually opposing each other.
Non-contradiction, therefore, is only a preliminary condition for
unity. Beyond that there is the need for the infra-doctrinal unity of a
common datum, Jesus Christ as known through the scriptural stories,

and the meta-doctrinal unity of obedience to a common norm, Jesus Christ as Lord. These three conditions, so I have argued, are sufficient for unity yet compatible with radical and irreducible doctrinal pluralism.

In conclusion, I can only repeat that it seems doubtful to me that these reflections have much immediate ecumenical relevance. Mass churches are incapable of being unified on this basis, and the *avant-garde* which professes to be clearing the road to the future is not interested in these questions. Yet if the Christian future will in fact be that of a minority diaspora, then our theme is the most urgent imaginable. The diaspora church will need desperately to be united—far more desperately than the church in the age of Christendom. But for that to happen, the problem of unity amidst diversity will need to be solved.

Secular Holiness: Loss or Gain of Christian Identity?

Harvey Cox

SAINTHOOD and holiness are two closely related concepts. The saint, in Christian history, is the one who leads a particularly holy and exemplary life. But what happens to sainthood when the criteria by which holiness is recognized and evaluated undergo radical and fundamental change? For this is just what is happening in Christianity today. The signal for this new stage came, perhaps, with the publication and widespread impact of Bonhoeffer's *Letters and Papers From Prison.* In one of the most memorable passages in that epochal collection of writings, Bonhoeffer confesses that he never really wanted to be a saint. His hope in life he said was to be a man, a fully human person. Following Bonhoeffer at least in this regard, let us begin this inquiry by stating that sainthood today does not mean the achievement of some particularly potent degree of religiosity. It means living an authentically *human* life, personifying in one's own life style those characteristics that define what it means to be human in the complex, rapidly urbanizing planetary culture of our time.

But is it possible to live a really human life in the world city of the late twentieth century? This oft repeated question conceals within it a host of related issues. Since the sustenance of persons requires a wide range of social and cultural resources, the question really requires a discussion of the structures of civilization. Since authentic personal life must be anchored in symbols of human hope and meaning, the question has far reaching theological overtones. No civilization, however impressive *en masse,* which does not somehow allow and encourage *individual* human fulfillment really succeeds. So despite its awesome complexity, Bonhoeffer's question of whether one can be a man today is rightly the central concern of our time. Can it be answered?

There can be little doubt that our epoch makes unprecedented demands on the individual. It hurls him into organizations so colossal he can barely envision their lineaments, let alone control their movement. Mobility and social change strip from him the dependable continuities of home and work which sheltered men in the past. At the same time the onrush of pluralism has splintered inherited meanings and secularization has emptied traditional symbols. No value remains unquestioned, no belief unchallenged. The individual person must live today in a more baffling world than ever, yet deprived of many of the securities which sustained him in simpler times.

For many observers this combination of threats to the person augurs his disappearance and thus the end of our civilization. As Yeats predicted, the center is broken and whirl is king, and the age of the ant-hill is here. For others however, ours is not the epoch of the insect but the age of the person *par excellence*. In different ways the thought of the maverick Marxist philosopher Ernst Bloch and that of Teilhard de Chardin both come out on the hopeful side. History has denied us the traditional answers to the question of what it means to be human, they argue, so we can now tackle it in a fresh way. The German sociologist and lay theologian Dietrich van Oppen in his book *The Age of the Person (Das Personale Zeitalter)* arose in a pre-personal stage of history. We must now tackle the question not as nations or as churches but *as persons*.

The argument between optimists and pessimists over whether the person can survive in the age of technopolis is not yet resolved. Both sides agree however on the issue. Ours is a time when the quest for significance in life has become a quest for personal style, a way of living which the individual person must achieve for himself and for which in the end he is himself answerable. Somehow a lot of people are beginning to understand this. Consequently, in addition to the collapse and confusion of conventional worldviews, we also see around us—often but not exclusively among the young—an impressive spirit of searching. It is a time of questing for a life which is not simply derivative, which, even if it makes sense to no one else, feels authentic to the one who lives it.

But is it legitimate in an age of global political crisis to talk about *personal* style? There are those who are apprehensive about it and claim it will inevitably result in a retreat from society, an abandonment of politics. The urgent issue of our time, they insist, is not the question of personal style, but the very survival of our world. The spectre of nuclear war and the curse of world poverty must be faced first. Only then can we afford the luxury of the quest for individual authenticity. The political must precede the personal or all will be lost.

The truth is however that the two must go together. One facet of any authentic personal style today must be some way of constructing the political conditions within which not only that style, but others, can be lived out to the full. And surely the objective of any political program worthy of serious effort is that it provide the material and spiritual conditions within which individual persons can live satisfying human lives. A personal style which overlooks the political dimension of existence is shortsighted and inadequate. A political vision which does not focus finally on the person is intolerable and unworthy. They belong together. Ignazio Silone once told an interviewer that only a mixture of saint and revolutionary could save the world from itself. The most admired religious figures of the twentieth century have been men involved in political struggle—Gandhi, Martin Luther King, Camilo Torres. Each evolved a political style that included the spiritual dimension and a religious style that encompassed the political.

The fact that the political and the personal are of a piece, however, does not mean that we must always deal with them all at once. A discussion must start somewhere. We start with the question of personal style partly because that is increasingly the way the question is posed today, recognizing the danger that this could lead to a kind of anti-social solipsism, but recognizing also that it need not and in the end must not. Our thesis is that the search for personal style has unavoidable political, cultural, and religious implications. We begin with the person in order to clarify these intrinsic dimensions of the quest, not to belittle them.

But why a personal *style*. By using this word we hope to avoid not only the discredited dichotomy between "form" and "content" but also the misleading distinctions between public and private morality, and between moral and aesthethic modes of action. By "style" then we mean a total way of being in the world, an orientation to life which guides perception, thought, and conduct. Style means a "way of life," but it carries the added significance of a way of life which is consciously arrived at, critically practiced, and capable of lending contour and identity to all that a person is and does. Yet by 'style" we also mean to suggest something we are not conscious of at every minute. Style is a habit. Like the style of an artist or an athlete, a life style functions best when it is not oppressively conscious but has become chronic. Still, a style is unique, it marks the person for who he is and it lends form and singularity to his approach to life.

Our urban epoch then is one in which the desire for sainthood has been transformed into the quest for structures of human justice and begins with the search for personal style. What are the chances that such a search can be successful? What obstacles does our society place in its path? What supports? What role, if any, does religious faith play in this quest? As we attempt to respond to these questions much of our discussion will focus on the artistic and cultural life of our time, including so called "popular culture." We turn to this lush source of motifs not to make aesthetic judgements but to explore the area where man expresses the exhilaration and the pain of his search for significance. With paint, light, stone, and song, through mimic gesture, dance movement, and dramatic action man conjures the themes and images by which his quest proceeds. Without for a moment suggesting that all artistic creation must have a discernible "content" or a deep meaning which can be translated into conceptual prose, we still believe that for our inquiry it provides a particularly fertile source of motifs and insights. We begin then by examining one of the newest and most suggestive art forms of our day, one that provides a particularly apt metaphor of the self in the new world city—the multimedia theatre.

THE MULTIMEDIUM WORLD

PICTURE a person in a large room enveloped by what is now called an "expanded cinema" or "multimedia presentation." Instead of watching just one screen as he would at a conventional movie, he finds himself surrounded by four, five, or sometimes as many as ten screens with different films flashing on each. In addition the walls and ceilings prance with color. Several contending sound sources vie for his attention while live dancers and eye-splitting stroboscopic lights escalate the complexity. It is a sensory circus. His entire visual and auditory environment throbs with spasmodic sounds and disjointed images. He feels inundated with thousands of unconnected messages. Yet he has probably paid to get in and even seems to be enjoying himself.

The multimedia presentation may or may not turn out to be a mere fad. Whatever its claims to artistic immortality however, it undoubtedly represents the imaginative recreation and intensification of the noisy, disparate and baffling urban environment itself. And herein lies its interest for us. The very fact that we do recreate this environment and that we even relish the chance to play with it is important. Man cannot cope with a new cultural environment until he becomes conscious of it. The multimedia theatre shows that we have now reached a level of consciousness about our world which may enable us to grapple with it more successfully. We are aware of the conditions under which personal life must be pursued. This is a hopeful sign.

But what is it that we are conscious of? First we are conscious of the *multiplicity of meanings* and values now available to us and therefore of the relativity of all of them. With seven projectors going at once we cannot possibly focus on one of the films and fail to notice the others. They relativize each other. Second, we are aware of the *mediated character of all experience* and are therefore skeptical about almost everything. Since we know the whole show has been selected and staged we have our guard up. We may enjoy it, but we won't be taken in by it. Thus the multimedia show represents both the rampant pluralism and prefabricated meanings of our day. It also represents the fact that we are conscious of these things and are capable of playing with them.

These two facets of today's world are not equally recent. Cultural pluralism, our confusing spectrum of alternative meaning systems with its resultant relativism, is a fairly new phenomenon. It is the product of radical social pluralism. We no longer hound each other to the stake for religious or moral differences, though we are still ready to incinerate cities for certain reasons. Our society is premised on tolerance. We give every contender with a meaning system to sell his booth in the market place. Harassed by so many hucksters, however, we don't believe the claims of any of them. A certain personal relativism is the price we pay for cultural pluralism.

The fact that all human experience is mediated however is not at all new. Only our awareness of it is. Since the dawn of human culture man has seen his world through mental images grafted into him by his society. We learn to see persons and things as they are already clothed in the values and meanings with which our culture endows them. The very fact that we think in words, that naming things connects us with them, means that we experience the world through language. Language however is at once society's gift to man and its way of sifting and mediating his experience. Men experience their worlds through the prisms provided by their cultures. They always have. The only difference today is that we know it and it bothers us.

This then is what the appearance of the multimedia cinema says about our contemporary world and our places within it: (1) it is a world brimming over with alternative meaning patterns which offset and neutralize each other; (2) it is a world of mediated experience whose images come to us indirectly and never unsullied by previous human minds and hands; (3) we are conscious of these conditions of life and though they concern us we at times enjoy playing with them and recreating them.

We now intend to look somewhat more carefully at these characteristic features of the world which surrounds us today and the mentality it engenders.

MULTIPLISTIC MEANING

MULTIMEDIA man is the pioneer of pluralism, an explorer on the frontiers of consciousness. A restless urban wanderer, he circulates among the different meaning worlds of work, travel, leisure, family life, trying constantly to be himself. He lives very day amidst a constant sensory bombardment from neon signs, TV, transistors, car radios, and thousands of publications of all types. He seeks to contain within himself seemingly divergent and even contrasting roles without flying apart. The fact that he does so with some success is impressive. It is a form of holiness. He is coping with a world whose power to bewilder and defeat him exceeds anything in previous history.

The appearance of multimedia man signals a new type of pluralism, what Johannes Metz calls the "pluralist consciousness." We should not be surprised by its appearance. As a society we have just about decided to embrace complete pluralism in religion, morality, and in the way we organize our institutions. What we should have noticed before this however is that we cannot have pluralism at one level without having it at another. They all go together. Pluralist culture means pluralist man, and the problem this creates for personal meaning is a considerable one. A radically heterogeneous culture may seem at first to provide a rich supply of ready-made, unified life styles to those who live within it. We have only to mention the numberless stereotypes invented and displayed in the mass media: the jocular consumer family of the TV commercials, the suave playboy, the emancipated jet set traveler, the buoyant teenager. But these partial and prefabricated styles really do not work in the end. When an individual identifies with one of them he loses just that authentically personal identity he set out to achieve. This is exactly what more and more people are noticing today and their dissatisfaction quickens their search for a style which is thoroughly personal.

Life in a religiously or morally unified culture is one thing. The individual simply accepts the meaning his society confers on him. Life in a world where highly variant meaning worlds and value systems jostle and compete is something else. The person who depends on a secure world view and a set of clear culturally approved values cannot survive as a person in an age of multiple meaning systems. The multimedia man tries to live without these securities. How?

Deprived of a simple and easily available life style not by "meaninglessness" but by a surfeit of contradictory meanings, multimedia man becomes an instinctive relativist. He distrusts the claims of any single religion or world view. But his relativism assumes a new and interesting form. Denied a ready-made meaning system to give contour to his life he begins to roll his own. He has gone beyond mere negative relativism and has begun to build his own individual life style out of whatever motifs and components he can gather together.

He is becoming an indefatigable syncretizer. His way of building a personal style is to select from the meaning motifs the world provides those which somehow connect and enliven his own experience. He then assembles his own set, living by it but constantly adding, discarding, and modifying. In religion this joyful reveling in the multiplicity of meanings produces results which puzzle and disconcert church leaders. Good Catholics practice Yoga, read Freud, and collect African ritual masks. The man of faith today is increasingly the one who assembles his own unique collage out of the multiple symbol systems which impinge on his spirit. The real question about all this do-it-yourself syncretism in religion and elsewhere is will it work in the end? Will it permit multimedia man to forge his own style?

The capacity to collect experiences and build one's own set of mean-

ings and values out of the disparate pieces with which the world bom-
bards us is particularly evident among the young. Our grandparents
were already aware, if only vaguely, that there were religions and
world views very different from their own. Their answer was to ignore them or to dispatch missionaries. Our parents kept the values of
their parents, though frequently soft-pedaling their religious sources,
and taught us to deal with other ways of life by being tolerant. Tolerance in fact was the great virtue, preached if not practiced, by the generation just before this one.

Our children however have gone another step. They not only want
to tolerate other life styles, they want to try them. They seek out and
collect experiences and life orientations the way a previous generation
collected bubble gum cards. While their parents were motivated by a
desire to have, they are more likely to exhibit a desire to be. Both
desires of course can become compulsions. One can be just as staggered
by the infinite multiplication of experience as his parents were by the
greedy accumulation of things. Still, the basic drive of the new urban
pilgrim to construct an authentic way of being, though it has its snares
and pitfalls, is a positive one as such. It represents the predominant
goal of the emerging man of our time.

MEDIATED MEANING

THE other characteristic of multimedia man is suggested by the word
medium. It reminds us of the recent discovery, popularized by sociology of knowledge and cultural anthropology, that nearly all of our
experience is mediated to us in one way or another by our culture. We
know from the comparative study of cultures that even the way we
see and hear things is not "instinctive" but learned. Even our most
vivid personal experiences come to us already clothed in cultural values
and interpretations. The mind is not a *tabula rasa* but more like a radio
with a built in frequency range. Again it should be emphasized that
this has always been the case as long as man has been man. What is
new today is that we are conscious of it, and this is what creates the
problem. The process of awareness can be illustrated by our changing
attitude toward the mass media.

His experience with the mass media, as well as his exposure to pluralism and his knowledge of the social conditioning of behavior have
made the man of today suspicious of everything. It is instructive to
notice how our attitude toward the media has changed. True, no one
probably ever quite fulfilled the stereotype of the slack-jawed, starey-
eyed total recipient of mass media signals that panicky cultural critics
once made him out to be. Opinion leaders in family, work, and other
places always provided him with at least some ways of checking and
testing what comes to him through the tube and the car radio. Nevertheless as society became more specialized, the mass media provided

a constant undertone of images and themes which helped organize man's experience. A good example is provided by the large number of television programs which depict life in different occupations. Doctors, nurses, lawyers, police, social workers, and school teachers appear on the screen week after week. In an occupationally segmented society these portrayals sometimes provide the only continuous experience anyone has of what goes on in these lines of work. Real doctors and policemen are not always satisfied, to say the least, with their television depictions.

In many other areas as well, television and the other mass media supply people with the information and images a previous generation garnered elsewhere—what's happening in the world outside. The media still attempt to do this today. News events today are scheduled with an eye to maximum mass media exposure. News preparation, packaging, and delivery constitute a colossal business operation. What Daniel Boorstein once called "pseudo-events" often crowd out "real" significant events, and news consumers find themsleves inhabiting a demiworld in which the persons and issues which make up their public world come to them wrapped in the opinions, adjectives, and camera cutting of the media man. Since our prophylactic age insulates most of us from pain and blood, movies and TV understandably focus a disproportionate amount of footage on violence. Political issues and natural disasters also come to us prepackaged via the vacuum tube. The result is a constriction of experience in which reality and the prepared portrayal of reality become confused. "Why are you bothering with that?" a teenage boy asked his friend who was valiantly attempting to peer at a solar eclipse through a piece of home-smoked glass. "It'll be on television at five o'clock." The process climaxes in the no doubt apochryphal story of the resident of a black ghetto who heard there was a riot in his neighborhood so broke into a shop and stole a TV set in order to watch it.

Many people still accept, more or less, the flickering grey world of the mass media as the real one. They try to live in it. It supplies the basic images and values that guide their lives. These people have not yet reached the critical level of multimedia man. For them the mass media do provide a roughly unified world view. They are really the tribesmen of technopolis, presecular men trying to cope with a secular civilization. The world of the mass media narcotizes them. Any exposure to a world which contravenes the conventional meanings of the TV world frightens and upsets them. For such people however the achievement of a personal style is simply out of the question. For them even the most vivid personal experience lacks an element of reality until it is given shape and context by the media. This represents a step back from merely watching the eclipse on television. One doubts the reality of the eclipse, or the riot or the strike, until it is reported and interpreted.

The man who interests us here however is not the one who drinks in the mass media world, but the one who views it with deep skepticism. This begins to happen when the person must cope with different media bearing different interpretations. Thus the pluralism we have just described contributes to skepticism. Those who read newspapers with very different editorial policies are struck by the surprisingly disparate accounts of the same event they publish. The more different viewpoints they see, the more skeptical they become. Thus the development of critical consciousness begins. The process is accelerated by travel to foreign cultures. Unless one camps in the local Hilton hotel, the assumptions of one's own society begin to seem questionable. The person begins to see that in a sense all experience on or off the media is mediated. It comes to him bearing cultural assumptions that seem increasingly relative.

There is nothing wrong with having a critical attitude. In fact it is necessary for survival. But when this critical attitude becomes a total life style, experience is constricted. The person views his world through a suspicious lens. He becomes incapable of spontaneous direct experience. The protective shell with which such people surround themselves sometimes produces a corrosive cynicism about the possibility of any real experience.

The true believer has settled into a more or less unquestioning acceptance of the media world. The TV-transistor landscape corresponds with his own mental landscape with very little friction. The skeptic doubts it all but must still live in a world where, despite all his precautions, events still come to him with prearranged interpretations. His cynicism may even reach out and engender doubts about his own cynical life style, thus leading to a vicious circle.

As the world of multiple meanings grows increasingly harder to avoid in a mobile world society, believers in a simple unified world will diminish in number and more agnostics will appear. Both however suffer from a kind of anesthesis, a loss of feeling and perception. The believer misses vast ranges of experience because his simplistic mass media world will not permit him to handle the jagged edges of life. The agnostic stands so far back in his critical detachment that although he is rarely fooled, he feels less intensely and may settle for a kind of misanthropic cynicism. He has not learned to live with gusto in a world of mediated experience. How to do so is one of the key dilemmas facing the individuals in the secular city.

The meaning market today bulges with rival nostrums and competing patterns. At the same time, our culture sifts and winnows the individual's experiences, but allows him to be aware of what it is doing. Multimedia man's method of coping with multiplistic meaning is to become both a relativist and a synthesizer. Quietly rejecting the total claim of any religion, ideology, or meaning system he simply patches together his own compound from whatever elements make sense to him. His way of coping with the obviously mediated nature of all his perceptions is to be equally suspicious of everything. He is "cool," provisional, tentative. He won't be fooled. As such he represents a creative adaptation to the new world.

He also however represents a crisis. Has his relatively unsuccessful attempt to survive in the secular city destroyed in him any real possibility of feeling and knowing himself as a unique person? Has it rendered impossible the human desire to live life rather than be lived by it? Has it erased individuality, stunted his capacity for celebration, numbed his ability to hope and love? How do his syncretism and relativism, his sophistication and his skepticism influence his quest for personal style? In political and social terms there are additional pitfalls inherent in this emergent life style. The true believer can easily harden into a fanatic. The agnostic can degenerate into a "cop-out," an alienated non-participant in the society.

At first glance the situation appears discouraging. To have a personal style means to have some dependable vision of what human life is, that is the style must be *authentic*. It cannot be simply a figment of fantasy, it must correspond in some way to what is going on "out there." But to have a personal style also means the style must be *personal*. It must in some real sense be *mine*, not just borrowed or inherited from someone else. My style must be *both* authentic and personal. But how can it be? If all the clusters of value and meaning our world projects are equally relative, each one undercutting the next, how can the one I have pieced together be worth living by? And if all experience is mediated and thus in part distorted, how can it be really personal? How can anything in life escape an element of phoniness and artificiality?

In this paper I have described the conditions within which secular sainthood, an authentic human life, would have to be lived in our epoch. The saint today must combine the personal and the political. He must find a way to embrace a degree of relativism without collapsing into nihilism. He must discover how to affirm provisionally without becoming a cynic. He must do it all with a spirit of playfulness and festivity. Can it be done?

Perhaps the model for man we need today must, in Nietzsche's words, be more dionysian and less apollonian, in Camus' phrase more "Mediterranean," in Sam Keen's words more the dancer, less the maker. Perhaps, as I have argued elsewhere, the clown and the harlequin will become better images for Christ, and thus also for man, than the king or the priest. The jester will not accept anything earthly as sacred, yet he is no cynic. He reminds us both of our baser selves and of the dimension of transcendence which breaks through to us in the grotesque and the comic. The clown is not fully contained by this world. He reminds us that if human authenticity is possible today, it is possible because of a dimension of reality that eludes empirical analysis. The secular saint and the religious saint have one thing in common. They both owe their sainthood to the mystery we call grace.

Church and State: the Orthodox Christian Experience with a view Towards the Future

Alexander Schmemann

I.

IN spite of the ecumenical encounter between the Christian East and the Christian West, encounter that has lasted now for more than half a century, in spite of an officially acknowledged state of "dialogue," in my opinion it is still very difficult for a Western Christian fully to understand Orthodoxy and not so much the officially formulated dogmas and doctrines of the Orthodox Church as the fundamental world view, the experience that lies beneath these formulations and constitutes their living and "existential" context. This of course is also often true of the Eastern Christian in regard to Western "experience." The difference here, however, is that whereas the West—its intellectual categories, its ethos and culture—has in some form or another permeated the whole world, has truly become universal, the experience of the Christian East is no longer a self-evident component of Western civilization and to a Western man remains extrinsic and even exotic. For us Orthodox one of the most agonizing aspects of the ecumenical encounter lies very often precisely in this inability of the "West" to grasp anything "Orthodox" unless it is reduced to Western categories, expressed in Western terms and more often than not, altered in its true meaning.

I begin my paper with this somewhat harsh remark not only because frankness and sincerity are the *conditio sine qua non* of any genuine ecumenical conversation, but also because this fundamental difficulty is nowhere more obvious than in matters pertaining to the very actual and burning issues of Church—World, Church—State and Church—Society relationship. Even many Orthodox following the Western dichotomy between "Faith and Order" on the one hand, "Life and Work" on the other, naively think that the "real" ecumenical difficulties being concentrated in the area of dogma, that of life or "practical" Christianity presents no major problems. This, I am convinced, is a very naive and superficial assumption, although I concede that it is not easy to show why the recent western pronouncements on these issues by the Second Vatican Council, the Upsala Assembly of the World Council of Churches, and the theologians of "secular Christianity," different as they may be from one another and in spite of some perfectly acceptable points, on the whole are representative of an orientation which is deeply alien to the Orthodox mind and from which the Orthodox "experience" is almost totally absent.

The difficulty is furthermore increased by what to a Western Christian may appear as a rather poor record of Eastern Orthodoxy in the area under consideration. He may ask, and not without justification: is it a mere "accident" that today some ninety percent of Orthodox people live in totalitarian, atheistic and militantly anti-Christian States? Does this not indicate a failure of the Eastern approach to the problems of the World? And, given that failure, what can the Orthodox contribute to the present passionate search for new or renewed guidelines of Christian action and involvement in and for the world?

To explain the Orthodox "experience," to answer these questions is not easy. They must be answered however and not for the sake of an "apology" of Orthodoxy, but because in answering them a different perspective, a different set of values may be disclosed, which are not it is hoped, totally irrelevant to the problems faced today by Christians everywhere. Now that the crisis of all Christian "establishments" has reached unprecedented proportions and requires, in order to be overcome, a tremendous effort—that of rethinking and reevaluating many of the presuppositions held hitherto to be self-evident—the Orthodox vision of the world and of the State, as well as of the Church's relation to them, may be of some help.

II

ALL historians would probably agree that the long and, more often than not, tragical history of the relations between the Church and the State has passed through three main stages: an open and acute conflict at the beginning, then a reconciliation that led to an organic alliance of the Church with a Christian State and finally, in our own "post-Christian era," a divorce between them resulting either in a more or less peaceful and "legal" separation or in a new conflict. But if these three stages are *grosso modo* common to both the East and West, the meaning given them, the way they were and still are "experienced" are without any doubt deeply different. Our first purpose then is to outline briefly the Eastern experience inasmuch as it differed from the Western one.

So much has been written about the conflict between the early church and the Roman Empire that we need not recall the bare facts. One point however pertaining not to facts, but to their interpretation does need our attention, for on it ultimately depends the understanding of the whole history of Church-State relationship, of its very basis. It has been often affirmed that the "rejection" of the Empire by the first Christians was rooted primarily in their eschatological worldview, in their expectation of an imminent Parousia. It is this eschatology that made the entire outlook of the Church a world denying one and prevented her from any participation and involvement in the "world." By the same token the subsequent reconciliation with the world, state, society and culture, a new and positive attitude towards them are ascribed to a radical change, a real *volte-face,* in Christian worldview, to its progressive liberation from the eschatological obsession of the earlier period.

This theory, in my opinion, is wrong on two counts: first, in its identification of early Christian eschatology with a mere "world-denying" attitude, and second, in its affirmation that this eschatology had to be therefore, and in fact was, dropped or at least radically altered before a positive Christian approach to the world and its components, state, culture, etc., could take shape.

The crux of the matter here is the very notion of eschatology so much used and also abused today. It seems to me that in no other area is modern theology more confused than in that of eschatology. This confusion may be to some degree explained, if not excused, by the fact that for many centuries Christian theology simply lost its eschatological dimension. There existed to be sure in manuals a chapter or rather an appendix entitled "de novissimis," in which all kinds of information about the end of the world and what comes after it was given. What disappeared however was eschatology as precisely a dimension, a coefficient of the entire theological enterprise, shaping and permeating the whole Christian faith as its dynamic inspiration and motivation. And thus when at first historians and then theologians rediscovered the tremendous importance eschatology had in the early Christian faith, they either rejected it as precisely "past"—a passing phenomenon characteristic of the primitive church, but of no value for our "scientific" theology—or then began to reinterpret and to "transpose" it according to their own understanding of modern "needs." Hence the paradox of the present situation: everyone seems to attach a great importance to eschatology—past or present—but there is no consensus as to what it meant in the past and ought to mean

for the Church today. To treat this crucially important subject, be it
only superficially, is obviously beyond the scope of this paper. But
since the whole problem of the Church and World, the Church and
State, ultimately depends on it, one must state very briefly our own
understanding of the meaning of eschatology in that development of
the Eastern "experience."

I submit in the first place that the eschatology in whose light the
early Church indeed judged and evaluated everything in this world
was not a negative, but a highly "positive," experience, not a denial
of the world but a certain way of looking at it and experiencing it. For
its ultimate content and term of reference was not the world, but the
Kingdom of God and thus rather than being "anti-world" it was a
"pro-Kingdom" attitude, in which it differed from eschatologies that
developed later. The Kingdom of God—announced, inaugurated and
given by and in, Christ—stands at the heart of the early Christian
faith and not only as something yet to come but as that which *has
come*, is *present now* and *shall come at the end*. It has come in Jesus
Christ, in His Incarnation, Death, Resurrection, Ascension and the
fruit of all this, the descent of the Holy Spirit on the "last and great"
day of Pentecost. It comes now and is present in the Church, the
"ecclesia" of those who having died with Christ in baptism can now
"walk in the newness of life," partake now of the "joy and peace of
the Holy Spirit," eat and drink at Christ's table in His Kingdom.
And it shall come at the end, when, having fulfilled all His dispensa-
tion, Christ will "fill all things with Himself."

Thus it is this experience of the Kingdom of God—and not a mere
doctrine "de novissimis"—experience centered on the Church's self-
fulfillment in the Eucharist, on the Lord's Day, that permeates the
whole faith and the whole life of the early Church and, supplying us
with the key to the initial Christian attitude towards the world and its
"components"—time, nature, society, state, etc.—explains the antinomical character of that attitude, the correlation within it of an emphatic *yes* to the world with an equally emphatic *no*. In the light of
the Kingdom the World is revealed and experienced on the one hand
as *being at its end*. And not only because the Kingdom of God, which
is the end of all things, has already been revealed and manifested,
but also because by rejecting and condemning to death Christ, the
Life and the Light of all life, it has condemned itself to die, to be
the world whose form and image "fade away" so that the Kingdom
of God "is not of this world." This is the Christian *no* to the world
and, from the first day, Christianity proclaimed the end of "this world"
and required from those who believe in Christ and want to partake
of His Kingdom that they be "dead with Christ" and their true life
be "hid with Christ in God." Yet, on the other hand, it proclaimed
that the world is redeemed and saved in Christ and that it is at its
beginning as "new creation," "Lo, I make all things new. . . ." This

means that for those who believe in Christ and are united to him, this very world—its time and matter, its life and even death—have become "means" of communion with the Kingdom of God, the sacrament, i.e., the mode of its coming and presence among men. "All is yours and you are Christ's!" This is the Christian *yes* to the world, the joyful affirmation that "heaven and earth are full of God's glory."

I have tried elsewhere to show how this antinomical correlation of the *yes* and *no* constitutes the very foundation, the initial *ordo* of the early Christian liturgy; how for example the *sui generis* Christian institution of the Lord's Day, the "first" and the "eighth" as the Fathers call it, far from being a Christian substitute for the Jewish Sabbath (this it indeed became in later piety), places the whole time in the perspective of the Kingdom, makes it "passage" towards the "day without evening" and thus fills each moment of it with meaning and responsibility; how Eucharist by being primarily the sacrament of the Kingdom, of Christ's parousia, i.e., coming and presence, refers the whole cosmos to eschatological fulfillment; how, in short, the fundamental liturgical experience of withdrawal from "this world" (Christ comes "the doors being shut") is understood not in terms of a spiritualistic or apocalyptic "escape," but as the starting point, the foundation indeed, of Christian mission and action in the world, for it is this experience that makes it possible to see the world in Christ. It is impossible here to reproduce the entire argument. Let me simply state that in the light of the evidence as I see it, the early Christian eschatology rather than rejecting the world posits the foundation of a worldview which implies a "positive" attitude towards the world in general, and the State in particular.

III.

THE State is to be sure wholly of "this world." It belongs to the level of reality which in the light of the Kingdom "fades away." This does not mean, however, that it is either evil or neutral, an enemy to be fought or an entity to be ignored for the sake of "spiritual values." On the contrary, it is precisely the experience of the Kingdom that for Christians gives the state its real meaning and value. The fall consisted primarily in the disconnection of "this world" from God and in its acquiring therefore a pseudo-meaning and a pseudo-value which is the very essence of the *demonic*, the Devil being "the Liar and the father of Lies." To redeem the world, or anything in the world, is then to place it in the perspective of the Kingdom of God as its end and ultimate term of reference, to make it transparent to the Kingdom as its sign, means and "instrument." The eschatological worldview of the early church is never a "static" one. There is no trace in it of any distribution of the various essences of this world into good and evil ones. The essence of all that exists is good, for it is God's creation, sanctioned for all eternity by His "very good." It is only its divorce from God and its transformation into idol, i.e., an "end in itself," that makes anything in this world evil and demonic. Thus as everything else in "this world," the state may be under the power of "the prince of this world." It may become a vehicle of demonic lies and distortions, yet, as everything else, by "accepting" the Kingdom of God as its own ultimate value or "eschaton," it may fulfill a positive function. As an integral part of "this world," it exists under the sign of the end and shall not "inherit the Kingdom of God." But its positive and indeed "Christian" function lies in this very recognition of its limit, in this very refusal to be an "end in itself," an absolute value, an idol, in its subordination, in short, to the only absolute value, that of God's Kingdom.

It is well known that from a purely legal point of view the crime for which Christians were condemned and denied the right to exist ("non licet vos esse") was their refusal to honor the Emperor with the title of *Kyrios*, Lord. They did not denounce, reject or fight any other "defect" of the Roman Empire be it, to use our modern "fixations," *injustice* (slavery), *"colonialism"* (the regime of Imperial *versus* the Senatorial provinces), or *imperialism* (expansion at the expense of other states and nations). Yet what by denying the Emperor the divine title of Kyrios they denounced and fought implied in fact much more than all this, for it challenged once and for all the self-proclaimed divinity of the State, its claim to be absolute value, a divine "end in itself." And it implied moreover not only a negation, but also an affirmation.

In the first place it affirmed the coming into the world, into time and history, of the one and true Kyrios, Jesus Christ. "Thou alone art the Kyrios" says one of the earliest Christian hymns and this means infinitely more than a general belief in Divine providence or a remote Divine government of the world. It means that the Kingdom of God has become the decisive factor of the "here and now" of the world's life and history and that human history develops from now on under the sign of the *kairos*, the direct Divine intervention into time and life. It lays thus the foundation for an ecclesiology, a doctrine of the Church including in its scope and perspective the whole cosmos and the totality of history.

,In the second place this denial affirms the state as also belonging to the dominion of the one Kyrios, Jesus Christ. In a deep sense it rejects the "separation" of Church and State if that separation is understood not in "institutional" or "legal" terms (the only terms ultimately retained in the West) but in those of a common perspective, a common reference to the same "end." Limited as it is by its belonging to "this world," the State is nevertheless capable of reflecting the ideal of the Kingdom, of living by it, of truly serving the Kyrios of the universe. Early Christian writings are surprisngly free from either cosmical or historical "pessimism." They resound on the contrary with a joyful expectation of a cosmical victory of Christ. Nowhere in them does one find any longing for a peaceful isolation of the Church into a purely "spiritual" sphere, a separation from the world and its "worries." Christians know of course that they are a "tertium genus." All home is exile for them and all exile a home, but this leads them to no indifference, or "neutrality" or pessimism. For their exile is in the Kingdom and that Kingdom has been revealed in the midst of the world as its true meaning, redemption and salvation.

Finally, that Christian "denial" proclaimed and affirmed the Truth as the very power and "mode of presence" of the Kingdom in "this world," as the criterion for both its negation and its affirmation, as the source of true charity and justice, as above all the criterion enabling men to "discern the spirits—whether they are from God. . . ." The "what is truth?" of Pontius Pilate and behind him of the whole Roman Empire implied indeed a distinction and a separation between Truth on the one hand and Authority on the other; it also implicitly denied the possibility for man to know the Truth and to be guided by it. Hence the absolutization of Authority and the divinization of Caesar. "What is Truth?" asked Pilate meaning the relativity of that concept and *therefore* demanding an unconditional obedience to the Emperor. "Authority *is* Truth," such was the significance of that demand. To it Christians answered by affirming that Truth is authority. Such indeed was the meaning of the Christian *martyria,* of the martyr's blood which ultimately destroyed the greatest, the most demonic of all idols.

Thus, in my opinion at least, early Christian eschatology, rather than "rejecting" the State, posited in fact the fundamental principles of the next historical chapter, that of a "Christian" state. But it posited them only inasmuch as it kept at the center of its "worldview" the radiant experience of the Kingdom of God.

IV.

THE different interpretation given that "worldview" by Western historians and theologians, who consistently view it as incompatible with the subsequent reconciliation of the Church with the world, a particularity of the primitive community soon to disappear under the pressure of reality, was not accidental. For it is here indeed that lies the fundamental difference between the two *visions* of the Christian world as they developed respectively in the West and in the East. I am convincd that basically, i.e., in vision and intention, in *theoria* if not always in reality, the Christian East preserved the eschatological perspective of the early Church, making it the basis of its attitude towards the world, whereas the Christian West replaced it at an early date with a different "vision," whose main ideological core and context can be termed *juridical.*

Is it not indeed characteristic of the Western ecclesiastical development that the relations between Church and State were virtually from
the beginning, understood, discussed and formulated almost exclusively in juridical or legal terms—as a relation between two *institutions,*
two *powers,* two *governments?* Is it not true that in spite of substantial differences such historical phenomena as the medieval struggle
between Papacy and the Western Emperors, Luther's doctrine of the
two kingdoms, and the modern theories of separation of Church and
State do ultimately belong to the same ideological level, for they all
share as their basic presupposition a "juridical" understanding of the
problem they try to solve. This legalism moreover is so deeply rooted
in the Western ecclesiastical mind that even when trying to understand
and to formulate other, non-Western, patterns of Church-State relationship, Western historians almost without exception begin by reducing
them in some way or another to "juridical" categories. Thus for
example when speaking of Byzantium, few of them fail to define it as
"Caesaropapism," i.e., to view it as a simple case of a total subordination of the ecclesiastical power to the imperial.

The truth however is that another type of Church-State relationship,
not exclusively juridical in nature and functioning, not only can, but
in fact did exist, rooted in the worldview which we termed *eschatological.* Such precisely was the Eastern or Byzantine "type." Just as
the initial conflict between the Church and the Empire was not a legal,
but an "eschatological" one, was focused not on rights and obligations,
freedom of conscience or freedom of cult, but on the decisive meaning
for the world of one Person, one Event, one Community, the subsequent reconciliation between Church and State could not in the
Eastern conscience, or maybe better to say "subconscience," have had any
other basis. It is this "eschatological continuity" which, in my opinion,
constitutes the starting point and the ultimate term of reference of the
entire Eastern "experience." The historical complexity, the tragedies
and failures of that experience should by no means be silenced or
minimized. But even their meaning cannot be fully grasped unless
they are referred to and seen in the light of the experience from which
they stem. To define that experience, be it only schematically, is thus
our next task.

V.

RATHER than with legal texts, this definition must begin with the
event which formed the spiritual and psychological foundation of
Byzantine "theocracy" and of its continuation in other Orthodox lands,
the spectacular conversion to Christianity of the Emperor Constantine
in 312 on the eve of the decisive battle at the Milvian bridge just
outside Rome.

We are not concerned here with what "really" happened to Constantine on that mysterious afternoon, not even with how he himself understood and later explained it. The unique and indeed crucial significance of that event lies in its acceptance by the Byzantine Christian tradition as the self-evident and sufficient basis for the Church's reconciliation with the Empire, or to use a Byzantine term, for their "symphony." Of the many and varied formulations of that acceptance one of the most explicit can be found in Byzantine liturgy, in that cycle of "Imperial" feasts and prayers whose constant theme is Constantine's vision of the Cross and its implications for both the Church and the Empire. It is here, in this emphasis on the election of Constantine "by God and not by men," that one grasps the continuity of the Byzantine experience with the early, "eschatological" attitude of the Church towards the Empire.

"Like Paul thou hast received the calling not from men. . . ." This in the eyes of the Eastern tradition is the decisive factor in Constantine's conversion. He is called directly by Christ, not even through the Church, and he is chosen not as an "individual," but precisely as Emperor, for the event of that election occurs at a crucial moment of his imperial career, his acceptance of Christ being the condition of his victory over his enemies. In him, thus, the Empire itself is called to accept Christ and to become His "politevma." But this means that in the person of the Emperor the Empire acknowledges as its own Kyrios the Lord of heaven and earth, places itself in the perspective and under the dominion of His Kingdom. Thus *ab initio* the alliance between Church and State is based not on any "treaty," bargaining and agreement, not on any detailed definitions of mutual rights and obligations, but on *faith*. One does not "bargain" with God, yet it is God who elected Constantine and in him revealed the Empire to be part of His "dominion." And in the eyes of the Church this act of faith leading to the new attitude towards the Empire not only by no means contradicted the earlier one, but was indeed in full continuation with it. For the Church, when she opposed the Empire, did it not because of any political or social principles, not for the sake of any particular doctrine of State, but uniquely in the name of Christ whom God made the Kyrios of all creation. In other terms she opposed the demonic "misuse" of the State by the "prince of this world," and her very refusal to acknowledge the Emperor as Kyrios implied, as we have said above, a positive attitude towards the State, faith in the possibility of its liberation from the dominion of darkness. Just as the primitive community in Jerusalem believed in the possibility of the Messiah's being accepted by the entire "house of Israel," the Church in the Graeco-Roman world never gave up her hope to see it accept Christ and His Kingdom. The heresies she consistently fought were heresies not of exaggerated "optimism" but those of dualism, docetism, escapism and pessimism in all its forms. The conversion of Constantine and its joyful and confident acceptance by the Church meant therefore no change in faith, no alteration of its eschatological content. To use a term well forgotten and dismissed today, but absolutely essential in the language of the early Church, the conversion of the Emperor and the Empire were of the order of "exorcism." The power of the Cross —the Church's essential weapon against the demons—liberated the Empire from the power of the "prince of this world." By crushing the idols, it made the Empire "open" to the Kingdom, available as its servant and instrument. But in no way, and this must be stressed, did it transform the Empire *into* the Kingdom of God. For it is the property of the early Christian eschatology that, while experiencing the Kingdom of God as an *immanent* factor in the life of "this world," it maintains intact its totally *transcendent* character. It is always the presence in "this world" of the "world to come," never the transformation or the "evolution" of the former into the latter. That this distinction was fully preserved is proved best of all by the fact that Constantine received baptism only on his death bed, some twenty-five years after his "conversion." And when he died on the day of Pentecost dressed in his white baptismal garment, it was as a Christian "neophyte," not as Emperor. Later on, the same symbol was preserved in the monastic tonsure received by the dying Emperors. The Empire may be Christian, i.e., serve the Kingdom, make it its own "highest value," but it is not and cannot become the Kingdom, which, although always present in "this world," remains forever "not of this world"—as its transcendent end and judgment, goal and fulfillment.

VI.

To remember all this is essential for the understanding of Byzantine "symphony." Whatever the motivations of Constantine's policy towards the Church—and they certainly changed and evolved, whatever the variations of the Imperial *raison d'etat*—and they were numerous, the Church, as we said above, asked for no formal or juridical guarantees, no agreements, but gladly surrendered herself to the care and protection of him whom Christ Himself chose and appointed to serve His Kingdom.

It is on purpose that I use here the strong term "surrender." For it is absolutely true that the Byzantine Church gave up her "independence" in the juridical connotations of that term. Administratively, institutionally, she indeed merged with the Empire to form with it but one politico-ecclesiastial organism and acknowledged the Emperor's right to administer her. In the words of a canonical text "the administrative structure of the Church followed that of the Empire," and this meant in fact a rather substantial transformation of the Church's organization on all levels—the local, the regional and the "universal." To analyse this transformation here is impossible, but it is certainly not a mere terminological change that is attested by the introduction into the ecclesiastical vocabulary of civil terms such as "diocese," "eparchy," "exarchate," etc. The spectacular rise of the hitherto unknown Bishop of Constantinople to the position of "ecumenical" (i.e., imperial) primacy is explicitly justified at the second Ecumenical Council by the fact that he "dwells in the city of the Emperor and Senate." The Emperor alone has the right to summon Ecumenical Councils, he legislates in matters of Church discipline and welfare, he appoints Bishops, and the formula of the imperial appointment is integrated into the ritual of episcopal consecration.

One could multiply *ad libitum* examples of this "surrender," and to Western historians they constitute as many unmistakable proofs of Byzantine "Caesaropapism," of the total subjugation of the Church by the State, of the Church's loss of "independence." In fact it is their subjugation to their exclusively juridical concept of Church-State relationship that prevents these men from discerning the true meaning of that relationship in Byzantium, to see it in its own light and according to its own presuppositions. They do not realize that for the Byzantine Church and precisely because of her eschatological worldview which made her accept Constantine's conversion, the problem of her relations with the Empire was situated on an altogether different level where, it can be said in all objectivity, she not only preserved what she meant by her "independence" but, to use Western categories once more, truly "dominated" the Empire.

To explain this, an ecclesiological footnote is in order. One of the reasons for the frequent misunderstanding and misinterpretation of Byzantine "Symphony" in the West is a surprising ignorance of Orthodox theology and more particularly of Orthodox ecclesiology, the doctrine of the Church. Thus it is very important to understand the difference that exists between the Western and the Eastern approaches to the whole institutional or jurisdictional aspect of the Church. Whereas in the West for a long time and for reasons that we do not have to analyse here, this aspect virtually absorbed the whole ecclesiology, in the East not only was it far less central, but the very approach to it was different. Here the Church was viewed primarily not as "power" or "jurisdiction," but as sacramental organism whose function and purpose is to reveal, manifest and communicate the Kingdom of God, to communicate it as Truth, Grace and Communion with God and thus to fulfill the Church as the Body of Christ and the Temple of the Holy Spirit. The Church, to be sure, is *institution* but of *sacramental,* and not *juridical,* nature. This means that it exists only in order to assure the Church's "passage" from "this world" into "the world to come," as the sign constantly to be fulfilled, as the "means" of the Church becoming all the time "that which she is." Essential as it is for the Church as *sign* and *sacrament,* the institution therefore cannot be simply identified with the Church. As institution the Church is of "this world," as fulfillment she is of "the world to come." This does not mean any separation within the church between "institution" and "fulfillment," for the whole purpose of the institution is precisely to make fulfillment possible, to reveal as present that which is "to come." The fulfillment is impossible without the institution, just as the institution receives all its meaning from that which it fulfills. What this means, however, is that the church's visible, institutional structure—episcopate, canonical order, etc.—is a structure not of power, but of *presence*. It exists in order to assure the fullness of that presence and its continuity in space and time, its identity and "sameness" always and everywhere. And this means finally, and we must stress this point, that the church claims no "power" in this world and has no "earthly" interests to defend. On the one hand the whole world, the entire creation belong to her because they belong to Christ, the Lord of creation, and are therefore in their totality the object of her mission. Yet, on the other hand, she does not *possess* them as her own "property," for her only mission is to reveal and to "represent," to make present in this world the Kingdom which is not of this world and for the sake of which those "who possess should be as if they possessed not."

Thus, in the Eastern perspective the relation of the church to the world is not "juridical" by its very nature and therefore cannot be expressed in juridical terms. There may be and there of necessity are "juridical persons" within the visible, institutional church—diocese, communities, monasteries, etc. But as such they are "of this world" and, in their relation to the State or society, live according to earthly laws and principles, inasmuch as these do not prevent the church from fulfilling her essential mission. If the church "abides" in a non-Christian State, she claims, as we know it already, nothing but the possibility to "be herself," i.e., to preach and to confess Christ, the unique Kyrios and His Kingdom, to offer salvation to all men everywhere. Yet in the case of a Christian state—the one which by definition shares her "scale of values," her eschatological faith—the church has no difficulty in leaving to it the "management" of her earthly life, the care and the administration of her earthly needs. And between the two attitudes there is no contradiction, for both are rooted precisely in the same "eschatological ecclesiology," in the same fundamental experience of the Church.

In the light of this "footnote," we may understand now why the basis for Church-State relationship in Byzantium was not a juridical principle but the notion of *Truth*. Juridically, let us repeat it once more, the Church indeed "surrendered" herself to the Empire and claimed no "independence" from it whatsoever. But, and here is the whole point, the one and absolute condition for that surrender was the acceptance by the Empire of the faith of the Church, i.e., of the same ultimate vision of God, world and history, and this we call *truth*. It was this Truth—expressed in doctrinal formulations, in the essential sacramental order, in worship, and last but not least, (a point which we shall elaborate later), in the freedom of each man to "leave" the human society in "this world" for the sake of the Kingdom—that in the eyes of the Church "guaranteed" her real independence, the fulfillment by her of her mission. As long as the Empire placed itself under Christ's judgment and in the perspective, essential for the Church, of the Kingdom of God, the Church saw no reason to claim any "juridical" independence from it and, in fact, gladly put the reins of ecclesiastical government and policy in the hands of the Emperor. In this care for the Church, in this function as the Church's earthly "habitation," the Church moreover saw the essential vocation of the Christian Empire, the very "note" of it being Christian.

But what in their digressions about Byzantine Caesaropapism Western historians seem to overlook is the unique and indeed crucial role played precisely by the notion of Truth within that new relationship. Not only can one say without any exaggeration that the "surrender" always remained contingent on the Empire's faithfulness to that Truth, but that, in another sense it was itself transformed into the Church's "victory," or even, more bluntly, into the Empire's "surrender" to the Church. Every time the Empire for all kinds of political motives "tampered" with the Truth, tried to "adjust" it to its pragmatic needs, the Church, be it only in the person of her best representatives, protested and fought the Empire, opposing it whenever necessary with the "martyria" of her blood and suffering. And ultimately each time it was the Empire, and not the Church, that "surrendered" and gave up its claims and demands.

From this point of view the great doctrinal controversies which almost without interruption disturbed the life of Byzantium from the 4th Century till the 9th, from Arianism to Iconoclasm, were a continuous crisis in Church-State relationship as well as a slow purification of Byzantine "symphony," the growth and deepening of that vision of Christian Empire which the Church accepted in the conversion of Constantine. And on this level the real history of the Church was made, her genuine consciousness expressed not by a perennially weak majority, not by Bishops and clerics always ready to pay with a compromise for another State grant or privilege, but by men such as St. Athanasius of Alexandria, the three great Cappadocians, St. John Chrysostom, St. Maximus the Confessor and so many others. Yet, and this is the crucial point, it was their *martyria* that ultimately triumphed. It was they who were "canonized," not only by the church, but also by the Empire as bearers of Orthodoxy. It was their "truth" that sooner or later triumphed and was accepted by the entire Byzantine world.

That the effort of those martyrs and confessors was not lost, that there was a slow but steady purification of the Byzantine mind from the ambiguity of its pagan antecedents, that in other terms the Church progressively imposed her view, her concept of the Christian state, can be seen in the Byzantine imperial legislation itself. Neither the code of Theodosius nor that of Justinian are free from the presuppositions and the categories of the old, pagan "theocracy." Accepted and exalted as it is, Christianity remains "ontologically" subordinated to the Empire, as the sign and means of its "victory," as a Divine sanction for its existence. From a purely legislative point of view Christian religion is given the place vacated by the old state paganism. In a way it is still Christ who is understood as "serving" the Empire. But in the 9th century, in a document like the "Epanagoge," or in later imperial iconography, the situation is altogether changed. It is the Emperor who, kneeling before the Christ-Pantocrator, offers and dedicates to Him the Empire. It is the Empire itself which, at least officially and symbolically, knows no other purpose, no other function but that of serving Christ and of being His "habitation." This victory is, beyond any doubt, the fruit of the long fight for Truth, of the Christian "martyria," which cleared the initial ambiguities of pagan theocracy, "exorcised" it from its impure elements. The very concept of "Orthodoxy," which at the end of early Byzantium becomes so central in Byzantine consciousness and forms henceforth the basis of all Byzantine "constitutions," is in fact a direct result of that long fight, its most significant and lasting consequence.

All this is said of course on the level of vision and theory. In reality, in practice, the theory failed more than once and was betrayed much too often. There is no need to recall here the history of these failures. It fills virtually every book on Byzantium. My purpose here is not to defend Byzantium or to "idealize" it. Anyone who would consult any of my other writings on this subject will readily agree that I am not guilty of any such idealization. My point here is simply to state that to see the history of Byzantine Christianity merely as an example of Caesaropapism, to reduce it to a surrender of Church to State, is not only to distort significantly the historical evidence, but also to miss, almost completely, the spirit and the psychological "make-up" of a society, a "world" which in more than a thousand years of its existence was Christian, not only in intention but also in content.

VII.

WE spoke of intentions, let us now consider the "content." In what sense, to what degree can it be termed "Christian"? It is clear, of course, that in the last analysis the answer to this question depends on the meaning given to the adjective "Christian," and it is precisely on this meaning that the mind and the conscience of Christians is deeply split today. The only objective approach therefore is to evaluate a society, an experience, in the light of its own criteria and presuppositions, and then to ask whether any aspect of that experience is of any lasting value.

For the Byzantines the term "Christian" as applied to the Empire meant, as we have seen, above everything else the acceptance by the Empire of a certain "truth," a definite vision of the world and of history. We have satisfied ourselves that the Empire indeed had *accepted* that vision. But now the question is: did it "apply" that vision and live by it? Where is the proof that the Church's understanding and interpretation of Constantine's conversion was not a naive one and that ultimately she was not "fooled" by her partner?

Here again the proof is to be found, first of all, in an event which, in my opinion at least, is as crucial for the Eastern "experience" of State as the conversion of the first Christian Emperor. This event is *Monasticism* or rather the place and the function it acquired almost immediately in the Byzantine "worldview." Here again, as in the case of Constantine's conversion, we are concerned not with the content of the monastic spirituality as such, but with the way in which the monastic ideal was incorporated into the Byzantine tradition.

One can consider as disqualified and abandoned the many more or less "radical" theories which some liberal historians of the 19th century formulated concerning the origin of monasticism. Several first rate studies have proved beyond any possible doubt the continuity which in spite of many differences existed between the early monastic ideal and the spirituality of the primitive church. For us here the main point is that this continuity was precisely that of the eschatological worldview, of the faith centered primarily on the experience, expectation and anticipation of the Kingdom of God. The difference was one of "situation," not of "content." The early Christian community because of the pagan context within which it lived was itself in many ways "monastic" as K. Heussi has pointed out. To be separated from the world one needed not to leave it physically. As to the monastic "exodus" and "anachorisis" of the 4-5th centuries it was motivated by the reaction of the same Christian maximalism to the spiritual dangers created by the "reconciliation" of the Church with the world, and, first of all, the very real danger of a nominal and "easy going" Christian life. What must be stressed, however, is the almost paradoxical mutual acceptance of monasticism by the Empire and of the Empire by monasticism, acceptance which constitutes one of the basic dimensions of the entire Eastern "experience."

On the one hand for all its maximalism and "world renouncing," monasticism did not either condemn or reject the very principle of the "Christianisation" of the world which began with Constantine's conversion. On the contrary it is, in a way, for the sake of that Christian world, in order to keep alive the "martyria," the testimony to the Kingdom of God by which the world is saved, that the monks "left the world," undertaking their spiritual fight. "How is the Church, how is the Empire?" is the first question addressed to a priest who came to visit her in the desert by St. Mary of Egypt, the great hero of Byzantine monastic literature, after she had spent some forty years in total solitude. The question is by no means a merely rhetorical one. Apart from some radical and quasi-Manichean trends, quickly eliminated, the classical monastic tradition is totally alien to any utopianism, millenarism, sectarianism, is nohow comparable to the later radical sects with their fanatical rejection of the State. Reading the texts in which this tradition was later formulated and, in a way, codified (cf. the Byzantine "Philokalia"), one is rather amazed by the wonderful balance, the absence from it of any exaggeration or "radicalism." The "world" which monks renounce is the one which all Christians, monks and non-monks alike, must renounce, for it is precisely the world which is an end in itself, an "idol" and "sin" claiming the whole man for itself. The renunciation is based on the same and eternal Christian antinomy: "*in* the world but not *of* the world." In itself however this renunciation and constant fight are directed not against the "flesh and blood" of the world, but against the powers of darkness that deviated God's creation from God. They are means of liberation and restoration, not of "negation" and destruction. All students of Eastern mysticism stress the positive, joyful and in a sense "cosmical" spirit that permeates it and which, as late as a century ago, shone so brightly in a simple Russian monk, St. Seraphim of Sarov († 1832). It is this spirit, the "joy and peace in the Holy Spirit," that for centuries attracted millions and millions of Orthodox pilgrims to monasteries where, while "in this world," one could taste of the ineffable beauty and bliss of the "world to come...." Monasticism thus was in continuation with that same eschatological worldview which made St. Paul and the early Christians, while fighting the Imperial "idol," pray for the Emperor and the "established powers."

Even more revealing was the attitude towards Monasticism of the Empire and the society it embodied. The Christian world born out of Constantine's conversion not only did not reject the monastic movement, but in an almost paradoxical way, placed the monastic ideal, the monastic "scale of values," at the very heart of its own life and consciousness. Very soon indeed the "Desert" ceased to be limited to the wilderness at the outskirts of the "inhabited world" (Oikoumene) and implanted itself, in the form of numberless monasteries and convents, in the "downtowns" of big cities, becoming thus centers of spiritual guidance, leadership and inspiration. The Fathers of the Desert became the "heroes" of the entire society and their *vitae* the "bestsellers" of Byzantine popular literature. The monastic liturgy, the monastic piety invaded and reshaped the liturgy of the whole Church, which, it can be said without any exaggeration, "surrendered" herself to monasticism, just as, in another sense, she surrendered herself to the Empire. Monasticism was thus "canonized" by the imperial-ecclesiastical organism as an intergral part and expression of that very Truth which, as we have seen already, formed the very basis of

Byzantine "symphony." And nothing reveals better the depth of that acceptance than the symbolic monastic tonsure of the Emperor at his death hour. This ritual symbolized indeed the "hierarchy of values" acknowledged by the Empire, its total subordination to the transcendent Kingdom of God, which the Empire as such does not inherit, of which it can be an instrument, or servant in "this world," but whose ultimate inheritance requires a total renunciation of everything "earthly."

My emphasis on monasticism as the main expression of the Byzantine world as Christian may seem strange and unconvincing to a contemporary man. What I am trying to say however is very simple. This "acceptance" of Monasticism meant, in fact, the recognition of the ultimate *freedom* of man, not of course in our modern and formal definition of that term, but as recognition of man's transcendent destiny and vocation, his belonging to God and to his Kingdom, and not to anything "in this world." It is not an accident that the Iconoclastic Emperors, the first proponents of a secular idea of both state and culture, led a violent attack not only against Icons but also and maybe primarily against Monasticism. They realized perfectly well that the latter's function within the Christian society was precisely to affirm the transcendent freedom of man from the State, to preserve the eschatological worldview which alone makes this world Christian. The Iconoclasts failed as failed all those in the East who tried to reverse the "hierarchy of values." Therefore, it can be said of the Empire that whatever its numberless failures, it lived by the "motto" inscribed by Justinian on the altar of Constantinople's Saint Sophia: "Thine own of Thine own offer to Thee Justinian and Theodora."

VIII.

A "BUILT-IN" tension and polarization between the Empire and the Desert, such could be the adequate definition of the Byzantine spiritual world, the context which makes it Christian. And the fruit of that tension, the tangible result of the "Christian politeuma," is a civilization, a culture whose depth and meaning are being rediscovered today. This culture, in spite of all its limitations, can indeed be called Christian, not only nominally, but essentially. It is a *sui generis* fruit of the Church in "this world." One must remark that the Western interest in the Byzantine civilization is of a relatively recent date. For too long the cultural and psychological self-centeredness of the West, its identification of Christianity with itself, prevented its seeing in Byzantium anything but an exotic and, to some, fascinating world. It is only today, through the efforts of a small group of Byzantinists, that the various aspects of the Byzantine experience—its art, thought, social and political organization, etc. slowly begin to recover their place in the Western "curriculum," And although it is evident that there is no room here for even a most superficial description or analysis of that culture, three points which are relevant to the theme of this paper must be made.

I mentioned above the concept of Truth as the basis of the Byzantine theory and practice of Church-State relationship. But it would be wrong to see in this concept a mere set of rigid doctrinal formulations or "symbolic" texts to use a term familiar to the West. In reality this concept of Truth permeates the whole life of Byzantine society, constitutes its essential Christian "coefficient." Not by accident the Byzantine period of Church history coincides with the partristic age, with the unique and truly unsurpassed effort of the human "logos" to "enter into the Logos of Truth," and, in a "synergeia" with grace, to find words "adequate to God." What from a purely formal point of view was a synthesis between Athens and Jerusalem, Christianity and Hellenism, meant on a deeper level the slow and creative transformation of the mind itself, the moulding of new fundamental thought forms, and not only for theology in the narrow, technical sense of this word, but for the entire intellectual enterprise of man. To the Byzantine mind Christianity is, above all, the revelation of Divine Truth but, by the same token, of man's "adequacy" to it, of his constitutional ability to receive it, to know it, to appropriate it and to transform it into life. All great theological controversies of the patristic age are never "abstract," merely "intellectual," they are always *soteriological* and *existential* in their ultimate significance, for they deal with the nature of man, the meaning of his life, the goals of his "praxis." This existential character of patristic theology, the certitude permeating it that Truth is always Life, the absence from it of any separation of the "theoretical" from the "practical"—all this it may be good to remember today when in the mind of so many Christians the "practical" alone is exalted as if it had no need to be rooted in the "theoria," the all embracing vision of God, men and world. When contemporary Orthodox theologians insist on a "return to the Fathers" (and it seems so often that theirs is a "vox clamans in deserto"), they call precisely to that vision and not to the contingent expressions of a past age. Together with the Fathers they affirm that "it all" ulimately depends on Truth, knowledge as life and transfiguration. To a modern man, even to a modern Christian, the endless Byzantine debates on the "enhypostaton" or the two wills and two energies in Christ may appear as the very example of the "irrelevant." In the Eastern mind it is in these debates, in efforts to "appropriate" the great theandric mystery, that are to be found the roots and the presuppositions of all truly Christian "humanism," of a Christian vision of the world. To dismiss them as useless for our problems and needs may be the great danger for today's Christianity.

The second aspect related to the first one, yet also distinct from it, is the expression, the embodiment of that same Truth as Beauty. It is the *liturgical* expression of Byzantine civilization. But liturgy here means more than just worship or cult. It is indeed a way of life in which the "sacred" and the "secular" are not disconnected from one another, but the entire life is thought of as a continuation, a "follow up" of that which is revealed and communicated in worship. For it is the very purpose of worship to manifest the Kingdom of God, to make people taste of its celestial beauty, truth and goodness, and then live, inasmuch as possible, in the light of that unique experience. It is enough to enter St. Sophia of Constantinople, even in its present "kenotic" state, to realize the vision and the experience from which it was born and which it aimed to communicate. It is indeed that of *heaven on earth,* of a Presence which transcends all human experience and categories, yet relates all of them to Itself and reveals the world as Cosmos in which heaven and earth are truly full of Divine glory. The paschal, doxological, "transfigurational" and, at the same time, deeply penitential character of Byzantine liturgy, which includes architecture, iconography, hymnology, time, space, movement and whose purpose is truly to take the whole man and in a way the whole world into its rhythm and scope, makes it much more than "cult." It is the experience in "this world" of the "world to come." It assumes the whole of creation—matter, sound, color—and it transfigures all of it in its sacramental *passage* and *ascension* into the glory of God's presence. As they leave the Church, the Orthodox sing: "We have seen the true light, we have received the Holy Spirit," and it is this light and that participation that are meant to act upon life itself, to transform it, according to one Russian religious thinker, into the "liturgy outside the temple." It is because in the liturgical mystery we are first given to see the *new* creation and to partake of it that we can then be its servants in "this world." When one considers in the light of that Eastern experience the modern liturgical chaos, the confusion about the very nature and purpose of Christian liturgy, one is tempted to say that maybe it is not the liturgy that we ought to make "relevant" to the world, but, on the conrary, it is again in the unique liturgical experience of the Kingdom—its Light, Truth, Beauty and Power—that the world could be rediscovered as a "relevant" place for Christian action.

Finally, a third aspect of the Byzantine Christian culture can be adequately termed *ascetical.* Man's sin and alienation from God, the radical illness of "this world," the narrow way of salvation—these are the essential components of Byzantine religious experience, shaping in more than one way the whole life of Byzantine society. It is, as I said already, a "monastic" society in the sense that it accepts the monastic ideal as the self-evident norm and criterion of all Christian life. The doxological spirit of worship, mentioned above, not only does not exclude, but on the contrary, implies as its very condition a deep penitential emphasis: "I see Thy bridal chamber adorned and I have no garment to enter therein. . . ." It would be a mistake however and

I have mentioned it already, to view this ascetical and penitential aspect as made up of fear and pessimism. To be properly understood it must be referred to and judged by its goal, by the theme, central in Eastern spirituality, of *theosis,* the deification of man by the grace of the Holy Spirit. For there is indeed no higher idea of man than the one by which Byzantine society ultimately lives and measures itself. Ascetisism here is the "art of arts," for it is the means by which man ascends to his true nature and calling, fulfills his eternal destiny. And if many a "modern" Christian rejects it today as "anti-human" and "anti-social" escapsim, it is because this modern Christian for all his obsession with being "man-for-the-other," with serving man and mankind, paradoxically enough does not seem to feel the need to ask the preliminary question: to serve *what* man and for the sake of what ultimate destiny of that man? Yet long before the vague terms "freedom" and "liberation" became the *passe-partout* slogans of modernity, they stood—but filled with very concrete, very high and indeed "difficult," meaning—at the very heart of an entire civilization, as its ultimate aspiration and goal.

It is true, of course, that there was much injustice and cruelty in the Byzantine society, that by our present standards it was "autocratic" rather than "democratic," that our concept of freedom and rights were unknown to it. Byzantium most certainly did not solve all its political, economic, social, and even "racial" problems. And yet to use the key word of our modern approach to these problems—there was no *alienation* in that society and this precisely because of the one and unifying *vision* of man, of his nature and destiny, a vision which in spite of all injustice kept the society together, as one body. For in that vision all men not only were equal but equally destined for the "honor of high calling." This vision they all received, day after day, week after week, in the "leitourgia," in this common and corporate celebration of and participation in the Kingdom of God. A full, and long overdue, study of the social texture of Byzantine society, a deeper analysis of Byzantine legislation, a fresh approach to Byzantine institutions, in short—a new evaluation, based on the entire evidence, would show, I am sure, that in spite of the apparent rigidity of its social and political system, there existed in Byzantium, and later in other Orthodox lands, a sense of community and inter-personal relationship, a spirit of "philanthropia," a constant opening towards a full human experience seldom achieved elsewhere. The rich, to be sure, were rich, and the poor much too often remained poor. Yet the poor, and not the rich, stood at the heart of the Byzantine experience as its inspiring ideal. One has only to read the funeral hymns of St. John of Damascus or the Byzantine Mariological hymnology to grasp the tremendous wave of compassion and solidarity, mercy and brotherhood that never completely died in the daily existence of the Byzantines. No doubt it was a pre-industrial "agricultural" aand "primitive" society. But whether these

definitions invalidate altogether *all* principles on which it was founded
and render them totally "irrelevant" for us today, whether furthermore
the principles and ideals which have replaced those of Byzantium
have not, in fact, mutilated something essential in man and are the
main reason for his present "alienation"—all this remains to be
seen. It is meanwhile my certitude that there is no reason to discard
disdainfully an "experience" which, when all is said about it, can still
teach and inspire us.

IX.

THE fall of the Byzantine Empire in 1453 meant by no means the
end of the Eastern "experience." The latter had its continuation
and also a creative development in states and nations which, having received Christianity from Byzantium, received it together with the Byzantine "theocratic" ideal.

Nowhere is this continuity seen better than in the self-identification
of each of these nations with a "Constantine" of its own, in the fundamental experience of its "conversion" as an act of Divine initiative
and election. Boris, the first Christian "Kaghan" of Bulgaria, Vladimir,
the Baptizer of Kievan Russia, St. Sava, the "Patron" of Orthodox
Serbia—each of them remained in the history and memory of his
nation as its "father in Christ," as the living symbol of its dedication to
Christ's mission in the world. We find here again the same philosophy
of history as in Byzantium, rooted in the same "eschatological" perspective in which nations and kingdoms are related to the church
not by "juridical" agreements but by a common "reference" to the
ultimate kingdom. Whatever the political motivations the historian
certainly finds behind many of those events, more important is their
progressive transformation into a national myth, their interpretation
by the nation's consciousness, interpretation which was the decisive
factor in shaping the very "psyche" of Orthodox nations.

The Turkish conquest put an early end to the theocratic dreams of
the Southern Slavs and thus it is the Russian "experience" that remains
the most significant and creative chapter in the history of the post-
Byzantine Orthodox world. Here only a few remarks concerning this
chapter can be made.

The Turkish "yoke" by isolating the Orthodox world for many
centuries and by depriving it of its freedom forced it into a kind of
"nonhistorical" survival, into an implicit rejection of history which,
as we know, was so central in the Byzantine theocratic consciousness.
The sense of the universal mission, of the cosmical and historical scope
of the Church, of her dynamic relationship with "this world," of her
responsibility for it—all this vanished if not "dogmatically," at least
psychologically, and was replaced with a kind of non-historical
"quietism" which moreover came to be viewed, by the Orthodox and

non-Orthodox alike, as the "essence" of Orthodoxy. Not noticing the tremendous political and cultural changes, the quick transformation of nearly everything in "this world," the Orthodox continued, and some still continue, to live in an unreal, imaginary, symbolic and purely "static" world, a static "Empire," all the more static since, in reality, non-existent. The early "eschatology" which gave birth to that world and whose main content was precisely its "openness" to history and to God's action in it, was now, so to speak, "reversed," aimed no longer at present and future, but at one particular "situation" of the past and thus voided of its meaning. The old imperial cities and, therefore, ecclesiastical centers—Constantinople, Alexandria, Antioch, now capitals of non-Christian states or sleepy Arabic villages—kept proclaiming their glorious ancient titles or claiming their "rights" as if "nothing happened," at if it were not the very nature of "this world" that its "fashion" always "fades away," as if God's purpose and will were revealed and decisively incarnated once and for all in one particular society, state and culture. The Orthodox historians and theologians, I repeat, do not seem fully to realize the depth of that metamorphosis of the Orthodox consciousness, of the tragical vanishing from it of that precisely which constituted its very foundation. And it is only against the background of that metamorphosis that one can grasp the unique significance and importance of the Russian "chapter."

Russia, alone in the whole Orthodox world, and even so not immediately, escaped the isolation and the historical "kenosis" imposed on it by the Turkish conquest and domination. Its political independence and growth on the one hand, the collapse of Byzantium and of Orthodox "empires" on the other hand, forced upon Russia a new historical awareness, challenged her with problems which in turn shaped its culture. Ultimately this challenge led Russia into a creative rethinking of the initial Byzantine "experience." This however would have never been achieved without another challenge, that of the West. For only through a restoration of the universal consciousness and perspective, through a return into "history" itself, could *history* become again the object of the Church's interest and mission, be related again to the central "experience" of the Kingdom of God. By his radical "Westernization" of Russia at the beginning of the 18th Century, the Emperor Peter the Great imposed on the Russian mind a search for identity, a radical reevaluation of both the "Western" and the "Eastern" historical and religious experiences, united and merged now within the same culture. And it is out of this search, of its agony and often tragical depth that emerged little by little a vision, a trend, a spiritual and intellectual perspective which permeates and unifies, in spite of all its internal diversity and even polarity, the Russian culture of the 19th Century and which Berdyaev termed "the Russian Idea."

There is no consensus yet about either the exact content of that "Russian Idea," or its meaning for Orthodox theology. Students of

Russian history and culture, theologians and philosophers disagree on it and interpret it each his own way. To some it means a creative progress of the Orthodox mind itself, to others a dangerous deviation from Byzantine patterns. No one denies however the fact itself of a tremendously meaningful, spiritual and theological revival that took place in Russia during the last century preceding the collapse of Imperial Russia. No one questions its general orientation. And this orientation is precisely towards a new synthesis between *eschatology* and *history,* towards a reintegration of "this world"—of action, creativity, and culture—into the perspective of the Kingdom of God. Whatever the value of answers given so far, the questions, the inspiration and the aspirations of this revival bring us back to the starting point of the Christian experience of the world, to the antinomical correlation of the *yes* and the *no* in the attitude towards it. The radiant and paschal spirituality of St. Seraphim of Sarov, the antinomical and prophetic world of Dostoyevsky's writings, the daring intuitions of Russian religious thinkers, the dreams of Russian poets—each of these components of the "Russian Idea" can and must be studied, evaluated and interpreted separately. All together, however, they unmistakably reflect and point towards a common vision, challenge us with the same "ultimate questions." And these are about God and the world, the Kingdom and "history." In this sense this Russian spiritual phenomenon is more truly in continuity with the real Eastern and Byzantine tradition, with its eschatological roots and inspiration, than the pseudo-conservatism of those who make Byzantium and the Fathers a closed, rigid and absolute "world in itself," requiring nothing but repetition and archeological cataloguing. This continuity moreover is proved by the facts. It was in Russia indeed that after many centuries of acute "Westernization" Orthodox theology recovered its genuine sources: the patristic thought, the liturgical tradition, the mystical realism of the spiritual "theoria." It is not an accident therefore that more and more of those who, in the "East" as well as in the "West," are thirsty and hungry for an authentic Christian vision, a vision in which the eternal and transcendent truth would at the same time be truly "relevant" for our age, begin to find it in this Russian "source."

But then what about the question we raised at the beginning of this paper? What about the historical collapse of that "Eastern" world, its catastrophic metamorphosis into the center of atheism and materialism, State totalitarianism and denial of all freedom? Does this not imply a failure also of the "worldview" by which it lived and which, as we tried to show, was its spiritual foundation? In trying to answer these questions, we encounter the last and at present probably the most serious Western misunderstanding of the "East," rooted again in the same inability of the Western mind to see the Eastern reality except through Western categories. It is indeed the West, and not the East, not Russia at least, that identifies Communism and the

Soviet political system with Russia and makes that identification the basic presupposition of all its dealings with the communist world. In Russia itself long before the revolutionary collapse, that collapse was prophesied and then interpreted and understood as precisely a "Western" phenomenon, the result of the rejection by Russia, in the person of both its imperial bureaucracy and its "intelligentsia," of its true historical and spiritual foundation, the result thus of a surrender to alien ideas and "visions." Here the blindness of the West, of its "experts" and "analysts," is simply incredible. They do not seem to realize that if there is anything deeply "anti-Russian" and "anti-Eastern" it is precisely the entire psychological, intellectual and even emotional "make-up" of men like Lenin and Trotsky, that if there is an example of a total alienation of a group of men from their roots and tradition it is that of "bolshevicks" and that finally, the deep motivation of "Bolshevism" was and still is a real, almost irrational, hatred for "Russia." Maybe if they knew Russian a little better, these "experts" would have discovered that even the Russian language used by the Soviet officialdom is a language deeply, if not radically, alien from that of Russian culture and always sounds like a clumsy translation from a synthetic and unidentified Western prototype.

All this does not mean at all that an attempt is made here to make the West directly responsible for the Russian "collapse" and to present Russia as an innocent victim of a Western "conspiracy." This collapse is a Russian sin and Russia bears the responsibility for it. What I am affirming however is that it is a sin *against,* and not a natural outcome and fruit of, the "Russian Idea" mentioned above. The sin itself, however, and this must be said, consisted primarily in a non-critical acceptance of a "Western" and not "Eastern" idea. It was the acceptance of the specifically Western eschatology without the "eschaton," of the Kingdom without the King, which reduced man to matter alone, society alone, history alone, which closed his spiritual and intellectual horizon with "this world" alone. This reduction of man, his progressive alienation from his divine and transcendent destiny began in the West at the time of the Renaissance, continued through the Enlightenment, and found its fulfillment in the "this-worldly" enthusiastic utopianism of the 19th century. And the fact is that throughout the entire 19th century, from Chaadayev to Dostoyevsky, it constituted the very focus of the critique of the West by the most creative and original Russian thinkers. Yet at the same time it was more and more enthusiastically endorsed by the "Westernized" Russian intelligentsia. The latter, as Berdyaev well put, "busied itself not with politics but with saving mankind without God," and this is exactly the scope and content of that Western "secularism" which today begins to engulf Western Christianity itself. It is time to realize that the Russian Revolution and the pseudo-messianic totalitarianism which grew out of it was the triumph on Russian soil of a "Western" idea, the *reductio ad absurdum* of a Western dream, the literal application of a Western program.

That this idea "succeeded" in the "East" and not in the "West," in Russia and not in Western Europe, was due to many and complex factors, one of which, it must be conceded, was indeed the initial acceptance by many Russians of the Revolution as fulfilling the "eschatological" aspirations of the Russian people, the interpretation of the "Western" idea in "Eastern" terms and this in spite of the total and outspoken frankness of the Bolsheviks themselves who systematically and violently rejected such interpretation. In his famous poem *The Twelve,* Alexander Blok, the most celebrated poet of the Russian poetical "Renaissance" of the 20th century, placed Christ as leading the twelve Red soldiers through storm and snow, blood and murder. But—and this is of crucial importance—while in Russia this confusion came to a quick and tragical end, it lasted, and in many ways still lasts, in the West, preventing it from simply seeing the present Russian reality. When he realized the depth of the spiritual lie which in his *The Twelve* he presented as truth, Blok literally died of despair and while dying kept asking his wife to destroy all copies of his poem. Esenin and Mayakovsky, the two other poets responsible for that confusion, committed suicide. Already in 1924 Berdyaev in his "Reflections on the Russian Revolution" denounced it as totally alien to true Russian tradition and affirmed that "Russia becomes that which it never was before...." But in the West the myth of the specifically "Russian" (if not "Eastern Orthodox"!) sources and nature of the Soviet reality remains the basic presupposition of all approach to and dealing with "Russian Communism."

The basic fact which the West and even the Christian West, because of its intellectual *a priori,* does not seem to acknowledge is the obvious fact of the *non-acceptance* by the Russian people in their overwhelming majority, and thus by "Russia" itself, of Soviet Communism. The evidence supplied by thousands of books and testimonies is so conclusive that, considering the amazing blindness of the West towards it, one is almost tempted to apply to it the words of the Gospel: "Even if a man rises from the dead, they will not believe...." Ironically enough, it may be a real disappointment for the Western Christians who, with their usual solemnity and seriousness, prepare themselves for a "dialogue" with Marxists to discover some day that there are no Marxists behind the Iron Curtain!

Thus we must reject as nonsense an interpretation of the Russian "collapse" in terms of that Eastern "experience" which we are trying to describe here. What happened in Russia is one event within the great crisis of Western civilization, a crisis which not only has not ended, but today enters its crucial stage. In Russia itself however, beneath the ruins of that spiritual collapse, one begins to detect a new and creative trend towards the recovery of the "Russian Idea" and the Eastern Orthodox sources that fed and shaped it. The return of the

"Westernized" Russian intelligentsia to its spiritual fatherland, a return which began before the Revolution but was limited to a few "prophets," becomes today an important, even if silenced, factor in the life of Russia. Pasternak and Solzhenitzyn, Seniavsky and Daniel, the mimeographed publications of the *Samizdat,* the renewed interest in Russian religious thought, and so many other "signs" are an unmistakable proof of all this as is also, on another level, the truly miraculous survival, after half a century of persecution, of the Russian Orthodox Church. It is obviously much too early to write off the Eastern "experience" or to consider it as disqualified.

X.

IF anything is obvious today, it is the impossibility of thinking of the future in terms of a "Christian state" or a "Christian society." The *secularization* of the world, i.e. its divorce not only from the Church but from all religious worldview as well, is a fact and is therefore a self evident presupposition of all Christian thinking and planning. It is however in approaching and evaluating this phenomenon of secularism, in reaction to it in thought and action, that the Christian West and the Christian East, rooted as they are in their respective "experiences," seem to come once more to different conclusions. To understand this difference, to "compare notes," to restore, if possible, a common Christian vision of the world and of Christian action in it, may constitute today one of the most important "ecumenical" tasks. As an Orthodox sees him, the Western Christian is increasingly preoccupied, not to say obsessed, with the world, society, history, etc. This preoccupation may be "radical" or "moderate," "revolutionary" or "evolutionary"; but a general consensus seems to exist as to the need itself for the Church's reorientation towards the world, its needs and its problems. Hence the acceptance if not of "secularism," at least of the "secular" as the self-evident term of reference of both Christian thought and Christian action, as the inner motivation and criterion of all Christian "renewal." This consensus, since it becomes more and more the exclusive context of the ecumenical movement, is forced, so to speak, upon the latter's Orthodox participants and it is here, no doubt, that a new ecumenical "malaise" is bound to develop even if at present neither the "Westerners" nor the "Easterners" seem fully to realize this: the Westerners because they have always assumed that their categories, theological fashions and approaches are *ipso facto* universal; the Easterners because with a very few exceptions they are theologically silent and ecumenically passive. There is a growing evidence indeed that behind this silence and this passivity a great majority of the Orthodox cannot help feeling that something is deeply wrong with what, to them at least, appears much more like obsession rather than preoccupation of their Western brothers with the "world"

and its problems. So far this feeling has not been expressed in theological terms, given a responsible theological interpretation and justification. As it so often happened in the past, the Orthodox reaction is
split between, on the one hand, so radical a rejection of the Western
approach that it distorts and vitiates Orthodoxy itself by reducing it to
a fearfully "apocalyptic" rejection of the world, and, on the other hand,
the search for a compromise which, as all compromise, only increases
confusion. There is thus an urgent need to transpose this "feeling"
into a more articulate and constructive critique, and this can be done
only by referring the present Western trend to the Eastern "experience"
in its totality.

Our initial distinction in describing the two "experiences" was
between the *juridical* and the *eschatological*. We termed "juridical"
the Western approach to Church-State relationships as it developed
after the conversion of Constantine and the reconciliation of the Church
with the Empire. Now it must be stressed that this juridical approach
was not limited to the state alone, but implied a much wider, in fact
an all-embracing, "worldview" which from the Eastern standpoint can
be defined as *non-eschatological*. The medieval Christian synthesis
in the Latin West was based indeed on a progressive elimination from
both the Early Christian "experience" and its theological formulation of the Early Christian notion of the Kingdom of God, elimination,
of course, not of the term itself but of its initial Christian understanding, the antinomical presence in "this world" of the "world to
come," and of the tension implied in that antinomy. For it is precisely
the antinomy and the tension inherent in the patristic notion of
mysterion that the West eliminated from its approach to faith, from
its ultimate "intuition" of God and creation, from sacramental theology
and the doctrine of sanctification, from ecclesiology and soteriology.
If all the old controversies between the Orthodox East and the Latin
West—those about *Filioque,* original sin, created grace, essence and
energies, purgatory, and even the Papacy—controversies which to so
many today appear totally irrelevant, were transposed into an "existential" key, explained in terms of their "practical" significance, it
would become clear that their "common denominator" in the Eastern
mind, is, first of all, the rejection by the West of the *mysterion*—
the holding-together, in a mystical and existential, rather than rational,
synthesis of both the total *transcendence* of God and His genuine
presence. But this mystery is precisely that of the Kingdom of God,
the faith and the piety of the Church being rooted in the experience
now of that which is *to come,* in the communion by means of "this
world" with Him who is always "beyond," in truly partaking of "the
joy and the peace of the Holy Spirit."

For reasons which we cannot analyze here, the West rationalized
the *mysterion,* i.e. deprived it precisely of its antinomical or eschatological character. It replaced the tension, essential in the Early Church,

between the "now" and the "to come," between the "old" and the
"new," with an orderly, stable, and essentially extra-temporal distinction between the "natural" and the "supernatural," between "nature"
and "grace"; and then, in order to assure God's total transcendence,
it viewed grace itself not as God's very *presence* but as a created
"medium." Eschatalogy became thus exclusively "futuristic," the
Kingdom of God a reality only "to come" but not to be experienced
now as the new life in the Holy Spirit, as real anticipation of the new
creation. Within this new theological framework, "this world" ceased
to be experienced as *passage,* as "end" to be transfigured into "beginning," as the reality where the Kingdom of God is "at hand." It
acquired a stability, almost a self-sufficiency, a *meaning* of its own,
guaranteed to be sure by God ("causa prima", "analogia entis"), yet
at the same time an autonomous object of knowledge and understanding.
For all its "other-worldliness," the Latin medieval synthesis was based
in fact on the alienation of Christian thought from its eschatological
source, or to put it more bluntly, on its own "secularization."

Thus even before the formal "liberation" of the world from the
Church's control and dominion, before its "secularization" in the
narrow meaning of that term, the "world" in the West was secularized
by Christian thought itself. In the early Christian worldview the
notion of "this world" is by no means identical with that of a "secular"
world. In its separation from and rebellion against God, "this world"
may be a sick, condemned, and dying world, it may fall under the
dominion of "the prince of the world" into a state of blindness, depravity and corruption, but it is never "autonomous." The term "this
world" depicts a state, but not the nature, of creation and for this
reason "this world" is the scene of the eschatological tension between
the "old" and the "new" and is capable of being experienced, in
Christ, as the transfigured "new creation." Eschatology is thus the
very "mode" of the Church's relationship with the world, of her
presence and action in it. By abandoning this eschatological perspective, the West rejected in fact the possibility of any real "interpenetra-
tion" of the Church and the world, or, in theological terms, of the
world's real sanctification. But then the only other possible relationship between the Church and the world is precisely the *juridical* one, in
the deepest sense of this term, as a connection in which those who are
connected remain ontologically extrinsic to one another. Within this
type of relationship, the Church may dominate and govern the world,
as she did in medieval society, or she may be legally separated from
it, as she is in our modern era. In both cases and situations, the world
as such remains essentially "secular."

From this point of view, the "secularization" which began at the
Renaissance and continued without interruption throughout the entire
"modern" era was in reality a second secularization, or rather, a
natural and inevitable result of the first one. For it was a "secular"

world that the medieval Church dominated politically as well as intellectually. If politically she claimed a power superior to that of the
state, and intellectually a source of knowedge superior to human reason,
both claims were essentially "juridical," i.e. extrinsic to the nature of
that which they claimed to dominate. The secularization changed a
relationship of "power," not of "essence." What the "world," i.e. state,
society, culture, etc., progressively rejected was an extrinsic submission
to the *authority* of the Church, the Church's ultimate "jurisdiction"
over them, but not an essentially "Christian" idea of state, culture, etc.
Revolutionary and criminal as this rejection may have appeared to the
Church accustomed as she was to her divine *power,* it meant no radical
change in the Western worldview itself. And in this perspective, the
Reformation with its radically "secular" concept of the world was in
fact more in continuity with the medieval synthesis than post-Tridentine
Catholicism with its belated struggle for power, dominion, and control.

It follows from all this that the true novelty of the present Western
situation lies not in "secularization" as the world's autonomy from
the Church's power and not even in "secularization" as culture's
autonomy from "religious values." It lies paradoxically enough in the
recent acceptance by the Christian West, or at least by Western theology,
of what could be termed the *secular eschatology* of the modern secular
world. This indeed is the new fact, the true focus of the theological
and ecumenical situation in the West. We call this situation paradoxical,
for it was, in fact, for the sake of the world's "stability" and "order"
that the Western Church gave up her eschatological worldview, replac-
ing it with immovable and absolute norms, making "this world" a well-
defined universe with a fixed and closed horizon. As a reward for
respecting, i.e., not transgressing, this "law and order," man was given
the promise of salvation in the "other world." Provided he preserved
that "stability," i.e., kept the required balance between his "secular"
and "religious" obligations, man could be at peace with God, the
Church, and the world. And yet this "solution" did not work. The
most ironic and probably the most tragical development of the entire
"Christian" history is this strange mutation of the eschatological worldview from the Church into the secular culture. It was indeed the
Church, it was Christian faith, that "poisoned" the human mind with
a certain vision and experience of cosmos and time, of matter and
history, that made the "world" a notion, an experience correlated to
that of the Kingdom of God and challenged man with a kind of "impossible possibility." And it was the Church in the West that "gave
up" that vision and replaced it with a universe in which no room was
left for history and movement, for the historically unique and irre-
versible, for the dynamic and disturbing *ruah* of the Spirit. But ban-
ished from the Church, the "poison" not only survived, but little by
little became the very spirit, the very motivation of the world's "secularization", i.e., liberation from the Church. From the medieval sects

and "revivals," through the Renaissance, Enlightenment, Rationalism, Romanticism, the social and political utopias of the 19th century, the idea of the Kingdom stood as the center of the secular mind, but a Kingdom, and here lies the tragedy, progressively deprived of its King, more and more identified with "this world" as such. A secularized eschatology, a faith in the imminent fulfillment by man of his dreams and aspirations, a belief in "history," "justice," "freedom" and other pseudo-absolutes—such was, such still is the secular faith of the secular man, a faith which miraculously survives and overcomes whatever wave of pessimism and disillusion shakes it at more or less regular intervals.

It is this "secularized eschatology" that the Western Christian, Catholic as well as Protestant, seems not only to accept but to accept on its own terms, i.e., as the criterion of Christian faith and action themselves, as the term of reference of all Christian "renewal," as a valid framework and content of Christian eschatology. As I already pointed out, after centuries of almost total neglect "eschatology" is becoming again fashionable among Western theologians. The fashion however is based not on an interest in the early eschatology in which the transcendent Kingdom of God and not the world is the "eschaton," but on the desire to find a common language with the secular world. Even where an attempt is made to preserve the transcendent Kingdom, it is preserved as a vague "horizon of hope" and not as the radical *reality* of all Christian experience. The obsession with "relevance" and "involvement," the incredibile discovery of Christ's social and political "radicalism," the enthusiastic "rethinking" of Christianity within the categories of secular utopian ideologies—it all looks as if having at first "secularized" the world for the sake of a totally transcendent God, the Christian West is about to give up the "transcendent" as the very content of Christianity.

XI.

IN the light of all that has been stated above, it hardly needs to be said that this whole perspective is alien to Eastern Orthodoxy. It is true that until now there has been no consistent and explicit response on the part of the Orthodox participants of the ecumenical movement, only a general feeling of alarm and anxiety about the seemingly growing surrender of the Christian West to "secularized eschatology." The purpose of this paper, however, was to show, be it only in general terms, that the deep reason for that anxiety is not the often-alleged Orthodox indifference towards the world and its problems, indifference rooted as some Westerners affirm in the "liturgical," "sacramental," and "contemplative" character of Eastern Orthodoxy, but in an entirely different worldview, a different experience and vision of the world itself. We call this worldview *eschatological,* but not in the sense given this term in the deeply Westernized systems of post-patristic theology. This eschatological dimension is to be found in the total experience of the Church and primarily in her liturgical experience as well as in her unbroken spiritual tradition. These indeed were the real sources and the living content of Patristic thought, which, when it is isolated from them, simply cannot be understood in its real significance. The ultimate meaning of that worldview can be expressed in a simple formula: to be fully *in* the world, to be of any "use" to it, to fulfill their historical, cosmical and any other "function," the Church and the Christian must be at the same time totally *not* of this world. This "not" implies no negativism, however, no connotations of escape, contempt, quietism, or, in short, no "spiritualistic" indifference. It is a highly positive notion for it means immersion in and partaking of the Kingdom of God, of the spiritual reality already "inaugurated" by the Holy Spirit, already given *now* although as one yet *to come*. Of this reality the Church, in "this eon," is the sign and the sacrament, the gift and the promise. Without this reality nothing in this world has any ultimate meaning or value. Thus that which to a Western "activist" appears to be the cause of Eastern "otherworldliness"— the "liturgical," the "sacramental," the "contemplative"—is, in fact, the very condition of any true discovery of the world and the source of any genuine theology of Christian action and involvement in it.

It is in a way irrelevant to ask what a return to that eschatological worldview and experience may mean in "practical" terms, how it can "contribute" to the solution of the world's agonizing problems. The whole point of our argument is that without the recovery of that experience, no clear pattern of Christian thought and action can be detected. As long as the Church is imprisoned by the world and its ideologies, as long as she accepts and views all "problems" facing humanity in their secular and worldly formulations, we remain within a vicious circle without any hope of breaking through it. Before it can be put to any "use," the notion of the Kingdom of God is to be purified of all "utilitarianism." As a young Russian writer recently condemned to hard labor in the Soviet Union put it: ". . . one mut believe in God not for any other reason but the simple one that He exists. . . ." It is when, in the words of an Orthodox Eucharistic hymn, we "lay aside all earthly cares" that the world and all its problems may be discovered again as the object of all Christian love, as the stage for Christian mission and action.

One thing, however, can and must be said. Only a recovery by Christians of their eschatology can, in the last analysis, be a response to the "secularized eschatology" of the modern world. One wonders indeed whether the Christian West in its enthusiastic endorsement of that "secularized eschatology" is not in reality misreading and misinterpreting its true significance. While Christians, in their eagerness to be "relevant," shift the emphasis from the "transcendent" to the "immanent," one detects in the world a growing thirst and hunger for that which can *transcend*, i.e., fill life with the ultimate meaning and content. Behind the sometimes cheap and romantically naive rebellion against "systems" and "establishment," behind the rhetoric of "revolution" and "liberation," there is a genuine longing not only for the Absolute but for *communion* with it, for its true possession. Behind the "juridical," it is for the "eschatological" that the modern man is longing and this means for the Kingdom of God. But have we not "seen the true light," have we not "partaken of the Holy Spirit"? Who else but the Church ought to be able to satisfy that hunger, to name the King and manifest the Kingdom?

The Theologian as Prophet, Preserver, or Participant

James M. Gustafson

THE title of this paper suggests three possible social roles for the theologian. The first is that of social critic; the theologian stands in a position which gives him distance and moral objectivity with reference to the society and the culture, and from this position he calls into question the moral and spiritual health of existing institutions. The second is that of social defender; the theologian stands within the society and the culture, offering theological warrants for the preservation of existing values and institutions. My intention is to develop the contrasts between these two social roles and a third possible one, that is, the theologian as participant. This role carries with it elements of the first two, but moves beyond them. In this role, the theologian would share in the processes of public opinion formation, of decision making, and the exercise of powers which are formative in the shaping of events in the course of social development. He would participate with others in the interactions of perspectives, technical knowledge, and moral beliefs, out of which come the convictions and actions that shape the future.

These three roles are ideal-typical; that is, they are constructs rather than empirical generalizations. No good theologian would find his activities confined to either of the first two. In his criticism of the culture the prophet is likely to be defending at least certain ideal values that are historically available, if not institutions that give social embodiment to these ideals. In his defense of culture, the preserver is likely to select certain values or institutions for his theological and moral justifications, and be critical of other trends in the society. As a participant in social and cultural development, the theologian is likely to be the critic of some and the defender of other values and institutions that are present in his time of history.

Each of the three ideal-typical social roles has certain attitudinal, institutional, theological, and moral correlates. A judgment about the proper social role of the theologian is likely to be correlated with judgments about, for examples, the relation of Christ and culture, the interpretation of the significance of history, and the role of the Church in society. Thus one would evaluate the conception of the social role in the light of the adequacy or inadequacy of these other correlates, and not merely on the basis of some subjective preference for one type or the other. The procedure of the paper will be to take each of the types in turn, and develop some of the significant correlates. In the development of the second and third types, I shall draw contrasts with previous exposition. It will be clear that the third type is the one which I would wish to defend as normative for our time in history.

I. THEOLOGIAN AS PROPHET

THE title of the paper indicates that the principal division to be examined is in the first instance a social one, not a theological or moral one. Prophet and preserver suggest relationships to the culture in which the theologian lives; they suggest the kinds of activities in which the theologian will be engaged with reference to institutions, cultural values, historical developments, and mores. Prophet, more than preserver, is a term with a long historical tradition in Western religion, and for certain purposes it ought to be conceived in terms of its Biblical foundations, in terms of the critical interpretations of the nature of prophecy as one finds it in the Bible. This major and proper task is not engaged in here; rather we are seeking to develop an ideal-type of the prophet for the purpose of contrast and insight into various options available to the theologian and the Church.

As I have indicated, the term prophet is used to designate the role of the theologian as a social critic. In this role he stands with and for God over against the existing society and culture, over against the spiritual and moral ethos of his time and place. He has a theological position from which he makes independent judgments about the spiritual and moral health of the society, and he calls men to return to the ways and will of God. He sees himself as God's appointed man in a society and culture estranged from God, and corrupted by its failure to obey God's commands, to be conformed to God's will.

The *attitude* of the prophet is likely to be a combination of sorrow and indignation. He observes the injustice of the world, the corruptions of human ends and purposes, the presence of moral evil in many and varied forms, and is likely to weep over Jerusalem, to mourn for the state of life in the community of which he is a part. He and the people know a better way, a higher way, to live, but they have not followed it. They suffer as a result of their own turning away from the path in which they ought to go. The prophet feels deeply both their suffering and its causes: lack of faith and obedience. But the prophet is not only a man of sorrows; he is also a man of moral indignation. He burns with passion in the presence of moral evil in the world. He hates the corruption of communal and personal life; he is angered by the gulf between what men know they ought to do and what they actually do, between what the possibilities for a just and fulfilling way of life are and the state of affairs that actually exists. He can lash out in word and deed, pointing to evil and its causes, blaming men for their failures, cursing them for their sins. He is likely to be impatient in his indignation; impatient with sloth, with the slow pace of change, with the technical requirements of new developments. He knows an order of righteousness and sees an order of corruption; he is sorrowful and he is indignant.

The prophet is likely to speak of *God* in terms of his righteous wrath and judgment. The impatience and indignation of the prophet are themselves expressions of the impatience and indignation of God. The sorrow of the prophet is the sorrow of God. God stands in perfect righteousness, in perfect justice, aware of the hiatus between what men have established and achieved and what they ought to be as his children. Men must suffer the consequences of their disordered lives; men must bear the burden of their failures truly to obey the way and will of God, truly to develop the way of life that God enables man to know and to fulfill. Men are responsible for the condition of their communities; they are actually guilty before God for the ills which they endure. Indeed, God's wrath and judgment are at least in part made known in the sufferings that befall men and societies that do not conform to the way of life, the way of peace, the way of justice.

In terms of H. Richard Niebuhr's typology of theological positions on *the question of Christ and culture*, the prophet is likely to take the stance of Christ against culture.[1] Christ, both in his deeds and his teachings, represents a "higher way," a way of life in contrast with a way of death. He demands obedience to him, and this obedience rules out compromises with the established orders of culture and society. The institutions of society, the mores of the community, the powers of the state are all things that have not yet been claimed by Christ, that are not in allegiance with his way and his life. They are to be brought under the judgment of Christ, and those who are faithful to him will at least be wary of these established powers. and perhaps also isolate themselves from their corrupting influences. Christ is not an ally of military movements, of imperial powers, of successful economic institutions, of middle-class mores, of entrenched political power, of white Anglo-Saxon Protestants, of ecclesiastical pomp and authority, of entrenched cultural values. Rather, Christ stands over against all these things, calling them into judgment, and calling his followers to live a different and higher way, an exemplary way that will by its own witness shame the world around it. The prophet speaks with and for the Christ who calls men to faithful discipleship to him, to take up their crosses and follow him, to be despised and rejected by the sophisticated and the successful compromisers and achievers in the established order, to witness to his perfect love in a spiteful and conniving society.

The correlative of these positions with reference to the status of *history and society* is that they are realms dominated by sin and its consequences of moral corruption and evil. The prophet is seldom, if ever, an optimist about the state of the world in which he lives, or about its future developments, short of some divine interventions. Whether he spells it out or not, he seems to believe that the fall of man has profoundly affected his capacities to be what God created him to be, and that the course of history is the story of sin rather than salvation, disorder rather than order, despair rather than hope, injustice rather than justice. He has no illusions about the achievement of an earthly utopia; he is not the purveyor of the message that human problems are relatively superficial, and susceptible to ready manipulation to bring about improvement. With the emergence of each new good quality of life, new level of justice, new mark of love, he readily sees the possibilities for new perversions and even the intensification of human evil and destruction. He knows that technical achievements do not alter the level of moral purposes, nor do they resolve the profound spiritual difficulties of the human condition. The prophet, though indignant in response to moral evil, is not surpised that it exists. History and society are realms of sin.

The prophet's view of the *Kingdom of God* is likely to be futuristic, and its coming apocalyptic. His trust and belief in God is not often shaken by the absurdities of moral experience and historical events; he believes in and expects God's decisive reign to come. But it is not now present in an historically effective form. Indeed, given the rebelliousness of men and communities against God, the rule of God will not be like the growth of a seed of moral renewal and spiritual regeneration. Rather, it will come through the devastation of the perverted old order. The more cataclysmic events in history become, the more likely some event will lead to the birth of the Kingdom, the new society and new man. We are living, in the prophet's view, between the times; in the hope of the coming future Kingdom we can struggle with the present historical evils, or at least abide their annoying existence.

The prophet sees the vocation of man to be faithfully *responsible to ultimate values.*[2] Max Weber describes the person who holds to the ethics of ultimate values in somewhat pejorative terms. "The believer in an ethic of ultimate ends feels 'responsible' only for seeing to it that the flame of pure intentions is not quenched: for example, the flame of protesting against the injustice of the social order. To rekindle the flame ever anew is the purpose of his quite irrational deeds, judged in view of their possible success. They are acts that can and shall have only exemplary value."[3] The prophet is more concerned to be faithful to the absolute claims of an absolute justice, an absolute righteousness, an absolute peace, an absolute will of God, than he is with calculating the kinds of compromises that will be required to achieve a slight moral gain in the complexities and vicissitudes of the social order. His words and his deeds express his sense of responsibility to the truth of ultimate values, even though they appear to be historically unrealizable in the eyes of realistic and sophisticated men of the world.

What is the prophet's position on *social change?* It is likely to be one of two. He might despair of history and its possibilities to the extent that he seeks merely to be the exemplary man, visibly manifesting a higher way, with an aspiration to be a forceful conscience among the masses of expediently oriented persons. Indeed, he might gather around himself an exemplary community which, while not taking a significant part in the development of the social and political affairs of men, demonstrates through the rectitude of its own life and structure the possibilities of another way of life. The prophet might, thus, withdraw from the human fray, to announce its futility and to witness to his ultimate values.

He might, however, be moved to instigate revolution in the oppressive, corrupt society to which he ministers. The contrast between the "ought" and the "is" is so vast, the historical evils so horrendous, the institutions of the world so oppressive, that in the name of obedience to God it is the duty of men to engage in revolution, to bring in the day of hope in the midst of despair, the day of peace in the midst of war, the day of freedom in the midst of oppression, the day of justice in the midst of inequality.

The *role of the Church* either might be an exemplary island in the sea of corruption, or the vanguard of God's army of righteousness, overthrowing the imbedded Philistinism of established social orders.[4] If the prophet moves toward the first, he is likely to identify himself with a community of people who are, like him, rigorously faithful to their ultimate values, and seek to provide in their own isolated conditions a bodying forth of a true community of justice, love and peace. The community would seek to avoid contamination by its contemporary Canaanites and their seductive Baals; it would be a true Israel for others to see. If the prophet sees the church as the vanguard in the struggles for a new order and a new life, he is likely to seek to bring the existing church into both a new internal moral and spiritual purity that matches its true norms, and a new zeal for radical change in the conditions of the world of which it is a part. In both views of the role of the church, a monastic- or sect-like discipline is the vocation of God's people. In the first its fruit is to be an example for emulation; in the second it is to be an agent involved in bringing in the Kingdom of Righteousness.

Theologians who take the social role of the prophet do so for reasons expressed by these several points. If one chooses to repudiate the social role of the prophet in the ideal-typical sense I have formulated, he would have to attack the validity of any, several, or all of the theological institutional and moral correlates of the role. He might bring scriptural and theological arguments to bear on certain of them, ethical arguments on others, arguments about actual social conditions on others. If one chooses to defend the prophet, he would similarly have to defend him for this variety of reasons.

II. THEOLOGIAN AS PRESERVER

OUR formation of an ideal-type of the preserver will be even more an essay in exaggeration than was the type of the prophet. It would be difficult to find any significant theologian, historically, who was the absolute defender of the *status quo*. But there have been, and are, theologians who call for the preservation of existing values and institutions. In this role the theologian stands with God against the forces which threaten the order of society, the established moral values, the practices and procedures of social institutions. He interprets the threatening events around him as onslaughts against the ways and will of God that are already embodied in the mores and structures of his time and place. He sees himself as God's appointed man resisting the forces that would alienate the society from God, that would corrupt it by turning to new gods, that would conform it to a will that he sees to be estranged from the human good now bodied forth in the social order. We shall examine the correlates of this type in the same order we did those of the prophet.

The attitude of the preserver is likely to be both defensive and combative. He may have indignation like the prophet, but rather than being directed at the present injustice, it is directed toward the forces, movements, and persons who seriously question and threaten the established order. He sees the forces of change as the forces of dissolution, breaking up and destroying the achievements so difficultly gained in the past history of man. He sees no promise of a higher and better way that would improve the human lot, and even the cost of attempting significant alterations in modes of life, structures of social organization, and mores seem too high to risk. He is stability-, rather than change-oriented. Like the prophet, he might also burn with passion, but it is a defensive combative passion, flaying at new ideas which threaten established patterns of thought, at new modes of participation by the many that threaten the autocracy of the elite few, at the radical questioning of the young and the disinherited. He appears to an outsider to be a person of closed mind; to him the outsider appears to be a person of no firm convictions or commitments. The established order of righteousness is imperiled by the proposed order of corruption; he is defensive and combative. He stands as the preserver of the tradition.

The preserver is likely to speak of *God* in terms of the creator and ruler of an order of life, established in the foundations of the world, known to men, and embodied to a high degree in the mores, the institutions, and the ways of life that now exist. The order that he defends is God's order, the laws that he seeks to preserve are God's laws, the values he wishes to continue to inculcate are the divine values. God stands for order against chaos, for truth against all thought that is not captive to traditional ways of thinking, for known virtues against all changes in moral development. God's people and the institutions they have founded are bulwarks against the powers of evil that threaten society in the forces of change that run amuck in the world. Life is to be conformed to the order of creation, the rule of God that is immutable, and that has already penetrated and informed the structure and customs of life that we know.

Perhaps the preserver adheres to a form of the *Christ of culture* position in Niebuhr's typology. He sees a present reconciliation of Christianity with culture. Christ himself is interpreted in terms of the preserver's own ideals, or the prevalent ideals of his own time. Christ represents the virtues of thrift and hard work, of scrupulous honesty and sexual virtue, of spiritual love for the poor and the oppressed. Christ has, through the impregnation of culture and society, informed what the preserver judges to be the best in human culture. He represents philanthropic love, as contrasted with power that seeks to bring justice into the world. He provides the forgiveness of man's sins more than the empowering of a new way of life. Any effort to change the values of the society is viewed as an attack on Christ and on Christianity. To be sure, there is a higher way that stands as the ideal toward which men ought to move, but the direction of social and intellectual development is slowly and inevitably moving toward that goal. The preserver identifies faithfulness to Christ with faithfulness to the things he approves of in the world in which he lives.

History and society, while struggling with manifestations of sin and evil, are already bearing the fruits of the redemption and creative purposes of God. Their orders are established in the goodness of their creation by God, and in the ruling purposes which he exercises through the institutions that nurture and preserve human society. The preserver believes in the goodness of what exists in history, especially when he sees it against the ideas, aspirations, and forces that would dissolve what he knows to provide a medium of justice, of order, of law, and of peace. Each slight improvement of justice bears testimony to the trustworthiness of God's work in and through the contemporary forms of social organization. Rather than seeing history as the story of sin, he sees it as the story of God's rule and power. The increments of forms of value are testimonies to the truth that God is still on his throne, and that he has not left his people without the aid of his

Spirit. Human problems are manageable within established channels
and procedures; the destruction of these is a threat to the reliable
forces of history that have brought us the successes we now enjoy. The
preserver reads the moral significance of history in a different light
than does the prophet.

The preserver might articulate his view of the *Kingdom of God* in
terms of the signs of its historical presence, and its gradual development and fulfillment. God's reign is not that which will come out of
the Armageddons of history, the holocausts of revolution, the aspirations for a more perfect future. Rather God's Kingdom is at work
like the mustard seed, growing and penetrating in its own good time
the laws, the institutional structures, the mores of the people. The
kingdom comes not through devastation of the old order, but through
the preservation and improvement of the existing order. The preserver's devil, the force that threatens the Kingdom, is not in the society
he lives in, but in the events that threaten it. He is the preserver and
defender of the marks of the Kingdom that exist—in the Church, in
society.

The preserver sees the vocation of man to be faithfully *responsible
to traditional, practical, and proved values.* He does not kindle the
flame of protest against the injustices of the present social order so
much as he calls attention to the achieved levels of justice that are
present in both law and informal social relationships. The claims of
absolute justice, absolute righteousness, absolute peace, appear to him
to be utopian and unrealistic. He will opt for what has come into being as a result of historical compromises; he will preserve the things
that have proved their rewarding significance in the real world that he
knows. The preserver will cite the good consequences that have
emerged from what persons have believed in and lived by in the past
as evidence for his point of view. He is the social realist, who understands how visionary are the dreams of the young, the aspirations of
the poor, the expectations of the oppressed. He will not give up the
established values if he judges the cost of the risk to be unpredictable,
not to mention high. His words and deeds express his responsibility
to the forming and stabilizing power of the tradition.

Social change is profoundly disturbing to the preserver. He is likely to be the defender of the *status quo.* Or perhaps he will concede
that change must come, but slowly and gradually in order to absorb
the social and moral costs that he perceives it to entail. His sense of
obligation to the society and the culture as a whole does not permit
him to develop such exemplary enclaves of a higher way that some
prophets choose. Rather, he sees much at stake for mankind as a whole
in keeping the brakes on revolutionary forces, in keeping control of
radical movements, in controlling the pace and the direction of social
change. The passionate and anxious traditionalistic preserver might
join the vanguard of opposition against the prophets and their move-

ments. He can be won by the forces of reaction, by the militants of the right, by the rhetoric of law and order, the purveyors of *Christian Economics* with their identification of Christian liberty with the freedom of the market. The moderate conservative preserver might avoid such extremes, but be what men call "prudent," weighing carefully and exactly what society is going to have to give up in order to effect something new. What is horrendous is the thought of revolution and radical change, not the imbedded evils in the historical past. The preserver has a psychological, moral, and theological stake in keeping the forces of social change in control of those who appreciate the values that are practical and traditional.

The *role of the Church* for the preserver is neither that of an exemplary community witnessing to a higher way, nor that of the vanguard of God in the struggle for new forms of life. Rather, it is the conserver of the religious and cultural tradition. The Church ought to be the defender of that which abides, rather than that which mutates. Even in the face of radical new problems emerging for humanity, it calls attention to the eternal verities, to the losses that will be sustained through innovation, to the values of authority and order. The church has a stake in the culture, in the preserver's view, not only for the sake of its self-preservation, but for the sake of the preservation of the qualities of life that it once imbued in society, the regulations it once imposed upon society. If the preserver should give up his aspiration to have the church effectively engage in the defense of the old, he might well cling to it as a source of spiritual and ideational inspiration for his personal sense of righteousness in the midst of a world destroying itself.

Just as the prophet has several kinds of reasons in defense of his stance, so does the preserver. One could properly repudiate his posiiton only by arguing against the different kinds of reasons, correlated as they are, that he gives for his adherence to it. Is Scripture in his favor? Does he understand properly the significance of God's creative and ordering work? the meaning of Christ? Does he read history properly? Are the values he defends justifiable ethically and theologically? To defend the preserver would require attention to these points as well.[5]

III. THE THEOLOGIAN AS PARTICIPANT

THE theologian as participant is not only an ideal-type in the sense of being a mental construct. It is ideal in two other senses as well. First, whereas one can find a number of historical examples of the prophet from which to build an exaggerated typical portrait, and one can find some examples of the preserver from which to do the same, there are few, if any, historical examples from which to construct the type of the participant. More than the other two, this type is a construct from almost no historical data. Second, it is a normative ideal; it is an ideal that I would wish to endorse as fitting for the theologian in our time for theological, historical and ethical reasons.

In one sense the participant stands between the types of prophet and preserver, in another sense it draws elements of each and moves beyond them. The participant is wedded neither to the condemnation of the existing state of affairs, nor to wholehearted support to them. He is, however, not a passive spectator of events and institutions, judging some to be worthy of endorsement and others to be worthy of re-orientation and reform. Rather, he is actively involved in the shaping of events and in the development and re-ordering of institutions. The participant shares in the processes of public opinion formation through his articulations of the ends and means that the human community ought to follow. He is involved in decision-making through his participation in political, educational, and other processes that have an impact on the course of human development. He seeks to influence the exercise of the powers that are formative in shaping the present and the future.

This theologian is not simply the sage generalist with great moral sensitivity and critical ethical acumen, though these are necessary gifts and talents. He also has a specialized knowledge and discipline of thought to bring to bear in the interactions of perspectives, technical knowledge, moral beliefs and opinions, out of which come the convictions and actions that shape the future. He represents a point of view about what the primary purposes of human existence in community and history are, about what the qualities of life ought to be, about what values are in accord with God's activity and intention for his creation. The participant is no less the theologian in conceiving of his social role in this way. He brings to bear the insight and wisdom of the Christian community's long historical reflection about the chief ends of man. The imagination, critical reflection, and historical awareness that have always been involved in the best of theological discipline continue to be relevant in this new role.

The participant is one partner among many in the human conversation that will give some determination to the ways in which men use their technical and political powers, their resources and talents in the development of history and society toward humane ends. The capacity to listen to and understand other points of view, to comprehend the basic options thrust up by political, technological and scientific developments, and to speak meaningfully and clearly from his perspective is at a premium in the theologian's function. While he thinks and speaks from a perspective that is theologically informed and shaped, he does not announce it as the truth. Rather he recognizes its limitations with reference to things that need to be known and done, and its relativity and partiality that need to be corrected by others. He neither stands with and for God announcing the failings of man, nor stands with and for God defending the achievements of society and culture. Rather, he is oriented toward policy and toward actions—those of persons and of centers of power, established and nascent—that give direction through purpose as men move toward God's future.

The *attitude* of the theologian as participant has been well described by Karl Rahner in an essay in which he reflects on the developments in the life sciences. "The Christian need not march forward as toward a hell on earth, nor salute the future as a this-worldly version of the Kingdom of God. Neither inordinate enthusiasm nor lamentation is consonant with the balance that should characterize the Christian."[6] This suggests that the theologian ought to have a sufficient measure of dispassion and objectivity to see clearly and to think carefully about the world in which he is active. Perhaps other terms can be used to point to the attitude. The participant is confident without being unrealistic; his poise is not sustained by rosey illusions about man's goodness or some view of the inexorable progressive development of life that will bring Utopia without suffering and evil. He is realistic without being defensive; his awareness of the actuality and possibility of costly human mistakes leads him neither to hide behind the fortress of the past, nor to fear about venturing into the future. He is hopeful without suffering illusions; he affirms the creative possibilities for man's historical achievements in both technical and moral realms without denying the treacherous character of the way toward human fulfillment. He is open without being uncritical; his willingness to listen and to learn from others does not lead to the surrender of his own worth and perspective, nor to a passivity that lets the thought of others simply carry the day.

Both the prophet and the preserver have a certitude about God's will and God's way that the participant finds excessive; both have a dogmatism which seems to foreclose the recognition of significant present values to be cultivated and developed in the case of the prophet, and significant emerging values to be explored in the case of the preserver. The participant, like the others, is a man of confidence, but his confidence is the kind that leads to creativity in his responses to events, persons, and institutions, rather than to sorrowful moral indignation or to defensive combativeness. He is not a man of fear or despair.

God, for the participant, is neither as much the wrathful Judge that he is for the prophet, nor the establisher of an immutable order that he is for the preserver. Perhaps he can best be spoken of as the active presence in the events to which men respond and which in turn they seek to direct. Several current modes of theological reflection lend support to this general view of God as active presence.

Karl Rahner provides one way in which theological foundations are established for the role of participant. "We mean first that God is not only above us, as Lord and horizon of history, but also that he is ahead of us as our own future, that future which carries history forward. For

Christianity proclaims that the absolute, eternal, transcendent God who is radical, infinite mystery gives himself to the world in absolute mystery and free grace as its innermost ground and ultimate future. He guides history as something truly his own, not as a process that he merely created."[7] God is the innermost ground and the ultimate future of the world, and he guides history, but not as an inexorable process. The theologian becomes a participant in the creativity that leads to the future that is open with many possibilities for man.

Rahner's is not the only theological and ontological option present in contemporary theology that supports the view of the theologian as participant. Daniel Day Williams, in the latest contribution from the "process theology" school to contemporary discussion, argues from a phenomenological account of the human experience of love by analogy to a conception of God's being as love. This account is built upon a critique of St. Augustine's view of the "absolute changelessness" of God. Williams' general point is that "process philosophy opens up for Christian theology a way of conceiving the being of God in historical temporal terms."[8] In this view God's function is not to make the future as certain as the past, but it is to give an ordered pattern to the creative life of the world, and "to bring new possibilities into existence in a real future." The work of God is a continual process of divine self-communication which presents men with the sustaining power of an involved and loving ultimate reality, and creates new possibilities of love.

Although a careful drawing of inferences from Williams' theology with reference to the vocation of the theologian and the Christian would lead to a somewhat different picture than one gets by drawing inferences from Rahner, Williams and the other process theologians would support a view of the theologian as participant. He is involved, as God is involved, in the temporal and historical existence of the human community, bringing it toward a more universal and loving communion of man with man. The theologian is to embody the spirit of love, searching for new forms of community in the life of men.

A recent exposition of Biblical ethics suggests that the fundamental structure of Biblical faith and morality would support our view of the theologian as participant. Freeman Sleeper states that "the structure of Biblical ethics deals with God's action in creating the conditions and possibilities for human community and with human action to fulfill those conditions and possibilities through an appropriate response." He argues that the meaning of the *imago Dei* is that men, "like God . . . are able to pursue the task of creating historical order."[9] Sleeper is in accord with both Biblical scholars and with theologians such as H. R. Niebuhr in seeing the vocation of man (including the theologian) to be the discernment of the appropriate human actions in society and history that are a fitting response to God's action in historical events. Here again there are grounds for the view that the theologian is the participant in response to the active and living presence of God. God is neither the uninvolved ideal-observer making judgments, nor is he the changeless ground of the established order, but the power that makes possible human creative and responsible action in directing the course of events.

Other modes of contemporary theological thinking could also be pointed to in this regard. Perhaps they indicate a rough consensus that the events in which man participates are ultimately made possible by the presence and activity of God in the historical order. In response to God's reality, and to man's understanding and comprehension of his reality, the participant seeks to be an agent among other agents in giving direction to the future. In the light of God's purposes for the redemption and fulfillment of men and history, the theologian makes his contribution to the society and culture in which he lives. God is seen to be bidding men to new responsibilities under new technical and historical circumstances, offering new possibilities for human development, ambiguous though they may be. The theologian is an interpreter of what God's active presence may be calling forth in the juncture in social and historical experience where men can intervene to restrain or redirect the course of events. God is not so much static being as he is active presence; he is not so much law as he is ordering and redeeming activity; he is not so much wrathful judge as he is the opener of new possibilities and the provider of the direction in which men ought to go. He wills neither the destruction of the old for the sake of its imperfections nor the defense of the old for the sake of its values, but rather he wills the development of human communities in which the qualities of life are present that lead to man's well-being.

Christ, to turn again to H. R. Niebuhr's typology, is the transformer of culture, rather than its radical critic or its defender. Christ seeks neither the defense nor the abolition of the historical orders; rather he seeks their renewal and re-direction, their conversion toward their proper end and their proper qualities. In Christ, man is acutely sensitive to the perversions of human society and personal life, to the ambiguities of human achievements. He knows and feels the pain and suffering of the world in which the hungry remain unfed, the oppressed remain shackled in the chains of indifferent and tyrannical social orders. He knows the potentialities for a fairer and more loving pattern of human relationships that remain unrealized because of the defensiveness and greed of those in control. But Christ seeks not the destruction of the perverse and the ambiguous, but their redemption and wholeness. He calls men not to flee from the world to form their exemplary sects and enclaves, but to be the agents of creative and redemptive action in the events in which they are engaged. He creates in men a vision of God's loving purposes, and he moves the wills of men to seek their fulfillment. He calls men to be as forgiving as they are condemning; he calls not so much for destructive action as he does for compassion and for positive participation oriented toward obedience to the claims of God's perfect reign, his Kingdom.

In Christ, man is conscious of the benefits of God's providence as he experiences them in all the realms of natural and social life. He acknowledges the forms of goodness and value that are his to be the gifts of God's love and grace in his creation and governing of the world, and is thankful. He is ready to support the achievements of justice and love in the human community against the encroachments of those who would undermine them; he is willing to protect actual spiritual and social freedoms against new oppressions and tyrannies. But Christ seeks not so much the defense of these qualities of life and community as he does their renewal and development, their extension and their intensification.

Christ provides the theologian his fundamental perspective or posture toward the world of persons, institutions and events in which he is living. He is the ground of confidence that the theologian has in the goodness of the ultimate power, source, and end of life. He enables him to see, be sensitive to, and affirm the reality and the power of the goodness of life wherever it exists and wherever it strives to come into existence. He is both the source and the symbol of the theologian's affirmation of the actual and intended goodness of human history and community. Christ provides the theologian with those dispositions of love and trust and hope that are so important in his participation in the life of the human community. He saves him from hate even in the presence of demonic forces in the world, from fear and distrust even in the presence of deception, coercion and injustice, from despair even in the presence of intransigency and failure. He is the ground of the theologian's freedom from the dead weight of the past, and from anxiety about the unknowability of the future. Christ provides the theologian his basic intentionality and direction. He orients him toward those ends that are in accord with God's purposes for human well-being and fulfillment in all the dimensions of existence. He shows the theologian positive norms of life that are the requisites of faithfulness both to God and to man, that are to be brought to bear upon the possibilities that emerge in the development of human life.[10]

History and society for the participant, in Rahner's words, will always remain both created and fallen, and the objects of both judgment and blessing.[11] There are two aspects of the view of history and society that need to be emphasized. First, they are the field of human action and human possibility. History, for the participant, is not the outcome of fated, inexorably determinative processes that are impersonal and absolutely beyond the powers of men to affect. Rather, there are interstices between institutions and events, between persons, which provide the occasions for the meaningful exercises of human and other powers to give direction to the world. The participant certainly does not move from this to some absurd view that each event is created out of nothing, that man's freedom is absolute in his capacities to alter the present and shape the future. He recognizes that the present possibilities for action are deeply conditioned by the past, and are limited to some extent by the present state of affairs. Not all options that his imagination might conjure are within the realm of the possible. But he does believe in a significant openness in the present and the future that enables human decisions and actions to conserve, alter, or overturn the course of social development according to human purposes. He has no illusions that human powers are great enough to determine all the effects or consequences of human innovations; he recognizes that his intended consequences interact with other factors to bring into being other effects not in accord with his normative purposes. But it is in accord with his understanding of persons as actors or agents, and history as a field of possibilities, to envision the role of the theologian as the participant.

Second, the participant understands the world to be the object of both judgment and blessing. It is not fated to human destruction by man's sinfulness and perversion. Institutions are not predetermined by man's disobedience to be repressive and authoritarian; morality exists not only as a provision of dikes against chaos. Man's knowledge is not only confined to his heritage from the past, to those beliefs that seem to have kept events and persons from sliding into the demonic. Nor is history predestined to a glorious fulfillment in the time of any one generation. The blessings of reformed political orders and of technological advances bear within themselves new possibilities of ill effects and subtler forms of coercive repression, as Reinhold Niebuhr taught a "liberal" Protestantism forty years ago. History and society will always be arenas both of achieved human good and of new possibilities for human evil.

They do, in the participant's view, offer the possibilities for significant human action, using various capacities and powers available to human agency in accordance with moral intentions and purposes. This action can be directed not only toward piecemeal change in the immediate and concrete circumstances, but also toward the development of juster, freer, and more loving orders of human community. Man can participate in the processes of life in a truly human and genuinely creative and effective way.

The perfect reign of God, his *Kingdom,* is a point of focus for the direction of human activities. The participant is oriented toward the fulfillment of God's creative and redemptive purposes, toward the development of a community of love and openness, toward an Omega which gives guidance and criteria for all his deeds. Man is not the defender of a Kingdom that already exists. He is not to identify the perfect reign of God's purposes with the actual achievements of the institutions and orders of society in which he exists, whether these be civil or ecclesiastical orders. Indeed, the outright identification of any historical order with the realization of the Kingdom of God is the utmost in idolatry, and can only lead to the myopic defensiveness that is characteristic of the preserver. Nor is man the proclaimer of a Kingdom that will apocalyptically break into being through the catastrophic events of history understood to be the action of God. He does not deny that revolutions might be necessary, that a painful wrenching from the established views might be in the offing. But the successes of no revolution will be equivalent to the arrival of the Kingdom of God as long as history retains its essential characteristic of possibilities, and man retains his essential characteristics as a finite, sinful agent.

Rather, the participant is a member of a Kingdom whose full reality is not perfectly manifest, yet whose power is at work in the actions of men that are in accord with its reality. The Kingdom is the orientation point that gives both the disposition of hope and the vision of human fulfillment. It provides the participant with the fundamental direction toward which he believes God's purposes are moving, and consequently toward which man's purposes ought also to be moving. The participant will run the risks of drawing inferences from his understanding of God's Kingdom for the direction in which society ought to move. Like the American theologians of the Social Gospel, he will hazard the opinion that social ethical correlates of the coming Kingdom can be determined. Thus, the Kingdom toward which he is oriented suggests that oppression must give way to human freedom, concentration of wealth to distributive economic justice, concentrations of power to the participation of the powerless in the determination of their lives, the ways of war to the insurance of peace, deprivation of opportunities to the availability of education, health benefits and other blessings of abundance. The participant is a creative agent in the formation of social and personal life in the direction of what man can become as a citizen in God's realm.

The participant is open to, and attracted by, emerging social and moral *values* as he shares in the development of man. In his freedom he is not compelled to deny the validity of existing values as the prophet might be, nor is he compelled to defend them as the preserver might be. He can appreciate the moral order that exists while he seeks a moral order that is to come into being. Perhaps it is not so much new "values" that he is sensitive to as it is the necessity and possibility of finding new embodiments of the values men have always been attracted to under new social and historical conditions. It is not that men's definitions of justice have fundamentally altered so much as it is the case that the claims for the extension of justice for more persons, and over a wider range of things, come to the fore and must be responded to positively. Scientific and technical developments extend the range of opportunity for human creativity, just as new awarenesses in the media of the traditional arts do. The participant is willing to experiment and to risk in his interest in finding new forms and patterns of all sorts of values. With his orientation toward the future, while not ignoring the past, he is aware of the necessity to compromise certain tradititonal principles and values for the sake of achieving those that are required under a new set of conditions.

He can be trained on the lodestar of such ultimates as love and perfect justice while setting his course through the murkiness of social and historical actualities. He is not overcome by nostalgia when he sees old patterns of life fading and falling away. Rather, he sees the development of new possibilities: in the patterns of political and economic ordering of urban life; in the responsible moral ordering of relations between the sexes and of family life under vastly altered social and technical conditions; in the organization of political units, cities, states, and nations, in relation to each other; in the development of medical technology. His openness to the new is not uncritical; he can warn about the losses of rights and values that will take place if various courses of action are pursued. The participant can alter his priorities of concerns and values that have existential and historical import under specific technological and social conditions. Traditional patterns of social order might have to bend in favor of the growth of freedom from oppression, as in situations where radical social reform and revolution appear on the horizons of the society. Individual freedom might have to bend in favor of ordered justice, as in the case of fair housing and fair employment laws. Restraints might be required on the actions of individuals for the sake of the common good, as in anti-pollution laws and perhaps in the future in the case of family size. Cherished notions of proper means of human relations might have to be given up for the sake of certain ends, as in the case of traditional anti-contraceptive morality in relation to population growth and to the personal fulfillment in marriage. The participant is sensitive and open to the kinds of responses that are required of human values as new possibilities and new threats emerge in the passage from past and present toward the future.

The theologian of our third type accepts *social change* as normal and necessary, even though its accelerated rate creates opportunities and problems in an order of magnitude not previously experienced in human history. He does not dread the ruptures that it brings, as change reverberates from one center of innovations across others and through the whole sea of human experience. Nor does he thrive on change for its own sake, or for the delight in seeing the old pass away. Rather he seeks to make as clear as possible the purposes that social change can most beneficially fulfill, and he seeks to judge those purposes in the light of his reflections on the Divine and human potentialities and demands that he knows.

The participant is under an obligation to know as best he can the nature of the processes of social change. For him the social and behavioral sciences are of great importance, as are the hard sciences with their technological effects on the social life of man. This obligation is a complex and often frustrating one, partially because of the vast growth in information about men and societies that we have been accumulating in the past decades. Like all persons concerned with policy and action, the theologian has to sort out the important from the unimportant information, that which is pertinent to the issues of human well-being which he addresses from that which is trivial. But this is not his only problem; there are the inevitable differences of opinion about which information is accurate, and what its proper interpretation is, even among the social and behavioral scientists who gather it. Like others, the participant is tempted to find and use the information that is congenial with his moral pre-dispositions, and ignore that which might question them. But he must keep the measure of detachment and disinterestedness that enables him to make the fairest possible judgments. He will necessarily find himself at least temporarily allied with others who interpret the practical significance of information in roughly the same way he does, but who work from different basic convictions and for different ultimate ends.

Since so many issues of social change abound, it is important that theologians find a division of labor among themselves. Not all will be equipped to engage in the conversation about economic development or about international relations, about public school problems in large cities or about changes in health care, about the population problems of the world or about race relations. Participants need to become at least lay experts in the arenas in which they concentrate their attention. This is necessary initially to gain access to the discussions being carried on among the experts in social change in particular areas, for they will not have patience to listen to uninformed judgments or to vague moral platitudes.

The participant is not so oriented toward the achievement of beneficial consequences that might come from change that he loses sight of the problem of the rightness and wrongness of the means. But he does not expect change to come without disruption, health without the pain of surgery, gain without the loss of cherished achievements, success without the possibility of costly failure. He will make his case for the illumination that can be gained from the past, and for the reckoning of potential losses, even while he seeks to be an agent among others in directing the course toward the future. He is not so fast in his commitments, however, that he rules out in principle the necessity for revolution. He is not dedicated in principle to the piecemeal social change that experts sometimes find themselves endorsing. And under certain circumstances he might be willing to endorse the exercise of violence.

The *role of the Church* for the theologian as participant is that of (to use a tired term) involvement. The people of God are not the isolated portrayers of an exemplary life in communities ghettoized from the frustrations and possibilities of events and institutions around them. Nor are they the last bastions against the hordes of change. Rather the people of God who acknowledge his Lordship are part of the whole family of man, all of whom are God's children. They work and live together with others, sharing aspirations and expectations, anxieties and suffering, striving toward the order of life that brings a greater measure of justice and love, peace and reconciliation, health and welfare. They share in the labors of the economic and political orders, the medical and scientific orders. They seek, through their participation, to bring these things to the glory of God, and the fulfillment of human life. The vocation of Christians is in the places where they do and can function in the framework of life, being agents of purposive action and manifestations of spiritual resources for humane ends.

One function of the theologian is this community is to be the leader of the moral discourse that is required if Christians are to be more effective actors. The congregations and assemblies of the churches become communities of moral discourse, where moral beliefs and consciences are formed, and where the ends and means of human action are clarified and discussed. The theologian recognizes that the lay members of the Christian community, by virtue of their jobs and professions, are generally in positions to influence policy and decisions in a way that he is not. Thus, internally within the community, he is both learner and teacher as the congregated Christians seek to discern what God's will might be for the particular occasions in which they are engaged. He is not the authoritative pronouncer of the obligations of all Christians under all circumstances, but rather a contributor from the point of view of his special knowledge toward the shaping of the collective and individual consciences of the Church. He recognizes that the Church has passed from a stage of moral teaching in conformity to highly specific and ill-understood rules of conduct to that of the moral educator who seeks to bring the consciences of its members to a sensitivity and knowledge that enables them to act as Christian participants in their societies.[12] They, like the theologian who hopefully gives them leadership, are creatively and redemptively present in the crises, struggles, and transformations of human existence.

This outline of the task of the theologian as participant needs more substantial justification and development than it has received here; indeed, it stands in need of critical examination and correction. Nor would I wish to suggest that every person technically trained in theology ought to be conformed to this type; the theological community, like other communities, benefits from pluralism of expert knowledge and divergent points of view. We can ask, as we did with the types of the prophet and the preserver, whether this type is warranted—scripturally, theologically, ethically, and socially. To some extent it is a depiction of a conventional consensus present in Christian thinking today. Be that as it may, it is also a call to a more demanding task than either the roles of prophet or preserver require.

It demands greater rather than less self-examination and self-criticism, for it lacks the simple certitude of the other types. It demands clearer and harder thinking, since its vocabulary and thought forms must communicate with and embrace the vocabulary and thought forms of other men, working from other perspectives, directed by other motives, and often seeking other ends. It demands at least as much courage and confidence as do the prophet and the preserver, for it requires that the theologian knows what he is doing as he moves into alien territories and strange seas. It demands the capacity to hear as well as to speak, to be receptive as well as to be active. Its sense of responsibility is more difficult, for its cannot rest on the traditional absolutes of the preserver or on the pure ultimates of the prophet, but must be accountable to the living God and to human communities. It requires imagination: the practical access to participation is not readily available, nor is much of the world breathlessly waiting to hear what the theologian has to say. It demands competence, for the theologian will not be attended to unless his words and deeds have the persuasiveness of excellence. But not all of the world has pre-judged that the theologian is without significance; he and his community must be prepared to grasp the opportunities that are being made available to them, modest as they may be.

NOTES

[1] See Niebuhr, *Christ and Culture*, New York: Harper, 1951, pp. 45-82. He discusses Tertullian and Tolstoy as illustrations of Christ against culture.

[2] Cf. Max Weber's distinction between an "ethic of ultimate ends," and an "ethic of responsibility," in "Politics as a Vocation," H. H. Gerth and C. Wright Mills, eds., *From Max Weber: Essays in Sociology*, New York: Oxford University Press, 1946, pp. 120 ff.

[3] *Ibid.*, p. 121.

[4] See Ernst Troeltsch's discussion of the relations of Christological beliefs, views of the Christian community, and relations of the community to the world in his famous passage on sects and churches, in *The Social Teachings of the Christian Churches*, Vol. I, Glencoe, Ill., The Free Press, 1949, pp. 331-43.

[5] I would like to call attention to an essay by Karl Mannheim that is not widely known in theological circles, but makes some useful general distinctions pertinent to this paper. It is, "Conservative Thought," and is printed in *Essays in Sociology and Social Psychology*, ed. Paul Kecskemeti, London: Routledge and Kegan Paul, 1953, pp. 74-164. In the course of the essay, Mannheim makes distinctions between "traditionalist," "conservative," and "progressive" forms of thought and behavior. "Traditionalist behavior is almost purely reactive. Conservative behaviour is meaningful...." (p. 98) My preserver is

meant to be more conservative than traditionalist, but I have allowed for more traditionalist and reactive elements at some points. "Traditionalism is a general psychological attitude which expresses itself in different individuals as a tendency to cling to the past and a fear of innovation.... This development of the traditionalist attitude into the nucleus of a definite social trend does not take place spontaneously: it takes place as a response to the fact that 'progressivism' had already constituted itself as a definite trend." (p. 99) In contrasting conservatism and progressivism, Mannheim writes, "One of the most essential characteristics of this conservative way of life and thought seems to be the way in which it clings to the immediate, the actual, the *concrete.*... To experience and to think 'concretely' now comes to mean to desire to restrict the range of one's activities to the immediate surroundings in which one is placed, and to abjure strictly all that may smack of speculation and hypothesis.... It is concerned with immediate action, with changing concrete details, and therefore does not really trouble itself with the *structure* of the world in which it lives. On the other hand, all progressive activity feeds on its *consciousness of the possible.* It transcends the given immediate present, by seizing on the possibilities for systematic change which it offers. It fights the concrete, *not* because it wants to replace it merely by another *form of the concrete* but because it wants to produce another *systematic starting-point* for further development.... *Thus progressive reformism tends to tackle the system as a whole, while conservative reformism tackles particular details.*" (pp. 103-04) "Where the progressive uses the future to interpret things, the conservative uses the past: the progressive thinks in terms of *norms,* the conservative in terms of *germs.*" (p 111) These statements about the conservative are fairly apt with reference to the ideal-type of the "preserver," and those about the "progressive" are somewhat apt with reference to the "prophet," and point toward the ideal-type of the "paricipant" as I shall develop it.

⁶ Karl Rahner, "Experiment: Man," *Theology Digest,* Sesquicentennial Issue, 1968, p. 61.

⁷ *Ibid.,* pp. 65-66.

⁸ D. D. Williams, *The Spirit and Forms of Love,* New York: Harper and Row, 1968, pp. 106-7.

⁹ Freeman Sleeper, *Black Power and Christian Responsibility,* Nashville and New York: Abingdon Press, 1969, p. 57, and p. 73. Part II of the book is an interpretation of the structure of Biblical theological ethics.

¹⁰ I have sought to elaborate on the significance of Christ for moral theology in *Christ and the Moral Life,* New York: Harper and Row, 1969. This paragraph is a condensation of the last chapter of that book.

¹¹ Rahner, *op. cit.,* p. 61.

¹² I have developed this theme extensively in *The Church as Moral Decision Maker,* Philadelphia: Pilgrim Press, 1970, especially pp. 83-85, 109-137.

From a Two-Nature Christology to a Christology of Presence

Piet Schoonenberg

I AM very happy to have this opportunity to speak to you, and, most of all *with* you at this Theology Institute. When I am preparing to lecture in a foreign country, I sometimes think of what Saint Paul wrote to the Christians at Rome before his visit to that city: "I am longing to see you either to strengthen you by sharing a spiritual gift with you, or what is better, to find encouragement among you from our common faith" (Rom. 1, 11). In Paul's time the Christian faith was in search of its first formulation, in search of words and concepts which were intelligible for the world into which Christianity was entering. We Christians are now once more searching for words and concepts for others, but also for ourselves, because the world is changing so rapidly that we now have to ask what it means to be a Christian in our times. All Christians are asking this, and certainly for the past decade we Roman Catholics have been among them. I am happy to be confronted with this question in the United States, where the Catholic Church is so much in movement. I hope to find the encouragement among you from the searching faith which is common to all of us.

Our faith is related to God and to Jesus Christ, to God in Jesus Christ. What does the person of Jesus Christ mean in our relation to God and to our fellow man? What is Jesus for us now? Among all Christians who are asking this question there lives a new kind of interest in the Scripture, especially the Gospels. Moreover contemporary exegesis, particularly the "New Quest of the Historical Jesus," summons us to reflect on Jesus' message and person. Thus we can best let ourselves be confronted with the image of Jesus as it is offered to us by the Gospels and the New Testament as a whole.

And yet I do not want to make Scripture my starting point here. I do hope to end up there, but my starting point lies somewhere between the time of the New Testament and our time. It lies in the Council of Chalcedon in 451 A.D. and in the Christology which was expressed in that Council and surrounded it. No Christian can read the Scripture fruitfully outside the Church and her tradition. For this reason, Christians take the doctrine of Chalcedon into account when reflecting on Christ, either by repeating or rejecting, by reinterpreting or criticizing that teaching. We Catholics least of all, along with many Eastern Orthodox, Anglicans and Protestants, can avoid confronting Chalcedon. The older among us can realize how much we have become used to the image of Christ as God and man, how much it has influenced our thinking and praying. And young people probably show the influence of this image of Christ on them in their resistance to it. Now it is in this image of Christ that the Church, the same Church as the one we belong to, tried to express her faith in Jesus Christ. If we are able to discover this, it will be a support for our faith today. We will perhaps also discover, however, that the form in which faith in Christ was once expressed no longer speaks to us, indeed, that it has become an obstacle for that same faith. In that case as well we must not simply repress the Christology of Chalcedon from our consciousness, since repression is always unhealthy; we must come to terms with Chalcedon, with whatever it is in Chalcedon that helps our faith, or hinders it. I think that such a procedure can make the Scripture and our entire relationship with Christ bear fruit.

Therefore beginning with the Christological model in which we grew up I would like to come to grips with the past and the present, with the biblical Christology that lies behind it and with the possibilities we have of seeing Jesus now and of making him intelligible for the future. I will first speak about the Chalcedonian model in Christology, about the difficulties inherent in it, and about the possibility of understanding the model. In doing this the path is opened for other Christologies; a Christology of the final salvific presence of God, a Christology of the final significance of the Man Jesus, a Christology of Jesus as Rabbi and Prophet, as Example and Pioneer. Thus my lecture divides into two Chapters: a discussion of the Christology of Chalcedon and the related Christological thinking, which I call the two-nature Christology, and a sketch of other Christologies.

A. THE TWO-NATURE CHRISTOLOGY
I. *A Short Outline*

CATHOLIC theology and catechesis represented Our Lord Jesus Christ as God and man. He is truly God and truly Man, fully God and fully Man, God like the Father and Man like us. In the terms used by the Council of Chalcedon, Jesus Christ is one person in two natures, the divine nature and the human nature. In this Christology as it has been presented to us one more point is important. The one person is not only indicated by the proper name Jesus or Jesus Christ, but he is also the subject of further qualifications: He is a *divine* person, the person of the Word or Son, divine and eternal, equally divine and eternal as are the Father and the Holy Spirit. This divine person has of course a divine nature which is proper to him with the Father and the Holy Spirit. In addition to that divine nature he assumed a human nature that originally was not proper to him.

Jesus Christ, then, is a divine person with a human nature which he has assumed. *He is not a human person.* The personality of the human nature is not proper to that nature, but is the divine personality of the Word or the Son. Expressing this in terms of salvation-history we can say: "The Word became flesh" by assuming the flesh or the human nature. In addition to his eternal birth from the Father, he was born in time from the Virgin Mary.

For the sake of brevity I will call this representation of Christ the "Two Nature Model" following the terminology of John McIntyre in his little book *The Shape of Christology.*[1] The two-nature model was familiar for centuries not only to the Roman Catholic Church, but also to the Orthodox Eastern Churches and to the orthodox streams in the Reformation and Anglicanism. It was not accepted by Nestorians and Monophysites and was criticized in the more liberal circles of the Reformation and Anglicanism. These liberal criticisms which started with historians of dogma such as Albrecht Ritschl, Harnack and Loofs became visible in systematic theology between the two world wars. In Anglicanism one can find examples of this Christological evolution in books written by Donald Baillie, John Knox and Norman Pittinger.[2] At the present time the critique has spread to Catholic thinking and Catholic theology as well. I think that the roots of this revolution and of practically all the revolutions in theology are to be found partly in modern exegesis, but principally in what we call modern thought, or the modern image of the world and man. For this reason the objections usually are expressed first by people who are not theologians.

At any rate the task of the theologian now is to give a precise formulation of the objections, to consider them critically and to search for an answer which fits in with both tradition and modern understanding. Therefore, I will now give a summary of the objections against the two-nature model.

II. *Objections or Difficulties Against the Two-Nature Model*

As I said, these objections are offered also by exegetes. The exegetes and many of their readers formulate the first objection thus:

(1) The two-nature model is not biblical; it is a Hellenistic invention. From this we get the second objection: (2) This model has nothing to do with salvation and salvation history. It is the fruit of static and essentialistic thinking ("essentialism" being one of the worst philosophical words of abuse nowadays, something like "establishment" in social matters). The third objection is formulated: (3) It is not only our salvation-history, but also the history of Jesus himself that has been covered over and made invisible by this model. It is applied in the same way to Jesus in his earthly life and to the risen Christ.

The fourth objection is more interior to the two-nature model and is the most serious of all: (4) The one Christ in two natures forces us either to deny a human person in Christ and thus his consubstantiality with us, or to admit the human person with the result that Jesus Christ is no longer *one* person.

Additional objections can be formulated against the two-nature model, especially against its epistemological presuppositions. The objections could be extended to the doctrine of the Trinity as well. However, let us now look at the four objections raised above. Certainly they are not all of the same gravity or importance, but I will say a few words on each of them.

First Objection: The model is a Hellenistic invention. First of all we will have to say something about this fact and then something about the proper appreciation of the fact. It is true that the two-nature model is not biblical. All the divine and all the human attributes the Council of Chalcedon gives to Christ are to be found in the New Testament except the distinction between the two natures. This is the product of a reflection by Hellenistic theology.[4] However, a strict opposition between a Hellenistic and a biblical way of thinking is misleading, for two reasons:

(a) Within the New Testament and already within the Old Testament there is already an encounter of Judaism and Hellenism;

(b) Jewish or Semitic thinking in itself is no more revelatory in character—as the term "biblical" suggests—than Hellenistic thinking.

Now we come to an appreciation of the fact: we have to admit the possibility of an evolution, and so of progression, in human thinking and also in theological reflection on revelation, which, after all, never existed without theology. This evolution can be an evolution for the better. Therefore, it seems to me illogical and unfair to stress, for example, the primitive character of the first man in the doctrine of Original Sin and on the other hand to search for the most primitive stratum in Christology as if, being the oldest, it were the truest. Here I want to consider three things:

(a) The interpretation of a fact or a person can become clearer in later times; it can also become fuller.

(b) The Holy Spirit is equally guiding the Church in the interpretation of the post-biblical tradition as he is guiding the Church in expressing her faith in the Scriptures. Jesus Christ is greater than all expression, and his gospel, the Good News, is the heart of both the New Testament Scriptures and post-biblical tradition.

(c) The same Spirit brought the Church from the Jews to the Gentiles. Therefore, He also guides the Church when she thinks in a Hellenistic way.

For these reasons a later evolution of Christology must not be rejected because it comes later. On the contrary, it must be positively appreciated because it can give a deeper and fuller interpretation. I deliberately said: it *can* give such an interpretation. The reason behind this is that in the evolution of thought as in all evolutions there is also a loss. All evolution is a specialization in one direction with the loss of others. So it may be that possibilities of the most primitive—the Jewish-Christian—Christology were lost and that precisely this loss accounts for the two-nature model with all its problems.

We must, therefore, explore the past history. There is a property of *human* evolution which will make such an exploration fruitful for the present. It is a characteristic of man that he does not limit himself in evolution through his specialization. He remains open in his history in order to bring the results of his specialization into a synthesis with the still undeveloped possibilities. Therefore, we must now ask, in order to find out if such a synthesis is demanded: "What are the deficiencies in the Christological position which we have developed?" The further objections against the two-nature model will probably give us the answer.

Second objection: This objection states that the two-nature model is static and essentialistic and has nothing to do with our salvation and salvation-history. We can omit the words "static" and "essentialistic" for the moment since they will be more relevant when we come to the third difficulty. What then about the assertion that the two natures have nothing to do with our salvation and salvation-history? It is clear that the formula "Jesus Christ is one divine person in two natures, a divine and a human one" is not yet an announcement of salvation in itself. Neither was the more elaborate dogmatic statement of Chalcedon a direct announcement of salvation. Nevertheless three things must be said about that statement:

(a) It is a synthesis of two statements defended on soteriological grounds by the great Fathers. Against Arianism, St. Athanasius and those who resisted against Arianism declared that Jesus Christ had to be the very Son of God, equal to God. Otherwise he would not be able to divinize and save mankind. But it is also true that if Christ is not fully human, if there is something lacking to his humanity, human nature is not assumed and so not healed and saved; "quod non est assumptum non est sanatum", as had been proposed in the struggle against Appollinarianism.

(b) The Council of Chalcedon not only supposed this soteriology but even spoke in soteriological terms, because it made its own the Credo of Nicea-Constantinople, two letters of Cyril of Alexandria, and the famous letter of Pope Leo to Flavian, each of which spoke of salvation.

(c) Finally the formula "The Logos (or the Son) assumed human nature" is more soteriological than we think. The assumption of the nature for Hellenistic believers united God's Son to *all* human beings.

For these reasons it is an injustice to deny all soteriological concern to the two nature model. We are still, however, faced with the total silence regarding salvation history; the place of Christ in the history of God's revelatory and saving deeds is not expressed in the formula. To retrieve this, modern theology has to return to Holy Scripture.

Third Objection: If Jesus Christ has a role in the salvation history of man, then he himself participates in that history. Here we meet the third objection to the two-nature model. It is expressed in particular by the Dutch theologian Hulsbosch.[5] The objection is that the model does not say anything about the history of Jesus himself. This points to its unbiblical character. While Scripture speaks of the earthly life and heavenly manner of being in Christ, of his self-emptying unto death on the Cross and his exaltation starting from His Resurrection, the Chalcedonian formula speaks only of two natures held together always in the same one person. Clearly the Chalcedonian formula needs to be supplemented at this point. It appears to be only a *schema* and must not be seen as the full content of our Christological treatises. The *schema* itself does not, I think, prohibit such thinking

Fourth Objection: Finally there is the fourth and most serious objection to the two-nature model. Traditional, or better, classical Christology always saw Christ as the divine person of the eternal and preexistent Son. What then about Christ being human and consubstantial with us in humanity? If the divine person excluded a human person, then we can still call Christ human or even man, but he is not *a* man, *a* man like us, a human being that exists in the only way that humans can exist—as an individual person. Then there seems to be in Christ no subject that is really capable of human consciousness, growth in knowledge and wisdom, no subject of real astonishment, fear and tears, nor of free historical decisions. In all that, the humanity of Christ is the instrument or tool, or even the puppet, of the eternal Word. The humanity cannot have an action which is its own because it has no personal being that is its own.

If we are to avoid this conclusion we must be prepared to admit an individual human act center, or a human 'I' in Jesus Christ. This is sometimes called a "psychological human subject" in Christ, but consequently it must be also an ontological one.

Then, however, another difficulty arises. We arrive then at two subjects in the same Christ, a divine subject and a human one, the Word and Jesus. We can affirm then that these two subjects are living together, that there is no struggle between them, nor is there any form of competition. But we can no longer say that there is only one person, because the subjects have opposed qualities, divine and human. Instead of one person in Christ we have then a dialogue of subjects.

These subjects are distinguished or opposed virtually or morally, since the eternal Son must be wholly equal to the Father in relation to the world. Like the Father and with him, the Son must be the First Cause and Last End, original 'I' and ultimate 'Thou' with respect to all creatures, even with respect to his own humanity. On the other hand, as a man he can only be the intra-worldly center of creation and not its source, the perfect mediator of our return to God but not its goal and end, remaining however source and end as the divine Son. This way of thinking can lead to the idea that the divine Son is the creator of his own humanity and that the man Jesus is the priest of his own divinity.

These few ideas may help for the moment as an outline of the dilemma that faces any Christology that starts from a divine person in two natures. I don't think I exaggerated the dilemma, since it has been a problem in Christology for centuries, certainly since the Council of Nicea. Between Nicea and Chalcedon it appeared in this form in the struggle between Alexandria and Antioch, ultimately in the clash between Nestorianism and Monophysitism. Chalcedon itself brought about a terminological balance between the two streams of Christology but failed to produce a final synthesis. After the Council of Chalcedon the opposition between the two became clear again. The question was now stated precisely: "Is the human nature of Christ a personalized or hypostasized nature or is it not?" Here we find the Antiochene stream in the Third Council of Constantinople with its dogma of the two actions and two wills in Christ. But on the other hand, we find the Alexandrian stream in the Second Council of Constantinople and in the Christology of Leontius of Byzantium. According to him, the humanity of Christ is ENhypostatic with respect to the Word ("en", the Greek word of "in"), but ANhypostatic with respect to itself, ("a" or "an" as a negation). Here we find the two-nature Christology as I proposed it at the beginning of this lecture: Christ is not a human person; the personality of the human nature is not the one which is proper to that nature but is the *divine* personality of the eternal Word itself; the human nature of Christ has its personality in the divine Word.

In this two-nature Christology the problem rises time and again how to conceive this humanity without its proper personality. I omit the discussions on this problem in the Western Middle Ages where the opposition between Alexandrian and Antiochene thinking showed up in a new form. Nor do I mention similar discussions in Protestantism which brought about a new model of Christology, the kenotic Christology accepted also by Russian and Anglican thinkers. The debate on the non-personal human nature of Christ reached its highest degree of subtlety in later Scholasticism. Here according to Capreolus and to Louis Billot in this century, a very ontological principle, namely, the created act of being (actus essendi), was denied to Christ. To this Thomistic opinion, Scotists have always been opposed. Between the two world wars an extreme form of Scotism came to the fore in the Assumptus-Homo Christology of the French Franciscan, Déodat de Basly, which was condemned by Pope Pius XII on the occasion of the 15th centenary of Chalcedon (DS 3905). The Assumptus-Homo theory is, however, only one of the new forms of Antiochene inspiration in modern Roman Catholic Christology.

After this historical survey, we can express the fourth objection against the two-nature Christology in more popular terms. It seems that we have to admit either a disguised Christ, a Christ who is, let us say, really God and only in the form, in the mask, of a man—or we must accept a divided Christ with two centers of action or two subjects within himself.

If we take a close look at the four difficulties against the two-nature Christology, it becomes clear that the first difficulty expresses in a general way what the following three specify further. It is a good thing that the message concerning Jesus Christ was translated into the thought-patterns of Hellenism, but this also reveals the necessity of translating the same message into the language in which we think. Thus what is ultimately at issue is not that we translate only the Hellenistic model but that we translate the *entire* message concerning Christ. We must pay attention to which points the Hellenistic model has developed in a restrictive way, and to what elements of the original witness are not developed in that model. The second and third difficulties point out these elements. Jesus' role in our salvation, especially in the history of salvation, and then Jesus' own history remain unexpressed in the two natures. The second and third difficulties indicated that the model has to be complemented. But the fourth difficulty gives us more work to do. It calls up a dilemma with which theologians have wrestled for many centuries. The question is whether we will be able to come to a solution. But perhaps we can point out a presupposition which is the cause of this dilemma and will then be able to perceive that that presupposition arose from the fact that Hellenism imposed a restriction on our thinking on Christ. For this purpose we will consider in the last section of this first part some simple hermeneutical principles.

III. *Genesis of the Two-Nature Christology as a Clue to Its Interpretation*

Hermeneutics is nothing else than the method of interpreting texts. It concerns the ways in which we can determine what a text wished to say and did not wish to say in its time. In this way, however, we come to understand also what this text has to say to us now or how the reality about which it speaks must now be expressed. This insight into the contemporary meaning of a text and the reality referred to by it rests on a certain intuition which is guided and developed by reflection, especially by philosophical reflection. Something of that will be necessary in the second part of my lecture, in which I will present various other Christologies. For the moment, it is more important to mention a few simple principles in order to understand what a text wishes to say and not to say in its own historical situation and then apply these to the two-nature Christology. I will limit myself to two.

1. We have to know what the words mean

This is the simplest principle. Yet it says more than appears at first blush. The entire *Theological Dictionary of the New Testament* edited by Gerhard Kittel,[6] was written in order to make clear what the meaning of the words of the New Testament is, particularly by showing their background in the Old Testament and in the Jewish and Hellenistic world. The studies of Christ's titles by Oscar Cullmann, Ferdinand Hahn and Reginald Fuller[7] have the same goal. The kerygmatic language of the Scriptures can evoke a great deal with one word. The same thing can also be the case in the later proclamation of the Church, and this is usually the case with the liturgy.

Does this hold true also for the key words of the Christological and Trinitarian dogmas which are not borrowed from Scripture, especially the words *hypostasis* (person), *ousia* (substance), *homoousios* (consubstantial) and *physis* (nature)? I am of the opinion that here the reverse must be said. We must watch out that we do not let the words here say too much. The reason for this is that these words have a clearly secondary function. They are not kerygmatic, nor evocative, but rather they clarify and describe the proclamation; they bound it off over against false explanations. This is clear in the case of the *homoousion* of Nicea, which was only accepted to express the equality of Father and Son thought to be in scripture (that the choice of the word was not particularly successful may probably be seen in the fact that the First Council of Constantinople did not use this word for the Holy Spirit). The philosophical terms in Chalcedon appear to have the same function. The text of the Council itself has two paragraphs in its middle section which say actually the same thing (DS 301f).[8] The first paragraph says, that "one and the same" or "the same" (these words are repeated many times) is truly God and truly man, one in substance with the Father according to the divinity and one in substance with us according to the humanity. The next paragraph speaks of the two distinct and unconfused natures which are joined in one person. Here the same thing is said as in the preceding paragraph, only in technical terms.

I wish in no way to deny that philosophical terms such as *essence, nature* and *person* have a history. I also think that this history can fertilize our theological thinking, in the further "thinking-through" of dogmas, although I do not myself consider them as promising as did the Thomistic and Neo-Thomistic theologians. But theologians must watch out for one thing. If they are going to reveal the immediate meaning of a dogma, the meaning which it had in its own historical situation, then they must above all see to it that they not read too many meanings from philosophical thought into the words borrowed from philosophy. The interpreter may not put too much of the preceding philosophical meaning into these words, and he certainly may not put later development back into the earlier period. He is not permitted to read too much of the previous philosophical meaning into words such as *nature, substance* and *person,* because they are only functioning as a means of clarification. Moreover, these words usually were borrowed from a popular philosophy by way of ecclesiastical writers, and they get their meaning only in their use by the Councils. This is certainly the case with words like *nature* and *person.* Here it is also obvious that a later development of the concepts can not be put back into an earlier dogmatic pronouncement. Of course, it is possible that this will lead to a theological development which is legitimate, but its results only have the value of a theological conclusion; they do not share the value of the dogmatic pronouncement itself.

What does all this mean concretely for the terms *nature* and *person?* We have said when speaking of the difficulties with the two-nature model that various realities go unexpressed in that model. Now we can say that they are not excluded. Hellenistic thinking had no interest in the historicity proper to man. Concepts like nature and essence certainly do not include this historicity, since for Greek thought history and change are accidental and not essential. But the Councils nowhere use the concepts nature and essence as opposed to history. They do not exclude salvation history; they even speak within a Church which albeit Hellenistic, had an understanding of salvation history, as appears from the typological method of exegesis with the Fathers. The same thing holds for the opposition of nature and person. Chalcedon did not say that Jesus Christ was not a human person; this was the development which Leontius of Byzantium and Boethius gave Chalcedon. Pope Leo's letter to Flavian, accepted by the same council, speaks of Christ's human nature as a subject of actions (DS 294), and the Third Council of Constantinople attributes to Christ's human nature a proper human operation and will (DS 556). From all this, it is clear that the terms used by Chalcedon do not *per se* call for an interpretation which denies a human person to Christ's human nature, and that they do not stand in the way of an interpretation which in this respect corrects the Christology in which we were raised. The latter possibility becomes even clearer when we begin to speak of the presuppositions of the two-nature Christology.

2. We must understand the presuppositions of a pronouncement

In the preceding remarks we spoke of the history of the words—and, of course, also of the concepts used. Of more importance, however, is the history or even the pre-history of the entire pronouncement, of the discussion in which it functions, of the question to which it offers an answer. More precisely put: the presuppositions must be understood. Within what vision of reality have the questions and discussions emerged which occasioned a certain formulation? Such a vision is always historically defined and, thus limited, it can be misleading, by raising false problems; it can be mistaken, whereby the problems become insoluble. This is the case, for example, in the discussion at the beginning of the seventeenth century between the Dominicans and Jesuits about the relation between the operation of God's grace and the free will of man: this discussion proceeded from the false presupposition that God and man are competitors, that what God does man does not have to do, and vice-versa. The same misleading and also false presupposition belongs as well to the pre-history of the two-nature Christology.

As I have already said, the New Testament attributes all that is divine and all that is human to Jesus, just as Chalcedon does. But the New Testament does not speak of a duality, not to mention two natures. How was that arrived at? The cause of this attribution of duality can be found in the transition from Semitic to Hellenistic thinking. It was already in the New Testament itself that this took place, and even more so thereafter. Within the theology of the New Testament there are three layers that can be discovered, that of the Palestinian-Jewish Church, that of the Hellenistic Jewish Mission and that of the Hellenistic Gentile Mission. This has been worked out for Christology by Reginald Fuller, in his book, *The Foundations of New Testament Christology*.[9] In the second century we still see a Jewish-Christian Christology alongside one that is Hellenistic, but since the third century Jewish-Christianity has practically disappeared as a counter weight and the Church thinks Hellenistically—up until today.

In the layers of the New Testament influenced by Hellenistic thinking we see that Jesus begins to be described and acclaimed as "God," although always with a clear distinction made vis-a-vis God the Father.

On the other hand, one is aware that Jesus is not a divine being in a way that makes him human only in appearance: the polemic with gnostic docetism appears clearly in the Johannine writings. There the humanity of Jesus, which was always presupposed as obvious, was emphatically expressed. Just think of Pilate's word "Here is the man" (John 19, 5) and on the other side, Thomas' cry "My Lord and my God" (John 20, 28). Ignatius of Antioch belongs to this tradition in the second century; on the one hand he called Jesus "God" even in his earthly life, and on the other hand he defended the reality of Jesus' human existence and suffering against the docetists. In him we find a summation of Jesus' divine and human attributes alongside each other. "One is the healing Lord: fleshly and spiritual, who became and did not become, in man God, in death life, from Mary and from God (Ign. to Eph. 7, 2). A century later Tertullian will describe Jesus as spirit and flesh, while he also speaks of him as God and man *"secundam utramque substantiam in sua proprietate distantem"* (*adv. Prax.* 20, 27). Here the two-nature doctrine finds its first formulation.

The transition from the two series of attributes to the two natures was rendered necessary by another factor, namely, the consideration of Christ's pre-existence. Jesus, just like the prophets, knew that he was sent by God, that he came from God to man. In the light of Jesus' resurrection this coming from God was applied to the entire life of Jesus from its beginning. Thus, the Gospels of Matthew and Luke begin by telling how Jesus was conceived by the power of the Most High, by the Holy Spirit. In the Johannine Gospel Jesus came forth from God and came into the world while God remains actively present in him. The last development of the New Testament Christology, that of the Hellenistic Gentile Mission, expressed this thought in a number of hymns which were inspired by what was said in the Sapiential literature about God's Wisdom. God's Wisdom is with God in the beginning, sometimes as his first creation, sometimes as the extension of God's personality; it works with God in all his creation and finally finds its resting-place in Israel. We recognize this scheme clearly in the prologue of the Johannine Gospel, where, in place of God's wisdom, his Word, his Logos is spoken of. The Logos was already with God in the beginning, he was himself God, he is the mediator of creation which brings life to men, light that shines in the darkness; and finally, the Word becomes flesh, man in Jesus Christ. Here too we meet duality: the Logos is God and becomes man: "The Word became flesh" (John 1, 14).

Yet we still have not arrived at the two natures. This only became necessary to the extent that the Logos was conceived in his pre-existence as person, as a proper *hypostasis*. One can also say: to the extent that the poetical personification of Wisdom in the Old Testament was conceived ontologically. We see this happen in the Hellenistic tradition. In Justin, the Logos is not only a power of God, but also his messenger and envoy. Hippolytus still hesitates to call the Logos "Son" before his incarnation (Contra haer. Noeti, 15), but it did happen soon, so that God's son had a double birth: in eternity from the Father, and in time from Mary. The Council of Nicea now says of the eternal Son of God, that he is one in substance with the Father (DS 125). He is thus a divine person with a divine nature. Now it becomes problematic how this divine Son of God is identical with the man Jesus. In the Alexandrian school the danger looms that the humanity of Jesus will not receive its due. The school of Antioch, on the contrary, defends the full humanity of Christ and accepts a human nature in addition to the divine nature. This was confirmed by the Council of Chalcedon which confesses Christ as one person in two natures, the divine and the human (DS 302). The two-nature Christology, with which Hellenistic thought was heavy for centuries, is now brought to birth in the middle of the fifth century.

Earlier we formulated four difficulties with the two-nature Christology, of which the fourth is the most serious. This difficulty became clear rather soon after Chalcedon. For who is now the one person of Jesus Christ? It is the divine person of the Word. Thus, one reasons, Jesus Christ does not have and is not a human personality. Leontius of Byzantium says that Christ's human nature has its personality in the divine (it is *enhypostatic* in the Logos) and for this reason is not itself a person (*anhypostatic*). We see this now as an Alexandrian interpretation of the synthesis between both schools which Chalcedon attempted to achieve. Just as before Chalcedon the Alexandrian Apollinaris had the Logos take the place of Christ's human soul, so Leontius says clearly that the divine person of the Logos or the Son takes over the role of Christ's human person. From this came the discussions we have just mentioned: either the man Jesus is de-personalized and Christ is—to put it roughly—a divine person clothed as a man, or the attempt is made, in a renewed Antiochene effort, to make Christ's human nature into a proper subject, center of acts, an 'I', and Christ is divided into two.

Yet from the pre-history and the presuppositions of the two-nature Christology it has become clear that this dilemma is not necessary and that the fight between Alexandrian and Antiochene Christology does not have to be an eternal one. We see that the root of the two-nature doctrine lies in a Christology which thinks in terms of the pre-existent Logos and the root of the *anhypostasis* lies in a conception of the Logos as divine person that imperils the human person. Let us also look at those Christologies which do not begin with the Logos, such as the Christologies of the Synoptic Gospels. And let us then correct the pre-existent Christologies in such a way that the Logos is not a competitor of the human person in Jesus.

B. THE POSSIBILITY OF OTHER CHRISTOLOGIES

IN the preceding part of this lecture we saw that the two-nature Christology arose through a progressive development within Hellenistic thinking. That development is a continually deeper reflection, and to that extent an advance. But it pays the price of any advance: it is a specialization and to that extent a limitation. While one aspect of Christ was developed and deepened in a definite way, other aspects remained in the dark. But they need not remain in the dark. The biological world which is below man cannot use at a later period possibilities which went unused at an earlier stage of evolution; if the whale, which as a mammal has lungs, becomes an aquatic animal, it cannot acquire gills again. But man can take up his unused possibilities and combine them with his present-day development. I do not say this because the older layers have importance in themselves, but because such a synthesis will enrich us now and in the future.

For this reason we will now speak about several Christological models which bypass the two-nature model. What is at issue is not the old models in themselves, but Jesus Christ himself: "the same yesterday, and today and forever" (Heb. 13, 8). We will begin with the model which is the nearest to that of the two natures: the model of Christ as the one in whom God is salvifically present, and this in an ultimate way. This leads us to ask how Jesus precisely as man differs from other men and is the source of salvation for them. Finally we must consider the form or way of life Jesus had in his earthly ministry, namely, that of rabbi and prophet, example and "pioneer" (Heb. 12, 2).

I. *A Christology of the Final Salvific Presence of God*
1. God's Presence in Christ

The problematic of the two natures and especially of the anhypostasized, non-personal human nature of Christ arose, we said, with the emergence of the personality of the Logos in theology. But we can stop before we have personalized the Logos in such a way that the human nature is thereby depersonalized. Then we stand by the prologue of John. But this can be viewed as a development of what is said in the Johannine Gospel about Jesus' origin from God and God's presence in him. This latter corresponds with Jesus' relation to the Kingdom of God in the Synoptics. Let us begin with this very early point.

Jesus preached the Kingdom of God. "Kingdom" here has an active meaning; it means God's reign, that is, his saving, healing 'whole-making' presence in his people and in his whole creation. This kingdom of God is, according to the apocalyptic writers of Jesus' time, that reality which we look forward to, that which God will realize as the crowning of all his work. Jesus took over this apocalyptic idea of the ultimate reign of God but he added something paradoxical to it. The future kingdom is already present: "Repent for the kingdom of heaven is at hand" (Mt. 4, 17). It is now being offered to men, and so the exhortation, "repent": it becomes real to the extent that men accept it: "Behold, the kingdom of God is in the midst of you" (Lk. 17, 21). It is in our midst through Jesus himself, through the fact that God is acting salvifically in him: "If it is by the finger of God that I cast out devils, then the kingdom has come upon you" (Lk. 11, 20). The presence of God's kingdom through Jesus thus rests on the effective presence of God in Jesus. It is precisely this which is shown us in the Johannine Gospel, again in the "works," that is, in Jesus' healing. "If I am not doing the works of my Father, then do not believe me; but if I do them, even though you do not believe me, believe the works, that you may know and understand that the Father is in me and I am in the Father" (Jn. 10, 37f).

Now this idea of God's presence was reproduced in the Hellenistic layer of the New Testament according to the scheme borrowed from the passages regarding God's Wisdom. In the Sapiential literature it was no longer directly God himself who was represented as actively present in his creation, but his Wisdom, which is, as it were, the extension, the presence of God himself. So in the New Testament, but with slightly different concepts, which link up more with Hellenism, especially the Stoa. In the Prologue of John's Gospel it is the Logos, which, however, is related also to God's *"dabar"*, his word and deed in the Old Testament. After his work in the preceding history the Word entered entirely into Jesus: "And the Word became flesh and dwelt among us, full of grace and truth" (Jn. 1, 14). In the letter to the Colossians God's fullness, his *Pleroma,* is present in Jesus. "In him all the fullness of God was pleased to dwell, and through him to reconcile all things" (Col. 1, 18). "In him the whole fullness of God dwells bodily" (Col. 2, 9).

As I said, I can admit up to here the development of the recognition of God's presence in Christ and I can participate in it. But not further: I do not want to make God's Pleroma or Logos into a person, at least not insofar as this would conpete with Jesus' human person or would crowd it out. Here we must realize that our word *person* has a much fuller meaning than the word *hypostasis* which the Greeks used for Father, Son and Holy Spirit. *Hypostasis* does not include the notions of a proper consciousness or freedom, which in fact in the West, especially in Thomistic theology, is not attributed to the distinct divine persons. The persons or the hypostases of the Word and Spirit I would rather not view as having their own independence, but as modes of being, modes of God's presence, extensions of the Father's being.[10] Thus for me the concept of presence is central, not only in Christology, but also in the doctrine of the Trinity. In Christology we should in any case not accept anything of a divine person that would crowd out Jesus' human personality. His human nature is not anhypostasized. Perhaps it would be better if the Logos were not called hypostatic. In any case we can do it insofar as the model of Leontius of Byzantium is turned the other way round, so that we say that the Word becomes a person in the man Jesus, instead of the human nature of Jesus becoming a person through the Logos. In him the Word "became flesh" and "flesh" includes our human personality.

2. God's Final Presence

The presence of God in Jesus Christ does not at all exclude the fact that God is salvifically present in other men. On the contrary, the texts we have cited suppose this: the kingdom of God is an eschatological reality; it is therefore the completion of God's presence in Israel and in the whole world. The Word was in the world, in his own, but it is in Jesus that it became flesh. In him the total fullness of God dwells and this bodily. That the *total* fullness of God dwells in Christ does not mean that God is present elsewhere partially. It means rather that no part of Christ's human reality, of his nature or of his history should be withdrawn from that presence. The Word is completely flesh in him, the fullness of God is embodied in him, tangible, so that Jesus can be called, in Gabriel Vahanian's words, "God's empirical reality."[11]

Because God's presence is embodied in Jesus, this very presence in him has a history. It does not remain in static fashion at the center of Jesus' person, while his history is restricted to outward manifestations. No, "Jesus increased not only in wisdom and stature, but also in favor with God and man" (Lk. 3, 52) and "he learned obedience through what he suffered" (Heb. 5, 8). "In every respect he had been tempted as we are, yet without sinning" (Heb. 4, 15), so that he was not protected beforehand against the temptations but was victorious through God's power *in* the temptations. Thus there exists in the New Testament not only the Johannine Christology beginning with the Logos, which can be called an Incarnation Christology, but also a Christology of glorification or even of adoption. According to this Christology Jesus has been made Lord and Messiah at his resurrection (Acts 2, 36), yes, he is even begotten as Son of God at his resurrection (Acts 13,33). This Christology was crowded out in the past by the Incarnation Christology, but we are making room for it by saying that God's Word and Fullness came to dwell more and more in Jesus, that he who was the Son of God also became this more and more, that the presence of God in him became more and more final.

This final presence we rightly call also unique. This unicity, however, is not exclusivity. It does not exclude anybody but is for all. "In Him the whole fullness of diety dwells bodily, *and you have come to full-*

ness of life in him" (Col. 2, 9f.). "The whole fullness" is destined for us, so that the writer of the letter to the Ephesians wishes for us "that you may be filled with all the fulness of God" (Eph. 3, 19). In the Lucan and Johannine writings this is represented by the Spirit, which rested on Jesus, being given to us as well. The presence of God in him and thereby he himself transcend us, but they are thus all the more *for us.* We can say the same thing when we speak now of the meaning of Jesus as man.

II. *A Christology of the Final Significance of the Man Jesus*

In the two-nature Christology it is possible to locate the transcendence and saving significance[12] exclusively in the divine person. He is a man like us, but what is special is that he is also God. An example of such a view is offered in the well-known words of Pope Leo I in the letter which he wrote shortly before Chalcedon: the divine nature "shines through the miracles," the human "undergoes humiliations,"— although this Pope also says that each nature acts in common with the other (DS 294). That community can in fact be conceived rather extrinsically, as in the Anselmian theory of redemption, where the divine person gives an infinite value to Christ's satisfaction by his human suffering. I do not think I am exaggerating when I say that the two-nature Christology is continually tempted to view Jesus' humanity as ordinary and to place the special element, that is the transcendence and salvific meaning, exclusively or almost exclusively in the divine person. That possibility is excluded if we replace the divine person with God's presence in the human person. The Christology with which we are concerned demands that we place all the transcendence and saving meaning of Christ in his human reality and no where else. Jesus is not an ordinary man with a divine person behind him, nor is he "only" an ordinary man. He is extraordinary, different from us and redemptive for us, but he is this precisely within that human reality which he shares with us, and in this way he may be called an ordinary man.

We human beings are—each of us—individual persons. This individual personality differentiates us from everyone else; it can elevate us and also isolate us. But we are able also to enter into community with others and this to the degree that we are not only individuals but persons. Particular differences or specialized traits first make the one who bears them a lonely figure, and only indirectly beneficial for the community; the genius and the hero challenge their fellowmen much more than they encounter them. That which is deepest in man, however, is love, which on the one hand surpasses everything: all prophecy, all knowledge and insight and even the heroic stature of the martyr; but it also forms community, by bearing all things, believing all things, hoping all things (cf. I Cor. 13, 1-7). Jesus is not a

genius (but still a "greater than Solomon" in wisdom: Mt. 12, 42).[13]
He is also not in the first place a hero (even though his prayer in the
Garden of Olives was an act of heroism to the extent that it lacked
glory). He is a saint, "the holy one of God" (Mk. 1, 24), "the holy
and just one" (Acts 3, 14). But not a saint of the extraordinary: "The
Son of Man eats and drinks" (Mt. 11, 19). He is one sanctified by
God's truth or fidelity, one who dedicates himself for the other
Jn. 17, 17f), in a word: the saint of love. For this reason the New
Testament saw in Jesus the fulfillment of the ideal figure of Yahweh's
Servant, who meekly goes out to men and gives himself for many, and
of the Son of Man, in whom God's plan for man is fulfilled.

If Christ's transcendence is situated so completely in the human
sphere, it is difficult to answer such questions as: is Christ essentially, or
only accidentally, different from other men? Is his transcendence absolute or relative? To say that Christ is essentially different from
other men is a misleading assertion, since it threatens to place him
outside the community of men; it threatens to deny the "consubstantial
with us" of Chalcedon. If one says that it is precisely Christ's sanctity
or fullness that is essentially different from ours, a similar misunderstanding threatens to arise. It then seems that another kind of holiness
is given to us, while it is precisely from his fullness that we have received and it is he who gave us the power to become sons of God
(Jn. 1, 12.16). Moreover, we can wonder whether sanctity is really
a perfecting of humanity, if Christ differs essentially from us in his
sanctity but not in his humanity. The term "essential" thus does not
appear suitable to describe the difference between Christ and us. But
are we then forced to call this difference an accidental one? This word
does not adequately express Christ's transcendence with relation to all
men and thus his saving significance for all men. Approximately the
same observation can be made with regard to the terms relative and absolute. The former term certainly says too little. It puts Jesus on one
plane with religious geniuses and the prophets, though he, compared
with them, is precisely God's *perfect* Word. For this reason he can be
called an absolute high point, but even then within the humanity and
within the human history of salvation. In order to express this last
fact we could use a more specifically theological and Scriptural term,
namely, "eschatological." Jesus Christ is the eschatological high point
of God's saving action and so of our salvation history. God speaks
through him to us "in these last days" or "at the end of the times"
(Heb. 1, 2); and so "the end of the times has come to us" (1 Cor.
10, 11). Yet the early Church had to give up the idea of an imminent
parousia and we not only see that after Jesus history simply goes on,
but our faith tells us that there must be a salvation history now as well.
Thus the eschatological aspect of Christ's place is to be understood in a
more qualitative sense: he is *definitive* in salvation history, God's

complete Word, speaking and spoken in the "fullness of time" (Gal. 4, 4; cf. Mk. 1, 15).

But the end of the times is not missing in Christ's eschatological character, since we confess him not only as the "first fruits of the dead" (1 Cor. 15, 20), but as the "first born from the dead" (Col. 1, 18). He already lives in the final completion and from there he remains for us, the bringer of salvation, life, freedom, love, sonship. These gifts of salvation are also attributed to the Spirit, but this Spirit is also his. So we read in John that the Spirit brings to mind all that Jesus said (Jn. 14, 25), that the Spirit receives from Christ and announces it (Jn. 16, 14), and Paul says: "the Lord is the Spirit" (2 Cor. 3, 17). Christ thus remains the completion, he himself through his Spirit.

In the preceding section I stated that Jesus and even God's presence in Jesus had a history and a fulfillment. Now we have to consider that it is precisely in his own fulfillment that Christ is our fulfillment. Or the other way round: Christ's fulfillment is never only his own fulfillment. His resurrection, his ascension and his giving of the Holy Spirit are not to be considered as separate events. It is only in the historizing theology of Luke that these three words clearly refer to consecutive events, separated by a period of forty days in the Acts of the Apostles (Acts 1, 3). Elsewhere in the New Testament these words are two expressions for the same thing that happened to Jesus, and which can also be expressed in terms of glorification, exaltation, or fulfillment. All words fall short in trying to represent what this event or condition really is like. The word *resurrection* expresses well that this fulfillment is a victory over Jesus' death and that Jesus himself, Jesus' person, and not only his program or his teaching, live on; on the other hand, the word *resurrection* suggests that Jesus returns to our earthly life and in that respect it has to be corrected. The word *ascension* offers this correction by saying that Jesus' life now belongs to the heavenly fulfillment, but it does not show sufficiently how much he, as Lord and source of salvation, is present on earth, in his Church and in the whole world. God has raised his Christ from death and corruption, but he allows him each day to conquer another kind of death, the death about which the book Ecclesiastes complains, the death of oblivion (cf. Eccl. 2, 16; 8,5). For the exalted Lord still takes the floor and speaks words of life, his Spirit, and in this he himself remains the witness and the leader, and in this way he is with us, he has a future in us until the end of time. But this is also a victory over bodily death, since we are allowed to hope and believe that the risen Christ will not die with the human race, but as the first fruits of the dead will lead all of us to ultimate fulfillment.

III. *A Christology of Jesus as a Rabbi and Prophet, Example and Pioneer*

Our Christology of God's presence forced us to place Christ's saving significance in his human reality. We have done this and so we have represented him as the eschatological, ultimate, definitive man, especially in his own fulfillment. This view is still rather formal, it has little content, it still does not say how Jesus is such a fulfilled man. We indicated this by not placing him in the category of hero or genius, but by representing him as the saint of love. Now we must explain more precisely what this involves and how we can conceive Jesus' influence on us.

To do this we reach back to Jesus' earthly life, since it is only from there that we can understand what kind of man he is for us. For the exalted Christ is not a heavenly being that descended into our history, but a man who lived in it having his own history. Jesus' fulfillment is precisely the fulfillment of what he did in that earthly life and what he remained in his passion. In this reaching back to the earthly Jesus we are allying ourselves with a movement in contemporary exegesis, known as "The New Quest of the Historical Jesus."[14] In the German exegete Rudolf Bultmann we find a certain high point of agnosticism regarding Jesus' earthly history. Bultmann accepts Jesus' historical existence as obvious, he recognizes several facts from Jesus' earthly life, even that Jeus cured men, but he emphasizes how much legend has covered these facts and especially, he thinks Jesus' earthly form of existence, his personal attitude, is unimportant for our faith, which lives only from the kerygma. Disciples of Bultmann such as Kasemann, Bornkamm and Ebeling, on the contrary, emphasize the fact that the historical Jesus remains important because the kerygma witnesses to him, because the community's traditions sometimes give access to his own words, and because even the legendary passages in the Gospels express traits of the historical Jesus. Supported by the arguments of these exegetes we will try to say something about the content of Jesus' deeds and words, and about the way in which he influenced his disciples and the way in which he still influences us.

1. Jesus' form ("Gestalt") and way of life

The first generation of Christians interpreted Jesus by applying familiar images to him, as that of Messias, Servant of Yahweh, the Son of Man. And we of the nineteenth and twentieth centuries see him according to our own ideal image: the ethician, the socialist, the revolutionary, and even the "provo", the "hippie" and the "fool." All of this is fine provided we are prepared to have the image corrected by the form ("Gestalt") of Jesus himself, as this breaks through all images and reports. If we are prepared to do that, we may see in Jesus a very modern characteristic: his love for all men, especially for the "outcast." He refused to be the Messias-King who used violence against the Roman domination, but he strove until his death against every form of religious and social discrimination or exclusion. He ate with tax collectors and sinners. He summoned the sinners and refused to judge the adulterous woman. He came forward for the right of the woman to expect fidelity from her husband (Mk. 10, 2-12). He spoke to "the people who do not know the law." He proclaimed salvation for the poor and sorrowful. He was good to and healed the lepers and the possessed. All of this is but putting into practice his own teaching that the commandment of love for the neighbor is like to that of the love of God.

All of this is an unsettling lesson for religious people. The letter of James later reproduced this lesson in these words: "Religion that is pure and undefiled before God and the Father is this: to visit orphans and widows in their affliction" (1, 27). But the secular man too, can learn something from Jesus' behavior. For Jesus acts this way from out of God, and is conscious of that. In Lk. 15, Jesus justifies his eating with sinners by telling three parables about God's attitude towards them. We are summoned in the same Lukan gospel to be merciful as our heavenly Father is merciful (6, 36). Jesus' relation to people is rooted in a relation to God. He can say "Father" to God free of any Oedipus-complex, and Jesus thus uses a familiar, confiding word: "Abba." He trusts in the Father until death. The faith to which Jesus summons men is not a faith in himself but in God, as is demanded especially in the miracle stories. Believing in Jesus from after the Resurrection supposes believing like Jesus. For this reason Ebeling sees faith as a dominant trait in Jesus. This is not in conflct with another exegete, Günther Bornkamm, who sees Jesus' *exousia,* his authority and moral power, as fundamental. For the *exousia* which causes him to set his own word against the letter of the law is an authority from God, of which he is conscious in his faith. By means of this faith he could live what he asked of us: "Do not be anxious about tomorrow" (Mt. 6, 34). He himself went forth with God's authority to act and speak, even when death threatened him.

2. Jesus' influence

After this much too short summary of Jesus' earthly life, we can say a few words about the way in which his influence spread out and is still spreading. We read in the Gospels that he had disciples and he summoned men to discipleship. He had disciples and so was a rabbi, a wandering rabbi. Jesus did not have all the traits of the later office of rabbi, and it is possible that Matthew has here accentuated the rabbinical traits in Jesus. But in some important points Jesus *was* a rabbi. The influence of a rabbi did not only consist in his teaching, but especially in the fact that he led an exemplary life as a just Jew, and

that his disciples took this over from him in their common life. Jesus
was a rabbi in this way. But at the same time he went beyond the
bounds of the rabbinate, most notably by his direct authority which
he acquired not from his teachers but from God himself. And so his
disciples saw him as their permanent rabbi and themselves as permanent
disciples. "The disciples" is the name which the Christians gave one
another, according to the Acts of the Apostles. And in the Jewish
community of Matthew the rule was: "You are not to be called rabbi,
for you have one teacher, and you are all brethren . . . Neither be called
masters, for you have one master, the Christ" (Mt. 23, 8, 10).

We can speak of Jesus as prophet in the same way. He was viewed
by the people as a prophet and saw himself that way. It was precisely
by his authority and the revolutionary effect of his words and deeds
that Jesus stands closer to the prophets than to the rabbis. The prophets,
too, do not appeal to predecessors. They say: "so speaks the Lord"; but
Jesus says: "I say to you." His community thus sees in him a very
special prophet, or rather *the* prophet who must come into the world,
the prophet who, according to an aggravated exegesis of Deuteronomy
18, 15 is to be the New Moses or the New Eliah, preceding immediately
the coming of God's Kingdom. Just as Jesus is recognized as the
permanent rabbi, so too, he is viewed as the eschatological prophet.

Even more than a rabbi, a prophet has an effect on others in that
his words are such as to unmask and summon, and his deeds and attitude
are contagious. Jesus' words do not merely convey information, but
awaken something in man, or better they cause a man to see what
powers he is subject to, they show ways in which love can realize itself,
and especially they bring man into community with Jesus himself which
causes them to experience the love of God. And so Jesus' word is redemptive when one accepts it and condemnatory when one refuses it.
This finds expression in John's Gospel: "He who rejects me and
does not receive my sayings has a judge; the word that I have spoken
will be his judge on the last day" (12, 48). "You are already made
clean by the word which I have spoken to you" (15, 3). The same
thing can be said of Jesus' example. This too does not consist in the
conveyance of information or an object lesson, such as one expects of
a teacher in physics or gymnastics. It therefore does not have to be
imitated in a material way. Authentic example is appealing: in this
a person witnesses to what a moral value means to him and so expresses an appeal, as we just described it.

The New Testament says of Jesus twice that he gave or left an
example (Jn. 13, 15; 1 Peter 2, 21); it does not say that he *is* an example. Instead of saying that, we can attribute the titles which we
just discussed—rabbi and prophet—to him, since they say something
like: a person who is an example in his life. This seems clear from the
fact that they are applied to Jesus. Moreover, the New Testament gives
another title to Jesus, which perhaps takes away the static aspect of

example and which sounds more dynamic. Jesus is called "archegos" three times (Acts 3, 15; Heb. 2, 10, 12, 2). The Revised Standard Version translates this word in the Letter to the Hebrews as "pioneer"; "The pioneer of their salvation," "the pioneer and perfecter of their faith." Jesus is the one who opens up the way, He is the forerunner, "chef de file" and, to use a word that calls up many special associations for Americans: "pioneer." A pioneer makes it possible for others to follow him, he clears a way; so it is with pioneers in new geographical regions, and even more is it the case for pioneers in search of freedom and human dignity, like the great Martin Luther King. In this last way, the way to the fulfillment of a dream, the way to the Kingdom of God, Jesus is the great pioneer, the pioneer leading toward the ultimate and so towards the real beginning.

Until now I have given special attention to Jesus' life, but the same thing can be applied to his death and resurrection. It is not necessary to view Jesus' death as a vicarious satisfaction to God, or at least this is not the only manner to clarify the salvific meaning of it. Such a view even threatens to obscure a good deal: the initiative of the Father's love and the necessity that we ourselves must go the way of love in faith. But in his death also we can see Jesus as example and pioneer, example of utter trust in God and so of faith and of obedient love for his Father, of utter fidelity to his mission and so to us. Then Jesus' death is redemptive just as his whole life was redemptive, liberating and healing. His death is then the last confirmation and completion of what was redemptive in his life, his last deed as teacher, prophet, example and pioneer. St. John considered Jesus' death as the love to the end towards his own who were in the world (Jn. 31, 1). Luke, however, shows Jesus praying for those who crucified him, "for they know not what they do" (Lk. 23, 34). Paul extends this love of God as it appears in the dying Christ to all of us precisely as God's enemies: "Why, one will hardly die for a righteous man—though perhaps for a good man one will dare even to die. But God shows his love for us in that while we were yet sinners Christ died for us" (Rom. 5, 7f). Of course, this "for us" means "on our account" and can be explained by vicariousness. But vicariousness seems to have no meaning if there is by no means an influence on those on whose behalf somebody acts vicariously. That God shows his love in the suffering and dying Christ can be explained so that Jesus is the example of divine loving at work in him, searching all people, breaking through all human limitations, forgiving enemies and finally liberating all those who accept this love, to love in the same manner. So Jesus is redemptive, saving and liberating in his death by being the example and the pioneer of this love.

The same holds true for the fulfillment or glorification of Christ. Just as Jesus' death does not have a saving meaning different from that of his life, so too his glorified life has basically the same saving significance as both his earthly life and death. The hymn of Phil. 2, 6-11

contrasts the earthly and glorified lives as those of the servant and of
the Lord, but the theology of the Synoptics links both of these in the
title "Son of Man." I think this is a good correction of the contrast
in the hymn. Jesus in his glorification has to be described not only as
the Lord, but also, and in my opinion with more truth, as the fulfilled Servant,[15] the one whose service to God and to man is more
powerful, whose love is made victorious by the Father. So all that Jesus
was in his earthly life is perfected, fulfilled, strengthened and made
victorious in his glorification. He remains the only rabbi and the
eschatological prophet as we saw already. He remains also the example
and the pioneer. He is not only an example of the past but he continues to speak and appeal. He "left" the example of his deeds and
sufferings (cf. 1 Peter 2, 21), but he is still in communication with us,
he himself and the Spirit who is *his* Spirit, and so remains our example
in the most stimulating way. In this fulfillment Christ is also the
pioneer, indeed "the pioneer and perfecter" (Heb. 12, 2), the forerunner of the age to come, the first man of the kingdom of God or
the messianic era, the first of the last time, "the first born of the dead"
and "the last Adam (1 Cor. 15, 20, 45). It is remarkable that the new
quest of Jesus' earthly life in our day is accompanied by theologies of
history and process, of hope and future. Here Moltmann's thesis is at
place that God by raising and glorifying Christ gives him future. God
makes him the source of an immense stream that goes on through this
age into the age to come, a stream of liberation, freedom, authenticity,
community or in a word: love. "For God is love. In this the love of
God was made manifest to us, that God sent his only Son into the
world, so that we might live through him" (I Jn. 4, 8f).[16]

NOTES

[1] Philadelphia: The Westminster Press, 1966. The author mentions
also the "revelation model" of Christology, which is near to what I
propose in the second part of this lecture.

[2] Donald Baillie, *God was in Christ*, London: Faber and Faber, 1960;
John Knox, *The Humanity and Divinity of Christ*, Cambridge Univer-
sity Press, 1967; Norman Pittenger, *The Word Incarnate*, New York:
Harper and Row, 1959; Idem: *Christology Reconsidered*, London: SCM
Press, 1970.

[3] A survey of some articles written in Dutch by A. Hulsbosch, E.
Schillebeeckx, and myself has been proposed by R. North, 'Soul-Body
Unity and God-Man Unity,' in: *Theological Studies* 30 (1969) 27-60.
The same author gives a methodological reflection in: 'Recent Christol-
ogy and Theological Method,' in: *Continuum* (Xavier College, Chicago)
7 (1969) 63-77.

[4] "Hellenistic" is not quite synonymous with "Greek" but refers to
the culture which came about in the reign of Alexander the Great and
his successor (the "Diadochs") and pervaded the Roman Empire in its
Eastern and Western parts. I wish to stress this broad meaning of the
word because it is very probable that Christian theology became more
hellenistic in the West than in the East, especially by the assumptions

of (Neo-)Platonic influences with Saint Augustine. This is the thesis of Dietrich Ritschl in his book *Memory and Hope, an inquiry concerning the Presence of Christ* (New York: The Macmillan Company, 1967), although Ritschl does not use the term "hellenistic."

[5] A. Hulsbosch, 'Jezus Christus, gekend als mens, beleden als Zoon Gods': *Tydschrift voor Theologie* 6 (1966) 250-272.

[6] Now being translated into English. Translator and editor: Goeffrey W. Bromley, Wm. B. Eerdmans Publishing Company, Grand Rapids, Michigan, since 1965.

[7] Oscar Cullmann: *The Christology of the New Testament*, Philadelphia: Westminster Press, 1959; Ferdinand Hahn, *Christologische Hoheitstitel*, Göttingen, 1966; Reginald H. Fuller: *The Foundations of New Testament Christology*, London: Lutterworth Press, 1965.

[8] "DS" refers to the editions of H. Denzinger's *"Enchiridion Symbolorum"* edited by Schonmetzer and published by Herder, Barcelona, since 1963.

[9] See footnote 7.

[10] Cf. A. R. Johnson, *The One and the Many in the Israelite Conception of God*, Cardiff, 1961; W. Wainwright, *The Trinity in the New Testament*, London: S.P.C.K. 1962, p. 10-20.

[11] G. Vahanian, *No Other God*, New York: 1966, p. 33.

[12] I join the words *transcendence* and *saving significance* in order to prevent that the transcendence of Christ may be conceived only as his distance from us. This is, however, not necessary. The transcendence of Christ as man consists precisely in his being more human and more personal and therefore also more communicating of himself. The same holds true for the transcendence of God, which does not consist in his alienation from us but in his ever surpassing communication, for God is able "by the power at work *within us* to do far more than all that we ask or think" (Eph. 3, 20).

[13] According to the 17th century course of theology known as the *"Salmanticenes"* (Tract XII, Dsp. 22, Dubiumm 2, W. 24), Jesus was the greatest philosopher, the greatest poet, the greatest mathematician, etc. It would be more true to say that in him was *something* of a philosopher, a poet and perhaps even of—a harlequin: cf. Harvey Cox: *The Feast of Fools*, Cambridge, Mass.: Harvard University Press, 1969, pp. 139-157.

[14] James H. Robinson, *A New Quest of the Historical Jesus*, London: SCM Press, 1968.

[15] This suggests that even God himself, precisely in his self-revelation in Jesus Christ, may be confessed not only by calling him Lord, but also by using the metaphor "servant." After all, "Lord" is no less metaphorical! So God is Father *and* Brother, powerfully healing and suffering, moving and moved, although not by need and imperfection but by giving love.

[16] I wish to express my gratitude to Fr. Brian O. McDermott, S.J., who translated this paper from the Dutch. A further elaboration of my christological views has been given in my book, *The Christ: A study of the God-Man Relationship in the Whole of Creation and in Jesus Christ*, New York, Herder and Herder, 1971.

The Experience of the Church in Holland: Authority as a Service in the Mutual Encounter

Bernard Alfrink

I<small>T</small> was with great pleasure that I accepted your invitation to outline the background of Catholicism in Holland in the first place, because a universal church which has become a historical reality in entirely different cultures has need of a mutually comprehensible exchange of precise and understandable information, and, secondly, I am sorry to have to say, because information concerning Holland as reported in the foreign press is often one-sided, and especially sensational.

It is not possible for me to give a complete picture, so I will limit myself to certain aspects which will enable you to better understand the present situation. In addition I will discuss in particular the manner in which the bishops exercise their authority.

Alongside the Catholics in Holland there is a very active group of Christians of the Reformation from many different denominations. In the last census all of the Protestant groups together totalled thirty-nine percent of the population, and the Catholics, approximately forty percent. According to the scientific study of religion, a situation like this one, in which sectarian groups are almost equal in size, is a factor which stimulates the vitality of religion. I am not sure this is true. In any case, the fact is that attendance at Mass, Saturday evening and Sunday, is very high in Holland when compared with other countries, even though there are only a few agricultural areas left in Holland and although the number of those who attend is decreasing.

In addition to these two groups, there is a third: the so-called non-sectarian individuals. In the census taken by the civil authorities every ten years, they report that they do not choose to belong to any church group. This group comprises about twenty percent of the population. A high figure you will say. And yet understandable, because Holland has never known an official national church, and an individual does not feel he is a social outcast should he not belong to a church. Dutch people are not slow to oppose a church and by this means, more clarity is certainly provided in the religious situation than in other countries. For that matter, the non-sectarian individuals cannot be considered the equal of atheists, or men without religion. Many of them believe in God; and a good number of them certainly call themselves Christians. They simply wish to have no definite ties to a Church or church-affiliated group.

The relationship between Catholic and Protestant has had a great influence upon the development of the Catholic Church. The Catholic Church in Holland was an underground church for centuries. The Protestant Reformation in the Netherlands was co-inspired by political factors. The Netherlands had to liberate itself from the Spanish occupation and by so doing, set itself to counter the Catholic religion as well. Protestantism replaced Catholicism as the religion of the established order and of public life. Catholics were deprived of Church buildings and possessions; they were excluded from public office and had to hold their church services in secret. The Catholics preserved their faith in the midst of this oppression, and they strengthened it. At the same time staunch group solidarity grew up, with a unity closed off to the outside, a piety which was introverted, and a close bond with the priests who literally risked their lives for the faithful.

What was the result of this historical situation? When the official equality of religions became a reality in Holland in 1853, about a century ago, therefore—and Holland again had a hierarchy of its own, there were very favorable conditions present for the flourishing of the Catholic Church in society.

By sheer weight of members—they were still one-third of the population—the Catholics formed collectively a group of some consequences, very active religiously, very faithful to their priests, bishops, and the Holy See. You are, perhaps, aware of the fact that Holland sent as many young men to Rome as the whole of France—three thousand, in fact—for the defense of the Papal States! Socially and culturally the Catholics set about taking care of themselves with their own political and social organizations, their own hospitals, own newspapers, own schools, and their own university. The number of vocations to the service of the Church was very high and thousands of young men and women went to the missions. Holland represents only one percent of

Catholics in the world. Until recently this small group provided ten percent of all missionaries. The country has only seven dioceses. At the Second Vatican Council, besides the bishops residing in Holland, there were sixty other bishops of Dutch origin, working in every area of the Church. Characteristic features, then, were a way of thinking which was too collective and almost passive under the direction of church authority, a life which was strong in aspects internal to the Church but with limited integration into Dutch life and society as a whole, and which maintained a defensive distance from Protestants, liberals, and socialists, a distance which, for that matter, was kept on all sides.

You must use this outline of the situation as a basis in order to understand the transition to present-day Catholicism. This transition occurred, for the most part, between 1940 and 1960, between the onset of the Second World War in which Holland, now after centuries, once again had to fight in defense of its freedom, and the beginning of the Second Vatican Council. In those five years of war, Dutch Catholics broke out of their isolation. In resisting foreign domination they declared themselves one with all fellow-supporters of that resistance, in solidarity with them without regard for religious views or philosophy of life. Cardinal de Jong was very courageous and was honored as a national hero of the resistance. As early as the 1930's, generally speaking, Catholics began to intensify the quality of their intellectual performance; many Catholic schools were built, and a Catholic University as well. The graduates of these schools began to take positions which criticized and opposed prevailing opinions often supported by episcopal authority. The most capable priests went to study at all of the great universities of Europe, and afterwards went to teach at their own seminaries in Holland. There arose more and more resistance to being closed off. There was also more and more openness with regard to Protestants in the ecumenical movement. The collective and more passive experience and way of thinking within Catholicism became more personal and more active. A person asked for his own responsibility, for his own freedom, for a genuine relatedness between faith and science, and a new technique for the exercise of authority. It is understandable that this situation implied a certain crisis, above all, a crisis of growth, in Dutch Catholicism. One was faced with a dilemma: either maintain the strong union and association of the group within itself, even in political and social life or send the faithful out into society with an apostolic mission to perform, and thereby set youself open to the influence of all kinds of currents outside of Catholicism. There is perhaps no country in the world where the transition from closedness to openness was experienced as rapidly and as dramatically as it was in Holland. This is really the great experiment of Dutch Catholicism, in which not just a few but large groups of priests and faithful are involved.

A number of general factors played a role in this crisis. The process of democratization has brought modern man to a degree of emancipation in which he finds it difficult to accept the fact that decisions concerning him are made without him. The democratic principle, as an attitude of mind, has penetrated into every facet of life: upbringing, education, recreation, work and profession.

Modern man wishes to be more himself, to go his own way, than to function merely as part of a group. He is indeed ready to accept a limitation upon his freedom, but has to be shown the necessity for it. This demands openness and a public airing of issues. These are values to which a Dutch man is very sensitive: freedom, openness, and public discussion with those bearing authority, even in the mass media.

In Holland, these factors also began to play an important role in judging ecclesiastical authority. The reaction was as follows: there was a heightened experience of the Church as a community of persons, as a community in which the principal concern is for values which the person interiorly recognizes and freely accepts, a community which is primarily an invitation to and witness to the Good News. An authoritarian regime in the Church is experienced by many, as men and as believers, as unworthy of and in conflict with the holiness of the community itself. The crisis concerning authority in the Church as a world church is also a deeply sensitive issue because that authority is exercised by men in office who live in a different culture and are of a different nationality. The position of the Church in society is also becoming more and more complicated. This demands many kinds of expertise in all of the various sectors of social life. It is a happy phenomenon that in Holland no gulf has ever separated the bishops and the Catholic laity in the professional schools. It was, however, especially among them that resistance was met when the Church proceeded to act all too managerially in areas where spiritual, religious, or ethical problems arose, marriage and the family, for example, care of the sick, social organizations, economics, and international politics. It is not a question of wishing to exclude the Church's competence in these areas, but of wanting to see clearly what the basis is for ecclesiastical authority intervening, and what the boundaries of it are; then assent may follow more easily.

The transitional phase which I have outlined here was especially stimulated by Pope John XXIII's initiative in moving the Church in the world to "aggiornamento," and to the Vatican Council. The figure of this Pope fits in entirely with the pastoral concept of invitation and the concept of the Church as a community of persons. As early as late 1960, the Dutch bishops published a letter in which the forms were presented in which authority in the church could be exercised in a new way. Dutch Catholics took tremendous interest in the development of new insights during the Vatican Council and saw it as a great event for the Universal Church. Their expectations ran very high.

After the Council, at the end of 1965, the Dutch bishops wrote to the faithful that the spirit of the Council had to to be kept alive: "It is a matter of giving forms to the basic insights of the Council, which are practical for Christian life and practical in the human community. The insights of the Council must not only become flesh and blood for us all, they must also become the foundation of the directive policy of the bishops. By basic insights we mean the following, to name but a few: reverence for and appreciation of the value of the human person; reverence for the religious convictions of others; the association in fellowship of God's people, priests and laity; the regulative use of democratic procedures in practical administration; common responsibility for the world and for the peace and happiness of mankind; the relationship among fellow-Christians, and that to non-Christians." To this was added that this new phase of growth in the Church of Holland would demand time and patience. The same letter also announced that the concepts which grew out of the Council would be applied in Holland by a Council for the Dutch Church Province.

In this Pastoral Council or pastoral consultative body, which convened for the first time early in 1968 and will end, with God's help, in 1970, the attempt was made to accommodate the real wishes and desires of the Dutch bishops, and on the other hand, to put into practice the ideas of Vatican II. In this, our primary consideration was the responsibility of the whole of God's people, priests, religious, and laity, for the renewal of the Church. In the Dutch Council, this shared responsibility was given expression in the following points:

—first, problematic issues on the pastoral level are to be studied by priests and laity, by experts in every field of theoretical knowledge together with experts in areas of practical application. In 1963, the bishops, to their advantage as administrators, created a separate institute for the organization of this scholarly and scientific work; this was the so-called Pastoral Institute. This implied recognition of the fact that bishops need advice for the administration of the Church, and that they invite the assistance of all experts in this task. This stimulates a wide sharing of life and work, and responsibility among priests and laity, all of them experts in their field. These commissions of specialists also prepare the reports of the Pastoral Council.

—secondly, all of the faithful are to be involved as much as possible in small group discussions of religious problems. Catholics in the Netherlands take their faith very seriously. They wish to discuss it with each other as adults. So approximately fifteen thousand Council discussion groups have come into existence; these have directors and report their findings to the Council. These discussions about faith strengthen an adult commitment to that faith, as well as one's sense of responsibility for the well-being of the Church.

—thirdly, the faithful who do not wish to take part in these groups can also make known their thoughts and views through their own

Catholic organizations, or by means of personal letters. We have had the contents of the first two thousand letters analyzed and they provide a good insight into what is going on among the faithful.
—lastly, in accordance with the decree, "Christus Dominus," upon which the idea of the Pastoral Council is based, each diocese has a diocesan Pastoral Advisory Board. These send representatives to the plenary meeting: seven laymen and three priests—seventy members in all. To these seventy are added ten religious, fifteen people directly designated by the bishops themselves, as well as the bishops and the Central Directorate of the Council.

And thus is the responsibility of God's people in pastoral consultation given expression. By this means, the Pastoral Council, the bishops arrive at a new method of exercising authority. It is not only the realization of a mutual dialogue among the bishops themselves, but also a dialogue of bishops, experts, representatives of priests, laity and religious with each other. This dialogue is public and the media, the press and television, are admitted. It is a remarkable and happy fact that in this open and public dialogue, as public as a meeting of a parliament, at times with almost one hundred journalists present and under television floodlights, the moral prestige of the bishops is not harmed, rather it is enhanced. This consultative process is one in which the bishops do not remain aloof, and they do not officiate as proclaimers of the faith having responsibilities which cannot be delegated. And as such, the process of consultation is taken extremely seriously by all concerned.

The Pastoral Council remains however, still an experiment. This is occasionally forgotten abroad. In the Church there existed no experience with forming opinions in common, no experience of the faithful and those in office arriving at decisisons together. Here, too, new rules of play have to evolve which will make possible and fruitful a dialogue within the Church between the people and administrators, and between different currents of thought in the Church.

It is now entirely clear to you that this Council, in its essence, is the realization of something, a serious effort to arrive at a new methodology in the exercise of episcopal authority, in dialogue and consultation.

The bishops of the Netherlands prefer to view authority as a service, performed by brothers, to proclaim, to make holy, and to guide. Totally in the Spirit of the Vatican Council's Pastoral Constitution on the Church, the bishops wish to exercise their authority with an attitude toward Christ and the People of God which attentively listens and gratefully receives.

It is, of course, self-evident, that in the process of growth and change, the bishops bear their own responsibility. They cannot, therefore, approve endeavors and developments for which they in conscience cannot find a place within the great endeavor of the universal Church to

make the Gospel continually authentic amid all the changes of circumstances.

But this does not yet mean that the bishops must mark the path at
every turn with concrete choices and preferences. Their special task is
rather to create the conditions under which the free and joint search
of the entire people of the Church has a chance, and under which, believing and acting in belief are acts which can constantly be posited
within the community as free acts. The bishops stand for giving the
process of a believing search and a searching belief, a venture at once
personal and communal, the best possible chance.

This demands creating a situation which at one and the same time
does right by personal freedom as well as by the responsibility we all
bear for each other. It is necessary on the one hand to give people
room and provide support for them because they have individual and
group differences in position and background which then also lead to
differences in their judgment of this age and in their vision of the future. On the other hand, it is also necessary to bring these persons and
groups into an encounter and dialogue with each other. In this mutual
encounter they can clearly assent to the answerability they need to have
for each other.

In our quest for authentic and meaningful Christian existence in today's world, it is not our intention to put ourselves forward as a model
community to be copied, and we do not wish to propagate our thought
and action as articles for export. We indeed want to leave other epis-
copacies free to judge whether what is here taking place is good, and
genuine, and whether it can be considered suitable for other countries.
In return we ask that we not be judged a priori, that one be willing
to leave us free wherever and whenever that freedom is in accord with
the Spirit and the letter of the Second Vatican Council.

The renewal which is everywhere underway in the Catholic Church
—which, in the nature of things, evokes all kinds of counter currents,
arising for the most part from a sincere concern which asks for serious
dialogue—this renewal is more or less grounded upon a series of
fundamental insights formulated in the Second Vatican Council. It
was first established that within the framework of the universal Church,
the particular churches had to be able to find the possibility and opportunity of showing forth their own particular physiogomy. The universality of the Church grew out of a multitude of patterns and a
wealth of traditions, all bound together in the unity of the authentic
faith of the Church. That is what makes acceptable the legitimacy of
pluriformity within the unity of the Church, a legitimacy which in
recent centuries was relegated to the background of events, because
the unity of the Church, in almost all aspects of its life, was in practice experienced as uniformity, especially in the Church of the West.
As a result, the people of the Church at every level, right up to the

present day, conceived of unity and uniformity as practically the same thing.

Thirdly, the Second Vatican Council has accepted a certain measure of democraticization within the framework of the hierarchical structure of the Church. That implies the acceptance of a principle which demands realization in every sector of Church life. The proper functioning of this principle will certainly require time. But new paths are being explored in every direction. Our Dutch Pastoral Council is one of those attempts to search for the correct theological form for a structure both hierarchical and democratic, a form which is at the same time supremely functional. Furthermore, the Second Vatican Council established a new openness toward the other Christian Churches and communities, and also toward other world religions and all groups of men with a philosophy of life. Even before the Council began, the trend was obvious. The Council broadened this trend, deepened it, and confirmed it. And finally the Church of the Second Vatican Council discovered this about herself: that by virtue of the evangelical task with which she is commissioned, she must be concerned that she sensitively engage the needs of the world and of humanity. She cannot isolate herself from men; by the Lord's own command, she must stand in the very midst of them. She will have to appeal to human conscience for the sake of peace, general welfare, social justice, human rights, and all of that is a secular context because the salvation the Lord wanted to bring to the world is not simply transcendent; it also has an earthly aspect, a dimension of the here and now. And what is more, it is intended for all of mankind; no one is excluded from it.

OPENNESS

TO

THE WORLD

Edited by Joseph Papin

Volume III

The Villanova University Press

Volume III
Library of Congress Catalog Number 76-155-103
Complete Series SBN 87723-007-2
Volume III SBN 87723-010-2

Printed in the United States of America by
Abbey Press
Saint Meinrad, Indiana 47577

First printing: 1000 copies
1-100 are numbered

The Churches' Contribution to World Unity and Community

Eugene Carson Blake

I BEGIN by recognizing the fact that at the present time there are many Christians in all the churches who sincerely believe that the task of the churches does not include contributing to world unity and community. There are many different reasons given for this position. Let me merely remind you of some of them. Some say "The task of the churches must be centered on individual salvation, that is, the eternal salvation of individual souls of men." These say "The task of the churches always remains centered on 'the other world' and the churches must not be diverted into the field of 'historical salvation.' "

Others, not going so far, suggest that it is most important that the church avoid using wrong means in its effort to achieve a world community or a world society. "The only means proper to the church," these say, "is to convert individual men and women from sin to Jesus Christ. Let these converted men make their social and political contributions to the solution of social and political problems as Christian citizens. The church, as church, should never become involved in social or economic or political questions since entering into these questions divides the church and weakens its ability to preach the gospel effectively."

There is a third group of church members who are unhappy about the church's activity in this field of historical salvation, not because of any general theory, but because they disagree with the usual ecumenical conclusions. These say "The trouble with the churches when they enter politics is that they swallow the socialist and communist positions on political and ethical matters. The churches should be active in this field but they should be anti-communist the way the Roman Catholic church was before Vatican Council II. Pius XII was the true Christian leader, not Leo XIII or John XXIII."

There was held in the Hague a Consultation on the Commission of the Churches on International Affairs during which this question was theologically discussed with specific reference to the churches' involvement in political and international affairs. This consultation of about 60 persons, widely representative of the churches of the World Council, agreed that the churches must concern themselves actively in the social, economic and political affairs of the present world. There was no opposition either from Orthodox or Protestants who were present. Their agreement was based upon their common interpretation of the Biblical imperatives (Old and New Testament), but they also noted that there did not exist an ecumenical consensus theologically which would enable us to express together that Biblical agreement. Four typical statements were formulated as follows:

1. Starting from the biblical testimony to the creation of the world by God and the divine providence in ordering it, the oneness of all mankind under the law of God is emphasized.

2. Starting from the creative and perfecting activity of God's grace in human history, the dynamic element in history, moving to a glorious consummation is stressed.

3. Starting from the message of the coming kingdom of God in Jesus Christ, the inspiration to action and the challenge this presents to our present imperfect and sinful world are revealed.

4. Starting from the Church's participation in the continuing threefold ministry of Christ in the world, the emphasis falls on priestly intercession, prophetic judgment, the arousing of hope and conscience, and the pastoral care for mankind.

Each of these was formulated by the whole group, but I call to your attention that paragraph one was out of a Lutheran theological background, paragraph two out of a Chalcedonian Orthodox statement, paragraph three out of a Reformed theology, and paragraph four out of an Oriental Orthodox point of view.

In my judgment, this was an important theological analysis even though no over-arching synthesis appeared except the original agreement that the biblical faith does require the church to be concerned in the social, economic and political questions of man within history. The church does not confine itself to questions of eternal salvation as if in the biblical perspective eternity had no roots in the historical.

If there were time, I could go on to argue the case for our involvement in the effort to establish a world community along the following lines which I shall merely state without setting forth any arguments supporting the statements.

1. In a time, such as ours, of rapid social change, the church will be

an entirely reactionary force unless it attempts to bring the moral insights of the gospel to apply to the moral decisions inherent in the changes being made in world society.

2. To make an absolute distinction between eternal salvation and historical salvation is a heresy. To make an absolute distinction between the 'spiritual" and the "physical" is to deny the incarnation.

3. To preach the gospel to a hungry man without giving him food is both futile and cruel.

4. To make Christian salvation a purely individual matter is to reject the Old Testament message and to forget that Jesus came preaching repentance in the context of the approaching kingdom of God.

On the other hand, let us be clear that the churches must avoid certain attitudes and positions as they interest themselves in political, social and economic affairs.

1. The revelation of God in Jesus Christ does not make Christians, as Christians, expert in technical questions.

2. The churches must avoid arrogance and triumphalism as they concern themselves in social, political and economic affairs.

3. The only absolutes of the Christian position are related to the Christian faith that every man is created in the image of God and is a potential son of God through Jesus Christ.

4. Unless Christian economic, social and political efforts are closely related to worship and mission, the churches' unique strength will be lost and their role distorted.

All these eight points are worthy of discussion but having stated them, I proceed to the central question of this address: The Churches' Contribution to World Unity and Community.

First let us distinguish two views with regard to world community which are not Christian, as such, but which have arisen out of Christian culture and because of their world-wide influence demand our attention.

1. The first of these is the Leninist-Marxist view. Let me describe by a simple statement its chief propositions:

a) World community will be established by world revolution which can only be introduced by the dictatorship of the proletariat and the liquidation or, at the least, neutralization of all capitalists and all men of religion.

b) There are no values except material goods.

c) There is no God.

d) The Communist state must be served by all citizens, whose rights are subservient to the rights of the state.

e) The evil in society can be eliminated and utopia established once the evils of private property and capitalist practices have been overcome.

2. Parallel to this romantic dream of a man-made utopia under the Leninist-Marxist programme is the romantic liberal humanistic hope

that education will solve the problems of world community. Its usual components are:

a) Man is naturally good and the goodness can be drawn out of him by education.

b) Man can be educated to act on self-interest, enlightened enough to include the self-interest of all other men.

c) The only problem in establishing a world community is to organize this enlightened self-interest to use the techniques that science and engineering now make available.

These two secularist hopes have much more in common than has been generally recognized during the half century since the Russian Revolution, especially during the height of the Cold War.

Their basic weaknesses from the Christian point of view are the same.

a) They recognize no transcendent God. This is not an unimportant lack. For, according to the Bible, man's essential danger and sin arises out of his rebellion against God. Pride is the most deadly of all sins. Idolatry in the Old Testament is the sin of worshipping the creations of man instead of Him who created man.

b) Neither of these secularist hopes recognizes sufficiently the universality of sin nor its radical nature. One wonders how many purges Communist states must go through before they will finally realize that men whose power is unchecked by God or man will use that power for their own interests as against those of the people they rule. When will Communists recognize in the ruling members of their parties and states the same human sins and selfishness that they so easily recognize in the propertied and ruling classes of capitalist societies? And equally when will the political leaders of the capitalist societies recognize in themselves the same sins of violence and selfishness to preserve their own positions that they so easily recognize in Socialist and Communist leaders?

As against these two types of humanist utopias which are presently competing throughout the world for men's allegiance, there are in my judgment two realistic schools competing for the support of men which may be labelled respectively the Cynical Realist and the Christian Realist. Let us look at them in order.

1. The cynical realist position is that which is most frankly described by Machiavelli in *The Prince*. The difference between Machiavelli and other cynical realists is that most such men have never so clearly analyzed their motives for political action nor so frankly revealed them.

Note first that these cynical realists, in sharp contrast to the Utopians, do take sin seriously although they do not ordinarily speak theologically. But it is because they clearly recognize the persistent and even demonic power of greed, fear, hate and lust in all men including themselves they reject as romantic all dreams including, for example, the dream of world unity or community which is the subject of this address.

In the second place, these cynical realists recognize the facts of power. They are never found supporting lost causes or underestimating the strength of their enemies. So when they have power they use it to protect their personal interests, or those of their families or friends or nations. Generosity or fairness are not values but tools to be used in place of harsher weapons which are sometimes less effective. And unlike Macchiavelli they normally write and speak in the most moral terms, cloaking their self-interest often in Biblical quotations.

As against these two kinds of romantic utopianism and this cynical realism, is it possible for the Christian Church to contribute to the unity of the world? I believe so, if in the light of the revelation of God in Jesus Christ, we will be realists. A Christian realist is however one who attempts to take into consideration all of reality and not just part of it. What is this total reality as understood by Christian faith?

1. First of all God. This is not just any god but the very specific God revealed in the Scriptures of the Old and New Testaments, namely the Creator and Redeemer, the God of both judgment and mercy. He is the Father revealed by Jesus of Nazareth whose almighty sovereignty is exercised in both love and justice, which are not understood as being in conflict with each other.

2. In the second place this Christian realism recognizes the reality of evil in the world and specifically in man. One does not read the Scriptures aright unless he discerns the satanic and demonic power of evil. I do not argue for a literal acceptance of Biblical demonology any more than a literal acceptance of angels. But I do insist that realism must recognize the persistence of evil, its frequent incarnation, its close connection with man's highest aspirations, and its ultimate mystery.

I have never been one who was willing to say that this whole revelation of reality is confined to those who accept the Bible. I have been rereading Homer's *Odyssey* recently and was impressed again with the deep though primitive classic grappling with this problem of the source and meaning of evil. One can do better by rereading the tragedies of Aeschylus and Euripides, Goethe's *Faust* or Shakespeare's *Lear* and *Macbeth*, none of whom are particularly biblical in their understanding of man and evil. My point is that a part of reality that must be reckoned with is evil, the knowledge of which is not confined to biblical Christians.

3. A third part of reality as understood by Christians is that man potentially and sometimes actually is also good. The cynical realist blinds himself to the good in man and the potential good of man who responds to God in Christ. There is a natural aspiration of man that is as real as his natural proclivity to evil. Love is as real as hate though perhaps not so common. Cynicism about man and his potential is the most blighting power in the world today and leads at last to a nihilism which threatens all mankind.

It is because I believe the Christian faith most fully comprehends the reality of human life and existence on this planet that I believe the churches have the task and opportunity of contributing to world unity and community.

Today it must be a world society simply because science and technology are rapidly making all men entirely interdependent. The hope, not of utopia, but of sufficient world community based upon a "rough justice" for all men everywhere is not a romantic dream but is a required development if man is to continue to live on this planet. Men have always, under the pressures of necessity, learned how to create larger civilized communities: from family to tribe to nation. There is no reason in logic why nations will not give way to world community.

If you believe in God, you will expect that in his sovereign grace He will continue using His right and left hands to establish sufficient justice to be the foundation of a world community of peace.

With his right hand, he stirs up prophets and seers, poets and statesmen, saints and martyrs, to see the vision and in sacrificial love to give themselves to that vision, and with his left hand we may expect God to continue to chasten evil and drive men away from folly and sin.

It is this two-handed God of mercy and judgment in whom Christians believe.

With all this as background, let me conclude rather quickly, describing briefly what the World Council of Churches is attempting to do to fulfill this task of the churches.

I think in this company I should emphasize particularly the programme of the World Council of Churches as it relates itself to the Roman Catholic Church. Ever since the establishment of the Pontifical Commission of Justice and Peace in January 1967, there has been a most intimate relationship between the World Council of Churches and that new Roman Catholic instrument which arose out of Vatican Council II. We are about half way through an experimental three-year period of a joint operation which is formally called the Committee on Society, Development and Peace of the World Council of Churches and the Pontifical Commission of Justice and Peace (commonly called SODEPAX). The considerable programme of SODEPAX with a small staff, headed by Father George H. Dunne, has encouraged all over the world joint action by Protestants, Orthodox and Roman Catholics in development education, which is to say to help the churches understand their role in promoting economic justice as the only strong basis for world community and world peace.

At this time, we have begun to look forward to the termination of the project ad experimentum, to see how we can best assure continuing cooperation in this field after the three-year period is concluded. One possibility is that the Roman Catholic Church will participate as a member in a new Commission of the World Council of Churches which has a responsibility of coordinating the whole effort of the churches of the World Council in participating in the development strategies of their nations and regions. Even before this new Commission was established by the Executive Committee of the World Council, I had the opportunity to lay the possibilities before His Holiness Pope Paul VI, so that he would be prepared for any recommendations that might come to him through the Pontifical Commission of Justice and Peace. As I speak, very friendly negotiations are going on. I think it is clear that in the next years the cooperation will be more and more intimate and wide spread toward a solution of this great problem of mankind.

I should conclude by calling to your attention the absolute necessity for this increase of Christian cooperation to work closely with men of other faiths, for example in the United States with the Jewish Community, in Indonesia with Islam, in Thailand with Buddhists, etc. Christians are a minority in the world. Christian triumphalism must be rejected. Christian service is the absolutely appropriate activity of Christians at all times and in all places.

A Need for Listeners

Charles A. Curran

CREATIVE REACTORS

IN approaching the topic, the need for listeners, one can quickly come up with a kind of nightmarish image drawn from Kafka or even Sartre's "no exit" conception of a world filled with people speaking furiously over telephones everywhere, into phones that are off the hook with no one listening. Perhaps no need is so dramatically emphasized in all the shouting that is around us as the need for someone to be genuinely, deeply and profoundly committed to listening to what is being said. It is listening that is the redemptive act. It is the Logos, the Second Person, the perfect understander that is at the same time the Redeemer out of whose relationship with the Father is generated perfect love. It is this kind of concept of the need for redemptive listening that we mean here. Redemptive listening means the deep convalidation that comes to me when someone genuinely hears what I say and deeply and sensitively understands it. This is someone of whom afterwards, in the glow of the worth that I feel about myself as a result of that experience, I can say with depth of meaning, "He truly understood me; he is a deeply understanding man." By such a word "understanding," I bring forth, in its resonances, to every hearer an experience of the most profound sort, an experience of compassion and misericordia in this kind of delicate and sensitive listening that heals wounds and cures, and which redeems with the sense of worth and value that it conveys to the person. It is in this sense then that we are going to focus on the need for listeners.

The title "A Need For Listeners" might be extended to mean something of what, in the Biblical sense, Solomon prayed for and received, namely, the understanding heart; or in the Hebrew, a listening heart. We might also make this title more formal, in the literal sense of the word "formal," by speaking of the art and skill of creative listening. We could even extend this further by talking about incarnate-redemptive listening or communication. Both these extensions could be considered facets of the title, "A Need For Listeners.

CREATIVE INCARNATE COMMUNICATION

THE kind of listening, or creative communication, which is both incarnate and redemptive, leaves both the communicator and the communicant filled with worth and positive motivation because it takes in the whole person as a communication—not merely an intellectualized segment of the person. This kind of communication does not come about naturally; it is an acquired, defined, concentrated, conscious and directed effort that skillfully engenders this communication process which is the end product of the art and skill of listening.

It is this kind of listening which is creative. It incarnates *both* persons and thereby renders them whole in their communication with one another. It also leaves them filled with a deep sense of convalidating worth. This is, then, a convalidating communication or a communicative convalidation. It is the kind of relationship which, between two or more people, is redemptive because it leaves each one enhanced in regard to his own significance and meaning in the Christian sense of having experienced what it means to be bought at a great price. It does this not only for the person himself, but also it enhances him in the appreciation of, and regard for, the validity and depth and meaning of his own ideas. These ideas were worthy of communication and they brought about a personal redemption when the person struggled to communicate them.

In speaking of the art and skill in creative communication, the person communicating his ideas becomes aware of the value of himself and of what he is trying to say because of the art and skill of the receiver and his response. What is being emphasized here is that redemptive communication, as an art and skill, is not something that just happens naturally but requires a conscious effort on the part of the listener to make it possible. The focal point here, then, is the nature of this ability to produce an incarnate-redemptive communication which is convalidating for both the person himself and his ideas.

PROTECTIVE COMMUNICATION

WHENEVER two people communicate together, whether in counseling or in a more superficial exchange, one of the main primitive motives that influences them, and therefore influences the communication, is a simple basic defense of the self. The result is that just the effort itself to communicate is very threatening so that in the very effort to communicate the person is simultaneously protecting himself from getting through to the other. In this contradictory position the person is defeated in his attempt to communicate. It is because of the fear of being hurt, because of some vague catastrophic anxiety, that it is necessary to consciously acquire an art and skill both in communication itself and listening. Otherwise the fear is enhanced and heightened not only on the part of the one communicating but also on the part of the receiver. And of course, the fear, both on the part of the communicator and on the part of the receiver, may well be justified since both, in fact, have been hurt in the past.

What we see here then is a double art and skill : the receptive person, the listener, must dovetail into and facilitate the art and skill of the communicator in order that the communicator may be able to overcome his defenses and protective linguistics, and consequently, genuinely trust himself to be open to the receiver.

This is communication viewed as an art that needs to be learned. But in the effort to practice this art, one is the victim of his own fear of the other's rejection, and so he fails to communicate at all. In calling it an art and skill that has to be acquired, we mean that one person has to learn to be open, to trust the other person. There is a dual kind of skill both in being able to be receptive to another and also in helping the other to be open. One of the reasons this does not come naturally is that its natural expression is inhibited by the fear the communicator has that he will be rejected.

THE REDEMPTIVE LISTENER

THE question to be raised now is which art comes first, that of communicating or that of receiving. I believe the answer to this is expressed in the title. The atmosphere, the matrix of the setting into which the communicator is about to project himself, must first reveal itself to him as non-threatening, as something in which he might at least be encouraged to risk communicating. To provide this atmosphere, the listener must communicate first his real listening capacity, since the communicator has a need for a listener, but he also needs some assurance that here is a true listener, a true understanding heart. It is into this true listener that he can take the risk of openly plunging himself in his communication, rather than turning aside in a protective, conflicting, and self-defeating way. Without the true listener, his communication will result in self-protection rather than an open commitment. There must be something in the listener's manner, and something in what he has first communicated that defines him as an understanding heart. It is only in this atmosphere that the communicator's need for a listener can be fulfilled.

Communication will not take place then unless and until the receiver shows that he is a person who can be trusted. Where non-convalidating communication exists, in the sense of ordinary communication, this atmosphere of trust must first be established by the receiver before redemptive communication can take place. It is paradoxical, but the only milieu in which the communicator can open himself up is one in which he feels the person is really receiving him, and then he is able to put aside his blocking and defenses and truly exercise his art of communication. In other words, he must feel a reciprocal milieu before he is able to do this.

It is important that the listener not only feel receptive but he must show this in some manner to the communicator. It is his, the receiver's gift of himself, that comes first. In this sense, it is the listener who loves first, in assuring the communicator that his need for a listener will be realized.

We have used the expression "incarnate-redemptive" communication, and both of these words are important. One might say, in using the word "redemptive" that whatever else the listener may communicate of himself, essentially what he must communicate is a redemptive atmosphere. By this is meant that he creates a quality and tone that allows the one in need of him, the communicator, to believe and trust and therefore begin to open up. So whatever he says, and in whatever manner he says it, as a result, the communicator will feel himself a worthy person in the receiver's mind, and therefore is redeemed. Consequently, whatever the communicator then says, he is assured in advance that it will be genuinely appreciated and worthily understood—it will not be distorted or misinterpreted or mishandled. One of the great impediments that prevent the communicator from openness is his fear that what he says will be segmented, distorted, twisted, and not really be redemptively received. And when what he says is not received in its true worth, he himself will be rejected as not *being* of any true worth.

The listener has to communicate the idea that he will accept the communicator and not distort him; that he will accept him for his true worth and give him his due value; that no matter what he says, this acceptance of him will continue. This atmosphere will give the communicator the assurance that he can take the risk of making a mistake in what he communicates and still be accepted. This is a redemptive atmosphere or a redemptive aura in which the acceptance of the listener is radiated back to the communicator. Thus, there quickly enters into the communication this redemptive atmosphere; this allows the communicator to take the risk. The receiver, then, takes an active role in creating an atmosphere in which the giver is free to let down his defenses.

NON-INVESTED COMMUNICATION

THE word "incarnate" is extremely important here also, because on of the most basic defenses that a person has is that of reducing communication to an abstractive intellectualizing. This does not really involve the person in any communication. Although he may give the appearance of communicaitng himself, in fact, he never really communicates himself at all. This type of intellectualizing is protective of the person because if what he said is misunderstood or distorted or twisted, he can rationalize out of it on the basis that he was not involved in the first place. He does not need to defend a position since he never really took one. All he did was make a series of abstracted intellectualizations; there was no incorporation, no incarnation, no deep self-investment in what he said. Consequently, the person's intellectualized statements afford him a maximum amount of protection. The most basic threat then to genuine communication is the subtlety with which the person can rationalize his suppressed anxieties about not being heard or validated or redeemed in a communication. He does this by intellectualizing, since this precludes self-investment.

Alternately, the person might speak in such a way that no one could include him in the investment of what he has said; for example, he might talk about things, or other people, or various kinds of facts that are neutral or scientific. But this in no way engages the person in self-commitment; a person may communicate generally in that way or teach in such a manner. In the incarnate sense, then, one of the defenses that can be assumed is that the speaker may go off into intellectualizing and factual information. In doing this, he does not invest himself, so that if what he says is not understood, he can simply say that he was talking about generalities or facts. But this is a way of keeping himself from becoming incarnate.

An illustration of this would be that non-self-invested teaching in which the teacher stays in abstraction and principles, or removed conceptions. Or conversely, one becomes very scientific, but scientific in the neutral, one-way-glass-mirror sense. Both of these kinds of masked communication are merely disguises for a communication that allows no openness into which the students can make an investment, since there was nothing really there in which to invest. They either understand or they do not, and the teacher grades them accordingly, but there is no risk or commitment involved on either side.

The difficulty with this is that the students will not likely really learn anything personally significant because they are not given anything redemptive in which to invest themselves. This seems to be one of the issues now being raised on university campuses, namely, that this protective kind of communication, appearing under the guise of intellectualized abstraction or scientific factual demonstrations, has totally depersonalized the student. The student feels this depersonalization confusedly without knowing exactly why. He is simply left with the feeling of not being able to commit himself personally; the communication itself does not allow it.

This depersonalization occurs because the teacher wants to protect his feelings from being hurt if he were to risk going out and reaching the student. This is the risk in becoming incarnate. Without this risk, the student never feels anything human; what he feels is impersonal scientific data or abstracted concepts being thrown out at him. The teacher who feels such a need for defense, might be thought to remain in the protective embryonic or pre-natal stage of personal commitment. He is afraid to be born into a genuine relationship with others because this would mean that he has to be seen as a human being. The communication is cut off on both sides: on the part of the teacher, in his refusing to become incarnate; and on the part of the student, in his lack of opportunity to invest in anything personal.

THE NATURE OF INCARNATE-REDEMPTIVE COMMUNICATION

BUT whether we speak of teaching and learning or of even more personal psychological encounters, the quality of the communications would be creative, would be incarnately redemptive, would be open, only if they would center on a listening heart in the emotional, instinctive and somatic sense of heart. If the communication is to be a communication of the whole self of the person who needs to be listened to, a great part of his need will be fulfilled if he is secure enough and free enough that he can begin to trust. But to do this, trust must be conveyed to him first. He can then begin to trust not only his own ideas and his intellectualizing process but his spontaneity as well. For his spontaneity to be trusted, he must allow his feelings to come through, he must let those ideas in which he is really invested show their self-investment by his own incarnate expression. He must get excited, and be allowed to; he must be free to be angry, and be allowed to; he must be free to let himself be depressed or frustrated or confused or elated or enthusiastic. All these concepts are of negative and positive feelings-incarnation. He must also be sufficiently trustful of the redemptive quality of the listener that his primitive instinct for self-defense is unhooked and he can let himself flow into the communication with some reassurance that he will not be destroyed.

EXPRESSION OF IDEAS THROUGH AFFECT

IN a word, the freedom that an incarnate-redemptive atmosphere would produce would allow the communicator to communicate himself spontaneously and without defense, in *affective* language. He would be able to let his affects flow in and through the idea that they are invested in. With this flow of both affect and ideas, what is of really deep value to him as a self, will be contained in this expression. Unless real personal values are hidden here, he would not have such deep feelings and the idea would not encapsulate him with its affective quality. Out of the spontaneous expression and then examination of such affectively packaged ideas will come an awareness of basic values which he can begin to disentangle and distinguish and so see their significance to himself. We are talking not only about affects, then, but about affects as they are communicated in and through spontaneous communication that contains ideas and personal self-investments as well.

It is relatively easy to communicate ideas alone, but in order for a person to communicate affects as well, he has to have some assurance that not only will his ideas be received but that his feelings also will be received. In this way he will be able to express together his ideas, his affects, and his values.

In order then for the creative self to come out, the affective self must be released. The person has to trust that his ideas will come through in his spontaneity. Within this is encapsulated his own self-investment, which at some point will reveal hidden values, but which are known only through his affect around these ideas. He cannot know himself in purely intellectualized versions of himself. This would only make him an oral character, in the traditional protective sense, and this never leads to self-knowledge, but rather to self-disguise.

In a sense a person does not become himself until he is free to express his feelings and those are accepted. Since the affects would not be present unless he were invested in the ideas they contain, by protecting himself from expressing feelings, he is protecting his personal ideas. This is why such ideas will not be communicated until he is free to communicate the affects around them. He will never then clearly see the ideas that he is invested in because he is too afraid to let his emotions spontaneously come.

CREATIVE SPONTANEITY

THE Surrealists understood well this protective device of intellectualization or rationalization or appearing to be logical or formal in the traditional poetic form. They rejected these because they felt no real communication occurred. However, they were misled in their understanding of form; what they were groping for was the notion that by genuine spontaneity one would reach genuinely self-invested ideas or, in other words, one would reach the truth of oneself, which would be indicative of a true communication.

What the Surrealists saw was that logic and form were not reaching the human person, and so they rejected these in an attempt to reach man through his spontaneous affects. Because logic and form and intellectualization could not reach man, they swung to the opposite extreme and placed all the emphasis on feelings. What they were groping for, however, was the realization that from a feeling will come one's personal values hidden like gems in the center. Somewhere in the unfathomed depths of the self, a real self-knowledge may be found. The process of creativity then is the process of this kind of discovery. Surrealist spontaneity alone, however, will not bring about this creativity because it does not go beyond itself. Rather, the spon-

taneity has to be distilled in order to get at the true communication of
self that it contains.

Another aspect of spontaneous communication which can be personally helpful, but which will not lead to the integrated self-awareness
that we are talking about here, is the concept of ventilation. The encountering of a warm listener who entices me to let my affects flow,
and in that way to ventilate my emotional self, is assuredly helpful.
It allows a catharsis and a release of the self which other structures
may not permit. But the difficulty with ventilation is that, somewhat
like a filling-station conception, one needs to do it repeatedly, that is,
it seems not to do anything about the situation in a fundamental way.
While it is relieving, it is relieving only as a release which will pile
up again. Thus ventilation alone, no more than surrealist spontaneity,
both of which have some worth, does not lead finally to this inner self-
integrative communication and knowledge.

The Surrealists' emphasis on acceptance of emotionality alone, then,
was not enough, nor is the simple conception of ventilation; both lack
"form." The listener does not really help someone find himself by
letting him ventilate only; rather, it takes some kind of creative listening—listening that has cognitive form as well as affect—to help a
person distill his real self from his affects. Ventilation is a one-way
communication in that the person empties himself of a superficial self
but does not fill himself with a real self. He simply ventilates the
covering, but he never uncovers the real self—he never *discovers*.

DISCOVERY OF THE SELF

ONE of the important things we have learned from research in
counseling and psychotherapy especially, but also from the other
communication arts, is an awareness of a double-language communication. The listener needs to acquire a profound and perceptive ability
to understand the implications, both affective and cognitive, of a person's communication. Both affects—somatic, instinctive and emotional
—and cognition—inner awareness of others and self, form an important part of any communication that is spontaneous and free on the
part of the secure and trusting communicator. This demands a highly sensitive ear that grasps what the affects are that are being communicated, that feels with them in the deepest sense of the Greek
"sunpathein," sympathy. At the same time this understanding penetrates into the self-investments which these spontaneous emotions encapsulate—penetrates them and therefore grasps what they genuinely
contain.

The speaker must feel free then, to make a total communication of
himself in order that he may become aware of what he says and is, or
in other words, to find that gem of himself hidden in his affect or
emotional self. In seeing the "gem" he will see the total relation-

ship and the gem all at one time. If he is angry and free to communicate it, the listener hears not only his anger, but gradually what is behind *why* he is angry, and he helps him to explore these. This is to say that the listener reaches, in his cognitive understanding, into the hypothalamic expression that comes up through the whole neurological system. This would be the instinctive somatic, affective, emotional world of communication, that the person has struggled in some cortical way to put into words. It is through those confused words that the listener sense his whole affective world. When the speaker then hears this expressed back to him, it fits his hypothalamic inner world and he feels the resulting relief. It is this core relief that gives the speaker the deep feeling of being understood. He usually expresses this relief by nodding, by a sigh and often "that's it!" or "Yes, that's just the way I feel" or "That's exactly it—that really fits!"

Such expressions convey almost an organismic relief. Because this response fits so well, the person feels his whole self validated. When the person hears that his affects are understood on a cognitive level he is then raised up to the cognitive level. From that level he can continue step by step, to discover himself.

The speaker needs, then, from the listener, an understanding of his language of affect; the listener must be a linguist in affective communication if he is to reach the subtle meanings of the speaker as he hears them. What would be misleading here, however, is simply to presume that the language of affect is the only language that he needs. It is this simplification which leads to a confusion between ventilation and constructive communication. If the only language that the listener has is the understanding of affect, he will largely resonate merely with his own affects at a greater or lesser level. He will have shared in some measure the same type of affect and he will say so or show so in his manner. But he then becomes a reverberating or resonant, affective object like the string of a violin. This however, will be no more than a resonating response that encourages ventilation. But it adds nothing further.

One must respond not just to the language of affect, but he must also be aware of other kinds of personal language as well and be able to respond to these. Speaking only affective language will allow continued ventilation but it will not reach the core being of the person.

INCARNATIONAL AND REDEMPTIVE COGNITION

THIS leads to another side of human communication—the cogntive intellectual side. If this is misstated, that is, if it is taken out of its incarnational quality, it will be what we seemed to reject, namely, an intellectualized formalism. But what will save us from that view is the notion of an incarnational cognition and its corollary, incarnational and redemptive symboliziation. This is not simply an intellectualization that is reflective and abstractive, but a process that is truly concerned with "flecting" and "tracting." By this we mean that such a cognitive process is incorporated in the actual experience of the whole invested self. The words "cognitive" and "symbolic," then, are meant here in an incarnate, redemptive sense and not in the formalized, abstractive, defensive, protective, intellectualizing implication that we rejected originally.

This incarnational cognitive process can lead to the discovery of self-value because by definition the person had to be invested in an experience for it to become hypothalamic and affective. It is not just cold intellectualism. It has to have an affective quality to it. While language of affect alone is not enough, and while the abstractive intellectualization is not enough either, the notion of an incarnational reflective intellectualization catches the idea of an inner value pursuit. But to arrive here, we must be considering "flecting" as well as reflecting. The awareness must be drawn out of the suffering, the elation, and the self-investment of the hypothalamic communication itself. We are talking then about reflecting on "flecting," and abstracting on "tracting." It is necessary to abstract on what one has been actually "tracting" and to reflect on what has also been genuinely "flecting" and not simply to intellectualize.

NEED FOR SYMBOLIZATION

WHAT is unique to man is that he needs to be symbolized in order to be free to understand himself. A symbol is a way of freeing one from the confines of one's unique individuation. One is unfree so long as he is bound to his unique self. One's affective bind has a person uniquely individualized in his communication. But when the understanding listener grasps the nature of the other person's affective communication, he responds not simply at the level of the uniqueness of his bind that he too has shared—thus resulting in two unique binds—but he responds with sensitively tuned cognition that adequately symbolizes the feelings in which the person is isolated. This allows him to go beyond himself; it frees the person to move out of himself. He can then begin to know, study, and reflect upon those self aspects that are encapsulated in the unique, highly individualized, emotional, instinctive, somatic components that were contained in his affective language.

One might say then, that the really creative listener who is incarnately redemptive of the other, first of all frees him by responding, not in the language of affect, but in the language of cognition. Such a response tries to give some kind of adequate self-symbols that the person can hold on to and which then enable him not simply to feel about himself but to begin to know about himself. This would lead not simply to "sunpathein" but to "gnosis."

The listener, by symbolizing the feelings of the other, frees him from his alienation and allows him a feeling of generic belonging. He is one with the human race when he is adequately symbolized, whereas when he is simply in affect, he is all alone. His adequate cognitive symbolization de-alienates him. It makes him human rather than alone in his unique feeling world.

REDEMPTIVE SYMBOLIZATION

THE listener who can do this, sets up a communication and a community through which the person is taken out of himself. The heart of the redemptive element in this is that it frees one from his "damned" aloneness and redeems him into belonging, into a state where he can begin to feel and understand that his uniqueness is now shared.

This redemptive quality of the listener's responses, takes the person out of the loneliness, alienation and confusion of his feeling world and leads him to an understanding of the nature of his feelings through a more adequate symbolization of them. But the responses go further. They also penetrate the nature of what it is the person is really seeking, wants, and cares about which lies behind his feelings. These are the goals, the purposes, the persons, the situations which he may not have clearly seen before but which are implicit in his feeling world— even when only the feelings are consciously known. This process leads the person to say, sometimes with surprise, "Yes, that is what I want; that is the reason why I was so depressed and that is why now I have been so delighted."

In other words, the person can feel anger, depression or joy and only implicitly recognize the cause. Its adequate symbolization on the part of the skilled cognitive listener, understanding his language of affect, leads him to the "why" of his feelings. The most widely used word among small children is the word "why." Spontaneously behind any affect is the need for this "why" of inquiring cognition. It is this need that the cognitive-affective understanding listener supplies in his responses, as well as the need for the person to have his affects understood. He supplies the person's need for "why." Why is he affective around this person, place or thing? This leads to personal values— to goals and purposes one has already invested in, even though unconsciously.

Affective communication is both verbal and somatic. The listener must take this into consideration and distill from it the cognitions that are there and give these back to the speaker. By such an affective-cognitive process the listener conveys the feeling that he has received the affect, but in symbolization he is also giving back to the person the "why." In ordinary relationships we are often woefully inadequate in regard to ourselves and others because either we simply see our-

selves as abstractive people, using abstraction as a protection from communication, or alternately, we see ourselves and others just as feeling
people and we get caught up in our own uniqueness of feelings. But
we are really "feeling-why" people. In the feeling is the "why." The
adequate affective-cognitive listener reaches not only the affects, with
all the hypothalamic reverberations that they contain, but he leads us
to the "why" of these affects, the "why" being the measure of one's
self-engagement to a goal, a person, a situation or a series of personal
values behind these affects. This allows a person not only to see them,
but having seen them, it can help him re-sort them, discharging and
disengaging himself from some, holding on even more preciously to
others and acquiring new ones. All affects then, are both goal-directed
and self-invested in some meaure or they would not be affects.

The communication comes from the lips of the speaker to the ear
of the symbolizer and it comes back to the one in need of communication both on the cortical level and also in a way that satisfies the
hypothalamus—the brain center of feelings and instincts—because it
fits. This is not only a moment of both ventilation and redemption
then, but it is also a moment of high humanity because it is no longer
just feelings; it is feelings at the very highest level of the person's
self-understanding, and this is integratively redeeming. While before,
he communicated as a segmented isolated person, he hears himself
back as an integrated whole and this is the heart of the redemptive
aspects of his incarnate communication, namely, that he has been
made whole in the most profound sense of the word "salvus."

The only way that the person can "pull himself together" is to first
go outside of himself and then come back in. While the element of
validation through the other is contained in the other's very listening
presence, more than this is necessary. It is a truly delicate skill that
enables one person to be genuinely redemptive of the other through
what he says. It is merely abstract, depersonalized and offensive, if
what the listener says is true but does not fit the hypothalamus of the
speaker.

UNCREATIVE LISTENING

THE art and skill of listening is in a very special way in demand
because in addition to the impediments of threat and anxiety that
the person needing to be heard has in his own openness, there is on
the other side an extremely aggressive need on the part of the other
person, not really to listen, but to be listened to. Or stated another
way, there are a vast number of people who need listeners and a very
few people who will discipline themselves to the art and kill of
listening.

One might even magnify this by proposing that there is all sorts of
shouting but nobody listening to any of the shouts. This could be a

room filled with shouters, or even a court room or open public area. The audience is not really an "audience" in the sense of listeners. They are either internally arguing with the speaker, whom they are hearing externally and not really trying to hear, or openly resisting him by opposing him, or subtly distorting and blocking the flow of what he is trying to say by devisive and misunderstood types of questions upon questions and argument upon argument. These lead not to a furthering of the speaker's ideas but to confusion and distortion. Algebraically designed, one might propose that the speaker intended to speak from point one to point five. But never gets to point two or three, not to mention five, because the questioner opposes number one by proposing a minus one and so forces the speaker into minusing, or answering with another minus, and the questioner minuses that equation of minus minus one, etc., with the result that point two is not yet reached. Usually then the speaker hurriedly, at the end of his allotted time, crowds in point three, four, and five. This leaves him and most of his hearers frustrated and disappointed or angry or depressed.

This results in a deep sense of not being understood. The hurt that he feels after such a humiliating experience leaves him as a speaker or as a teacher reluctant to risk himself openly like that again. One might say that he is hurt by such misunderstanding in proportion as he genuinely tried creatively to invest himself in what he said. The end product is that often what appears to be speaking or lecturing or teaching is, in fact, a form of intellectualized abstraction which is protective of the speaker's self. The speaker is never truly open because he is too afraid of the cruelty he will meet with when he tries to be genuinely open. He therefore goes through the appearance of an open presentation but in no way is he self-invested.

The end affect is a sort of depersonalized, aggressive power-control which protects against any real inner relationship with others under the guise of teaching them or alternately, under the guise of student learning. This is similar to the experience of an audience going through the appearance of a communication with no genuine listening. Here we are at the heart of our topic—the need for listeners.

THE RISK OF COMMUNICATION

EXPERIENCED circus people say that the one act that all circus people watch and have a never-tiring, ever-fascinating interest in, is the trapeze act. Now one might consider that the reason that act would never be tiring is that it so profoundly corresponds to the kind of openness that would be related to any truly creative communication. One person takes the risk of letting himself go. He is suspended in air. He can always fall no matter how many times the act has been performed before. There is no instance, no matter if they have done the act one hundred thousand times, where in that trapeze act, one of them cannot fall and hurt himself badly; he must trust the other person to catch him. It could be that right here is the reason it is so fascinating for even the most experienced of circus workers. Each time any person truly lets himself go, he can fall and be gravely hurt. Each practice never lessens the skill and art and concentration required because every practice is also real. It is somewhere here that we are not only talking about the need for listeners if one is to really live in and through others but, in addition, the need of the concentrated skill of the one who "catches."

When we speak of the need of listeners we speak of two fixed categories of people: one who is in need of being listened to, and the other which constitutes the listeners. In this sense, the counseling analogy or the psychotherapeutic analogy can be misleading because we think of the same person as the counselor or the therapist, and as a differing person, one who is in need of counseling or therapy. But in creative relationships these change. What we are implying here is a kind of rhythm that people have towards one another; almost like the diastolic and systolic action of the heart; or like breathing. This is the rhythm of life.

Consequently we mean that at any point one needs to be listened to with a listening heart. But at another time the other person may equally need to be listened to with the same understanding. There are no fixed categories, but a kind of breathing rhythm when, at the right moment, the listener knows that he is the listener and the speaker knows that he will be delicately, sensitively and artistically listened to. We mean it in this flowing creative rhythm together, rather than the fixed dichotomized categories of counselor-client; patient and therapist.

THE HUMAN CONDITION

THE issue can be raised then as to why this redemptive communication would not occur spontaneously—why would we need an art and skill to bring this about? Would it not seem the most natural thing in the world for one person simply to communicate to another at the deepest level of the self? Why should one person be afraid of another? Indeed, why should not the one person wish to get out of his alienation? For example, one does not mistrust others by going around with his eyes closed, even though his eyes may be exposed to many unsightly views or even hurt seriously sometime. Why cannot the person keep his trust open in the same spontaneous way he keeps his eyes open?

Traditionally there have been many explanations, basically theological, offered for this. Perhaps no other explanation of original sin is as compelling as this simple fact, namely, that it was natural for one to be open, but something in a primeval sense has happened to the human race that has injected some kind of mistrust into our being. This could be considered as some primal sin that we are born with. This leaves us then already born into an anxiety-ridden untrustworthy relationship with others.

WORLD OF LIARS

IN this theological sense, then, one might say that it is the result of some original sin. This is so convincing that even now sophisticated people can believe this. Indeed, for many centuries some sort of primal sin has been presupposed. The reason that makes this statement somewhat tenable is that it has always been one of the most convincing of human experiences.

This idea has been carried further and if we were to give a title to this special phase of this discussion, it might be called "Satanism Revisited," or even "Satanism Internalized." The reason for this is that another way of dealing with the situation that we are talking about, namely, one's fears of being open, one's need to protect himself, one's need to disguise oneself, is that he is under the influence of and strongly in the control of one who has been called a liar and The Father of Lies. The Prince of this World, in other words, is a liar. Consequently, there are primal forces against one's being open and trustful and genuine and outgoing. These primal forces are so strong in others, in the way that they would overtake one if he were so foolish as to be open, that he must realize that he is living in a world of liars, controlled by The Prince of Darkness who is The Father of Lies. This makes logic of one's being very careful of what he says and to whom he says it because these liars will pounce on him and smother him and, in so doing, they will destroy whatever was worthwhile.

To leave the human race with some dignity, the great value of satanism is that it is not exactly vicious people who do this to other persons; there is a prior force, a force of principalities and powers, a satanic force beyond human awareness that works towards this evil and, consequently, Satan is present everywhere. So every time one attempts to communicate oneself, he meets first of all the effects of satanism in what other people do to him.

Traditional spiritual writing, in asking the question, "How do you know the presence of Satan in a situation?" gives an interesting description of the actual human situation. The answer goes something like, you know that Satan is present when one person or a group of people, arriving for an obviously good work, for something that is obviously fine, meet marked and unreasonable resistance. They explain that this potential good so proposed, engenders in Satan a resistance and envy so that, in proportion as he sees a good work emerging and realizes the extent and dimension of this work, he mounts against it forces of evil; he ensnares as many people as he can within these forces. What this good work will, then, immediately face, as soon as it attempts to communicate itself, is derision, distortion, segmentation, and miscontruction. Satan's whole effort—so they explain —is to discourage the person who represents this good work, to cause him to give up, to lose his courage and not try any more; thus Satan has succeeded.

In this view, we have something that is not internal to the human race but comes to it from the outside. There is an apparent kindness here from this viewpoint. In my hurt, for example, I can still feel that it was not your evil, something that you destructively and viciously did to me; it is just that Satan tempted you and you became his creature in that process. In this view, then, the reason we have this mistrust in ourselves is that we were born with the imperfection of original sin. This explains our mistrust and our difficulty in getting out of the suffering of our alienation. Original sin also impedes us from knowing where our true selves could have been before we were afflicted with original sin. This is expressed popularly in such expressions as "Let's get the devil out of here," so that we can communicate without the devil; or 'Let's beat the devil out of him." These indicate the basic desire to communicate without interference, misunderstanding, and distortion.

PSYCHOLOGICAL AWARENESS

DRAWING from psychological developments of the past fifty years, there is, however, another way of explaining this human situation which corresponds to the shrewd observations of these spiritual writers of an older age. For the situation that they described was one that is very real and endlessly encountered. But we can leave the Satanic aspect out of it and look at the psychological factors that are involved.

The spiritual writers were speaking of an experience we know to be true. This is an experience in which, whenever forces arise that seem to have worth and significance, one is first of all in a deep struggle with himself to have the confidence to dare trust to communicate them. And secondly, when he does dare, having struggled with himself to arrive at the courage to do so, the probabilities are that he will encounter only rarely any kind of creative, constructive response; rather the probabilities are in favor of his encountering a discouraging, depressing response. Many creative people, for example, never speak to anyone about what they are doing until it is formed and viable in the sense of a fetus after seven or eight months, and so their project cannot then be easily hurt by the response they might receive.

MAN'S PRIMAL CONDITION INTERNALIZED

MODERN psychological writers, beginning with Freud, have treated somewhat differently this same state of distrust and fear of others: man's primal condition. They have "de-Satanized" it and internalized it. In his *Beyond the Pleasure Principle*, Freud deals with this under the aspect of death and life. He suggests that inside of each person is a force for death almost as powerful as any force towards life. He proposes a strong death instinct in man. But Freud goes a step further than this in the way he reasons. Rather than the simple notion that it ought to be easy for us to open ourselves up to life and trust one another, he proposes that nature has a different intent; that everything born has as its goal to die. Consequently, nature has already provided inside the self of each man, an instinct which, at the moment one is born, begins to prepare a person to die. The moment one begins to live, he begins to die. His goal is death. His purpose is death. His end is death. The whole nature of the organism is to die. And so, buried inside of everything else that the person is, is a powerful instinct to die; to wish death. This is the Freudian death wish.

Man's inability to be open to communicate then, can be described in terms of such a death wish. One has to struggle within himself to bring anything alive because to bring anything out of himself that is true, meaningful or valuable, is to strive against his own death wish. Strong forces in him are aimed at keeping him dead, for then he will be closer to his goal. That is, any life force within him is, in a certain sense, against his nature because it is against what he is born for, namely to die. It is, then, only with great effort that a person struggles to make the first thrust to express himself positively. Rather, then, for it to be natural for the other person to respond creatively, he is also born to death. Hence, the person's success in bringing something to life and communicating it only arouses the forces of death in the other. All his death instinct is lined up against the person who has succeeded in presenting something constructive and positive.

DEATH-WISH DECEPTIVENESS

FROM the point of view of the death wish, let us look at a common type of intellectual process that often results in self-defeating learning relationships. Early in the counseling therapeutic experience we grew to see that the counselor or therapist had to be completely open to the client, that he had to accept the client at whatever level of personal expression the client wished to communicate himself. What we learned was that the best way to form a genuine relationship with another person is to avoid approaching the person with preconceived intellectual ideas of what he ought to be, how he ought to express himself, or what he ought to say he intended to do. These can

distort a communication and prevent a genuine relationship. Such pre-
conceptions most often seemed to produce either non-cooperation or a
submissive passivity which, by appearing to do what the therapist or
counselor told the person to do, simply masked a supine dependency
that was really a negative, passive resistance. We learned, rather, that
the best approach to a genuine relationship was an open committing
of oneself to whatever it was that he chose to communicate, and then
making an effort to cognize and understand this communication.

Transferred to learning, we have the conception of the teacher not
as counselor but as client. Let us propose then that the learning situation does not, as we popularly think, view the teacher as the counselor
who understands the student. Rather the teacher, seen as the client, is
in deep need of being understood himself. He needs to be received
and accepted by the student or students at the intellctual or emotional
level of his struggle for creative communication with them. Reversely,
the student is not, in this conception, in the client-patient role, but
rather in the counselor or therapist role. It is the teacher who is suffering with ideas that are welled up within him and that he needs to
express and have understood. It is the student who can be in the therapeutic position of understanding and genuinely relating to the teacher
as he unfolds, often with painful intensity, the ideas that he is invested
in.

Seen this way, we have a situation similar to what we learned in
counseling and psychotherapy. By intellectual arguing, the student will
not, in the first instance, understand the teacher or anything that the
teacher has really invested in. On the contrary, this type of intellectual
argument runs the danger of the death-wish, self-defeating system.
It appears to have an intellectual component that is constructive and
positive. But this is deceptive. The student, hit with the first excitement of hearing the teacher's self-invested ideas, spontaneously re-
acts by questioning. The danger here is that the student's spontaneous
reaction, under the guise of intellectual questioning, arguing or some
similar intellectual process, will actually impede his impulse to learn
because he has not yet really understood. As a result the teacher's
spontaneous freedom to communicate at the deep level of his own creative experience is blocked and frustrated by this initial misunderstanding. Before he is argued with or questioned, the teacher needs—like
the client—to be genuinely responded to, accepted and understood.

Consequently, we see applied to the learning situation the same subtlety that we have learned from counseling and psychotherapy. It is
the teacher, who is in need of a genuinely affective-cognitive listener.
The student's art and skill of affective-cognitive listening will heighten
the learning experience for himself and heighten the creative expression of the teacher.

In counseling and psychotherapy, insofar as learning is occurring,
it is the therapist and counselor who are learning about the client

from himself, from the deep painful process of his exploring his own creative self-world. The client himself begins to learn all sorts of depths and dimensions of his own self that he did not know in his initial attempt to express himself and to be understood.

Applied to learning, then, it would be the creative teacher who is suffering and in need of being understood. The sensitive understanding art of the student makes him a skilled learner. Once this kind of deep affective-cognitive understanding has occurred between the teacher-client and student-learner, we then can make way for a second exchange. Here having grasped what the teacher has creatively invested himself in and has been struggling to communicate, the student-learner may then make his own reverse investment in what he has learned. He is then understood by the teacher, in his own creative reaction, and by other students.

In this we see a creative dynamic, flowing first through the understanding of the student-listener to the creative teacher who needs to be understood. This process needs to be fulfilled to the complete satisfaction of the teacher's need to be listened to and affectively and cognitively responded to. Then the learners themselves become clients. As a result of the creative process that has been engendered in them, they now need the listening attention and accepting responses of the other learners and of the teacher.

This recalls an observation of Aquinas, representing a long tradition, that one should never argue with another person until one has thoroughly understood him and his ideas. Only when the other person totally accepts our presentation of his ideas, are we in a position to argue and disagree. This kind of traditional observation is similar to the creative learning relationship we are describing.

CONTROLLING THE DEATH WISH

WHERE the death wish defeats the learner is that, in his first impulse to learn, all his life forces are brought forward by the excitement of a new idea. But at the same time, all his death wishes are impelled with equal or greater strength. If he gives in to his first spontaneous urge here, it tends not to be really constructive but impeding. Under the appearance of intellectualizing he actually presents a series of negative arguments and resistances which really reject what the teacher has painfully struggled to present. This rejects and frustrates rather than helps.

In the situation where the student controls his death-wish urge to argue and intellectualize and actually submits himself to the learning experience, he strives to understand as the counselor tries to understand the client. Here intellectual argument does not occur. What actually occurs is the flowering in the learner of the seeds of what he has received from the creative teacher. It is a flowering of a new self in himself. But this is not expressed in intellectual argument or resistance. On the contrary, it comes out with the same need to be understood and listened to and with the same intense, creative excitement as was originally expressed by the creative teacher. Consequently, at this stage it is the student himself who becomes the teacher of his own creative ideas. These are engendered in him, not in an intellectualized, argumentative process but in a deeply painful struggle with the new awarenesses that are being born in him as a result of the previous learning insemination.

A familiar illustration of death-life impulses which may be helpful here is the drowning swimmer's relation to the life-saver. The death wish contradicts the life wish in the drowning person. With his life-wish need he shouts for help. But with a death-wish, self-defeating, instinctive urge, when the saver-teacher comes forward, he reaches out and tries to grab the throat or head and shoulders of the saver. If this process succeeds it can end in nearly drowning, if not drowning, both the life-saver and himself.

The skilled life-saver is trained to recognize this death impulse and the grab-at-the-throat gesture and dive under the floundering person and come up behind him. By momentarily surprising him in order to get him on his back, the hope is that the life-wish impulse will again assert itself and the drowning man will realize that this is his path to being saved. In a similar way, the learner realizes that the path to learning is not argumentative resistance but commitment to a trusting understanding of the creative teacher.

ABANDONMENT OF THE SELF

SEEN this way, the path to learning is not aggressive resistance but a kind of abandonment of oneself to the creative teacher. Once this is done, the student, like the panic-stricken person, experiences security and confidence in the realization that the teacher does know what he is doing, and that one can trust oneself to him. In this process, then, both the teacher and the learning person are going safely into the threat of learning as the person is pulled to the shore.

Genuine learning, coming after a commitment to the learning experience, is in contrast to the death-instinct resistance which is self-defeating because one succeeds in impeding one's real impulses to learn. He is peacefully dead because he is the same as he was before; he has learned nothing and has not changed. He has defeated learning because he has submitted to the death-wish threat of change. In this sense he has negated Newman's phrase that "to grow is to change and to grow really mature is to change often."

MAN: A THEO-PSYCHOLOGICAL BEING

THIS leads to the conception that, in order to justify the strength and power of the life instinct in man, we have to talk about the source of life-forces in psychological man. Psychological man, by definition, is a man oriented to death. In other words, one aspect of nature's wish for any man is that he be dead long before he is buried. This would be the best way for nature to prepare man for what is his evident end. Those people might be thought to die best who have been dead a long time before physical death. Nature, considered in one way, would want this.

To justify the power of the life instinct in man we have to consider nature as going beyond death in man. One way to define this is to say that man is a theo-psychological animal. By this we mean that man is not simply a being in the process of becoming. If we say that he is a human being becoming, we have to say that the thing he is becoming is dead and his whole bent is towards death. That is the apparent goal of his natural becoming. But man is a being whose life urge pushes him to a goal beyond death by definition. It is this goal which explains his life forces and validates the art and skill necessary in him and in others to bring these life forces into fruition. By definition then we are talking about a beyond. If we accept Eliade's definition that any beyond-the-self is a kind of approach to God, then we are in a theo-psychological area. This would be our reason for calling this concept of the beyond in man, a theo-psychological definition of him.

From this point of view, we are rather seeing that nature leads man to death. We have to say then that there is a kind of special effort required in man in his struggle to stay alive. It is not simply "natural" to him. What we have here in another form is the profound decision of the Prodigal Son's turning and coming back to the father. That is, the person does not have to respond to the life impulse of returning again to the source of life; he can defeat this, as the Prodigal Son could defeat it. In the terrible realism of the contrast between Peter and Judas, we have Judas hanging himself, not because he was not sorry or not because he was not convinced of the meaning of Christ in his life, but because he could not stand the hatred that he had for himself in his own death-wish. Fittingly, then, the Gospel record has him in the death-fulfillment of hanging himself. Peter, whose sorrow was not nearly as sharp or intense, had sufficient strength of life impulse to turn and come back and face Christ again. That is the basic difference between the two of them.

In summary then one aspect of Satanism has been internalized in the death wish. What spiritual writers have observed in man, psychologists have also observed and have given their explanations. The death instinct is for the person to want to kill what is created in the other before it has a chance to come out; he does this by giving a destructive, negative response to the other in place of genuine understanding. In each person there is some sort of balance between life and death: if the person overcomes his own death wish, he still must encounter the death wish in the other, whose impulse is to be threatened by the forces preserving death in himself; but in destroying the other, both are relieved of the threat of life. Death has its own kind of peace, as a cemetery surely is peaceful.

Anything alive in man, has two forces against it: one's own death wish and the other person's death wish. The one person's overcoming his death wish threatens the other person in the peace of his death. He is immediately threatened that he will be challenged to this perverted life action. Nature, knowing that one's end is death, has prepared man to want death, to be comfortable and even at peace with it—if one does not struggle for life.

WILL TO POWER

Adler called this same thing the will to power. What will happen is that when the person succeeds in communicating life, he will appear to give, in his openness, power to the other person to destroy him. That is, once the person has foolishly opened himself up to a life-urge expression, the other person's will to power cannot resist crushing him. Consequently, the person will have to exercise a powerful effort with himself to control his will to power to destroy the other when he was so foolish as to open himself up.

Other psychologists, in using the term "self-defeating," meant that in having once revealed oneself, the other will destroy him because of his will to power or his death wish. And he may succeed in destroying the person. But it is self-defeating because he also destroys himself, because his defeat is in death. In death there is no self. There is no extension beyond. There is nothing so alienating as death.

Whether we use the concept of will to power, death instinct or self-defeat, they all try to describe the same solution that spiritual writers were describing. There must come forth on the part of the listener, not something that is simply "natural" to him, but something that, in a sense, is highly unnatural to him, something that all his inner forces are leagued against. By holding on to life when he hears life, by holding on to communion and community when he finds them, by holding on to his own self and by embracing the self of the other, he is doing something in a way unnatural because it is beyond himself.

CONCLUSION

It is here that we see meaning in the concept of the art and skill of listening, or the art and skill of the listening heart. This is not something that is natural at all; on the contrary, it is something against which all of one's life forces are leagued. Therefore unless the person does have some reassurance that the listener has some skill that will make this warm, understanding, affective, cognitive, incarnate, creative, redemptive relationship possible, he is a fool to take the risk of being open. He is a fool to risk his openness to the tenacious death wishes of the other. For the listener to give the other that reassurance demands the highest art of communication of his open, warm, receptive, self to him. At the same time it demands skill in both affectively understanding the person when he makes the communication and also a profound cognitive skill which enables the person, by adequate linguistic symbols and cognition, to abstract and reflect on the "why" of his feelings. So, little by little, he arrives at an increasing grasp, not only of a security feeling with himself, but also a genuine knowledge of himself, or "gnosis."

Through the incarnately, redemptive cognitive symbolization by the listener of the affective world of the speaker, a person is able to arrive at the "why" of his affects and the subtle implicit and explicit self-investments and personal value systems that they contain.

The Religious Tradition or Traditions in a Traditionless Age

Abraham I. Katsh

THE current international scene demonstrates how the civilized world continues to violate those humanizing spiritual principles that mankind at its best has often aspired to implement. But the consequences of violating these principles at this time is more serious than ever. For a world of science without a heart will inevitably lead to a heart without a beat.

Because our situation is so serious it behooves us to look into the following:

What has happened to the basic principles of the Judeo-Christian ethics which we have evolved over the centuries and which are the foundation of our Western civilization? Why are they being violated?

Why are the thin, small voices of the prophets of Israel ignored? Why is the Golden Rule being sneered at and honored more in violation than in observance? And why, in the twentieth century, is the ideal of "peace on earth to men of good will" a far-off Utopian dream?

Our astronomers have expanded our universe. But science has contracted our globe. Not only has the jet plane annihilated space, but militancy has made mud out of moderation, and the man of measured thought has been replaced by the man of precipitate action. Many have little regard for tradition and custom, and the result is that one of the greatest casualties of our era is the good we inherited from yesteryear. The new Politics, the New Moral codes, and the New Art Forms, are mostly impatient with the past. As a result of this impatience with our spiritual legacies, no one may speak of the quasi, if not of the full, demise of the Judeo-Christian tradition, which is that remarkable amalgam of religio-ethical values that up to the present has survived as the single most humane power in the Western world.

As one academically trained and nurtured in one of the traditions which form the Judeo-Christian heritage, I would plead for the importance of this common tradition as a foundation for a society unable to resolve problems of war, race, and environment, while attempting to thrust men toward the outer reaches of our solar system. Yet I would caution that this tradition can only be meaningful when the contributors share in its formation, responsibilities and benefits, and when the commonalities are not employed for the purpose of establishing authority or theological aggrandizement. This tradition can only be viable insofar as the contributing parties are engaged in a true dialogue, where differences, as well as similarities, are recognized, learned and appreciated. I stress this openness, for tragically, it has not always been so. Indeed, I would argue that one of the fundamental reasons for the decline of the religious tradition in our time has been the sometimes careless, sometimes willfully evil manner in which it has been put to use through the years. Regretfully the record of the great religious leaders in the crucial problem of attaining peace is badly tarnished. Their deeds have seldom matched the dedication to peace and true brotherhood expressed by them as a prescriptive ideal.

Perhaps if we examine together the history of the relationship between the two contributing parties to the Judeo-Christian tradition, we shall be able to discover where we have gone wrong, what potential strengths reside in the tradition, and how we can make it a force for good in an increasingly traditionless world.

Our coming together today testifies to the unique nature of the relationship between Christians and Jews, and to the resilence and hopefulness in the Judeo-Christian teachings. Whenever one talks of Old and New Testaments, law and grace, coming of a Messiah, or expectation of such a coming, or any other topics which relate to a core of sharing or commonality of ideology and practice, he points up the singularity of the relationship between the two faith communities.

The greater part of this 1900 year old relationship has been at best tenuous and problematic. At its worst it has been marked by persecution and violence. In a historical sense one can define several stages in the development of the relationship. In the early period Church and Synagogue struggled for survival both against a pagan Roman jurisdiction and many mystery cults from the East. It was in these years that a Christian tradition of teaching concerning Jews and Judaism was born. This tradition, expanded and embellished down the long centuries of developing Western civilization, was to have the most ominous consequences for Jews far removed in time and place from the ear of the New Testament authors and Church fathers.

After the Fourth Century and the political triumph of Christianity, Jews suffered under legal, economic and social restrictions imposed by Church law. In the medieval and early modern period the image developed of the Jew as agent of Satan, Christ killer and obdurate enemy of Christendom, leading often to the dehumanization of the Jew as a person and causing widespread death and destruction. Our own generation has witnessed the unthinkable horror of the Holocaust and the systematic extermination of six million Jews, men, women, and children. Indeed, Israel Zangwill was right when he said, "The people of Christ became the Christ of the people." I must be frank and say that I believe the strains evident in the historic relationship of Christians and Jews contribute today also to much Christian misapprehension over Jewish concern for the State of Israel.

I should like, therefore, to touch upon the historic Jewish-Christian relationship. With this as a setting, I will discuss the Holocaust, the new State of Israel, and the biblical foundations of American democracy. Finally, I will attempt to suggest how, through Jewish tradition an answer may be found to the polarization and to the tensions which grip our society.

A. JEWISH-CHRISTIAN RELATIONS

THE period between 250-450 C.E. was crucial in determining the attitude of the Church toward Jews and Judaism. Father Edward Flannery, in his pioneering work, *The Anguish of the Jews,* writes:

> [From the third century dates] the emergence of a teaching not yet fully formulated but clearly enunciated . . . that Jews are a people punished for their deicide who can never hope to escape their misfortunes, which are willed of God. This thesis formed the first seeds of an attitude that would dominate Christian thinking in the fourth century and greatly contribute to the course of anti-Semitism.[1]

It should be noted that not only did this tradition assign to the Jews responsibility for the crucifixion and its resultant judgment, but it also acted to denigrate Judaism as a religion and the Jew as an individual. Thus Father Flannery continues:

> . . . the Church's belief that Judaism, unfaithful to its calling and rejected as a vessel of universal salvation, was, by selective and figurative use of the Scriptures, converted into a belief that the Jews were always a wicked and despicable people, rejected by God from the beginning and prepared as if by compulsion for the murder of Christ.[2]

Out of this tradition came a crucial formula propounded by Gregory the First after the Roman Empire accepted Christianity. Church and State then became synonomous, and no non-Catholic could have survived unless he gave up his paganism. With the Jew, however, it was different. He could not be considered a pagan, since his religion preceded the new faith. Hence a special formula was propounded, and in retrospect, I may refer to it as a humanitarian approach to enable the Jew to survive as a Jew within the conclave of the Roman Christian Empire.

The formula deeply entrenched in Christian teaching was as follows:

(1) The Jew is a living witness to the truth of the new religion.

(2) He cannot be molested.

(3) However, he is guilty of a nefarious crime—the crucifixion of Jesus, for which he is forever accursed and must suffer.

(4) Jesus will return to His glory only if a remnant of the Jew will accept Him voluntarily. (What it really advocated was that as long as the Jew lives Jesus will never return).

Two effects resulted from the formula: (a) The Church was forced to recognize another "protecting" faith, inimical to its own teachings; nevertheless, it was indeed a pioneer step for Religious Pluralism; (b) Painful as the principle for the Jew to be a living witness was, the liability also served as a means of survival. Paganism and most non-Christian practices were obliterated within the confines of Christian power. The Jews, however, survived. Somehow or other they lived. They may have survived on no better than sufferance, and they may have continued to be only because their own will to live transcended the embarrassment that the clergy had imposed upon them. But the living witness idea did at least give them the conditions that allowed their will to live to be realized. The living witness principle then, was not entirely cruel. It did indeed contain an aspect of humanitarianism. Its humanitarianism may not have been loving and kind-hearted in theory, but pragmatically it worked as a kindness. In a pagan Europe only the good Lord knows what may have happened, not only to the Jews, but to the Biblical ethics upon which Judaism is founded.

On the other hand, accusing the Jews as "Christ Killers" (and in insisting that Jesus' return depended on a remnant of Jews accepting him voluntarily as their savior) made living for the Jew unbearable.

However, the Christian missionary approach in converting the Jew to Christianity resulted not so much in saving the Jewish soul, but rather in helping bring his Savior again. Christianity never embraced the new convert as a total Christian. The Jewish convert succeeded merely in changing his label from an "accursed" to "convert," to a "Hebrew-Christian." He was never restored to a human being, born in the image of God, on a par with others. Labeling the Jew as "accursed" made many of the Christians numb to Jewish sufferings, and from the psychological point of view, made them feel that the Jew is punished by his own God. In their hatred, some Christians at times rationalized that they were in reality helping God. Since the crime against the Jew was considered a *collective* one, all Jews were responsible. The position of the Jew as time went on became worse and worse. There was a systematic attempt by the ruling clergy to separate Jews from

Christians—socially, politically, and, of course, religiously.

The Crusaders' attempt to fight the infidel Moslems in the Middle East brought additional horror to the Jewish homes. Whereas, under the feudal system no outsider could have invaded a neighboring territory and molest its people, the feudal rule was not followed as far as the Jews were concerned. Instead of traveling to Palestine to kill the Moslems, the Crusaders decided to kill the "infidel" Jews at home, and thus invaded their territory and murdered thousands of people. This had an adverse psychological effect on the non-Jewish neighbor. It taught him that feudal practices apply to any group, but not to the Jew. The fate of the Jew became hopeless, and any stranger could enter his home, molest and massacre him.

Something of the flavor of these happenings in those times can be seen in the comments of one of the Crusaders, Richard of Poitiers:

> You are the descendants of those who killed and hanged our God. Moreover, God Himself said the day will yet dawn when My children, will come and avenge My blood! We are His children, and it is our task to carry out His vengeance upon you, for you showed yourself obstinate and blasphemous toward Him.[3]

Even the French Revolution, with all its beautiful slogans, did not significantly improve the Jewish position, though it enabled individual Jews to "feel" emancipated; for no individual is really emancipated unless his people, as a whole, are emancipated first, and this depends on whether his country is emancipated fully, otherwise it is merely academic. Also, even where attitudes were changed toward the Jews, there was not a similar attitudinal change toward Judaism. A millenium and a half of negative indoctrination and persecution against the Jew needs intensive re-education in order to "undo" the harm and damage. And this has not been done!

Even in their absence, the hatred of Jews lived on. In England, for instance, from which country the Jews were expelled by Edward I, and from where they remained absent for 365 years, the sentiment against them was seldom abated. The Passion plays, full of burning hatred against Jews, kept alive the animosity toward Jews, allowing for a Shylock character of Shakespeare to come into being, and for a Fagin to emerge, allowing for Marlowe's denunciation of the Jewish personality in his diatribe (*The Jew of Malta*) to come into being. The survival of the hatred of the people, as well as the survival of the people itself, went hand in hand, as a result of the "living witness" idea.

The late 19th and early 20th centuries witnessed the growth of racial anti-Semitism. H. S. Chamberlain, Drumont, Gobineau, and even Paul La Garde, all had their activist followers, ever ready to harass Jews and disrupt the fabric of Jewish experience. Some of their doctrines, as well as the more esoteric philosophy of the Viennese Lanz

Libenfels, influenced the frustrated architect and painter from Linz, Adolph Hitler. His anti-Jewish fulminations owed much to the racialists, yet one can see that in terms of the practical working out of an anti-Jewish policy, his administrators and legal experts relied heavily on Church legislation for precedent. Raul Hilberg, in his massive *The Destruction of the European Jews,* was perhaps the first to systematically compare the infamous Nuremberg laws with canon law. The following chart will indicate the degree of relationship between church law and National Socialist edicts affecting social intercourse, economic activity, ghettoization, and the wearing of a distinctive insignia:[4]

Canonical Law	*Nazi Measure*
Prohibition of intermarriage and of sexual intercourse between Christians and Jews, Synod of Elvira, 306	Law for the protection of German Blood and Honor, 15 September, 1935 (RGBI I, 1146)
Jews not allowed to hold public office, Synod of Clermont, 535	Law for the Re-establishment of the Professional Civil Service, 7 April 1933 (RGBI I, 175)
Jews not allowed to employ Christian servants or possess Christian slaves, 3rd Synod of Orleans, 538	Law for the Protection of German Blood and Honor, 15 September 1935 (RGBI I, 1146)
Jews not permitted to show themselves in the streets during Passion Week, 3rd Synod of Orleans, 538	Decree authorizing local authorities to bar Jews from the streets on certain days (i.e., Nazi holidays), 3 December 1938 (RGBI I, 1676)
The marking of Jewish clothes with a badge, 4th Lateran Council, 1215 Canon 68 (copied from the legislation by Caliph Omar II (636-44) who had decreed that Christians wear blue belts and Jews yellow belts)	Decree of September 1, 1941 (RGBI I, 547)
Compulsory ghettos, Synod of Breslau, 1267	Order by Heydrich, 21 September, 1939 (PS-3363)
Christians not permitted to sell or rent real estate to Jews, Synod of Ofen, 1279	Decree providing for compulsory sale of Jewish real estate, 3 December 1938 (RGBI I, 1709)

Today, it is fashionable to characterize the statements of Hitler, Rosenberg, et al. as the rantings of lunatics, but in actuality what they said concerning Jews was but an embellishment of a traditional Jewish experience. The great British Christian scholar James Parkes summarized the tragic 20th-century climax to the relationship of Jews and Christians when he wrote:

> And the old falsification of Jewish history itself persisted unto the present time in popular teaching. Scholars may know of the beauty and the profundity of the Jewish concept of life. They may know that (some) Jews were responsible for the death of Jesus. But the Christian public as a whole, the great and overwhelming majority of the hundreds of millions of nominal Christians in the world, still believe that "the Jews" killed Jesus, that they are a people rejected by God, that all the teachings of their Bible belong to the Christian church, and not to those by whom it was written, and if on this ground so carefully prepared modern anti-Semites have reared a structure of racial and economic propaganda, the final responsibility still rests with those who prepared the soil, created the deformation of the people and made these ineptitudes credible.[5]

The difference in the interpretation of biblical concepts also affected greatly the relationship between Jews and Christians. Judaism teaches that everyone in his daily actions of righteousness and mercy becomes a martyr for God. Christianity teaches that God (Jesus) became a martyr for man, and faith in Him exculpates the individual from original sin. To the Jew the ushering in of the Messiah may be more important than the coming of the Messiah. For in his attempt to accomplish the former, man perfects himself, and constantly responds to the task of being a partner to the creation. In Genesis, God ends each creation with the words "And it was good." The exception is only when man was created. The words "and it was good" were left to man himself to complete through perfect conduct and good deeds—through man's humanity to man and man's humanity to God (e.g. Kiddush Hashem—the sanctification of the name of God). In Judaism no compromise is possible when it involves theological tenets, regardless of the exigencies of time.

Judaism stresses freedom of will to choose between good and evil. This is a divine choice (Deut. 30) and man has the choice to elect what is good for him. For free will to exist, evil, too, must exist, in order to teach man the choice he should prefer. In choosing, God doesn't interfere in man's deeds. Any interference by God would make "free will" meaningless, nor would blind faith or ignorance of Jewish practices lead to a genuine choice between good and evil. Such a blind faith may even lead to "spiritual idolatry," which is anathema to Judaism.

Yet there were ambivalences in the relationship. It is also interesting to note the fact that despite unhappy experiences in Christian lands, Jews chose to settle in these lands where at least some kind of biblical tradition was honored, rather than to settle in countries where such tradition was unknown. During this period, the Judeo-Christian tradition had an opportunity to develop, and I hope that it will be clear from the following that the Jewish contribution to this tradition did not end with the Old Testament. It has been an ongoing process throughout the ages.

We must also bear in mind that not all Christians always shared this official bias of the clergy against the Jew. And in contemporary times, this unfortunate bias has been so lessened through the historic influence of Pope John XIII and present-day churchmen that it is quite obvious that strictures against the Jewish people are neither essential to the structure of the Christian religion's position, nor do they any longer impede the possibility of constructing a bridge of good will and cooperation to advance the cause of ethical education fashioned out of Jewish and Christian components.

Our spiritual values, our conceptions of justice, love, and benevolence, in public as well as in our private lives, all stem from the Judeo-Christian inheritance. And I hope that the Judeo-Christian inheritance that determines the life we are living today will also form the pattern in which life will be lived tomorrow.

The Jewish contribution to civilization comes in two parts. One from the Hebrew Bible, the Old Testament, and the other from Jewish scholarship through the Jewish communities as they settled all over the globe. Jewish thoughts and ideas as they were interpreted through generations by sages and philosophers gave new vitality to the ethical and moral teachings of the Bible.

A good example is the misinterpretation by non-Jews of the biblical reading "an eye for an eye, a tooth for a tooth." This phrase is supposedly characteristic of the biblical (Hebraic) teachings, forgetting that the talmudic lore which every Jew must follow in order to live as a Jew explains that these words were never meant in Judaism to have a literal reading or a verbal adherence to the text. The sentence actually meant monetary compensation commensurate with the injury inflicted upon the individual. Otherwise, the rabbis claimed, if one has one eye and the other two eyes, the one with the one eye, if he loses it, will be totally blind. Not so with the one who had two eyes.

There is no exaggeration in stating that every social reformer in European history took his vitality and spiritual stamina from the Jewish prophets, and even though individual laws were constantly misinterpreted, it was the Jewish sense of law that was stressed.

Unlike the ancient Greeks and Romans, the Jewish people remained a vibrant, dynamic force in the midst of Occidental Christendom.

The philosophies of Aristotle, Plato, and other Greek thinkers came to Western civilization filtered through the minds of Moslem, Jewish and Christian theologians. The seeds of these philosophers and the great Alexandrians, which had lain so long dormant and inactive, began to fructify and blossom in the Middle Ages, producing marked advances in all fields of science, mathematics, medicine and philosophy, and, to the Jewish scholars, we owe the survival of many a classic text.

Greek works were translated from Arabic into Hebrew, and many of the Greek and the Arabic versions were lost. As a rule those which were translated into Hebrew survived for Western civilization.

The Jews, dispersed among the peoples of the Orient and the Occident, were the only ones who served as an international educational bridge at a time when other nations warred. In striking contrast to an intellectually frozen world in the Middle Ages, the Jews manifested a burning zeal for education and considered it essential to their survival. A knowledge of reading and writing was a normal possession of every Jew. As a link between East and West, the Jews were excellent educational carriers for the benefit of mankind.

The best example is the famous philosopher and physician, Moses Maimonides, who lived from 1135 to 1204. He was an outstanding Talmudist, and was equally at home in Arabic and Hebrew. His major philosophical work, *The Guide for Perplexed,* translated into Latin and European languages, in which he endeavors to harmonize the philosophy of Aristotle with Judaism, strongly influenced Albertus Magnus and Thomas Aquinas. Cassaubenus writes, "He treats religiously matters of religion, philosophically all that pertains to philosophy and divinely all that is Godly." *The Guide for the Perplexed* has been translated innumerable times into Hebrew, Latin, German, Spanish and English.

Maimonides' fame extended far beyond the confines of the Moslem world where he was born and he declined an invitation from Richard the Lion Hearted to become his physician. Instead, he settled with his family in Fostat, a suburb of Cairo, Egypt, in 1165, where he was appointed physician at the court of Saladin. We know of ten medical works of Maimonides all written in Arabic. All of them have been translated into Hebrew, some into Latin and other European tongues. These have exerted great influence upon European medical science. Israeli scholars are now editing several of his works written in Judeo-Arabic. He also wrote important medical works under the title *Aphorisms According to Galen and Aphorisms of Hippocrates.* A very popular work of his during the Middle Ages concerned poisons and antidotes. These writings lose their medieval aspect for so much of them are in accord with modern practice. Maimonides was not only a philosopher and physician of distinction but was a philosopher in medicine and a physician in ethics and philosophy. The same applies to Solomon Gabirol's book, *On the Improvement of the Soul.* This book, the first Jewish philosophical treatise of magnitude, was from its very publication a tremendous influence upon Christian philosophy and theology. Numerous other books can be cited.

There were actually three main centers for Jewish activity as interpreters to Europe of Graeco-Arabic science. One was in Spain, during the period commonly known as the Golden Age of Spain. Another was in Naples under the auspices of the house of Anjou. The third was in Provence, the link between France and Spain, where local Jewish scholars translated large numbers of literary works from the Arabic and Judeo-Arabic into Hebrew. These works were frequently rendered into Latin at the request of Christian scholars.

The late Professor George Sarton of Harvard University, the renowned historian of science, claimed that the great cultures of the Moslems and the Jews in the so-called dark ages were responsible for the preservation of the great cultures of the Greeks and Romans. He, therefore, maintained that it was they who laid the foundation for modern social structures, and therefore suggested that the modern investigator or student of European civilization should learn Arabic and Hebrew, instead of Greek and Latin, in order to probe sources of what came to be known as the Renaissance and Reformation.

The influence of Jewish thinkers upon Christian scholarship was vast. Roger Bacon (1213-1294) believed, as did others in his day, that Hebrew was the medium through which God had revealed Himself and all wisdom to humanity. Bacon chided both the theologians and the laity for their ignorance of Hebrew. He distrusted the Bible in translation, for "wine is purer in the original cask than when poured from vessel to vessel." Not only was St. Thomas Aquinas immensely influenced by Maimonides, but many other theologians such as Martin Luther were affected by the teachings of the Jewish commentator Rashi and other Jewish philosophers and scholars. Indeed, the Hebrew language was an important component of the Reformation and later biblical scholarship. If the 19th-century higher criticism became, as suggested by Solomon Schechter, higher anti-Semitism, it also was a major force of renewed interest in Hebrew thought and life.

I would suggest that the concept of intellectual interchange can work to diffuse polarization and build bridges to understanding. It was Johann Reuchlin (1463-1494) who strongly urged the study of the Talmud, so nobody would have to burn it. He felt that a keen understanding of Judaism and the talmudic teachings would shed much light on Christian ideas and doctrines, as well as to explain obscure portions of the Hebrew Scriptures.

As we, in retrospect, examine the historic relationship of Jews and Christians, we can point to the positive experiences of academicians and seekers after truth who profited from mutual contact and understanding. Thus, despite the tragic past, there is yet a foundation upon which to construct a meaningful relationship. Franz Rosenzweig may have been correct in his statement that "before God, the two, Jew and Christian, are workers in God's cause. He cannot do without either." For, as

Jacques Maritain states: "Hatred of Judaism is at bottom hatred of Christianity."

We have gone a long, long way in ecumenism. Witness the reply to question II which I received in 1954 as a result of a private audience I had with His Holiness Pope Pius XII.

I.

a. What is the attitude of His Holiness toward modern Hebrew?

b. In view of the fact that the knowledge of the Bible and archaeological discoveries bearing on Biblical studies are now written in modern Hebrew, is it not important to encourage the study of spoken Hebrew in order to foster an acquaintanceship with the new research?

c. Actually, the teaching of Biblical Hebrew in the institutions of higher learning is limited to grammar only, making it a dead language. Would His Holiness favor the introduction of modern methods used in the teaching of modern Hebrew in order to encourage more students to study Biblical Hebrew?

II.

a. The present Catholic theory relative to the Jews which was inaugurated by Pope Gregory I, was a humanitarian measure to allow the Jews to survive within the framework of the Roman Empire, which did not accept non-Christian enclaves. The reason for Catholic toleration of the Jews was never fully understood through the ages. But now that a State of Israel is reconstituted, is there a possibility for the Church to re-evaluate this humanitarian approach and thus eliminate the stigma of anti-Semitism often attributed to the Church?

Answers received April, 1954.

The Holy See is not able to do otherwise than to value highly all methods of study which lead to a deeper and more genuine knowledge of the Sacred Scriptures.

Furthermore, the Secretariat of State reminds us of the Pontifical charities, especially in recent years, extended to numerous Hebrews. The Church has acted in behalf of the persecuted and has favored laws in some countries that would benefit them. As a consequence, a Representative of the United Jewish Appeal expressed gratitude to the Holy Father in an audience on February 9, 1948. On that occasion the Sovereign Pontiff pronounced the following discourse:

> "This is not the first group of your much-tried people we have been pleased to receive here at the home and heart of the Christian Family. We welcome the opportunity of your visit to tell you once more how deeply Our Paternal heart has been moved by the manifestations of gratitude for what We were able and so happy to do to lighten the burdens of your people among so many others in the dark days of the war."

"The commission which God has given Us opens Our heart to the sufferings of all His children, and more especially today are we eager to save the little ones who so sorely need a Father's protections and care and assistance. They were always so dear to the Heart of Christ."

"We gladly invoke the blessing of God Most High on all the charitable endeavors you may undertake in His name. May His grace and love help all men to purge this divinest human sentiment and duty of all that could be unworthy of its Author, and thus bring peace back soon to His great human family and Ours."

The answer by the Pope regarding anti-Semitism and Israel was a statement made by him before the State of Israel came into existence, and naturally was not germaine to the question.

However, in 1965 the Vatican Declaration not only acknowledged the Jewish roots of Christianity, and emphasized that the Virgin Mary, Jesus Himself, and his early disciples sprang from the Jewish people, but also stated that even though most Jews did not accept the gospel "God holds the Jews most dear for the sake of the Fathers . . . what happened to Christ in his Passion cannot be attributed to all Jews, without distinction, then alive, nor to the Jews of today." Furthermore, the Church "deplores hatred, persecutions, displays of anti-Semitism directed against the Jews at any time, and by any one."

B. THE HOLOCAUST

A few moments ago, I alluded to the Holocaust. I would like now to discuss the Holocaust from a Jewish standpoint, and to assess its influence on the modern development of the Judeo-Christian tradition. For the Holocaust was not a sudden phenomenon. It was the product of a kind of teaching that enabled a cruel leader to amass followers who were attuned to his preaching. Just as today the vicious utterances in the United Nations by Soviet Russia are often accepted without indignation or rebuff.

To live is one thing, to will to live is another. To live is an assignment to which we are conscripted. To actually will to live is instinct and choice. But then to will to live with a firmness of purpose, to will to live with courage, to will to live with a taste for life, even in the face of pain, frustration, and adversity, is something of a resounding vote of open-eyed confidence in the act of being, because it is an enlightened exercise of preference for life over death.

Thirty-one years from the outbreak of the Second World War it is difficult to realize the magnitude of the fear which Hitler spread over the entire world, how deep was the trepidation he planted in the hearts of the allies and how the Jewish population sank in a sea of horror and cruelty.

One is not certain who was the real hero—the soldier who marched in battle with a war song, well equipped with modern arms, or the isolated Jew living in the misery of the ghetto, but imbued with a zeal for life and with a faith in the indestructability of his people. The pious Jew who spat in the face of a Nazi, the people in the ghettos and concentration camps who, at the risk of the immediate collective death penalty, observed the Sabbath in secret, lighted the Hanukkah candles, gathered for communal prayer, organized schools for children, projected cultural programs—each one in his way expressed resistance to cruelty—each one showed a magnificent struggle to retain a spiritual, religious and educational life with hope for basic survival, even though there was no hope. For the Jewish inmate in the concentration camp, there was not merely flagrant and barbarous cruelty, starvation, exposure to freezing cold, shooting or hanging, but also murder of Jews as a day to day occurrence. This struggle to resist tyranny and to retain dignity and integrity as human beings, at a time when the conscience of the world seemed mute, evidenced the noblest expression of the will to live.

It is true that the Jews were not the only ones to be exterminated in the course of history. Many nations suffered fates like theirs, but the difference came in the nature of the struggle for survival. With the Jewish people in the Nazi concentration camps were some five million inmates, representing every European nation from Norway to Greece, from France to Russia, and regardless of how better their conditions in the camps were as compared to the Jews, life for them too was horrible and inhuman, yet there was no active rebellion or even self-defense on the part of these non-Jews. The non-Jewish population in Warsaw, in Lidice, in the Ukraine, in White Russia, or in France did not revolt. It would seem that the only people, *as civilians,* who actually revolted were the Jews.

One would be embarking on a hopeless task, writes K. Shabbetai, were he to search in history books for examples of successful revolts by a civilian minority against a majority. Open rebellion by a minority without a scintilla of hope never existed. Wherever such sporadic outbursts of minorities against majorities occurred, they were inevitably doomed to end in failure for the minorities. If some success occurred, it was merely transitory. The reason for that is that the scope of action is exceedingly limited. No defeated group, even a majority, can ever revolt, for defeat and revolt are mutually exclusive. "Defeat means the fall of the people. The victor disarms the people, robs them of power and, what is more important, the potentiality of revolting in the future. All that is left to the defeated is silent resentment. The defeated nation has no alternative except to bide its time, for time may heal its wounds, renew its spirit and infuse it with new strentgh."[6]

When Hitler invaded Poland, the best of the Polish people, intellectuals, scientists, and leading businessmen were either murdered or sent to concentration camps without the people resisting. The enemy looted their treasures, exploited their wealth, made slaves of their sons, and still they remained silent. The Polish underground government settled as a government in exile, in London, but in Poland itself there was scarcely a sign of resistance. Five long years had to pass before the Poles, in 1944, revolted in Warsaw, but even then it would not have happened without the Stalingrad defeat which was followed by the overthrow of Mussolini, by the landings in France, and by the presence of Soviet forces at the gates of Warsaw itself. Without this hope, even false ones, nothing would have happened. Revolt thus finds expression only after the period of terror has passed and a new era begun, an era of liberation and weakening of the terror.

But the Jewish people were a small, weak, impoverished minority between two powerful majorities (the local population and the invading enemy), both equally terrifying and both aiming to destroy them. One common point united the enemies, the conquerors and the conquered, the determination to wipe out the Jew completely. History cannot recall such a predicament as this, in which they found themselves as a minority in Europe, helpless, despised and ostracized, vulnerable to attack on all sides, and lacking in any potentiality for self-defense.

No foreign enemy ever heard from German lips what Jews heard constantly, "The last bullet will be for a Jew." With all the doors closed to him within, and without weapons of defense whatsoever, there was naturally no escape from German hands. In contrast to this hopeless situation of the Jews, the world saw how a Western army equipped with the best and most modern weapons in the world was facing Hitler, and yet it took six years of war, with the concentration of all forces and strategic intelligence, to finally overcome the Nazis.

The will to live in a tragic situation unparalleled in history is clearly described in my book, *Scroll of Agony*—a detailed diary by Chaim A. Kaplan.[7] Kaplan lived in Warsaw with dignity even under the indignities of the Nazis, and he wrote there a chronicle that could be called a pragmatic poem, which, while it deplored the evils about him, also cheered the existence of life and toasted the life of existence.

In the Warsaw about which Chaim Kaplan wrote from 1939 to the end of 1942, there was forced labor and starvation, there were brutal words and murders, there were insults and suicides, there were false arrests and sadistic beatings, there was fear, insecurity, and sexual depravity. Kaplan records them all honestly and grimly in his daily entries.

"In the eyes of the conquerors we are outside of the category of human beings. This is the Nazi ideology, and its followers, both common soldiers and officers, are turning it into a living reality. Their wickedness reaches the heights of human cruelty. These people must be considered psychopaths and sadists, because normal people are incapable of such abominable acts."

"The gigantic catastrophe which has descended on Polish Jewry has no parallel, even in the darkest periods of Jewish history. First in the depth of the hatred. This is not just hatred whose source is in a party platform, which was invented for political purposes. It is a hatred of emotions, whose source is some psychopathic malady. In its outword manifestations it functions as physiological hatred, which imagines the object of hatred to be unclean in body, a leper who has no place within the camp."

Kaplan was a principal in a Warsaw Hebrew school and an author of excellent textbooks, some of which are still used here in America. When the Nazis came into Warsaw in September 1939, his intellectual and spiritual commitment to Judaism neither capitulated, flagged, nor failed. Instead, he stopped his personal diary, took pen in hand and wrote down the story of his days of misery so that the record of them could be read and understood in future days. Kaplan knew without doubt that there would be a tomorrow.

And here now our today is his tomorrow. Kaplan no longer breathes, but the pulse of his passion for life still beats in the diary bequeathed to us. It was found in a kerosene can on a farm twenty miles outside of Warsaw long after the Nazi oppression had been defeated. Written in flawless Hebrew, Kaplan's diary is an imposing document, each paragraph having been composed with a sense of danger; for had the manuscripts been discovered by the German invaders, its author would undoubtedly have paid bitterly for his words. But he chanced the consequences for our sake, and though Chaim Kaplan is believed to have died in 1942 or 1943, we have the treasure of his responses to ghetto living, the war, and the Nazi hegemony. And it all boils down to an overpowering, indomitable and inimitable will to live.

Man's inhumanity to man makes even atrocities hard to describe. Kaplan writes, "If anyone in the democratic lands is attempting to write a book on the nature of Nazism, I know without seeing it that the author will not be able to express the truth of Nazism's cruelty and barbarism. Nazism has two faces. On the one hand, it is full of hypocrisy and submissiveness when it is necessary to obtain some benefit from someone; and on the other hand, it is full of brutal strength, trampling all humanism under foot, hardening its heart against the most elementary human emotions."

"Descriptive literary accounts cannot suffice to clarify and emphasize its real quality. And, moreover, no writer among the Gentiles is qualified for this task. Even a Jewish writer who lives the life of his people, who feels their disgrace and suffers their agony, cannot find a true path here. Only one who feels the taste of Nazi rule in all his '248 organs and 365 sinews'; only one who has bared his back to the lashes of its whips; only one who has examined the various nuances of its administrative and legal tactics in relation to the Jews, unequaled in hard-heartedness, sadistic cruelty, warped sensibility, petrification of human feeling, and stupidity—only such a writer, if he is a man of sensitivity, and if his pen flows, might be able to give a true description of this pathological phenomenon called Nazism. Only those afflicted with a disease of the soul are capable of being joined to a party such as this. Only one who has a defect of the soul and of the senses is able to be numbered in its ranks. It is not impossible for an entire class of human beings to suffer a mental illness, and attempt to put into practice a diseased, unclean ideology by such barbaric means as the human race has never recognized and never known, and which it would have been incapable of inventing even in the remotest Dark Ages."

In Warsaw, the urge to help others and the implementation of this urge was no less fulfilled than in better-equipped communities. In poverty, hunger and fear the Jews of the Warsaw ghetto systematically looked after each other, Kaplan tells us, and as such their self-help organization with its charitable activities and its spiritual base stands out as a high and magnificent monument to what the prophetic ideals and the rabbinic principles really mean.

What Kaplan had to say about Churchill's elevation to power and Chamberlain's resignation, about the military situation in North Africa and the significance of the other Eastern European countries is positively astounding. How a man, incarcerated in a ghetto, removed from a free press and out of touch with the great world could be able to piece the political facts together and make good sense out of them is amazing. And yet Kaplan must have gone through whatever propaganda came his way, sifted it, weighed it, and edited it, and then came to conclusions. No one without convictions about life would have bothered. Only a man with an involvement in life could have understood the issues so shrewdly. And Kaplan, like his people before him, was rich both in convictions about life and in a shrewd understanding of its complications.

The will to live was there and is beautifully expressed in Kaplan's words, "Logically we should be dead. According to the laws of nature, we ought to have been completely annihilated. How can an entire community feed itself when it has no place in life? There is no occupation, no activity which is not limited, circumscribed for us. But here again we do not conform to the laws of nature. A certain invisible power is embedded in us, and it is this secret which keeps us alive and preserves us in spite of all the laws of nature: if it is impossible to live by what is permitted, we live from what is forbidden. This secret power works wonders in us; as evidence, we don't have cases of suicide."

"This fact, that we have hardly any suicides, is worthy of special emphasis. Say what you wish, this will of ours to live in the midst of terrible calamity is the outward manifestation of a certain hidden power whose quality has not yet been examined. It is a wondrous, superlative power with which only the most established communities among our people have been blessed."

"We are left naked, but as long as this secret power is still within us we do not give up hope. And the strength of this power lies in the indigenous nature of Polish Jewry, which is rooted in our eternal tradition that commands us to live. Polish Jewry says, together with our poet laureate Chaim Nachman Bialik:

> "One spark is hidden in the stronghold of my heart,
> One little spark, but it is all mine;
> I borrowed it from no one, nor did I steal it,
> For it is of me, and within me."

This will to live was with the people throughout, because there was stamina and faith in the divine image through which man attains a certain sanctity, and so Kaplan was right when he said: "Never were we so hopeful of the final Nazi downfall as during these days, days in which our tribulations grow worse from hour to hour. The transports do not cease, and the Nazi sword rests against our throats, wreaking havoc amongst us. But we were always a nation bound by hope—and so we shall remain. Jewish faith is marvelous; it can create states of mind that have nothing to do with reality. Like the believing Jewish grandfather who in anticipation of the Messiah always wore his Sabbath clothes, so we too await him, 'and, though he tarry, I will wait daily for his coming.' "[8]

C. ISRAEL

TODAY, one cannot understand Jewish fears, or aspirations, outside the context of the Holocaust. Yet the central Jewish force of life to 1970 is the State of Israel. It is here that Jewish minds and hearts are anchored with the greatest intensity, and it is here that Jews look to the Judeo-Christian tradition as a potent force in helping to solve a critical problem.

The relationship of the Jewish people to the tiny Mediterranean coastal strip known as ERETZ YISRAEL is something of a "mystery." The Jews were the first people in the ancient world, according to Professor R. J. Zwi Werblowsky,[9] to hold to the faith in one God, a faith which, with a few exceptions, seemed incomprehensible to the other nations, a faith for which they suffered terribly. The Greeks called them a "Godless people", because they found no statues of the God in their settlements. The Romans accused them of idleness, because they did not work one day of the week and observed the Sabbath.

Twice independence was destroyed. Once in 586 B.C.E., and once in 70 C.E. But the Jews, who were exiled to Babylonia 2500 years ago, had taken an oath by the waters of Babylon: "If I forget thee O

Jerusalem, may my right hand forget its cunning; may my tongue cleave to my palate if I do not remember thee, if I do not prefer thee to my greatest joy." That oath was kept to this day. And all this took place before Paris, London, Moscow, New York, and other such cities even existed.

During their vicissitudes in many countries, a number of Jews abandoned their faith under coercion. Threatened with torture and death, many Jews were unable to withstand this threat. But on the whole, the Jews resisted, and remained steadfast to their faith, and often died for it.

History does not know of any other people that was exiled from its land and dispersed among the nations of the world to be hated, persecuted, expelled and slaughtered, that did not vanish from the earth, did not despair or assimilate (though many individual Jews did), but yearned incessantly to return to its land, believing for 2000 years in its messianic deliverance—and that indeed, in our own times did return to its homeland and renew its independence. We know, too, that no people that ever lived in "Canaan", in "The Land of Israel" (Eretz Yisrael) identified its life with the country so completely, legion though its conquerors were. This land was never the *sole* and *unique* homeland of any people in the world except the Jewish people. Remove the land from the Jews, and you have a "torso" Bible. Modern archaeology attests to this relationship.

To the Jew, whether barren or desolate, the land was always a good and beautiful land, a land with "streams and springs and lakes . . . a land whose rocks are iron and from whose hills you can mine copper . . . a land flowing with milk and honey." At all ceremonies from the day of birth to the day of his death, the words Eretz Yisrael were part of the Jewish ceremony. Wherever a Jew is buried—in the East or in the West, a handful of dust or earth from the Holy Land is laid in his grave or coffin. After all, one wants to be buried "at home."

In Jewish experience, rightly states Dr. Werblowsky, "the land actually preceded their existence as a people." For the Lord had said unto Abraham, "Get thee out of thy country, and from thy kindred, and from thy father's house, unto a land that I will show thee" (Genesis 12:1). Again when Abraham arrived in Shechem, the Lord said: "Unto thy seed will I give this land" (Genesis 12:7). And when Abraham aged, the Lord made a covenant with him and promised: "and I will give unto thee, and to thy seed after thee, the land wherein thou sojournest, all the land of Canaan, for an everlasting possession" (Genesis 17:8). Moses' task as the leader of the people was redemption from slavery, the revelation on Mt. Sinai and the restoration of the people to the land (Exodus 3:7-10). The attachment to the Promised Land which became an organic part of the faith and the notion of a "return" thus became a basic element of Jewish self-understanding and of the interpretation of their existence in the Diaspora, and this bond could never be severed!

The Jews were always saturated with a faith that in the fullness of time, God would remember His covenant with his people and remember the land. In the meantime, travelers and pilgrims throughout the ages reported with a remarkable degree of consistency the picture they had formed of the land. How one of the most fertile regions of the ancient world, a land of milk and honey, had become a waste and malaria-ridden area; and how after the Turkish conquest in the 16th Century, the desolation of the land reached its peak and in the 19th Century, when the population of the world was everywhere expanding, that of Palestine dropped to less than half a million.

The Reverend Philip Schaff in his book, *Through Bible Lands,* writes as follows: "A word about the Jews. They have four holy cities in Palestine: Jerusalem, Safed, Tiberias, and Hebron. They still look forward to the restoration of their race and country. Their number in Jerusalem is growing rapidly and amounts fully to one third of the whole population. They are divided into three sects—the Sephardim of Spanish and Portuguese origin, the Askenazim, from Germany, Hungary, Poland and Russia, and a small number of Karaites, who adhere strictly to the letter of the written law and discard the rabbinical traditions. There are no reform Jews or rationalists in Jerusalem. They are all orthodox, but mostly poor and dependent on the charity of their brethren in Europe. Many come to be buried on holy ground, and outside of the Eastern wall on the slopes of the valley of the Kedron, which are covered with tombstones. The Jewish quarter is forbidding. It ought to be burned down and built anew. The Polish Jews look dirty and shabby, and wear curls, which give them an effeminate appearance. The Hebrew language is used in Jerusalem as a conversational language, and there only. The Spanish and Portuguese Jews, whose ancestors emigrated after their expulsion from Spain under Isabella I (1497), still speak a Spanish dialect. The German, Austrian, Polish, and Russian Jews speak a corrupt German. Baron Rothschild and Sir Moses Montefiore have done much for them by building hospitals and lodging houses. They ought to buy Palestine and administer it on principles of civil and religious liberty.

"Every traveller ought to visit the 'Wailing Place of the Jews' at the foundation wall of the temple, just outside the enclosure of the mosque El Aska and near 'Robinson's Arch'. There the Jews assemble every Friday afternoon and on festivals to bewail the downfall of the holy city. I saw on Good Friday a large number, old and young, male and female, venerable rabbis with patriarchal beards and young men kissing the stone wall and watering it with their tears. They repeat from their well-worn Hebrew Bibles and Prayer books, the Lamentations of Jeremiah and suitable Psalms (the 76th and 79th)."[10]

Hence, it is understandable that the impressive achievement of the

Jewish pioneers in reclaiming the land and "making her wilderness like Eden, and her desert like the garden of the Lord" (Isaiah 51:3) should have biblical effects.

Today, Israel is no longer a pious wish "to be fulfilled on the basis of hopes, expectations and biblical promises, or in the response to acute persecution of Jews in the Diaspora. As far as the Jews are concerned, Israel exists by right of history and not by right of conquest. The conquest was incidental, forced upon Jews, although, *post factum,* its importance can hardly be over-estimated." But Israel today, though fighting for its survival, has not become a warrior state. For Israel's victory is not a mere celebration of conquest. It is a victory for world justice to enable nationhood to a people most desperately in need among an international community of 130 states. To the Jew, Israel represents the righting of age-old wrongs of unbearable misery and long humiliation and the constancy of the people's faith and hope. To deny Israel's right to live its corporate life as a nation is to deny its right to exist and its importance to contribute and share in the welfare of nations. To invite the Jews to live as Jews, and to be faithful to "Judaism" without fulfilling their existence as a people with a land, is sheer hypocrisy. All Israeli life is affected by the memories of Auschwitz and Dachau. The history of 2000 years of pogroms, massacres, slaughter, murder, and burning is deeply rooted in the minds and hearts of all citizens. Those who appeal to Israel to relinquish this claim actually invite it to relinquish its identity, and to commit corporate suicide—or to have themselves massacred once more. It is an appeal so outrageously immoral that Israel can accept it neither from its enemies nor from its "friends." For Jewish history has taught that everything horrible is possible when it relates to the Jew, regardless how incomprehensibly outrageous and horrifying the mind can invent.

At the time of Hitler's reign, the doors of the world were sealed for Jews. Not one country was gracious enough to welcome them so that they could survive with safety and dignity. (Remember the British General's remark, "What will I do with a million Jews?") The leaders and statesmen in whose hands lay the destiny of the 6,000,000 Jews and in whose hands lay the key to their deliverance closed their ears and conscience and as a result the destroyer massacred without hindrance.

For centuries Jews were singled out by bigots and despots, and mainly for one reason only—because they lacked a home, a center, roots.

Thus we see that the very genesis and formation of the State of Israel were different from all other states whose driving forces sprung from territorial elements. In Israel, the driving forces were spiritual which, in turn, engendered the material factors requisite for independent statehood. This reverse process was dictated by the reality of the peculiar Jewish world position. Were it not for a spiritual propelling force which derived its power and inspiration from the eternal quality of the Jews, it would have been impossible for the people scattered throughout the world to ingather and to achieve redemption. As a substitute for roots in the land and for earthly values which each homeland bestows tupon the children, the Jews in the Diaspora had to substitute forces of a higher order of strength and vitality. These were the spiritual forces of Israel's Torah and Jewish culture which nourished the people throughout all of their wanderings. And if in an earlier generation or generations those forces preserved in the hearts of all Jews everywhere a tie with the yearning for Zion, they crystallized in recent times into a will to action which spurred them to redemption through the return of their homeland.

The beginning of Jewish colonization and settlement in Palestine was linked not only with a passion for acquisition of land, it was rooted deeply in spiritual ideals. The people rebelled against a city life, wanted solid ground under their feet, much like any other nation, but the desire that stirred them was derived from the noblest spiritual inspiration. These dictated the paths to be followed and the forms to be adopted in the idealistic lives of the early pioneers, the Halutzim. It is difficult to conceive the heroism of those settlers unless it is realized that it had its origin in the great values which sustained Judaism through many generations and which drove these new heroes to establish a land where the spirit of Israel can again blossom and bear fruit. It is these spiritual forces and the realization that in Israel and in Israel alone can one live as a normal observing Jew that encouraged many people, even from the Western countries, to settle in Israel. The fine spirituality of Israel is therefore not a chance occurrence; it constitutes, on the contrary, a natural path of development, and the creation of the State is an expression of the greatness of Israel's culture and spirit.

The Christian thinker Pierre Von Passen wrote at the time of the emergence of the State of Israel: "In Israel there will live a prophetic people, which, no matter how small, will lift its voice in the world assembly of nations in support of justice and humanity, because over a long period of time, this people has itself been a victim of injustice and inhumanity. The history of the people of Israel is the history of mankind. The State of Israel is the laboratory of mankind, a laboratory where, the problems of society will, at least in principle, be solved with toil and sorrow, and at the same time, with joy of faith."

American students of government, sociology or international education who visit today's Israel find unlimited possibilities in studying group dynamics in Israel. The normal living as a Jew, the tremendous task of rehabilitating human beings, the emphasis on the negation of profit for all, the heterogeneous environment where cultural pluralism is a reality—all these factors offer a perfect soil for the student of human relations.

Jewry in Israel today and throughout the world was recently pre-

occupied with the basic question, "Who is a Jew?" In this connection
there is a great polemic about the mission of the State of Israel. Will
Israel be the land governed by the Halakhah (rabbinic law) or will
the legal authority be based on the foundation of civil law and juris-
prudence? But however sharp and penetrating the issue, divisive as
it is at the moment, one cannot say that any group, even one which
advocates the higher authority of civil law, sees in Israel a State
estranged from the traditional ways of Judaism. Israel will always remain a Jewish state and not merely a state of Jews.

Israel's Jewry as it is developing in large population sectors of the
State does not follow the dictates of orthodoxy as in the past, but neither
does it uproot traditional Judaism. On the contrary, the varied impres-
sions one would get in Israel regarding the observance of the Sabbath
and Holidays are indeed deeply spiritual. There one can find their
observance in all its details as dictated in the Shulhan Arukh (code)
as well as what amounts from the orthodox point of view to the pro-
fanation of the Holidays. But even those who do not observe the Sabbath and Holidays preserve the beauty of these days and give them a
spiritual character and meaning not to be found anywhere else in the
world.

All homes have fairly substantial libraries containing the choicest
Hebrew and world literature. Collections of this sort are possessed only
by select families throughout the world. In America Bibles are as a
rule found in hotel rooms but not in too many individual homes,
whereas in Israel each home has a Bible, which is used for spiritual
uplifting, as well as to understand the geography of the country. Nor
do I know of any country in which the press, essentially commercial,
engages in the spread of classical literature, national or universal, to
the same degree as in Israel. Morning and evening newspapers all
distribute Hebrew classics from the Bible, the Talmud, Maimonides,
Shulhan Arukh, and Midrashim to modern literature and encyclopedias.
The distribution of these volumes is usually in the form of prizes to
subscribers. Hebrew books are published at the rate of one a day,
originals, translations, science, research and classical works. In their
beauty, quality of printing and technical excellence, these can match the
best books published anywhere. The size of the reading public is out of
proportion to that of any other country. In Israel, the "People of the
Book," connotes not only the Jews of the past but those of today. Books
symbolize the character of the new State of Israel.

The same can be said of the country's leadership. Perhaps nowhere
else are statesmen and political leaders also the spiritual helmsmen of
the people to the extent that they are in Israel. Engaged in high political
activities in defined areas and cultures, these leaders are also the
elite of the realm of thought, science and spirit, persons of stature in
the cultural treasure house of its people.

Israel is probably the only country in the world where twice a month on Saturday evenings, in the President's home, the President of the country, a Supreme Court Justice, the Minister of Education, the secretary of the Chief Rabbinate, a President of a University, and several other university scholars convene to discuss solely the teachings of the Bible, to understand properly the true meaning of the word "Shalom."

Israel today is no longer a dream. On the contrary, Israel has proven that in a single lifetime we have passed from a world in which the existence of a free Israel seemed inconceivable into a world which seems inconceivable without its existence.

To the Jew Israel means that the flag with the Magen David is no longer a symbol of degradation or martyrdom but a symbol of creativity and glory, a symbol of joy and respectability.

To the Jew Israel means that more than two thousand years of martyrdom was not in vain and every "ani maamin," (I believe) or "Shema Israel" (Hear O Israel) uttered by a martyr was true and prophetic.

To the Jew Israel means that a Jew in America like any American has been restored to his historic address, and he is here not by sufferance, but by choice, given the opportunity to choose to live in a great democracy in the United States of America or in a new democracy—Israel.

To the Jew Israel means that the Jews, the only people in the world to belong to an ancient people whose lineage was never severed, are no longer *servants* to humanity but *contributors* to civilization.

To the Jew Israel means that the image of the Jew, degraded and vilified for centuries such as Shylock, Fagin, etc., now stands out boldly and nobly as that of a member of an old and honorable nation with an abundant, venerable culture whose contributions to the universal fund of arts and sciences have never ceased.

To the Jew Israel means that for the first time since emancipation, the majority of the Jews in the Diapora and especially in America are in a position to be exposed to their ancestral heritage in a normal way.

To the Jew Israel means that for the first time in two thousand years the Jew has a place under the sun where the term majority may also include the Jewish people.

To the Jew Israel means that in the United Nations and in the public schools and on all occasions where the Israeli flag is included, the Jew too is also *counted* on equal terms.

To the Jew Israel means that in America the Jew is not only a member of a major faith, but a member of an historic nation as well.

To the Jew Israel means that the world must now recognize the Jewish definition of "What is a Jew" rather than the one imposed upon him by his enemies and his detractors.

How beautiful it is to be a master of our own destiny, how beautiful it is to be able to stand up erect and be counted, how beautiful it is to be able to express our own thoughts and ideas in the United Nations rather than to ask and beg strangers to express our hopes and aspirations.

I visited Russia several times in the past years and I tremble when

I think what would have happened to our brethren over there without the State of Israel. There would be no Talith (Prayer Shawl), there would be no Siddur (Prayer book), there would be no book of Jewish content, there would be no hope and nobody would be able to talk to the Russian Government with the words which Moses spoke to Pharaoh a long time ago, "Shalah et ami" (Let My People Go!).

How beautiful and how meaningful it is to live in a great democracy in the United States and at the same time feel that because of Israel our culture too is represented without any need for apology. How exciting it is to feel that we, too, are represented in the exhibition of books, in the halls of learning, in the exhibition of stamps, in the jet planes, in the collection of coins, in the challenge for the spiritual enrichment of mankind. How beautiful is the feeling to watch how the State of Israel has forced the American press and publishers to take cognizance of Jewish culture and Jewish civilization. Let us not forget that more books dealing with the understanding of Judaism have appeared in the past twenty-two years than in the three centuries of Jewish life in America.

I am rather concerned at recent tendencies within some of the churches to view the Moslem guerrilla movements as legitimate agents of the third world liberation movement, as well as the activities of some churchmen in promoting the creation of a Palestinian state which would mean the political dismantlement of Israel. There are fourteen Arab sovereign states today with a population of 100,000,000 covering an area of 4,000,000 square miles and of unlimited wealth and opportunity. Israel's security certainly overrides moral imperative in the conflict.

For twenty-two years Israel has welcomed all Jewish refugees who were driven out of Yemen, Iraq, Jordan, North Africa, etc. No Western organization or country, political or civil, allowed the refugees in Europe after World War II to rot or used them as political pawns. But no Arab organization ever made an attempt to solve the problem of the Arab refugees. Shouldn't brothers be interested in relieving the misery of their next of kin? Instead, they have been used for political demagoguery!

I would hope that Christians would interpret Israel along the lines I have indicated in my remarks thus far, as a major factor in the continuity of Jewish tradition, in better understanding the Judeo-Christian heritage, and in the hope of being able to contribute to man's humanity to humanity. Too often in the past, what has been most important to Jews has been least important to Christians. Hopefully, we have reached a point in our relationship where sympathy and understanding are basic in our contacts.

D. TRADITION AND DEMOCRACY

ONE of the most significant victims of our increasingly traditionless age has been democratic political theory, and indeed, as recent events testify, practice. There is a keen relationship between Judaism and democracy. Both Judaism and democracy teach the unity of the human race. Both are motivated by moral considerations. Both aim to create, to build, to contribute, and to share. Both regard the divine character of human personality. Both command respect for the religious convictions of others, and the practice of charity toward all. Both aim toward walking humbly with God, and in modesty among men. Both emphasize the conscientious observance of the laws of the state, respect for, and obedience to the government. Both are based upon the natural right of a person to be different. Both stand for a government by the consent of the governed. Both recognize the fact that material and spiritual benefits of society belong to the whole of society; that the focal point of social processes is in the individual and not in the state. These are the things Judaism and democracy have in common.

Every democracy has been greatly influenced by the biblical and Hebraic teachings. The United States of America is an excellent illustration. The Puritans went to the Hebrew Bible for their political ideas and governmental procedure. There they found inspiration for their antagonism to the principle of "divine right of kings."

In the matter of polity, an outstanding parallel between the ideals of the Old testament and those of the American republic was drawn by an eminent clergyman, Dr. Henry M. Field, in his book, *On the Desert*. Dr. Field found in the Jewish polity much that was adopted by the Constitution of the United States. "Perhaps it does not often occur to the readers of the Old Testament that there is much likeness between the Hebrew Commonwealth and the American republic. At the bottom there is one radical principle that divides a republic from a monarchy or an aristocracy, and that is the natural equality of man ... which is fully recognized in the laws of Moses as in the Declaration of Independence. Indeed, the principle is carried further in the Hebrew Commonwealth than in ours, for there was not only equality before the laws, but the laws aimed to produce equality of condition in one point. And there is a vital one—the tenure of the land, of which even the poorest could not be deprived, so that in this respect the Hebrew Commonwealth approached more nearly to pure democracy."[11]

Samuel's abhorrence of monarchy was often the mouthpiece of the clergy in advocating the separation of the colonies from England. Jonathan Mayhew, a leading clergyman, frequently referred to as the father of civil and religious liberty in America, in a sermon delivered in Boston, May 23, 1766, on the repeal of the Stamp Act, declared: "God gave Israel a King (or absolute monarchy) in his anger, because they had not sense and virtue enough to like a free commonwealth, and to have himself for their king—where the spirit of the Lord is, there is liberty—and if any miserable people on the continent or the isles of Europe be driven in their extremity to seek a safe retreat from slavery in some far distant clime—Oh, let them find one in America."

Our present world, which is divided by two divergent camps of mistrust and hatred, if it wishes to survive, must turn to the teachings of the prophets, who maintained that in the fundamental ideas from which social justice springs, there is a clear understanding and a sympathetic appreciation of the natural rights of man who is born in the image of God, being a partner with God and not a bystander.

When the supreme occupation of the highest type of man as conceived by Aristotle, the greatest mind of Greece, is with his own personal status, when his primary concern is with the honors due him, and when such a person must be always watchful to see that the line of demarcation between him and inferior fold be ever kept clear, then *no* democratic fellowship can ever develop. Against the Aristotelian theory that the human race must be divided into two classes, free men and slaves, the Hebrew prophets taught that all are children of *one*-father.

To all this kind of thinking Jeremiah shouted:

> "Thus saith the Lord,
> Let not the wise man
> glory in his wisdom.
> Neither let the mighty man,
> glory in his might.
> Let not the rich man,
> glory in his riches.
> But let him that glorieth
> glory in this—
> That he understandeth and knoweth Me,
> That I am the Lord who exercise mercy,
> Justice and Righteousness in the earth;
> For in these things, I delight SAITH
> the Lord."
> (9:22-23)

Every individual has a right to be different, and must not be penalized for his inalienable right—and this is the essence of Democracy.

Every difference is a vibrating note of the divine symphony of life. We differ in our thoughts, appearance, actions and makeup; but we all can and must work with honest intention and effort for the common welfare of our fellow citizens whose fate we share, and upon whose cooperation our mutual success depends. Fellowship is the law of survival. Mutual assent does not mean agreement. It means that we are making an effort to remove the distrust on one hand, and acquire the feeling of the immediacy of togetherness on the other.

With all our progress, modern scientific accomplishments failed almost completely in achieving human happiness and ushering in peace to the world. It is left for the Judeo-Christian teachings to become the magnetic power which would galvanize humanity into a world of righteousness and peace, a world where every one of us is our brother's keeper.

The non-religious society has been achieving its goal with religious zeal, but the religious community has failed to concretize the prophetic teaching of morality and justice. The Biblical sentence, "Love thy neighbor as thyself," ends with the words, "I am thy Lord." The correct translation of this Hebrew sentence is "Thou shalt love thy fellow-man, for he is as thyself." Only if we make an effort to inject love in our daily life, with an appreciation of differences, does the divine attribute in us manifest itself.

From Genesis on throughout the Bible, the stress is that *man* was created in the image of God, and one statute must be for the native and the stranger. Rightly does the prophet exclaim: "Have we not all one father, hath not one God created us? Why do we deal treacherously against one another?"

With the creation of *one* man, human history began, hoping that humanity will do no evil nor deal corruptly.

The spiritual nature of man is shared by the entire offspring of Adam, the father of the human family, and not by a particular race of men. The differences must never create permanent divisions and irremovable barriers.

No genuine democracy is possible when the individual is incapable of identifying himself sympathetically with the suffering and failures of others.

Abraham challenged God's righteousness for planning to destroy Sodom and Gomorrah. "I am," he said, "but dust and ashes." But the moral urge within him added dignity to the divine image in him.

The Jewish tradition, the Christian tradition, the democratic American tradition have a common heritage. This heritage is symbolized here in Philadelphia on the Liberty Bell inscription—an inscription taken not from Greek philosophy or Shakespeare, but from Leviticus 25:10— "And ye shall proclaim liberty throughout all the land unto all the inhabitants thereof."

Similarly, the words of Micah adorn the walls of the Library of Congress—"What does the Lord require of thee, only to do justly and to love mercy and to walk humbly with thy God."

It was the same prophet Micah, who expressed in immortal words the final triumph of peace, democracy and brotherhood when tools of destruction will be converted into construction. They are music to the soul and solace to the body.

"But in the last days, it shall come to pass, that the mountain of the house of the Lord shall be established in the top of the mountains, and it shall be exalted above the hills, and people shall flow unto it."

And many nations shall come, and say, "Come, and let us go up to the mountain of the Lord, and to the house of the God of Jacob; and he will teach us of his ways, and we will walk in his paths; for the law shall go forth of Zion, and the word of the Lord from Jerusalem."

"And he shall judge among many people, and rebuke strong nations afar off: and they shall beat their swords into plowshares, and their spears into pruning hooks: nations shall not lift up a word against nation, neither shall they learn war any more! But they shall sit every man under his vine and under his fig tree: and none shall make them afraid: for the mouth of the Lord of hosts hath spoken it. For all people will walk every one in the name of his god, and we will walk in the name of the Lord our God for ever and ever."

True brotherhood will be achieved not by lip service, but by a meeting of the minds and hearts and by the realization that we are all endowed with divine rights.

Let us not forget that the fault has largely lain with our religious leaders, whether we think of Christianity or of Judaism. And it is certainly true that it lies with us who believe in God to regain our contact with the world around us, for the world will not make the first advance. May it not be said by our generation that we have shut up the Kingdom of Heaven against men, when it was our task both by our lives and our teaching, to reveal it.

If by tradition we mean the axioms which were evolved by time and experience, then even a rebellious world must accept tradition in order to survive. For a careful study will show that the traditionless world has adopted traditional nomenclature. Witness the communistic reference to Lenin—a substitute for Jehovah—"he was, he is, and he will be", or the usage of Isaiah's statement about achieving peace, used at the United Nations and in communistic countries. Russia, an atheistic country has made "atheism" a religion, ignoring the source and the postulates upon which the original theories were based.

At all times in America's history men in high positions have been open to criticism, from the press, from the people, from vocal dissenters. Based on biblical teaching, freedom of speech became a basic tenet of our democratic society.

Yet our society is in a state of turmoil, and, according to Andrew Hacker, (*The End of the American Era*) "the American character has become incapacitated for community membership." Those who compare themselves to the prophets of old do not realize that even though the criticism of the prophets was directed not only against the establishment, but also against the "average person" in the street, the methods used to criticize, and the outrageous language uttered, differed greatly.

True, the prophets resembled the dissenters of today, but differed much in the theological source and substance of the message. With the prophets, there ran the thread of *mercy* and *compassion* in the dissent—always indicating a way of deliverance from suffering. This our modern dissenters ignore: The leaders of American democracy looked for guidance in the Bible in order to develop a unique democratic system and it is my conviction that even a rebellious and violent world, if it accepts the Judeo-Christian tradition, will succeed in paving the way for a world to peace, spelling out the true meaning of "Shalom," completion in spirit and in mind, in justice and in righteousness, so that "the earth shall be full of the knowledge of the Lord as the waters cover the sea."

In conclusion, to undo a tragic wrong we need reinvigorating of the Judeo-Christian tradition and just as the two rubbed shoulders with each other for the past 1900 years so we need an approach with an eye to constructing a harmonious and mutually respectful future. I hope that Christians will see Israel as a major factor in the continuity of the ethical traditions of Judaism and the humanizing power of political tradition. I hope that Jews and Christians can work together, can understand each other in the light of truth, can respect each other's differences, and appreciate each other's similarities. I hope that the Jews and Christians of the world can continue to be a moral force in the history of mankind, and can be a more harmonious and a more idealistic union than ever. And, most of all, I hope that this is not a vain fancy, but that it is so practical a possibility that its realization will constitute the rock foundation upon which that vision of greatness inspired by God's Fatherhood and man's brotherhood, will be realized.

NOTES

[1] New York: The MacMillan Co., 1965, p. 43.

[2] *Ibid.*, p. 61.

[3] Norman Cohen, *The Pursuit of the Millenium* (New York, 1961), p. 52.

[4] pp. 5, 6.

[5] *The Conflict of the Church and the Synagogue*, p. 366.

[6] K. Shabbetai, *As Sheep to Slaughter?*, pp. 17-22.

[7] *Scroll of Agony—The Warsaw Diary of Chaim A. Kaplan*, ed., and trans. by Abraham I. Katsh, 3rd ed. (New York, 1966), p. 130.

[8] *Ibid.* p. 131-2.

[9] *Israel: The People and the Land.*

[10] Philip Schaff, *Through Bible Lands* (New York: American Tract Society), p. 250.

[11] Quoted in *Hebraic Foundation of American Democracy*, p. 47.

BIBLIOGRAPHY

Ben-Gurion, David. *Rebirth and Destiny of Israel.* New York: Philosophical Library, 1954.

Cohen, Norman. *The Pursuit of the Millenium.* New York, 1961.

Eban, Abba. *The Voice of Israel.* Horizon Press, 1969.

Eckardt, A. Roy. *Christianity and the Children of Israel.* New York: King Crown Press, 1948.

Flannery, Edward H. *The Anguish of the Jews.* New York: The MacMillan Co., 1965.

Grayzel, Solomon. *The Church and the Jews in the XIIIth Century.* New York: Herman Press, 1966.

Hay, Malcolm. *The Prejudices of Pascal.* London: Neville Spearman, 1962.

Herford, R. Travers. *Christianity in Talmud and Midrash.* London, 1903.

Hilberg, Raul. *The Destruction of the European Jews.* Chicago: Quadrangle Books, 1961.

Katsh, Abraham I. *Hebraic Foundation of American Democracy.* New York, 1952.

————. *Judaism in Islam.* New York: New York University Press, 1954.

Klausner, Joseph. *From Jesus to Paul.* New York: The MacMillan Co., 1943.

Parkes, James. *The Conflict of the Church and the Synagogue.* London: The Soncino Press, 1934.

————. *The Foundations of Judaism and Christianity.* London: Vallentine, Mitchell, 1961.

————. *The Jew as the Mediaeval Community.* London: The Soncino Press, 1938.

————. *Judaism and Christianity.* Chicago: The University of Chicago Press, 1948.

————. *Prelude to Dialogue.* New York: Schocken Books, Inc., 1969.

Pearlman, Moshe. *Ben-Gurion Looks Back.* New York: Schocken Press, 1970.

Pulzer, Peter G. J. *The Rise of Political Antisemitism in Germany and Austria.* New York: John Wiley & Sons, Inc., 1964.

Sandmil, Samuel. *The First Christian Century in Judaism and Christianity.* New York: Oxford University Press, 1969.

Schaff, Philip. *Through Bible Lands.* New York: American Tract Society, 1878.

Shabbetai, K. *As Sheep to Slaughter? The Myth of Cowardice,* Bet Dagon, Israel, 1963.

Silver, Abba Hillel. *Where Judaism Differed.* New York: The MacMillan Co., 1957.

Werblowsky, R. J. Zwi. *Israel: The People and the Land,* reprint, 1971.

Wolfson, Harry A. *The Philosophy of the Church Fathers.* Cambridge, Mass., 1956.

Zeitlin, Solomon. *Who Crucified Jesus.* New York: Harper & Row Publishers, Inc., 1947.

————. *The Rise and Fall of the Judean State.* The Jewish Publication Society of America, Philadelphia. Vol. I, 1968, Vol. II, 1969.

The Hebrew Sage and Openness to the World

Roland E. Murphy

IT is imperative at the outset that we agree in a general way on what we mean by openness to the world and why we limit ourselves to the wisdom literature of the Old Testament.

We understand openness to the world to mean an attitude begotten of *reflection* upon the wide gamut of human experience, and a *discernment* of values therein. Man finds himself continually exposed to the impact of his environment: his family, his friends and nature itself. His experience of the environment leads him to form judgments how to cope with it—judgments that also imply positive or negative evaluations. These evaluations are not always moral judgments about the ethical goodness or badness of things or actions. Lying just outside the realm of ethical decision is a whole area that contributes to the formation of man: his aesthetic reactions, his alertness to changes in nature about him, his acceptance or rejection of reality.

The preceding paragraph succeeds in spelling out in greater detail I trust, a description of "openness to the world" offered by Thomas Merton: "True Christian 'openness to the world' proceeds from a genuine respect for being and for man, and for man's natural and historical setting in the world. But to 'respect' man in his historical situation today without taking account of his need, his anguish, his limitations, and his peril, above all without consenting to share in his guilt, ends only in a cruel mockery of man."[1] Merton has chosen to emphasize the human factor in the world to which we must be open: man's anguish and peril. He is echoing here a genuine Old Testament concern, as anyone who has read the Psalms of Job or Ecclesiastes, well knows.

Taken in its general thrust, the Old Testament is more concerned

219

with the Israelite than with the *goyim*. While it is true that a genuine
universalism emerges in the Yahwist interpretation of Israel's pre-
history (cf. Gen. 1-11) and in the vision of Deutero-Isaiah (Is. 40 ff.);
the vision of faith provided by Yahwism deals primarily with the
Israelite and his role in the covenant community. For this reason we
shall evclude from our consideration the specific faith reaction of Old
Testament man to the actions of the Lord in his national history
(*Heilsgeschichte*). Instead we will concentrate on universal human
experience—the realm which is the preserve of the wisdom literature of
the Old Testament. The Hebrew sage applied himself to the created
realities that came within his daily experience. What was specifically
Yahwistic—a reflection of his covenant faith commitment—was excluded
(Sir. 44-50, the "praise of the fathers" which treats of the heroes of
the faith, and Wis. 11-19, dealing with the Exodus events, are notable
exceptions). The sage did not cease to be a Yahwist, for the Lord controlled the realities about which he pondered. But the sage formed
his reflections within a relatively narrow sphere, that of human experience. He avoided cultic questions, and the meaning of God's
action in the history of the patriarchs and the people. This does not
imply that he was without a sense of history. Even wisdom had its
history, and the sage knew himself to be locked into the development
of the wisdom doctrine. But his was a theology that looked to experience, rather than to the salvation history, for insight and direction.
Other parts of the Old Testament, such as the historical and prophetical
books, could also be used to document the insights of the sages, but
since they were particularly concerned with the saving history and the
covenant obligations of Israel, we leave them aside in our consideration.

The books with which we shall be most often dealing are: Proverbs,
Job, and Ecclesiastes, and among the so-called apocrypha, Ben Sira,
and the Wisdom of Solomon. We will also include the Song of Songs,
because this has been traditionally considered by the Church as part of
the wisdom literature, and especially because there is good reason to
think that it owes its preservation to the Israelite sages. All this literature can be generally characterized as post-exilic, i.e., written after the
return of the exiles to Jerusalem in 539 B.C. The single certain exception to this is the various collections of sayings in Proverbs, Chapters
10 ff. The generally accepted view today is that Proverbs 1-9 forms an
introduction to the collections in chapters 10 ff., which go back in large
part to the royal period, perhaps even to Solomon. While it is difficult
to date the book of Job, we can for our purpose accept a post-exilic
date. The Song of Songs may well comprise poems which are pre-
exilic in origin, but it is very likely post-exilic in its present form. There
is no question about the post-exilic origin of Ecclesiastes (4th-3rd
centuries), Ben Sira (or Ecclesiasticus, in the first half of the second
century), or the Wisdom of Solomon (written in Greek, probably in
the 1st century B.C.).

The post-exilic dating of these books should not mislead us. Wisdom is old in Israel. Most likely it has its origin in the family or tribe, since it would be quite unreasonable to assume that it began only with the monarchy under David and Solomon. As we shall see, an earlier stage of modern research, captivated by the undeniable similarity between Israelite wisdom and Egyptian wisdom, associated the wisdom movement with the Jerusalem court on the model of the Egyptian court. The professional scribes and bureaucrats of the Jerusalem court did have a large role in the development of the wisdom movement. But it would be shortsighted to eliminate other sources of wisdom in Israel. Indeed, the fact that the wisdom books are to be dated in the post-exilic period is a healthy warning against identifying wisdom simply with court teachings. For there was no monarchy after 587, when most of this literature assumed its present literary form, or was actually composed. In the case of Ecclesiastes and Ben Sira we are dealing very particularly with religious teachers who would have had their school or disciples in the post-exilic age.[2]

From this summary it is clear that the development of wisdom in the Old Testament reaches across several centuries and perdures through all the vicissitudes of Israel's life. For our purposes it is better to adopt a topical rather than a chronological treatment, and we will ask the following questions:

1. How do the sages look at nature, the created world?

2. What does the empirical wisdom of the sages suggest for openness to the world?

3. How does openness to the world fit into the theological wisdom of the sages?

Finally, we will attempt to state some conclusions.

1. HOW DO THE SAGES LOOK AT NATURE, THE CREATED WORLD?

ISRAEL came to recognize the Lord in history especially the historical actions by which he delivered Israel. Thus the deliverance of Israel in the Exodus is the pivot of what is called "salvation history." What happened was interpreted as the action of God by the prophetic leaders of the people. It is not to be denied that Israel shared this attitude with other nations which also viewed their gods as active in their history,[3] but none of them have bequeathed to posterity such a fixed view or such a unique corpus of historiography as Israel. It would be wrong to infer that the historical framework was the only one in which Israel understood the Lord. We may distinguish and even oppose the realm of history to that of nature, but the biblical attitude unites them under the sovereign dominion of Yahweh. The Lord himself lays claim to nature as well as history in the complaint that is voiced through Hosea:

> Yes, their mother has played the harlot;
>   she that conceived them has acted shamefully.
> "I will go after my lovers," she said,
>   "who give me my bread and my water,
>   my wool and my flax, my oil and my drink."
> Since she has not known
>   that it was I who gave her
>   the grain, the wine, and the oil, . . .
> Therefore I will take back my grain in its time,
>   and my wine in its season. . . . (Hos. 2:7,10-11)

Israel was not to pay homage to the nature deities of Canaan; it was the Lord, the same God who acted in history to deliver her from Egypt, who was also the dispenser of the gifts in the land promised to the forefathers. He was not to be confused with the *baalim* worshipped in the fertility rites of Canaan.

This understanding of nature is rooted in the Hebrew view of creation, presented to us in Genesis 1-2 and reflected throughout many other books (e.g., Pss. 8, 104; Is. 40 ff.). The obvious emphasis of Genesis 1 is not only that the Lord is responsible for the created world, but that world is *good*. Man's role is to "fill the earth and subdue it," to have dominion over it. This direction of thought is not to be opposed to the "historical" or *heilsgeschichtlich* orientation reflected in most of the Old Testament. But it does clearly stake out an area of interest for Israel, and it is with this area that the Israelite sages were preoccupied. As the noted Göttingen scholar, Walther Zimmerli, has remarked, "Wisdom thinks resolutely within the framework of a theology of creation."[4]

The association of wisdom and nature appears particularly in the famous characterization of Solomon as the wise man:

> Moreover, God gave Solomon wisdom and exceptional understanding and knowledge, as vast as the sand on the seashores. Solomon surpassed all the Kedemites and all the Egyptians in wisdom. He was wiser than all other men—than Ethan the Ezrahite, or Heman, Calcol and Darda, the musicians—and his fame spread throughout the neighboring nations. Solomon also uttered three thousand proverbs, and his songs numbered a thousand and five. He discussed plants, from the cedar on Lebanon to the hyssop growing out of the wall, and he spoke about beasts, birds, reptiles and fishes. Men came to hear Solomon's wisdom from all nations, sent by all the kings of the earth who had heard of his wisdom. (1 Kgs. 4:29-34; MT. 5: 9-14)

Interestingly enough, there is relatively little of this explicit nature wisdom preserved in the corpus of Old Testament literature. The most outstanding examples are in Job. 38-41, Proverbs 30:15-31, and several passages in Ben Sira and the Wisdom of Solomon. Scholars are inclined to situate this nature wisdom in the ancient Near Eastern tradition of *Listenwissenschaft* or onomastica.[5] The Sumerians made lists containing the names of animals, fish, plants, minerals, etc., which served as aids in scribal training. From this developed the *harra-hubullu* bilingual (Sumerian and Akkadian) tablets which deal with many topics: trees, wood, reeds, earthenware, leather, metals, various kinds of animals, plants, fish, birds, etc. Such lists served vocabulary purposes, and perhaps one may detect here an attempt to recognize a kind of order, a classification of related things in groups.[6] The Egyptian counterpart to the Mesopotamian lists are the onomastica, such as that of Amenemope, which lists over six hundred objects: heaven, stars, waters, earth, etc. The Old Testament itself has no such precise lists, but the enumeration of natural phenomena such as we find in Job 38, Psalm 48, and elsewhere, fits into this tradition.

More important, however, is the Old Testament attitude towards nature. Because it was created by God, the world was God's arena, in which he was directly operative. When Jacob is asked by Isaac how he found game so quickly, the answer is that God let him come upon it (Gen. 27:20). The land promised to Israel is described as "a land which the Lord, your God, looks after; his eyes are upon it continually from the beginning of the year to the end" (Dt. 11:12), and if Israel is faithful to the Lord, he will carry out his promise:

> I will give the seasonal rain to your land, the early rain and the late rain, that you may have your grain, wine and oil to gather in; and I will bring forth grass in your fields for your animals. (Dt. 11:14-15)

Any secondary causality fades away against the background of the divine cause operative in every event. In such a context one can easily understand the Israelite view of divine retribution: fidelity to the Lord brought material prosperity in the land, while infidelity brought famine, drought, and other catastrophes. We shall return to evaluate this idea of divine retribution.

It is not surprising, therefore, to find that nature is frequently the frame of reference in the experiential wisdom handed down by the sages. Human conduct could be explained and illustrated by natural phenomena:

> When the clouds are full,
> they pour out rain upon the earth.
> Whether a tree falls to the south or to the north,
> wherever it falls, there shall it lie.
> One who pays heed to the wind will not sow,
> and one who watches the clouds will never reap.
> Just as you know not how the breath of life
> fashions the human frame in the mother's womb,

So you know not the work of God
which he is accomplishing in the universe. (Eccles. 11:3-5)

Like a cool water to one faint from thirst
is good news from a far country.
Like a troubled fountain or a polluted spring
is a just man who gives way before the wicked.
Like snow in summer, or rain in harvest,
honor for a fool is out of place. (Prov. 25:24-25; 26:1)

It was natural for the Israelite to exult in the gifts of God's creation
which had been so definitively characterized as good in Genesis 1. The
biblical man evidences a beautiful poetic feeling about creation. Creation is not a once for all action—it goes on. The Lord keeps chaos,
personified in such monsters as Leviathan and Rahab, in check (Pss.
74:14; 89:11). His breath in living things accounts for their con-
tinuance (Ps. 104:29-30). Israel was thus basically oriented towards
acceptance of this world, its joys and blessings, which spoke to her of
God. It is here, free from any Gnostic or Jansenistic taint, that the
Bible provides a fundamental insight into openness to the world.

The sensitivity of the sage to the mysteries pervading this world is
illustrated by the reflections upon the "smallest" things on earth which
are yet "exceedingly wise";

Ants—a species not strong,
yet they store up their food in the summer;
Rock-badgers—a species not mighty,
yet they make their home in the crags;
Locusts—they have no king,
yet they migrate all in array;
Lizards—you can catch them with your hands,
yet they find their way into kings' palaces. (Prov. 30:25-28)

The famous numerical proverb in Proverbs 30:18-19 portrays wonderment as well as a desire to penetrate mystery:

Three things are too wonderful for me,
yes, four I cannot understand:
The way of an eagle in the air,
the way of a serpent upon a rock,
The way of a ship on the high seas,
and the way of a man with a maiden.

There is no unanimity as to the precise meaning of the saying. Most
would agree that the sage enumerates mysteries in nature in order to
illustrate the mystery which forms the climax. The form is the well
known numerical proverb: x and x plus 1, with the final item carrying
the emphasis. But is the "way" (*derek*), repeated in each case, a
significant repetition or not? If it receives due emphasis, then the point

is not merely that the eagle defies gravity, but that the path of his flight is not recoverable—and similarly for the other examples. Then in the final case there is wonderment not merely at the mystery of sexual attraction, but at the whole sequence of events (no longer recoverable) which issue in the union of a man and a woman.[7]

We have already noted Thomas Merton's emphasis on "taking account of his (man's) need, his anguish, his limitations, and his peril, above all . . . consenting to share in his guilt." It is particularly in the book of Job (as well as the Psalms) that these factors in human existence receive expression:

> Is not man's life on earth a drudgery?
>   Are not his days those of a hireling?
> He is a slave who longs for the shade,
>   a hireling who waits for his wages.
> So I have been assigned months of misery,
>   and troubled nights have been told off for me. . . .
> My days are swifter than a weaver's shuttle;
>   they come to an end without hope.
> Remember that my life is like the wind;
>   I shall not see happiness again . . . .
> As a cloud dissolves and vanishes,
>   so he who goes down to the nether world shall come up no more.
>   (Job 7:1-9)

And there is the magnificent parody of Psalm 8, which underscores the weakness of the human condition:

> What is man, that you make much of him,
>   or pay him any heed?
> You observe him with each new day
>   and try him at every moment! . . .
> Though I have sinned, what can I do to you,
>   O watcher of men?
> Why have you set me up as an object of attack;
>   or why should I be a burden to you?
> Why do you not pardon my offense,
>   or take away my guilt? (Job 7:17-21)

It is true that the sages made a sharp distinction between the wise man and the fool, between the just man and the wicked. But they remained sensitive to the struggle that is intrinsic to every man:

> A great anxiety has God allotted,
>   and a heavy yoke to the sons of men;
> From the day one leaves his mother's womb
>   to the day he returns to the mother of all the living,
> His thoughts, the fear in his heart,
>   and his troubled foreboding till the day he dies— . . .

are of wrath and envy, trouble and dread,
terror of death, fury and strife. (Sir. 40:1-5)

2. WHAT DOES THE EMPIRICAL WISDOM OF THE SAGES SUGGEST FOR OPENNESS TO THE WORLD?

WHEN one speaks of ancient Near Eastern wisdom, it is primarily empirical or experiential wisdom—considerations about human conduct—that is meant. Here, in the practical order, one can perhaps best appreciate the biblical openness to the world. How is one to act vis-à-vis the different types of men? How does one cope with the varied situations that life presents? As we have already said, these questions do not, of themselves, always involve moral judgments. There is also a grey area of human conduct not explicitly covered by moralizing: what is to be one's attitude to work, to silence, to friends? It is this world of experiential wisdom that emerges most often in Old Testament wisdom literature.

The wisdom sayings are usually associated with the Jerusalem court. The precedent for this was indicated already in the style of the Egyptian wisdom literature—the "teachings" which a prime minister or a king would prescribe for his student. Similar emphasis appears: praise of diligence, self-control, proper kind of friends, etc. When Israel adopted the kingship "like other nations" (1 Sam. 8:5), she imitated the bureaucracy of Egypt, and the training of courtiers became necessary. The example of the Egyptian wisdom teachings was so strong that most scholars agree there is clear evidence of the wisdom of Amenemope in Proverbs 22-24. It is no surprise, therefore, to find several "king" proverbs (Prov. 16:10-15; 25:2-7). On the other hand, several sayings scattered throughout the historical books suggest that Israelite wisdom has a much broader base than the sayings cultivated at the court. One can point to what is usually called popular or folk wisdom —such proverbs as "from the wicked comes forth wickedness" (1 Sam. 24:14); "a man's strength is like the man" (Jgs. 8:21). Hence one is prompted to ask what are the origins of the wisdom movement in Israel.

J.-P. Audet was the first to suggest that both law and wisdom ultimately are to be traced back to family customs and tribal practices.[8] Neither law nor wisdom is a strictly literary phenomenon; both have their origins in the sociology of a group. Such works as the Wisdom of Ahikar and the book of Tobit (Tob. 4:1-19) demonstrate how wisdom was transmitted within the family; observations concerning life, lessons of experience, were handed down from father to son. The counsels and commands relative to life's varied situations were preserved in the family structure before they became differentiated into the laws that developed within the larger framework of societal development, and into the wisdom that was cultivated in the schools. This common origin of wisdom and law has an important bearing on Old Testament theology and therefore on openness to the world.

These humble origins of the wisdom teaching have been confirmed in recent scholarly studies which underscore the "tribal" wisdom crystallized in the admonitions of the Torah itself as well as in such passages as Proverbs 22-24. This common base also tells us something about Israel's attitude to the world. Wisdom did not come from heaven; it is the people's view of how a man should act in the society of his fellows, the virtues (honesty, diligence, etc.) he should practice and the vices he should avoid, the societal values that were to be honored. Such values were begotten of human experience and the prevailing mores of the tribe. They constituted the daily life style which came to be accepted within the social unit. They were subject to the change wrought by Yahweh's encounter with the Lord, who made certain demands upon his people. But revelation did not replace Israel's orientation to all the values that had taken root among the people. The thrust of wisdom, reflected among the lawgivers and the sages, remained.

The important theological implication here is that our modern distinction between profane and sacred law breaks down when it is applied to the biblical material. It has been customary to characterize the apodictic laws of the covenant as sacred (especially because they were proclaimed in the celebration of the covenant feast) and the wisdom tradition as profane (especially because it is empirical and rational). Basically the roots of Israelite law and wisdom are identical, and the identification of Wisdom with Law by Ben Sira (Sir. 24) is an insight that is probably more brilliant than he realized. It is true that the Sinai revelation became the pivot about which Israel's laws were clustered. The all-embracing dominion of the Lord swept them into his imperious claim upon Israel's fidelity. But they did not thereby change from being profane to sacred. They were as they always were: the experiental insights of the tribe, testing the world in which it lived. This has an obvious bearing on our topic, "openness to the world." If much of the societal practices of Israel eventually became the "holy law," we must then recognize that God is also active in and through the daily lives and experiences of people. The attitudes and values that are formed within the heart of a people need not be opposed to a Sinai revelation.

The *purpose* of a proverbial saying is different from the question of its *origins*. What is the saying trying to achieve—or better, what is the sage reacting to when he forms a proverb? The collection and preservation of the sayings suggest that they have a didactic purpose. But one can postulate an even more primary intent: the saying itself is an effort to impose a certain basic order in the chaos of experience. Gerhard von Rad has described this aspect of empirical wisdom: "Empirical and gnomic wisdom starts from the unyielding presupposition that there is a hidden order in things and events—only, it has to be discerned in them, with great patience and at the cost of all kinds of painful experience. And this order is kindly and righteous ... Wisdom thus consisted in knowing that at the bottom of things an order is at work, silently and often in a scarcely noticeable way, making for a balance of events. One has, however, to be able to wait for it, and also to be capable of seeing it. In such wisdom is something of the humble—it grows through having an eye for what is given, particularly through having an eye for man's limitations. It always prefers facts to theories."[9] Therefore, the wisdom saying is an insight into a range of experience, from which it draws a steady generalization. If one observes the frequency with which proud persons are discomfited, one can control this experience with the tag: "Pride goes before a fall" (Prov. 16:18; 18:12). A certain regularity in events and in their circumstances can be translated into a pungent saying. While the regularity may strike us now as a commonplace, the original discovery must have been exciting: What is the permanence of goods hastily acquired?

> Possessions gained hastily at the outset
> will in the end not be blessed. (Prov. 20:21)

Is an argument really as strong as it first appears?

> The man who pleads his case first seems to be in the right,
> then his opponent comes and puts him to the test. (Prov. 18:17)

How is one to interpret an ambiguous silence?

> He who spares his words is truly wise,
> and he who is chary of speech is a man of intelligence.

> Even a fool, if he keeps silent, is considered wise;
> if he closes his lips, intelligent. (Prov. 17:27-28)

However, one should beware of exaggerating the world order which the sage is concerned with. Not all proverbs, particularly those preserved for us in the Old Testament, are to be explained in the light of this mentality. There is nothing rigid about empirical observations, as von Rad himself notes; one has to be open to whatever occurs. The Israelite view is not to be equated with the Egyptian view of *maat*, or world order.[10] In the Egyptian wisdom literature, *maat* (translated as "justice," "truth," etc.) is a key concept, for it represents the divine order to which man's ethical conduct should correspond. It is cosmological in that it is the world condition as established by the creative act of God. It is ethical in that one lives according to *maat*, aligning conduct with world reality; thus one establishes *maat* in the world. Although some characteristics of *maat* (e.g., association with life) appear in the biblical description of wisdom, there is no justification for transferring the Egyptian experience of reality to Israel.

It must be confessed that many of the sages overshot the mark. They laid out their conclusions too patly, and in so doing were unfaithful to the care and sensitivity supposedly intrinsic to the wisdom ideal: the right word at the right time. Overcome, as it were, by their own didactic purpose, they tended to freeze the "teaching." As the sages developed their understanding of divine retribution, they became complacent. Perhaps this result was inevitable. Any gnomic conclusion relative to God, world, and man needs a balancing corrective. Eventually the author of Job and also Ecclesiastes supplied a corrective to the sages' one-sided view of divine retribution.

By retribution we understand the blessing or reward that attaches to wise conduct, and the misfortune or punishment that folly encounters. How did the Israelite conceive of the relationship between action and result? The interpretation offered by Klaus Koch, with the support of G. von Rad, has won many supporters. He places human acts in a "fate-producing" context. A human act contains within itself, as the seed does its fruit, a good (or evil) effect. An act infallibly tends to good or bad effect in harmony with its own quality. Hence one is not to conceive of the Lord intervening to punish or to reward; rather, this result is intrinsic to the act. A wicked deed necessarily results in doom; God merely watches over the deed as a kind of mid-wife. This mentality seems to lie behind such statements as:

> A kindly man benefits himself,
>   but a merciless man harms himself. (Prov. 11:17)

> He who digs a pit falls into it;;
>   and a stone comes back upon him who rolls it. (Prov. 26:27)

> He who conceived iniquity and was pregnant with mischief,
>   brings forth failure.
> He has opened a hole, he has dug it deep,
>   but he falls into the pit which he has made.
> His mischief shall recoil upon his own head;
>   upon the crown of his head his violence shall rebound.
>   (Ps. 7:15-17)

However, the biblical emphasis on the *reaction* of God to man's conduct (cf., e.g., Dt. 4:3-4; 5:9-11) does not leave room for the hypothetical reconstruction advanced by Koch. The biblical description of reward and punishment is anthropomorphic to be sure, but it is the only way of asserting God's personal involvement in man's responsible action. And for the Israelite, nothing could escape the all-pervasive causality of God. In this view, however, it was also easy to fall into a rigid understanding of divine activity. The Lord *must* reward the good and punish the evil. Such is the basic attitude reflected frequently in Proverbs and Ben Sira, as well as in the classical example of Psalm 37:

> The Lord watches over the lives of the wholehearted;
>> their inheritance lasts forever.
> They are not put to shame in an evil time;
>> in days of famine they have plenty.
> But the wicked perish,
>> and the enemies of the Lord, like the beauty of meadows,
>> vanish; like smoke they vanish. (Ps. 37:18-20)

Some sages showed an awareness of the mystery of God's dealing with men:

> The discipline of the Lord, my son, disdain not;
>> spurn not his reproof;
> For whom the Lord loves he reproves,
>> and he chastises the son he favors. (Prov. 3:11-12)

But the logical outcome of this mechanical view is the blindness typical of Job's Three Friends, who are forced by their own narrow understanding to accuse Job of wrongdoing. Only thus can they defend the justice of God, and their defense in effect puts God in a bind, restricting the divine sovereignty and freedom.

In the light of this fixation on divine retribution, we can appreciate the vision provided for us in Job and Ecclesiastes. Both of these works attack the traditional wisdom doctrine. The author of Job can find no assurance against life's adversity; he knows that the traditional guarantee of prosperity for the just does not work out in life. He can do nothing but acknowledge God as his Master and finally yield himself to the Almighty who appears to him (Job 42:5). But how deeply attached to life he is, we learn from the words of Job himself:

> Oh, that I were as in the months past!
>> as in the days when God watched over me,
> While his lamp shone above my head,
>> and by his light I walked through darkness;
> As I was in my flourishing days,
>> when God sheltered my tent;
> When the Almighty was yet with me,
>> and my children were round about me;
> When my footsteps were bathed in milk,
>> and the rock flowed with streams of oil. (Job 29:2-6)

Ecclesiastes recognized that "the sinner does evil a hundred times and survives" (Eccl. 8:12). The worst thing is that "things turn out the same for all" (9:3). And along with this he urges man to accept any pleasure in life, for this is a gift of God: "to eat and drink and enjoy the fruit of all his labor is a gift of God" (3:13).

We must recognize that these two voices in the Old Testament speak for the mystery of God, for his freedom in his dealings with mankind. The Lord of the Old Testament was not one to be painted into a corner by the persistent formulations of the sages. He had to have an ample margin of freedom to act, as one of Israel's earliest traditions (the "testing" of Abraham, Gen. 22) inculcated. In the development of the movement, Ecclesiastes and the author of Job struck a blow for divine freedom, and in such a way that man should learn not to over-interpret the world and its goods against the mystery of divine Providence.

We have described empirical wisdom as being open to whatever occurs. There is a curious ambivalence in the sage's judgment of what "appears to be." On the one hand he will warn against the villain who "winks his eyes, shuffles his feet, makes signs with his fingers" (Prov. 6:12). External appearances should be a guide to human reflection:

> He who winks his eye is plotting trickery;
>> he who compresses his lips has mischief ready. (Prov. 16:30; cf.
>> Sir. 27:22)

On the other hand, the truly wise man will not let himself be deceived by appearances:

> Sometimes a way seems right to a man,
>> but the end of it leads to death!
>
> Even in laughter the heart may be sad,
>> and the end of joy may be sorrow. (Prov. 14:12-13)

The point is clear: the sage looks hard at the reality that is offered to him.

What did he expect from reality? Life—in all its aspects. That is why wisdom is described as a tree of life (Prov. 3:18; cf. 11:30) or a fountain of life (Prov. 13:14; 14:27):

> My son, forget not my teaching,
>> keep in mind my commands;
> For many days, and years of life,
>> and peace, will they bring you ... (Prov. 3:1-2)
>
> Long life is in her right hand,
>> in her are riches and honor;
> Her ways are pleasant ways,
>> and all her paths are peace. (Prov. 3:16-17)
>
> With me are riches and honor,
>> enduring wealth and prosperity.
> My fruit is better than gold, yes, than pure gold,
>> and my revenue than choice silver. (Prov. 8:18-19)
>
> The reward of humility and fear of the Lord
>> is riches, honor and life. (Prov. 22:4)

On the other hand, folly has only death and calamity to offer:

> The man who strays from the way of good sense
>   will abide in the assembly of the shades. (Prov. 21:16)

The polarity of life and death is sharpened by the fact that there was
no *real* life after death: "there will be no work, nor reason, nor knowledge, nor wisdom in the nether world where you are going" (Eccl.
9:10). Clearly the emphasis on the earthly values is heightened by the
bleak prospect awaiting a person in Sheol (cf. e.g., Sir 14:11-16).
This point of view was shared by Mesopotamian and Israelite alike, as
can be seen in the following comparison between the advice given by
Ecclesiastes and the admonition given to Gilgamesh:

> Go, eat your bread with joy and drink your wine with a merry heart,
> because it is now that God favors your works. At all times let your
> garments be white, and spare not the perfume for your head. Enjoy
> life with the wife whom you love, all the days of the fleeting life
> that is granted you under the sun. This is your lot in life, for the
> toil of your labors under the sun. (Eccl. 9:7-9)

> Gilgamesh, whither rovest thou?
> The life thou pursuest thou shalt not find.
> When the gods created mankind.
> Death for mankind they set aside,
> Life in their own hands retaining.
> Thou, Gilgamesh, let full be thy belly.
> Make thou merry by day and by night.
> Of each day make thou a feast of rejoicing.
> Day and night dance thou and play!
> Let thy garments be sparkling fresh,
> Thy head be washed; bathe thou in water.
> Pay heed to the little one that holds on to thy hand,
> Let thy spouse delight in thy bosom!
> For this is the task of mankind! (*ANET* 90)

There are positive accents here: life is to be seized and lived. Although
Ecclesiastes several times characterizes life as a vanity of vanities and
a chase after wind, he recognizes that God may *give* man some
pleasures:

> Therefore I commend mirth because there is nothing good for man
> under the sun except eating and drinking and mirth; For this is the
> accompaniment of his toil during the limited days of the life which
> God gives him under the sun. (Eccl. 8:15)

The acceptance of life and its activities may be conditioned, but by no
means cancelled, by the absence of any personal eschatology. Thus the
recommendation of Qoheleth can even appear in St. Paul:

Anything you can turn your hand to, do with what power you
have ... (Eccl. 9:10a)

Whatever you are doing, whether you speak or act, do everything
in the name of the Lord Jesus ... (Col. 3:17a)

Paul's motivation is, of course, the eschatological motivation—what God
has done in Christ. Lacking this eschatological thrust, Qoheleth settled
for what God had done in the here and now:

However many years a man may live, let him, as he enjoys them all,
remember that the days of darkness will be many. All that is to come
is vanity.

Rejoice, O young man, while you are young
    and let your heart be glad in the days of your youth.
Follow the ways of your heart,
    the vision of your eyes ... (Eccl. 11:8-9d)

The recommendation of Qoheleth to "enjoy life with the wife whom
you love" is further concretized in the teaching of the sages on marriage and in the Song of Songs. The preoccupation of the sages with
adultery is striking. The introductory chapters of Proverbs (5-7)
discuss it at length, and Chapter 7 contains an episode told by the
sage as a warning to youth. We can best understand this emphasis from
the nature of the wisdom literature, which, as it was collected, was
directed primarily to young men. But the frequency of this topic, even
as late as Ben Sira (e.g., Sir 9:3-9; 23:22-26; 25:9-12) is somewhat
inexplicable. It may be said that the personification of wisdom as a
woman (Prov. 1, 8, 9), and therefore as a woman to be courted and
sought after (Wis. 7:1-14; 8:2-16), created the possibility of under-
scoring infidelity. And perhaps the unhappy history of sacred pros-
titution in Israel is another reason why this admonition could have
become a regular topos in the wisdom literature.

The Israelite attitude to sex is to be seen in a larger context than
these frequent warnings. It is surely significant that Israel, settled in
the midst of the sacral sexual culture of Canaan, reacted so strongly
against the fertility rites, yet at the same time turned to the marriage
union, human love, in order to express the covenant relationship. This
was a narrow line to tread, but the marriage imagery is expressed with
great beauty and theological depth in the Prophets (Hos. 2; Is. 1:21;
62:1-5; Jer. 2:1-2, 20-24, 32; 3:1-5; Ez. 16 & 23). This fact alone
shows that sex could be evaluated very positively, and hence the characteristic warnings of the sages in this area have to be put in context.
It also remains true that elsewhere in the Old Testament sex and marriage are viewed primarily in terms of fertility (e.g., Ps. 128:3),

and even in the wisdom literature women are judged from a male
viewpoint. A good wife is a gift from the Lord (Prov. 12:4; 18:22;
19:14; Sira 26:1-4). The description of the ideal wife in Proverbs 31
is motivated by the fact that she provides for the needs of her husband
and children. Here the relatively servile position of women in
the ancient Near East is reflected.

There is all the more reason, therefore, to hear the tones of mutual
love that are sounded in the Song of Songs. Many scholars believe that
the preservation of the Canticle is due to the sages. After all, it expressed the great value which they tried to inculcate: fidelity. The very
language of the Canticle is reflected in the advice given in Proverbs
5:15-19:

> And have joy of the wife of your youth,
>   your lovely hind, your graceful doe.
> Her love will invigorate you always,
>   through her love you will flourish continually.

Here we are introduced to an aspect of male-female relationship seldom
made explicit in the Old Testament. The tenderness of the language
in the Song of Songs illuminates another side of marriage; the mu-
tuality of sexual love in the Canticle balances the man-centered thrust
in the wisdom literature:

> I am a flower of Sharon,
>   a lily of the valley.
> As a lily among thorns,
>   so is my beloved among women.
> As an apple tree among the trees of the woods,
>   so is my lover among men. (2:1-3)

There is also a frank joyous acceptance of sexual pleasure which is a
happy corrective to a Jansenistic and false asceticism:

> Now let your breasts be like clusters of the vine
>   and the fragrance of your breath like apples,
> And your mouth like an excellent wine—
>   that flows smoothly for my lover,
>   spreading over the lips and the teeth.
> I belong to my lover
>   and for me he yearns.
> Come, my lover, let us go forth to the fields
>   and spend the night among the villages.
> Let us go early to the vineyards, and see
>   if the vines are in bloom,
> If the buds have opened,
>   if the pomegranates have blossomed;
> There will I give you my love. (7:9-13)

3. HOW DOES OPENNESS TO THE WORLD FIT INTO THE THEOLOGICAL WISDOM OF THE SAGES?

OUR consideration of the wisdom of the sages would be incomplete were we to neglect the "theologizing" of wisdom. We wish to sketch the development and the meaning of the radical change which took place toward the end of the Old Testament period (cf. Prov. 1-9, Sirach, Wisdom of Solomon), when wisdom departed from court for the school. Four directions of this development will be noted here: wisdom as "fear of the Lord," as the Law, as "divine," and as means of revelation. These aspects, it will be seen, develop rather than negate our theme. Wisdom teaching becomes more explicitly religious, but the openness to the world remains.

"Fear of the Lord" in early Old Testament literature suggests a reverence for the numinous, and it expresses the loyalty of the God-fearer within the covenant context.[11] But it comes to be appropriated by the wisdom literature: Fear of the Lord is described as the "beginning" or "chief part" of wisdom (Prov. 1:7; 9:10; cf. Ps. 111:10; Sir. 1:14, 16, 18; 19:20; 21:11). It is practically identified with "knowledge" (Prov. 1:29; 2:5; cf.19:10; 30:3) in the concrete sense of action, and it is generally associated with such terms as wisdom and understanding. The moralizing aspect of fear of the Lord is due surely in part to the moral values implicit in the wisdom instructions. Integrity, diligence, avoidance of evil—such values came to be seen as characteristic of the men who reverenced Yahweh. The growing emphasis on the Law contributed to this development.[12] In Deuteronomy (4:7), Israel's observance of the laws is viewed as giving evidence of her "wisdom and intelligence" to the nations who witness it.

Observance of the Law embraced all man's activities, and hence Wisdom and Law are identified in Sirach:

> He who fears the Lord will do this;
>   he who is practiced in the Law will come to wisdom. (15:1)

> He who hates the Law is without wisdom
>   and is tossed about like a boat in a storm. (44:2)

The most striking text is Sirach 24:22, where after describing the divine origins of personified wisdom, who claims to have "struck root among the glorious people" (24:12), Sirach remarks:

> All this is true of the book of the Most High's covenant,
>   the Law which Moses commanded us
>   as an inheritance for the community of Jacob.

And at the end of the wisdom poem in Baruch, the same identification takes place:

> Since then she [wisdom] has appeared on earth,
>   and moved among men.
> She is the book of the precepts of God,
>   the Law that endures forever;
> All who cling to her will live,
>   but those will die who forsake her. (Bar. 3:38-4:1-2)

This description of wisdom serves to introduce the third direction taken in late wisdom literature: the divine origins ascribed to her in the famous personifications (Prov. 8; Sir. 24). It is a remarkable fact that not until late in the Old Testament is God consistently thought of as wise. True, he "gives" wisdom, and Solomon is described as having received it as an answer to his prayer (1 Kgs. 3:4-14; Wis. 6:22-9:18). Isaiah described the Lord as "wise" in the sense of being able to outwit and punish the Israelites who fail to rely upon him (Is. 31:2), and the psalmist recognized that he could be astute and outfox the crooked (Ps. 18:27). But this anthropomorphism is not frequent. The Lord is seldom directly described as wise; it is almost as if wisdom was too much identified as a human trait to be applied to him.

Human failure—man's recognition of his inability to acquire wisdom —seems to have promoted the association of wisdom with the Lord. Ecclesiastes admits this: "I said, 'I will acquire wisdom'; but it was beyond me. What exists is far-reaching; it is deep, very deep: who can find it out?" (7:23-24). Several of the proverbs recognize that wisdom cannot prevail against the Lord:

> There is no wisdom, no understanding,
>   no counsel, against the Lord.

> The horse is equipped for the day of battle,
>   but victory is the Lord's.

> In his mind a man plans his course,
>   but the Lord directs his steps. (Prov. 21:30-31; 16:9)

The magnificent poem in Job 28 points out there is a place for all things—silver in mines, iron in the earth—except for wisdom. Wisdom cannot be purchased, it cannot be found:

> The abyss declares, "It is not in me";
>   and the sea says, "I have it not."
> Abaddon and Death say,
>   "Only by rumor have we heard of it." (Job 28:14,22)

Man cannot attain to wisdom because it is with God alone:

> God knows the way to it;
>   it is he who is familiar with its place.

> For he beholds the ends of the earth
>> and sees all that is under the heavens . . .
> Then he saw wisdom and appraised it,
>> gave it its setting, knew it through and through. (Job 28:23-24,27)

Wisdom is therefore inaccessible because it is with God (cf. Baruch 3:15, 23-36). This association with God leads to the expression of its role in creation:

> The Lord by wisdom founded the earth,
>> established the heavens by understanding;
> By his knowledge the depths break open,
>> and the clouds drop down dew (Prov. 3:19-20)

Jeremiah (10:12) describes the Lord as

> He who made the earth by his power,
>> established the world by his wisdom,
>> and stretched out the heavens by his skill.

The most explicit witness to wisdom's relationship to the Lord is the personification of wisdom in Proverbs 8 (cf. Sir. 24):

> The Lord begot me, the firstborn of his ways,
>> the forerunner of his prodigies of long ago;
> From of old I was poured forth,
>> at the first, before the earth.
> When there were no depths I was brought forth,
>> when there were no fountains or springs of water;
> Before the mountains were settled into place,
>> before the hills, I was brought forth;
> While as yet the earth and the fields were not made,
>> nor the first clods of the world.
> When he established the heavens I was there.
>> when he marked out the vault over the face of the deep;
> When he made firm the skies above,
>> when he fixed fast the foundations of the earth;
> When he set for the sea its limit,
>> so that the waters should not transgress his command;
> Then was I beside him as his craftsman,
>> and I was his delight day by day,
> Playing before him all the while,
>> playing on the surface of his earth
>> (and I found delight in the sons of men). (Prov. 8:22-31)

Christian tradition has exploited this in the direction of Trinitarian theology; but this exaggeration should be avoided as eisegesis. The sages intended no distinction in the Godhead. The passage from Sirach (24), quoted previously, shows the orientation of their thought. What was the supreme communication which God made of himself? The

revelation of his will in the Law. Hence the conclusion could be
drawn by Sirach that this wisdom was told to dwell in Israel and was
described as resting in Jerusalem (Sir. 24:8-11). Whatever the origin
of the idea of wisdom's divine origins, the idea itself is turned to the
glory of the Law. Sirach, whose wisdom teachings go far beyond the
Law in their explicit recommendations, described himself as a rivulet
from the great stream of wisdom or Law (24:28-29). He was not
aware of doing anything more than inculcating the Law by his teaching.

The final point—wisdom as an agent of revelation—is closely related
to what we have just said about the divine origin of wisdom. Wisdom
now emerges as a means of divine revelation, speaking with the authority of the Lord, calling for acceptance and obedience under the
threat of death (Prov. 1-8). This contrasts with the old style wisdom,
which relied upon the tradition of the sages handed down from generation to generation, and which looked to human experience for verifica-
tion. As G. von Rad remarks, "Nevertheless, one can say that she
[wisdom] is the form in which Yahweh's will and his association with
man (in other words, salvation) comes to him. She is the essence of
what man needs for a good life, and of what God gives him. But most
importantly, wisdom does not present herself to man as a thing, or
a teaching, or guidance or salvation, etc., but as a person, an "I" who
calls. Hence wisdom is really the form in which Yahweh makes himself
present and in which he wants to be sought after by man. 'He who finds
me finds life' (Prov. 8:35). Only Yahweh can speak this way."[13]
The old advisory tone of the sages has yielded to the insistent claim
of personified Wisdom that claims authority from the Lord and reveals
his will—the Law, the teaching of the sages.

The "theologizing" of wisdom appears to be the fruit of the theological reflection to which the several trends just described made their
contribution. Wisdom now assumed a bolder tone, a prophetic stance,
and challenged man to listen to her, to love her beyond all things.
She could guarantee life and full prosperity. But in no instance was
the typical emphasis on the values of this life lessened. Although there
is a break-through in the Wisdom of Solomon (Wisdom, or justice,
is seen to be a title to immortality, Wis. 1:15), this eschatological thrust
was not allowed to dim the realities of this world. Indeed, Wisdom is
the teacher of Pseudo-Solomon:

> Cycles of years, positions of the stars,
>   natures of animals, tempers of beasts,
> Powers of the winds and thoughts of men,
>   uses of plants and virtues of roots—
> Such things as are secret I learned, and such as are plain;
>   Wisdom, the artificer of all, taught me. (Wis. 7:19-22)
>
> And if prudence renders service,
>   who in the world is a better craftsman than she?

Or if one loves justice,
  the fruits of her works are virtues;
For she teaches moderation and prudence,
  justice and fortitude,
  and nothing in life is more useful for men than these.
Or again, if one yearns for copious learning,
  she knows the things of old, and infers those yet to come.
She understands the turns of phrases and the solutions of riddles;
  signs and wonders she knows in advance
  and the outcome of times and ages. (Wis. 8:6-8)

The Book of Wisdom strikes an admirable balance between the values of this world and those of the next.

4. CONCLUSIONS

1. This analysis of the Old Testament wisdom literature has indicated that Israel was essentially open to the world because all things were good, created by the Lord, and man himself had received the commission to rule the earth. The sages of Israel developed—lived out, so to speak—this basic datum. The point is not to canonize certain views of the sages as absolutes, transcending time and space, and determining our conduct in the twentieth century. My purpose is more modest: Is the biblical *attitude* to the world and its values relevant to us? I think it is. One inevitable objection is that the Old Testament follows a time-table different from our own, that is, its basic orientation is to this world, and not to the next.   But is this really an objection? Doesn't it rather suggest that Christian preoccupation with the next world has to be re-examined? The Israelite, for all his preoccupation with *this* world, never lost sight of God. Essential to his world view is the possession of God in this life; "the fear of the Lord is the beginning of wisdom." He may have been tempted, as human beings are, to throw it all over when he failed to understand God's action in the world. So the author of Psalm 73 "almost slipped" when he was confronted with the contradictions of human existence. But he had a vision of faith to sustain him:

Yet with you I shall always be;
  you have hold of my right hand;
With your counsel you guide me,
  and in the end you will receive me in glory.
Whom else have I in heaven?
  and when I am with you the earth delights me not.
Though my flesh and my heart waste away,
  God is the rock of my heart and my portion forever. . . .
But for me, to be near God is my good,
  to make the Lord God my refuge. (Ps. 73:23-28)

The vision of Deuteronomy is one of life and death, and man is invited to choose life, because it is here to the midst of creating things, that he experiences God (Dt. 30:15-20). Event if the Lord gave little evidence of working out traditional sanctions of good and evil, Qoheleth did not fail to glimpse that there was always the divine gift of life to reckon with, the "portion" that God gave to man.

The antithesis between the Old and New Testament eschatology is not to be absolutized. Paul himself was called upon to relativize the eschatological absolute of the Christian message in I Corinthians 7. He conceded that the Corinthians had a right to marry, even though the parousia was imminent, and even though he himself preferred that they not marry. The message of Luke is likewise a relativization; the Lucan theology provides a vision of the way Christian life is to be in view of the delay of the parousia. Church structure (Acts) and reflection upon the meaning of Christian life in the secular world (Gospel) emerge. The history of the early Church displays a gradual accommodation to the practical demands of this world. Church history shows also how unevenly Christian thought has evaluated the goods of this world. There has always been the danger of the so-called "spiritual" or "supernatural" snuffing out "material" and "natural." This merely highlights the inevitable tension in human evistence. A truly Christian experience keeps the two worlds in correct balance, and the Old Testament emphases are very helpful in this respect.

2. What claim does the Old Testament evaluation of the world exert upon the Christian? We have to admit that the biblical message is time-conditioned. But we cannot, as it were, peel off these external trappings in order to reach an alleged "essence." Neither can we exalt biblical mentality over any other kind of mentality. The Christian takes the position that the biblical record of God's revelation of himself to Israel does convey a normative message. The Christian must hear the word of God that is the Old Testament, but the hearing is not indiscriminate. The Christian is absorbing the word through the filter of New Testament values, and also through the experience of man (Christian and non-Christian).

Those who read the Bible in the twentieth century do not read it in a vacuum; they read it against the background of the interpretation and discriminating evaluation made over past centuries. The history of exegesis is a valuable guide which the current preoccupation with historico-critical methods tends to neglect.[14] I do not mean we should turn the clock back and forsake these methods which have given us such better understanding of the historical meaning of the ancient texts. One cannot escape the duty of capturing the precise message of the biblical text, against which current values are to be measured. Nonetheless, we can learn much from the earlier exegetical traditions which attempted to interpret the Scriptures within the Church, and to give an answer to the question: What *does* the text mean (and not merely an antiquarian question: What *did* the text mean?). The very mistakes and excesses in the earlier exegetical patterns are a help in our appropriation of the text to our present needs. What is time-conditioned was not always successfully filtered out in the process (one thinks of the "holy war" obsession that is justified by some from the pages of the Old Testament). Such mistakes are inevitable in the experience of man; Christian understanding must constantly undergo a process of purification.

In this process, one looks not only to the Bible. We must take into account the revolution in human understanding and knowledge that has taken place over the last two centuries. The insights of psychology and philosophy and history provide new vantage points from which to interpret the Bible. Man raises new questions (slavery, revolution), and the Bible can speak to these issues. We must trust as well as test this new situation if we are to grow. Israel herself kept re-interpreting the sacred traditions throughout her long history. We would be wise to emulate her. In this context we propose that the wisdom literature provides insight into human attitudes to the world. We must listen to these and be inspired by them.

3. This essay can perhaps best terminate by entering into dialogue with two positions represented in current theology by Walter Brueggemann[15] and Karl Rahner.[16]

Brueggemann's purpose is to re-affirm the relevance of biblical wisdom literature. Modern biblical theology has tended to restrict itself to certain key themes and even to certain books within the canon, in such a fashion that a "canon within the canon" is established. Thus, one portion of the Bible is made the cutting edge of theological ideas, to the neglect of other biblical witness.[17] There is no reason to deny that some parts of the Bible are more "important" (although much here depends upon one's vantage point) than others. But we cannot afford to neglect the many options which the Scriptures offer—options that have been well expressed by Brueggemann: "the *trust* motif of creation, the *responsibility* motif of wisdom, the *joy* motif of Deuteronomy, the *affirmation* motif of the Pauline letters, the *humanity* motif of the Gospels." He goes on to point out that the wisdom perspective is not in conflict with the salvation theology which the Bible underscores: "Grace means not only help for the sick and depraved. It means the full affirmation of our life in all its forms and parts. It means we are delighted in and not resented. We are trusted but not abandoned. It means we have great expectations placed on us and God does not give up on us. Graciousness is not condescending paternalism but a healthy affirmation of our worth and importance."[18] He urges us to break out of the "salvation-history-prophetic-creedal stance" and recognize another style of biblical faith—the wisdom tradition—which serves as a critique or corrective of the normative theology that is so specifically Yahwistic or Christian. Surely the recognition of wisdom theology as creation theology provides the basis for the glorious affirmation that life is good, and to be enjoyed. So Sirach thought:

> So from the first I took my stand,
>   and wrote down as my theme:
> The works of God are all of them good;
>   every need when it comes he fills.
> No cause then to say: "This is not as good as that";
>   for each shows its worth at the proper time.
> So now with full joy of heart proclaim
>   and bless the name of the Holy One. (Sir. 39:32-35)

Karl Rahner's theology is particularly pertinent to our consideration of Old Testament wisdom. We have stressed that for the most part there is nothing specifically Yahwistic in this wisdom; there is nothing of typical "creedal" style. We did not bother to document the similarities between Israelite wisdom and that of the ancient Near East, but such documentation could easily be supplied. The tendency of theologians has been to downplay what Israel thus had in common with other peoples. The nod is given to the salvation-history theology as against wisdom theology, and a canon within the canon is created with the result that no serious consideration is given to wisdom, which becomes an embarrassment in biblical theology. If I understand Rahner correctly, he has put the question on an entirely new level, while he also preserves the integrity and the supernatural and inspired character of the wisdom literature.

Rahner argues: "Salvation-history and profane history are distinct because God has interpreted a particular part of this profane and otherwise ambiguous history by his word (which is a constitutive element of salvation-history itself), by giving it a saving or damning character."[19] There is a general salvation- and revelation-history, distinct from the salvation history recorded in the Bible. In it, man is in contact with God on the level of a faith response. This is not to be opposed to biblical salvation history, which is constituted by God's interpretative word. While Rahner does not take up the specific nature of the wisdom movement within the people of Israel, his theology provides a proper locus for understanding the wisdom literature as salvific —and not only the wisdom literature of Israel, but of other peoples as well, in so far as they are caught up in this general salvation- and revelation-history. In his view, we can better understand and evaluate the sage's struggling with creation, human experience, and proper conduct. Essentially this is salvific because it participates in the *de facto* supernatural order of faith in which all men find themselves. We have seen that wisdom developed in its own way in Israel, with particular Israelite emphases. But its origins, like the origins of the wisdom of its neighbors, is already a response to the God who communicates himself to man.

NOTES

[1] T. Merton, *Conjectures of a Guilty Bystander* (New York: Doubleday, 1966) 202-03; cf. also 183-184 where Merton comments on a passage from Bonhoeffer's *Ethics*. Bonhoeffer writes: "Eating and drinking do not merely serve the purpose of keeping the body in good health but they afford natural joy in bodily living. Clothing is not intended merely as a means for covering the body but also as an adornment for the body. Recreation is not designed solely to increase repose and enjoyment. Play is of its nature remote from all subordination to purpose.... Sex is not only the means of reproduction, but independently of this, it brings its own joy, in married life, in the love of two human beings for one another. From all this it emerges that the meaning of bodily life never lies solely in its subordination to its final purpose. *The life of the body assumes its full significance only with the fulfilment of its inherent claim to joy."* On this Merton comments: "This is genuine Christian humanism, and Catholic, too, when understood in its context (his [Bonhoeffer's] doctrine of the earthly life as 'penultimate,' deriving its dignity, seriousness, and meaning from its ordination to the ultimate coming of Christ). This is a 'Christian worldliness' with which I thoroughly agree.... Note, he [Bonhoeffer] bases this on quotes from *Ecclesiastes* (2:24; 3:12; 9:7 ff, 11:9; 2:25), often thought to be pessimistic. *Ecclesiastes* is critical of enthusiasms and facile idealisms, not of true wisdom based in the realities of life as God has made it."

[2] The pertinent literature supporting this position can be conveniently summarized by reference to O. Eissfeldt, *The Old Testament. An Introduction* (New York: Harper and Row, 1965), and to R. E. Murphy, "The Wisdom Literature of the Old Testament," in *The Human Reality of Sacred Scripture* (Concilium 10; New York: Paulist Press, 1965) 126-140, and "Assumptions and Problems in Old Testament Wisdom Research," *Catholic Biblical Quarterly* 29 (1967) 101-12 [407-18].

[3] Cf. B. Albrektson, *History and the Gods* (Lund: Gleerup, 1967).

[4] See "The Place and Limit of the Wisdom in the Framework of the Old Testament Theology," *Scottish Journal of Theology* 17 (1964) 145-58, esp. 148.

[5] Cf. A. Alt, "Die Weisheit Salomos," *Theologische Literaturzeitung* 76 (1951) 139-44.

[6] A. Leo Oppenheim, *Ancient Mesopotamia* (University of Chicago Press, 1964) 244-48; he registers his doubt about "such a quasi-mythological concept as *Ordnungswille*" (248).

[7] For details, see R. E. Murphy, "The Interpretation of Old Testament Wisdom Literature," *Interpretation* 23 (1969) 289-301.

[8] "Origines comparées de la double tradition de la loi et de la sagesse dans la proche-orient ancien," *International Congress of Orientalists* (25th) (Moscow, 1960) I, 352-357.

[9] *Old Testament Theology* (New York: Harper and Row, 1962) I, 421, 428.

[10] The conclusions of both H. Gese and H. H. Schmid seem to go too far in this respect. Cf. Gese, *Lehre und Wirklichkeit in der alten Weisheit* (Tubingen: Mohr/Siebeck, 1958); Schmid, *Wesen und Geschichte der Weisheit* (BZAW 101; Berlin: Töpelmann, 1966) 156, 159, 181.

[11] Cf. J. Becker, *Gottesfurcht in Alten Testament* (Rome: Biblical Institute, 1965).

[12] Cf. M. Noth, *The Laws in the Pentateuch and Other Essays* (London: Oliver & Boyd, 1966) 1-107.

[13] *Old Testament Theology* I, 444.

[14] Brevard S. Childs, *Biblical Theology in Crisis* (Philadelphia: Westminster Press, 1970) 139-147.

[15] "Scripture and an Ecumenical Life-Style. A Study in Wisdom Theology," *Interpretation* 24 (1970) 3-19.

[16] See especially the essays on salvation history and non-Christian religions in *Theological Investigations V* (Baltimore: Helicon, 1966) 97-134, and "Observations on the Concept of Revelation," in K. Rahner and J. Ratzinger, *Revelation and Tradition* (Quaestiones Disputatae 17; New York: Herder & Herder, 1966) 9-25.

[17] This position has been advocated strongly for the New Testament by E. Käsemann, "The Canon of the New Testament and the Unity of the Church," *Essays on New Testament Themes* (London: SCM, 1964). London: SCM, 1964). It can be illustrated, for the Old Testament, by G. E. Wright, *The Old Testament and Theology* (New York: Harper & Row, 1969) 166-185.

[18] The quotations in the text are taken from the article of Brueggemann (see note 15 above), pp. 17-18.

[19] *Theological Investigations V*, 106. See also p. 104: "...this supernatural elevation of man which is granted by God's universal saving purpose already has of itself the nature of a revelation.... It follows then that there is a history of salvation, revelation and faith which co-exists with the general profane history. We have called (this) the general salvation—and revelation-history."

Christians as a Minority in a World Community

Joseph H. Fichter

L AST winter I flew to the Holy Land and visited the sacred spots
to which millions of other people—Jews, Christians and Moslems
—had gone over the centuries. As the plane hovered over the Mediterranean coast I meditated about the fact that the cradle of Christianity,
the land where Christ lived and taught and died, had long since ceased
to be a Christian country. I recalled that Israel and Egypt, the Near
East and Asia Minor, had once seen flourishing churches and dioceses
and had had a population in which the majority followed the teachings
of the Saviour. Later, as I visited the cities and towns of Israel, I
saw clearly and everywhere that Christians are a minority among the
people of the country where their religion originated.

FAILURE OF MISSION

T HE relative disappearance of Christianity from the Holy Land and
the Middle East generally may be attributed to many factors like
military invasions, political turmoil, large migrations of people, as well
as religious conversions. There are other parts of the world where
Christianity never penetrated, or where it barely set down its roots
and then failed to grow. Added to this is the observation by some that
the large traditional Christian nations of the West are no longer Christian. Quite aside from the plethora of books about secularization and
the decline of religion in general,[1] there is the oft-quoted remark of
Arnold Toynbee, who said that Western civilization has now become a
"post-Christian or ex-Christian civilization."[2]

Let us try to keep a balanced perspective in the rapidly changing
world of religion. The Marxist, secular, and "scientific" predictions
on the decline and death of religion have been disproved. The great

religions—like Hinduism, Buddhism and Islam—have grown and not declined. "There has been no capitulation; and ready assumptions of their disintegration, for example in the nineteen-twenties, have miscarried."[3] The confident remark of Christopher Dawson was already out of date when he said "if Christianity were just one among the other world religions, then it too would fail and fade as they are doing."[4] What seems closer to the truth is an invigorated religious competition by the Eastern religions accompanied by a proportionate decline in Christianity.

Hans Küng deals with this problem from a doctrinal point of view focusing on the axiom, *extra ecclesiam nulla salus,* but he also employs available demographic data.[5] He says that if the human race is more than six hundred thousand years old, why did Christ come so late and how did salvation reach the untold millions who never knew anything about Christ. Even now only about one-third of the total world population can be called Christian. For the future, the comparative annual birth rates and population growth indicate that Christians will constitute a decreasing proportional minority. In other words, Christianity always was, is now, and always will be a minority religion.

Are we to take it then that universal evangelization, the spread of the Gospel message to all mankind, is a colossal and historical failure? Was it from the beginning a "mission impossible?" Should we say rather that two thousand years is just a short span of time and that in the long-ranging providence of God we are only at the dawn of Christian world civilization? Obviously, we have no empirical evidence that can provide satisfactory answers to such questions, but the matter is of such grave importance that we are forced to probe the data and speculate on the probabilities.

We should not be called simple and unsophisticated if we believe that Christianity was intended to be a universal religion, that the message of divine Incarnation was to spread throughout the world, that the redemptive sacrifice of Christ on the cross was for the benefit of all human beings. I leave it to the scripture scholars to explain what Jesus meant by the promise of one fold and one shepherd, and what he meant when he said there are "others who are not of this fold."[6] The ordinary reader of the Bible thinks that this was a prediction of an ultimate world-embracing religion of Christianity.

Lest we make our problem too complex we had better talk about Christianity in its broadest definition rather than about the Roman Catholic Church. This sidesteps the problem that professors of dogmatic theology may have with the *Unam Sanctam* of Boniface VIII, which in November, 1302, declared that "there is one holy Catholic and apostolic Church, outside of which there is neither salvation nor remission of sins."[7] There was also the more recent *Syllabus of Errors* published by Pope Pius IX (1846-1878) which said it was erroneous to hope for the eternal salvation of people who are not members of the true Church of Christ.[8]

Even more recently the Fathers of the Second Vatican Council declared that "it is through Christ's Catholic Church alone, which is the all-embracing means of salvation, that the fullness of the means of salvation can be obtained."[9] In another document, however, hope of salvation is held out to those who do not know Christ and His Church. "Those also can attain to everlasting salvation who through no fault of their own do not know the Gospel of Christ or His Church, yet sincerely seek God and, moved by grace, strive by their deeds to do His will as it is known to them through the dictates of conscience."[10] We need not delay on this sticky doctrinal point which now seems at last to have been satisfactorily solved.

From an intentional point of view there can be no doubt that the universal mission of organized Christianity has been a relative failure. The true believer still holds that the intention of the Incarnation was universal salvation through Christ's redemptive grace. The immediate disciples of Christ seemed to understand well this divine intention. Christianity from the beginning, as Fustel de Coulanges remarked, "was not the domestic religion of any family, the national religion of any city, or of any race. It belonged neither to a caste nor to a corporation. From its first appearance it called to itself the whole human race."[11]

The embarrassing fact, embarrassing for literalists and fundamentalists—if not for expert theologians and scripturalists—is that something went wrong in this universal missionizing effort. One must be careful to distinguish between the original intentional ideology of Christianity and the historical and contemporary efforts to implement that ideology. One dare not suggest that two thousand years are not enough time in which to Christianize the world, or that the Providence of God is somehow at fault in this failure. Given these considerations in the present context of Christianity in the world there is wide room for the speculations of social scientists and demographers. It is from this point of view that I should like to discuss the minority status of Christians in the modern world.

RELIGION IS CULTURE-BOUND

ONE of the unavoidable verities about religion is that it becomes institutionalized in the culture where it exists. This is not peculiar to religion, but must be said also of the familial, educational, political and economic institutions. In sociological terms, a cultural system is the sum of its institutions, which in turn are made up of the shared, repetitive behavior patterns of the people. Institutionalized religion cannot escape culture because it is a constituent of the cultural system. This means that Christianity, like any other world religion, is always culture-bound, but it does not mean that it has to be bound to only one cultural form or system.

If Christianity then is to be universal it must also be flexible enough to be institutionalized differently in a variety of cultures. This is similar to the concept of the organized Church, as explained by the Fathers of the Second Vatican Council. The Church which is "sent to all people of every time and place, is not bound exclusively and indissolubly to any race or nation, nor to any particular way of life or any customary pattern of living, ancient or recent. Faithful to her own tradition and at the same time conscious of her universal mission, she can enter into communion with various cultural modes, to her own enrichment and theirs too."[12]

The fact that Christianity presents itself in a variety of cultural forms is abundantly apparent when we look at the cultural pluralism of Catholicism itself. Even within the United States, how else can one explain the differences in religious attitudes and behavior among Catholics of Italian, Polish, German and Irish background? Unless one makes unscientific racial or biological assumptions about human behavior, how else can one understand the diversities (and even conflicts) in the last century between American Catholics of German and Irish descent?[13]

It is generally agreed that American Catholicism has been fashioned more by Irish influence than by any of the many other religio-cultural influences that came with European immigration. By sheer weight of numbers of Irish people in the Catholic population, and of Irish clergy and bishops, religious Sisters and Brothers, this cultural predominance was to be expected. We need make no value judgment, of either boast or blame, concerning this historical development (although there are those who seem to feel that "Irishness" is at the root of most American Catholic problems).[14] The point of these remarks is simply to underline the sociological fact that Catholicism, like any other organized religion, is significantly affected by the socio-cultural system in which it exists.

The typical Catholic tourist from the United States visits Mexico and finds Catholic religious customs "strange." He is assured by the tour guide that these people really are "Roman" Catholics but he still feels that they do not act like Catholics. He would probably agree with the remark of Raymond Panikkar: "It is obvious that the same religion that has undergone different cultural, historical, temporal and spatial experience, takes on completely different forms, which from the point of view of an outsider may be interpreted as completely different religions."[15]

It is this cultural coloration that people see when they note that the religious behavior of British Catholics differs so greatly from that of Italian Catholics. Both England and Italy, however, are within the larger framework of European Christian civilization. Can one say that all cultures are receptive to Christianity, or are some cultures clearly hostile, or at least alien to the Christian religion? It is suggested, for example, that the religion and culture of India are so inseparably interwoven that "assimilation of the Indian culture means at the same time assimilation of Hindu religion,"[16] yet one-third of the population of the State of Kerala in India is Christian.

To use another example, one may suggest that the Christian religion cannot adapt to the Communist culture, but this conclusion probably emerges from a misunderstanding of the definition of culture. Certainly, Christian religious practices have existed alongside totalitarian political institutions, rigid educational institutions and non-capitalistic economic institutions. The fuzziness in the analysis of the relation between Communism and Christianity comes from a failure to distinguish between a cultural system and a social structure.

What we are talking about here is the flexibility of cultural forms and not about the cooperation, indifference, or antagonism of the organized political structure against either the organized religious structure or the cultural religious institution. The failure of Christianity to adapt itself to the cultures of India, China and Japan exemplifies the point I am trying to make here, and not any antagonism against Christianity on the part of the social authorities of India, China and Japan.

RELIGION IS CULTURE-ADAPTIVE

LET us clarify this distinction by looking again at modern Israel where religion is both culturally and structurally tied into the total system. Here we see a repetition of the "Church-State" problem that has plagued so many Western countries. "Obviously the present relation is unsatisfactory," says Mordecai Kaplan. "Religion cannot be free to develop, as long as the leaders of an entrenched Orthodox minority exercise exclusive authority over a large area of civil law and religious practice for the entire population."[17] Objections to the current arrangement in Israel are raised also from an extremely Orthodox group called the "Neturei Karta," who label Zionism nothing more than "Gentile nationalism." They argue that the Jews, having been exiled by Divine Providence must lovingly accept their sentence and "should not seek to enter *Eretz Yisroel* in a body before the predestined time."[18]

Both the non-Orthodox Jew who wants the separation of Church and State, and the deeply Orthodox Jew who opposes Zionism, seem to be making the same argument but from different points of view. Judaism as a religion should not be identified with a place and a government. The eternal spiritual message of Judaism is universally adaptive and transcends any particular cultural system and social organization. What bolsters their argument is the historical fact that without a homeland for almost two millenia, the Jews continued to exist religiously in a variety of cultures. One can appreciate both the nostalgic "homesickness" of the Jew in the diaspora and the tremendous pride of the Jew who is now building the State of Israel, but at the same time one can appreciate the practical desire to keep the Jewish religion from becoming nationalized.

From the point of view of cultural assimilation, what is happening in Israel in bringing together religious Jews from different ethnic backgrounds is analogous to the American Catholic experience in bringing together immigrant Catholics from various national backgrounds. The intention in Israel is to develop a distinctive national culture within which religion is a supportive and integrative institution. If this is the case, then to be a Jew means to be an Israel, and vice versa, whereas in the United States one cannot say that to be a Catholic means to be an American. Furthermore, there is still a large Jewish diaspora in which a religious Jew can be culturally French, American, British, or whatever. Alfred Lilienthal makes this point when he says that "Jews are individuals who profess Judaism," some of whom may be Israelis and some may be Zionist, but to be a Jew does not necessarily mean to be also an Israeli and a Zionist.[19]

It appears that the more historical a religion is—like Judaism, Christianity and Islam—the more likely is it to be culturally adaptive. These three are called the "western religions" by Christopher Dawson, but there is no reason to believe that the "eastern religions," Hinduism and Buddhism, are not also essentially and potentially culturally adaptive. One does indeed note a growing interest among westerners in these eastern religions and an increasing willingness on the part of their representatives to make contact—as well as converts—among Europeans and Americans.[20]

The historical, and frustrating, evidence that Christianity need not be imbedded in European civilization, and that this religion is adaptve to other cultures, was in the work of the Jesuit missionaries to China and India in the sixteenth and seventeenth centuries. What they did was to "purge our Christianity of its Western accessories," and this is what Toynbee says is the first thing we must do in our approach to the non-Christian religions.[21]

The Jesuits realized they were in the presence of a high and ancient Chinese civilization, for which they developed great respect. They not only adapted the Christian liturgy, celebrating Mass in Chinese instead of Latin, but also interpreted architecture, music, philosophy and theology in accord with the Chinese culture. Malcolm May judges that China, "with an ethical tradition four thousand years old, with a unity of spirit both national and continental, was ready at the end of the sixteenth century, to absorb Christianity."[22] Although these innovations were officially approved by Pope Paul V in 1615, they were rescinded by Pope Benedict XIV in 1742, and all missionaries were ordered to take an oath against Chinese rites.[23]

This brilliant anthropological approach, and the controversy that accompanied it, are now only historical monuments to an ethno-centric European Christianity. We need not recount the complicated story of its suppression, but we may well ask whether even at this late and enlightened date the principle of cultural adaptation of religion has been accepted. To be sure, Africans and Asiatics have been raised to the episcopacy, and emphasis placed on the training of native seminarians and statements made about entering into "communion with various cultural modes."

In spite of all this, the decree of Vatican II on the *Missionary Activity of the Church* is very cautious about creative adaptation and initiative, and still stresses the importance of jurisdiction and organization and supervision. In commenting on this decree, Eugene Smith remarks that "the missionary call of every Christian—inescapable in his faith and baptism—is rightly stressed. The participation of the laity in mission, however, is to be channeled by the hierarchy. Fulfillment of the missionary obligation which the Christian discovers in Christ demands opportunity for individual creative initiative and experimentation which the hierarchical controls assumed in this document seem severely to restrict."[24]

WESTERN DOMINANCE

THE uneven distribution of Christians in the world's population of today, as well as the large cleavages within Christianity, may be largely attributed to non-doctrinal and non-theological factors. The so-called Great Schism between East and West in 1204 was surrounded by important cultural competition and power struggles. The rejection of papal authority by Henry VIII and the subsequent autonomy of the English Church from the mother Church cannot be fully explained unless we recognize the contemporary political, military and economic rivalry between the English and the Spaniards. One need not belabor this point by discussing all the "national" churches that sprang up in the wake of the Reformation and the subsequent sectarianism that still constitutes what H. R. Niebuhr called the "scandal" of Christian disunity.[25]

Aside from these internal dislocations, there is the broad historical fact that Christianity has been predominantly Europeanized. This was the case with the Roman empire especially at and after the time of Constantine's Edict of Milan (A.D. 313). From then on it appears that wherever European civilization penetrated it brought Christianity along with it. The ecclesiastically inspired Crusades of the eleventh century attempted to "restore" the true religion to the Holy Land by making use of the military, economic and political resources of Christian Europe. Centuries later, the explorers and colonizers out of Europe brought their culture-bound religion to the New World of North and South America.

It was a European religion they disseminated, and this seems to be a large reason why Christianity was never really Africanized, nor took root in China and India. Can we fault the organized *ecclesia* for not penetrating the East, for not reaching the untold millions, for historically binding itself almost exclusively to Western civilization? Was it a mistake to localize and Europeanize the Christian religion? Obviously, religion is institutionalized in every culture, but does this mean that religion has to be organizationally tied in with particular forms of political, economic and other social structures?

We see it now as a mistake that religion was identified with a national system, or for that matter with an imperial system of government and society. The mistake of Christianity was not that it became an organized *ecclesia* but that this organization tied itself in with exclusively Western forms. It was natural then, and a historical accident, that the tremendous power and influence of the Western world carried along with it the influence of Christianity. One need not be disloyal to the message and intent of Christ if he says that Christianity spread less on its own merits than on the force of Western civilization.

The cross and the flag went with empire and conquest and colonization, whether the empire was Spanish or Portuguese, French or British, even though there were often bitter disagreements between bearers of the cross and bearers of the flag. As Kenneth Cragg remarks, "Their relation has been more complex and ambiguous than western assumption or non-western accusation has generally recognized. Yet that they were broadly parallel is not in doubt. European commercial expansion provided the occasions of Christian mobility and imperial authority, in its turn, utilized, or shielded, or answered missionary imagination. 'Their gain,' Drake had said of the penetrated lands even in the sixteenth century, 'shall be the knowledge of our faith, and ours such riches as their country hath.' The priest and preacher could not long exclude the merchant, even when they had preceded him."[26]

Bishop Cragg's remarks may well be applied to the missionary experiments among the Paraguay Indians in the seventeenth century. An adaptive culture and society were there established under Christian auspices with the direct intention of protecting the Indians from exploitation. The Paraguay Reductions ultimately succumbed to economic greed, governmental neglect and military power. It was another in a list of failures to demonstrate the socio-cultural flexibility of Christianity which could have flourished outside Western and European dominance.[27]

Bringing the good news of Christianity to all the "new" lands implied a kind of Christian optimism that westerners could bring enlightenment to the heathen darkness everywhere, and thus "raise" even ancient civilizations to our own bright level. This was an illusion, as Abrecht says, "the product of both political and theological errors.

The political miscalculation was to assume that these countries would remain for years under the control of Western 'Christian' governments which would provide the umbrella for the Christianizing process. The theological mistake was to identify Christianity and a particular civilization. Today the umbrella of Christian culture has unexpectedly folded."[28]

Must the theological error persist even after we have recognized the political error? The collapse of empire, the birth of new nations in Africa and the re-birth of independence in India and China, as well as the establishment of the United Nations—all of these have meant a realignment of power relations throughout the world. In a sense, out of the re-shuffling of the last half century the United States has emerged at a position of enormous power, wealth and influence. In spite of the "bad image" as the new economic imperialist and exploiter, and as the military blunderer in Southeast Asia, the United States, by its sheer technological success plays a predominant role in the modern world. This technology is what the rest of the world wants; we like to think that they should want our concept of personal freedom and civil rights.[29]

Even this kind of remark indicates a certain prideful optimism that we of the Christian West are accustomed to display. We have so much that the rest of the world wants. This pride extends sometimes to the conviction that we, and only we, possess the true religion. Arnold Toynbee has suggested that contemporary Christianity ought to show some repentance for its presumed monopoly of God's grace. In commenting on this point, Hocking declares that "what has chiefly stood in the way of the message of the Nazarene in the Orient has been less the political and economic tempers of imperialism, than a certain lack of contrition on the part of many of its messengers. For Christianity is not something we *have,* and can therefore transmit: it is something we have continually to seek, knowing that it is forever beyond us."[30]

Repentance and contrition imply a willingness to make reparation, but basic to all this is the repudiation of ethnocentrism, especially the kind that has set up an idolatrous self-image of Western Christianity. "We are always relapsing from the worship of God into the worship of our tribe or of ourselves; and therefore we Christians, whether we are Western Christians or Eastern Christians, tend to treat Christianity as if it were the tribal religion of our particular civilization. In the West we tend to treat it as something that is inseparable from the West, and even as something that derives its virtue not so much from being Christian as from being Western."[31]

THE WORLD AND THE WEST

THERE is no question that perceptive thinkers have changed this ethnocentric attitude, or have had change forced upon them by the realities of the modern world. With the growth of instant communication we have come to learn more about the global situation than ever before. With the knowledge that more than one nation now possesses an accumulation of destructive power that can devastate the whole world, we begin now to question even our capacity to survive. There are indeed hopeful people like Robert Slater who "see new prospects of world community which offer hope of something more than survival. In this situation what are significantly called the forces of religion—forces manifestly resurgent today—cannot be ignored."[32]

The "One World" of Wendel Wilkie and of the United Nations was not to be a new form of imperialism; neither is Hocking's "world civilization," nor Slater's "world community." The new People of God is meant to be universal and whatever is meant by the "coming of the Kingdom" it is yet to be realized. Vatican II said that "earthly progress must be carefully distinguished from the growth of Christ's kingdom. Nevertheless, to the extent that the former can contribute to the bettering of human society, it is a vital concern to the kingdom of God."[33] Before lapsing into optimism about either worldly or religious unity we had better look at the contemporary facts of disruption and disunity.

The encyclical *Progressio Populorum,* of Pope Paul VI, sees the dilemmas that have resulted from the maldistribution of the world's resources. "Social conflicts have taken on world dimensions. The acute disquiet which has taken hold of the poor classes in countries that are becoming industrialized is now embracing those whose economy is almost exclusively agrarian: farming people too are becoming aware of their 'undeserved hardship.' There is also the scandal of glaring inequalities not merely in the enjoyment of possessions but even more in the exercise of power. While in certain regions a small restricted group enjoys a refined civilization, the remainder of the population, poor and scattered, is 'deprived of nearly all possibility of personal initiative, and oftentimes even its living and working conditions are unworthy of the human person.' "[34]

The Pope does not employ revolutionary rhetoric but he is pointing out the same harsh facts discussed in stronger language by revolutionary writers and orators. The harsh fact is that eighty percent of the world's resources are in the hands of only twenty percent of the world's population. These are the citizens of the First World, formed in the European Christian civilization, mainly Caucasian and well-educated, technologically advanced and holding power over large-scale organizations. In broadest terms, this First World is made up of the nations that are sometimes called the North Atlantic Community.

The Second World, typified by Russia and Japan gets along well without Christianity, escapes the domination of the First World, has appropriated much of the technological expertise and is now in the process of developing its own resources. It is the so-called Third

World, largely Asian, African and Latin American, that contains the suffering masses of humanity. Its people are poor, multi-racial, with little training in technological skills, victims of exploitation and oppression. The geographical lines we draw are a little too neat to express reality. Pockets of the Third World are represented by many Blacks in the United States. Pockets of the First World are represented by the ruling classes of Latin America.

The vast inequalities between the First and Third Worlds are a matter of concern to all conscientious people, and they pose a large moral problem especially to committed religious people. Insofar as Christianity allied itself with the First World and promoted the social order of the West, it must take organized responsibility to lessen the appalling differences between the rich and poor segments of the world. But beyond that, as Barbara Wards says, "Christians are called to see behind all the efforts of reform in aid and trade the deeper effort to redeem their vast and accumulating wealth, to give their material resources a soul of compassion and to introduce into their planetary societies the instruments of love, without which any society is little more than a herd or mob or system of controlled injustice."[35]

In spite of weakness and ignorance and failures, Christianity has always been attuned to the hopes and fears of mankind. One of the documents of Vatican II starts with the words, *gaudium et spes.* "The joys and the hopes, the griefs and the anxieties of the men of this age, especially those who are poor or in any way afflicted, these too are the joys and hopes, the griefs and anxieties of the followers of Christ."[36] People everywhere, in the First World as well as in the Third, should be the object of Christian solicitude. "In the twentieth century," writes Professor Slater, "these hopes and fears are very largely concentrated on what may happen in a world which is so closely drawn together that the prospect before mankind is often presented in terms of one world or no world at all." [37]

What is going on in much of the Third World today is the gigantic shift from colonial to national status. At the very time when transportation and communication are drawing us together, when the possibility of economic and political cooperation seems within our grasp, when representatives of the world religions are moving in an ecumenical direction—at this same time the former colonial people are setting up independent nations. The European Christian First World that now repents of having kept these colonies dependent and submissive and would like to help them join the global community is met by fierce resistance and a determination for liberty and independence. There is neither the desire nor the ability on the part of the West to suppress nationalism, especially in Africa and Asia, nor will the movement be abandoned from within.

ECUMENISM AND PLURALISM

IN spite of this insistence on national independence, it seems that the process of so-called "westernization" is taking place more rapidly than it did under colonization. When cross-cultural borrowing becomes voluntary it becomes selective. We have to say now, and probably with some regret, that westernization, or Europeanization, does not necessarily mean Christianization, as was often the alleged intent during four centuries of Western domination in Africa and Asia.[38] Religion as an imported cultural item is not nearly so desirable as the institutions of political freedom and industrial technology.

If it is true that the Third World, and to some extent also the Second World, are avid for Westernization but indifferent to Christianization, then we probably have to take a different view of Christianity as both a western religion and a world religion. On the one hand we have to come to grips with the fact that Christianity should never have been identified as a western religion, and on the other hand, with the probability that Christianity will never be the universal world religion.

This is a hard saying and cannot be accepted gracefully by everyone. The notion persists that Christianity *must* eventually convert or displace all other religions. Even Panikkar, who is very much at home in the Eastern religions, feels that religious pluralism is a temporary phenomenon and that it "continues generally only because the religions have not yet achieved their maturity and perfection." He says further that "the growing demand for unity of the religions that we can recognize in our times, is a healthy and positive sign of human vitality and is itself a religious truth."[39]

There can be no question that modern ecumenism is a strong impetus for inter-religious cooperation, and even for religious unity in the mergers of some Christian churches. The prospect, however, of a single American Christian Church, or even of complete unity of all American Protestant churches, is so remote that it is hardly worth speculation. A curious fact is that the most zealous ecumenists are also usually the staunchest members of their own church. Professor Brown had already noted this as a kind of "threat" to the ecumenical movement when he said that "alongside an ecumenical concern for the reunion of Christendom is a growing denominational self-consciousness that threatens to perpetuate the ancient divisions."[40]

Ecumenism, defined as positive cooperation and respectful understanding across denominational lines, is likely to succeed in a country where the experiment of religious pluralism has itself succeeded. Religious pluralism, in turn, needs as a prerequisite the kind of separation of Church and State that exists in the United States. Here we have come full circle in the discussion and I return to my premise that religion is culture-bound and culture-adaptive but flourishes best when it is not society-bound. In other words, those countries where organized religion is tied in with the organized society (Israel, Argentina, the Scandinavian countries) are not the places where religion is likely to flourish.

At the risk of sounding chauvinistic, we may suggest that Christianity as a minority religion in the world could well look to the model of Catholicism as a minority religion in the United States. It neither enjoys privilege nor suffers persecution, and we might recall the remark of Murray: "It would be difficult to say which experience, privilege or persecution, proved in the end to be more damaging or gainful to the Church." He explains also that "the American government has not undertaken to represent transcendental truth in any of the versions current in American society."[41]

It was long before the Second Vatican Council that Murray lectured approvingly about religious pluralism, separation of Church and State, and freedom of religion, and he had very little official support from Catholic sources. Nevertheless, he felt that America offers a "pattern in miniature" for the development of a "religiously pluralist international community."[42] That support was finally and officially forthcoming in the Council documents, which he had a hand in formulating. "It is highly important, especially in pluralistic societies, that a proper view exist of the relation between the political community and the Church . . . The role and competence of the Church being what it is, she must in no way be confused with the political community, nor bound to any political system."[43]

It ought to be clear that American Catholics, while they rejoice in the vindication of Murray's—and their own—approval of religious pluralism, do not think of this thesis merely as a compromise or as a temporary arrangement until the time is ripe for Catholicism to capture the American society. Like most other Americans they hold it as a positive value that is conducive to good citizenship. They firmly believe that the political structure should be separated from *all* ecclesiastical structures and that there must be an underlying guarantee of freedom for *all* religions.

In spite of the continuing problems with which the theologians and scripture scholars must wrestle, it seems perfectly logical to a sociologist to suggest that the American model ought to be usable on a world scale. If Catholicism here can exist happily as a minority religion alongside Protestantism, Judaism, Orthodoxy, it does not seem illogical to suggest that Christianity can also do so as a minority religion in the whole world. The principle of religious freedom is upheld by the United Nations, and wherever this principle is concretized there should appear an approval of both religious pluralism and ecumenism.

NOTES

[1] One of the sociologically interesting of these is Talcott Parsons, "Christianity and Modern Industrial Culture," in Edward Tiryakian, ed., *Sociological Theory, Values, and Sociocultural Change* (Glencoe, Free Press, 1963) to which a response was made by the late Pitirim Sorokin, "The Western Religion and Morality of Today" pp. 9-43 in *International Yearbook for the Sociology of Religion* vol. 2 (Koln and Opladen, Westdeutscher Verlag, 1966).

[2] Arnold Toynbee, *Christianity Among the Religions of the World* (New York, Scribner, 1957) p. 46. Christopher Dawson remarks that "the tendency to the secularization of culture is continuous and universal and there is no sign of any return to the ideal of a positive Christian culture, such as T. S. Eliot has described in his *Idea of a Christian Society*. Everywhere, Christians, whether Orthodox, Roman Catholic or Protestant, are tending to be self-conscious minorities set in an alien or hostile world." *The Movement of World Revolution* (New York, Sheed & Ward, 1959) p. 76.

[3] Kenneth Cragg, *Christianity in World Perspective* (New York, Oxford University Press, 1968) p. 67, who says also that "Christianity is rapidly losing ground, dwindling from perhaps a third of humanity in the nineteen-fifties to less than a fifth three decades hence when the millennium turns." p. 66.

[4] Christopher Dawson, *op. cit.*, p. 176.

[5] Hans Küng, *Christenheit als Minderheit* (Einsiedeln, Benziger, 1966) pp. 9-11. This was published in English as "The World Religions in God's Plan of Salvation," pp. 25-66, in Joseph Neuner, ed., *Christian Revelation and World Religions* (London, Burns and Oates, 1967) The latter is a collection of four papers delivered at a conference in Bombay in November, 1964, and published originally in *Indian Ecclesiastical Studies*, vol. 4 (July-October 1965).

[6] John, 10/11-16.

[7] English text in Anne Fremantle, ed., *The Papal Encyclicals* (New York, Mentor-Omega, 1963) p. 72. The concept of exclusive unity is furthered with the statement: "In this Church there is one Lord, one faith and one baptism. There was one ark of Noah, indeed, at the time of the flood, symbolizing one Church; and this being finished in one cubit had, namely, one Noah as helmsman and commander."

[8] *Ibid.*, p. 145. The list of eighty itemized errors are on pp. 143-152.

[9] *Decree on Ecumenism*, art. 3. Samuel McRea Cavert quotes this passage unhappily and then says, "Associated with this is the further assumption of the primacy of Peter and of his jurisdiction over the whole Church. These assumptions seem to indicate that the Roman Catholic understanding of ecumenism is unchangeably Rome-centered." p. 369 in Walter M. Abbott, ed., *The Documents of Vatican II* (New York, Angelus Books, 1966).

[10] *Constitution on the Church*, art. 16. In footnotes to both this and the previous passage, Abbott, *op. cit.*, pp. 35 and 346, points out that a letter from the Holy Office in 1949 to the Archbishop of Boston had already clarified the question of *extra ecclesiam nulla salus*. See Denzinger, 3869-3872.

[11] Fustel de Coulanges, *The Ancient City* (London, Mayflower, 1956) p. 522.

[12] *Constitution on the Church in the Modern World*, art. 58.

[13] See Colman Barry, *The Catholic Church and German Americans* (Milwaukee, Bruce, 1953).

[14] Edward Wakin and Joseph Scheuer, *The De-Romanization of the American Catholic Church* (New York, Macmillan, 1966).

[15] Raimundo Panikkar, *Religionen und die Religion* (Munich, Hueber Verlag, 1965) p. 83.

[16] *Ibid.*, p. 85.

[17] Mordecai Kaplan, *Questions Jews Ask* (New York, Reconstructionist Press, 1956) p. 414, answers the question: "What should be the relation of the State of Israel to Jewish religion?"

[18] Yerachmiel Domb, "Neturei Karta," pp. 23-47, in Michael Selzer, ed., *Zionism Reconsidered* (New York, Macmillan, 1970) p. 44.

[19] Alfred Lilienthal, *What Price Israel?* (Chicago, Regnery, 1953) p. 243. Kaplan, *op. cit.*, p. 475, makes a similar distinction when he says that "this Reconstructionist principle is intended to counter the assumption that the State of Israel is synonymous with the Jewish People. It is the antithesis of the claim that Jews of the Diaspora are disloyal to Judaism, if they do not plan to settle in Israel, or train their children to settle there."

[02] "Hinduism is rapidly changing from its traditional provincialism, and claiming for itself a universal validty." Philip Ashby, *The Conflict of Religions* (New York, Scribner, 1955) p. 169.

[21] Toynbee, *op. cit.*, p. 92.

[22] Malcolm Hay, *Failure in the Far East* (London, Spearman, 1956) p. 169. The author is unhesitating in blaming "the disruptive influence of Jansenists and their fellow travellers and the administrative incompetence of the Roman Curia." p. viii. In Appendix C, pp. 190-192, he reprints the decree of the Sacred Congregation of Propaganda of December 8, 1939, which finally rescinded the oath on Chinese rites.

[23] See Columba Cary-Elwes, *China and the Cross* (New York, Kenedy, 1957) chap. 4, "The Jesuit Age," pp. 73-180. "The tragedy itself is the loss of China for the Church and, in merely political and cultural terms, the failure of the marriage of two minds." (p. 147).

[24] See Abbott, *op. cit.*, p. 631, where Eugene Smith gives the "Protestant Response" to the decree on the missions.

[25] See *passim* H. Richard Niebuhr, *The Social Sources of Denominationalism* (Hamden, Shoe String Press, 1954).

[26] Kenneth Cragg, *Christianity in World Perspective* (New York, Oxford University Press, 1968) p. 19.

[27] See the account of R. B. Cunninghame Graham, *A Vanished Arcadia* (New York, 1924); also H. Storni, "Reductions of Paraguay" in *New Catholic Encyclopedia* (New York, McGraw-Hill, 1966) vol. 12, pp. 165-166.

[28] Paul Abrecht, *The Church and Rapid Social Change* (London, SCM, 1961) p. 199.

[29] In fact, the struggle against imperialism was largely a demand for freedom and self-sufficiency. "The political prisoners of the decades of resistance became the presidents and premiers of the new order. When the gears shifted from the negative eviction to the positive replacement of the foreigner, ideologies and their religious sanctions were necessarily attuned to the same mood of self-sufficiency." Cragg, *op. cit.*, p. 69.

[30] William E. Hocking, *The Coming of World Civilization* (New York, Harper, 1958) p. 166.

[31] Arnold Toynbee, *op. cit.*, p. 94.

[32] Robert L. Slater, *World Religions and World Community* (New York, Columbia University Press, 1963) p. 1. Hocking, *op. cit.*, p. 51, says that "today we seem to stand on the threshold of a new thing,

civilization in the singular." This optimism, especially the theory of religious "reconception," is roundly criticized by A. C. Bouquet, *The Christian Faith and Non-Christian Religions* (London, Nisbet, 1958) pp. 364-371.

[33] Pastoral Constitution on the *Church in the Modern World*, art. 39.

[34] Pope Paul VI, *Progressio Populorum, Encyclical* (1967) art. 9.

[35] Barbara Ward, Commentary on *Progressio Populorum* (New York, Paulist Press, 1967) p. 26.

[36] Pastoral Constitution on the *Church in the Modern World*, art. 1.

[37] Robert L. Slater, *World Religions and World Community* (New York, Columbia University Press, 1963) p. 201.

[38] Abrecht, *op. cit.*, p. 95.

[39] Panikkar, *op. cit.*, p. 169. In another place he tells what he means by a non-Christian religion "coming to maturity." He points out that Christianity in India "should not be an imported, full-fledged and highly developed religion, but Hinduism itself *converted*—or Islam, or Buddhism, whatever it may be. It has to be added immediately that this converted Hinduism is substantially the same as the old one and yet something different, a new creature." See section IV, "The Relation of Christians to their Non-Christian Surroundings," pp. 143-184, in Joseph Neuner, ed., *Christian Revelation and World Religions* (London, Burns & Oates, 1967).

[40] Robert McAfee Brown, *The Spirit of Protestantism* (New York, Oxford U. Press, 1965) pp. 216-217. The same phenomenon was discovered in an empirical study by James Kelly, *Attitudes Toward Ecumenism in a New England Suburb* (1970) Unpublished Dissertation in Harvard University Widener Library.

[41] John Courtney Murray, *We Hold These Truths* (New York, Sheed and Ward, 1960) p. 74.

[42] *Ibid.*, p. 75.

[43] Pastoral Constitution on the *Church in the Modern World*, art. 76. This quotation should be read alongside two other statements: "A wrong is done when government imposes upon its people, by force or fear or other means, the profession or repudiation of any religion, or when it hinders men from joining or leaving a religious body." Declaration on *Religious Freedom*, art. 6. Also in the decree on *Ecumenism*, art. 4, we read that "this Sacred Synod, therefore, exhorts all Catholic faithful to recognize the signs of the times and to participate skillfully in the work of ecumenism."

The Universe of Man

Bernard L. Bonniwell

EXISTENCE

EXISTENCE is an eon-timed universe in which man appears tentatively and in disparate self unity for a brief moment of magnifi-
cence to again quietly rejoin the ultimate universe of timelessness.
Existence, then, is formed and formless energy. Nature is energy in its
many forms. Man, Nature's most complicated form, is conscious energy.
His uniqueness is his awareness, primarily of his awkward aloneness in
a world of events which support him, enrich him and ultimately
re-gain him. Contemporary man may die out or may evolve in higher
and more complex forms: planets may vary and dissolve within time
and be replaced by substantially new and unforeseen forces: yet all
of this—the perceivable and unperceivable—seems to eventuate from
time, just as the phenomenal life of a single man eventuates from the
dark womb of existence.

Personal existence is anti-statistic. It is the phenomenal realization
of a material improbability. The whole charade should have ended
long ago in the mean presence of uncompromising non-ness. In the
galaxy of events involved in the attainment of meaningful life, there
is too much of chance to allow even the hope of a plausible developmental scheme. Reasoning so, man is led to the ultimate absurdity:
that life is indeed without value, goal, or personal meaning. Perhaps
he arrives at this conclusion because he is something of an inexperienced
newcomer in a relatively ancient world of existence. Thus, T. Dobzhansky cautions: "This universe runs according to precise and inexorable laws; the more comprehensible of these were discovered by
Newton, while Einstein and other modern physicists and cosmologists
added some less comprehensible ones. And finally, man himself is
very much of a newcomer; he inhabits a vanishingly small bit of the
cosmic scene, for at most 2 million years, while the scene itself is
somewhere between 5 and 10 billion years old."[1] Against this ordered
universe, the intellectual absurd becomes the only absurdity. Absurdity
is of man's own making. Given a choice, the order of materiality,
from which man evolves, is the superior order, for man eventually

returns to the final care and keep of Nature itself. Man has, in this instance, selected the lesser of two criteria. Psychologically, absurdity is personal. It is a point of view; it can be a way of life. But it is not a law of the universe. It is, rather, a miscalculation of damning proportions, passed on to others in the guise of philosophic faith. The challenge for man is clear. Let life be made over in the fullness and wisdom of the complete man who seeks only contentment. When one is content, the universe is meaningful. But the secret of contentment is varied and differs with individuals—and perhaps it is out of this melange of contradictions and difficulties that the personal absurdities of life in general arise. Rather unfortunately men are prone to conclude that the same incomprehensible generality must also be the truth of their personal existence.

In the trackless universe of science, man lost his way and fled to the darkness of alienation. With the steady ascent of science, man became less and less secure in the reason for his own being. Fortunately, in retreating to the world of subjectivity—where he exists in reflective aloneness—he found freedom from harassment and once again reorganized his understanding of the universe. Simply stated by Rollo May in *Man's Search for Himself:* "Freedom is man's capacity to take a hand in his own development. It is our capacity to mold ourselves."[2] In technical terms, Hans Jonas, 1966, presenting a series of essays directed towards the necessity of a philosophical biology, removes the final barrier: "So it happened that in the hour of the final triumph of materialism, the very instrument of it, "evolution," implicitly transcended the terms of materialism and posed the ontological question anew—when it just seemed settled. And Darwinism, more than any other doctrine responsible for the now dominant evolutionary vision of all reality, turns out to have been a thoroughly dialectical event. This becomes increasingly visible as its teachings are philosophically assimilated."[3] In retrospect, it seems that whatever rule of thumb is applied to the understanding of total existence, most certainly *chance* seems remarkably unsuited to the task of solving the riddle. Even such common concepts as selection, hybridization, inbreeding and mutation, all half brothers to chance, appear to be fearfully limited in accounting for the overall scheme of things. It seems strange, too, that whatever evolution *is,* it appears to consistently advance with time, moving constantly towards higher and higher forms of complexity. In addition, the cumulative activity seems predictably to attain a final expression of fullness, for either a species or an individual, and then abruptly thrusts to a destructive end. All this does not seem characteristic of chance. Theoretically, there would seem to be no valid reason why evolution, having attained a highly manifest form of biological or phenomenological achievement, should not be found to regress, purposively and selectively, to lower and more proficient forms while keeping pace with observed environmental changes. In effect, a mechanically perfect correlation would continually function between the life form and the material environment, regardless of the direction of the advance. If the advance was positive, proficiency would be marked by complexity: if the advance was negative, proficiency would be characterized by simplicity. Thus an appropriate relationship, via positive evolution or negative evolution, would be maintained and the struggle for survival would be, scientifically conceived, both logical and meaningful. On the other hand, if absolute and unstructured chance is to explain the evolutionary process, then the various classifications presently observed would hardly be likely to occur. Instead, a vast array of minor differences would be found in such profusion that classifications would defer to individuations of an almost incalculable number. Then, again, the locking-on of evolution upon the living fossils rubs elementary logic to distraction. Somehow there is too much directional and predictable order, and the clear hint of pre-arranged emergence, to hold that blind chance is the sufficient explanation. A remarkable preview of the new and emerging concept of a man-directed evolution is tentatively suggested by T. Dobzhansky of the Rockefeller University. He writes: "An evolutionist need not be a Pangloss or a Pollyanna; he may recognize that the absurd is widespread. Evolution is not predestined to promote always the good and the beautiful. Nevertheless, evolution is a process which has produced life from non-life, which has brought forth man from an animal, and which may conceivably continue doing remarkable things in the future. In giving rise to man, the evolutionary process has, apparently for the first and only time in the history of the cosmos, become conscious of itself. This opens at least a possibility that evolution may some day be directed by man, and that the prevalence of the absurd may be cut down." The geneticist continues with the same optimistic view in regard to modern evolutionary biology: "Evolution comprises all the stages of the development of the universe: the cosmic, biological, and human or cultural developments. Attempts to restrict the concept of evolution to biology are gratuitous. Life is a product of the evolution of inorganic nature, and man is a product of the evolution of life. In a sense, the discovery of evolution reinstates man in the station from which he was demoted by Copernicus: man is again the center of the stage—at least of the planetary, and quite possibly of the cosmic, one. Most important of all, the stage and the actor not only have evolved but are evolving."[4] In extended evolution, then, there arises a new horizon for the freedom of man. The hand of man is proposed as the shaper of evolution. Unlike the ancient and mythological Atlas, son of Iapetus and Clymene, condemned to stand at the western end of the earth, bearing the sky upon his shoulders, scientific man dares to hold that ultimately there shall be no enslavement of his kind. Surely the hope exceeds the resolute strictures of history, and yet—and thus hope is reaffirmed—man has unearthed a staggering sum of knowledge while restructuring

both his environment and himself. No longer dominated, he has become dominant in a fabulous universe of intercoiling mystery and
science, and with good reason and cause is sometimes appalled at the
monstrous role he may inadvertently play. Even the most confident
man may wonder at the power granted him: the freedom to flower
deserts or to destroy civilizations.

Some appreciation of the incredible bio-physiological emergence of
man is suggested in the introduction to *Perspectives in Psychology*
by E. J. Shoben and F. L. Ruch: "Man is a puzzling animal. Neither
the strongest, the swiftest, nor the most self-sufficient of the beasts that
populate the globe, he has nevertheless come to dominate the earth.
He has changed the courses of great rivers to irrigate his fields; where
once impregnable forests stood, he has built his cities; and, like the
Prometheus of legend, he has plundered the dormant sources of energy
in his universe—coal and oil, the power of steam and electricty, and
the potent forces of the atom and of the sun's rays—to drive his cars
and planes, light his towns, operate his enormous factories, and let
him communicate almost instantaneously by radio and satellite-relayed
television across thousands of miles. At the same time, he has shown
himself to be the only organism preoccupied with both creation and
the appreciation of art. Wherever one finds people, one finds a concern for adornment and decoration, a notion of beauty or elegance
to set beside a concept of utility or efficency. The human conquest of
the planet has often involved an ideal of loveliness as well as a yearning
both to wrest secrets from nature and to make the land, sea, and air
yield a less toilsome or dangerous way of life."[5] Collectively, then,
man has written his exploits in the pageantry of time with superb
confidence. Individually, however, each man must face the certainty of
his own existence to attain the threshold of faith in self: it is a singular,
individual and brief journey, phenomenal and personal, and co-existent
with the order of the universe. It is the extension and projection of
one's own self with the marvel of the supportive and surrounding
environment, the complete surrendering of the self to the incalculable
and infinite possibilities attendant to life. It is a purposeful freeing
of the spirit, uninhabited by the passiveness of mechanical laws and
stultifying social norms; it is the intended seeking of the unknown that
it may be challenged and forced to relinquish its hidden gifts; it is
the positive strength gained by testing the stronger foe; it is striving
to learn, through defeat, that similar defeat will never occur again.
Beyond all measure, it is the willingness to think the creative thought,
attempting to share with all men the quality of life beyond the margin
of conventionality. It is the interweaving of self with time, where all
of history is humanity in change, and the linkage of every individual
in the chain of existence is of consequence. It is the profound merging
of the internal life with the external universe in such a fashion that
they become indistinguishably one and mutually desirable. In a certain

philosophic sense, there is neither beginning nor end for man. He is enriched by his knowledge that his personal time, his awareness, is limited and so endowed with a special sense of urgency; he is blessed with the faith that he shares the timelessness of the universe, flattered that he was once honored with the brief, luminous touch of human life. Free of personal vanity, for he is one with existence, the contented man shares with de Chardin the evident truth that life is not an accident in the material universe, but the essence of the phenomenon.[6] In parallel fashion, the all-pervasive unity of existence is perceptively described by Loren Eiseley in *The Mind and Nature* in the imaginative terms which characterize his genius: "Directly stated, the evolution of the entire universe—stars, elements, life, man—is a process of drawing something out of nothing, out of the utter void of non-being. The creative element in the mind of man—that latency which can conceive Gods, carve statues, move the heart with the symbols of great poetry, or devise formulas of modern physics—emerges in as mysterious a fashion as those elementary particles which leap into momentary existence in great cyclotrons, only to vanish again like infinitesimal ghosts. The reality we know in our limited lifetimes is dwarfed by the unseen potential of the abyss where science stops. In a similar way the smaller universe of the individual human brain has its lonely cometary passages, or flares suddenly like a super nova, only to subside in death while the waves of energy it has released roll on through unnumbered generations."[7]

In the opening stages of the 21st Century there is now perceivable an evident melding of bio-philosophy and science, presaging the development of a meta-evolutionary theory consistent with the harmonic presentation of a single universe of existence. The very welcome interest in the phenomenal aspects of matter—such as awareness, motion, motivation, interest, intelligence, decision, and human affection—represents a wholesome and advanced concern with the reality of human behavior. Thus the prestigious American Association for the Advancement of Science, meeting in 1969, lists the following unlikely title for discussion: The Identity and Dignity of Man—a scientific and theological dialogue on issues emerging from behavioral, surgical and genetic interventions. Again, the explorations of outer space, where the individual and the machine in perfect rapport, with equal contributions, turn to the Sea of Tranquility and message back to the Earth the moment of triumph, reflect the pragmatic research temper of the new century. Science and philosophy—the unlikely teaming of the hare and the tortoise—are successfully combining their diverse talents in the more extended search for truth. Man undoubtedly possesses the liberty and the ability to make the new judgments and attain security in a world of change. The necessary freedom is confidently noted in the casual remarks of Gabriel Marcel when commenting upon the philosophy of existentialism: "Strange as it may seem, I do not think that my concern with maintaining the primacy of action has ever expressed itself, as it has with others, in a philosophy of liberty. The traditional problem of liberty has never worried me to any great extent: I have always held that man could not but have the liberty which he required, and that, consequently, there was no real problem."[8]

Human responsibility applied to scientific truth, structures man's behavior towards an ever increasing sense of individual worth, dignity and security. Psychologically, the roots of personal freedom sustain and hold firm the human being. The underlying value system, however, requires a pervasive and totally meaningful personal life philosophy. Such a philosophy is not imposed, but accepted. It is the slow outgrowth of experience. In the fullness of personal awareness, it is ultimately the basic values which give purpose to life. It is the coming to grips with the problem of material existence and phenomenal existence. It is the ultimate directive which makes sensible the fine relationship between these two indiscerptible units of being. In the past, the directive has been theology. In the present, it is science. And the shift from biblical text to scientific text, although intellectually necessary, has not been satisfactory. The relatively new scientific freedom, though invigorating, has failed to satisfy man's eternal longing for the richly endowed purpose which seems inherent in the total universe as well as for the sentient purpose of man's individual life. Yet man must learn to live with transition, however violent, for it is a part of man's destiny to share the convulsions of change which always precede a new order of understanding.

The epi-center of existence for the individual, then, is freedom and contentment. Ultimately, it is contentment with life and satisfaction with death, for both are elements of the universe and constitute the profoundness of an individual's being. To understand contentment, to possess it, is to sense a deep awareness of the purposiveness of all life and all the events which impinge upon it, for Nature is abundant with her gifts to those who love her deeply, to those who approach her openly and with compassion for her beauty and her agony.

PHILOSOPHY

PHILOSOPHY is the summing up of wisdom. It is the existential product of art, science and behavior, consistently fused in time. It is absolute in its presence, relative in its expression. It is modifiable but imperishable for it attains neither apex nor climax; it is the spin-off of the enduring evolutionary process continually subjected to humanistic interpretation. In turn, the process of extended *evolution* draws incessantly upon the systemic energy of the cosmos, accurately assessing through endless eons the singular characteristic of unity undergoing change. The unfortunate research error is to attribute, at least by implication, the possibility of dis-unity in a universe of unity: thus, to indicate that the universe consists of the animate and the inanimate, suggesting that these are essentially different unities rather than simply different aspects of the total universe. In the 21st Century, it appears reasonable to predict, the distinction between living and non-living will be dropped in favor of the principle of observing universal *matter* at various evolutionary levels. The unitary theory is not surprising, having been inferred by scientist-philosophers for some time. An interesting illustration of the principle is contemporarily presented in the *Journal of Theoretical Biology* by Dr. P. Fong, who states that life phenomena can be analysed on a physical basis: "Thus life phenomena is not intrinsically different from physical phenomena. The only difference is that they are rare, special cases that occur only in rather special circumstances. The interplay of the special circumstances and the development of life is what we call the evolutionary history. The understanding of the life phenomena is thus closely tied to the problem of evolution." Concerning the definition of life, he notes that "Since life phenomena are not intrinsically different from physical phenomena, there is no need nor is it possible to make an exact definition to demarcate life from non-life. Thus any definition of life may be made only for the sake of convenience. Actually, different forms of life have different characteristics and no single definition is equally appropriate for all." Dr. Fong perceives the implications of his research as impinging upon civilization conceived as generalized life, stating that "As a matter of fact, the present world minus the physical world is nearly all life (biological) or life-like (social and humanistic). The life-like part comes into being by the same evolutional principles that bring life into being . . . human beings are a part of the biological world, and therefore human activities cannot be isolated from the principles of the biological world. In fact, biological studies cannot avoid human activities and will not be complete without them."[9] In attentively auditing these remarks, acceptance of the data is not to be inferred. To audit is not to give assent. Perhaps, if the preceding principles are intellectually or even theologically offensive, the contemporary and related proposals of Teilhard de Chardin[10] are equally intriguing. "Who knows," writes de Chardin, "whether the ultimate solution of the paradox of transformism will not be found in a conception of a universe wherein the main zoological types would find their continuity in the fact that they radiate and spread about starting from a common power of organic development localized in the total unity of the earth. In this hypothesis that which is plastic in the world of living beings, that which moves, that periodically diverges into newly formed branches would no longer be the elements (they are locked up within variations of low amplitude), but it would be the physical power which envelops all the elements." The philosopher, Joseph Donceel, in commenting on de Chardin's observation, says: "The problem, therefore, is not so much one of the passage from one species to a higher one. What we must explain is the steady upward trend of evolution as a whole, which is manifest especially when it crosses what Teilhard called the thresholds, that is, when it passes from matter to life, from life to consciousness, and from consciousness to reflection. Even if we stay within the animal realm, it is evident for the philosopher that the ape-like creature in which evolution culminates stands on a higher level of ontological perfection (Being) than the amoeba-like creature from which the process may have started a billion years ago. The contrast is even stronger when we widen the scope of evolution in both directions and compare inorganic matter with rational man. The passage from such humble beginnings to such a lofty end requires an explanation, demands the intervention of causes other than the material energies at work in the starting point in the environment."[12] May it be added, this is precisely the problem confronting modern science. Perhaps there is only one science: the science of discovery. And only one problem: the problem of universal unity. In this sense, the only true object of study is *matter* conceived in its many manifestations and presently unperceived potentials. In digest form, the fundamentalness of matter—capable of emergence—is emphasized; geophysical matter—to bio-physiological matter—to conscious matter —moving upward to the phenomenal level of thinking matter. The spiral remains unbroken. The evolutionary potential of man-matter is unpredictable although it seems reasonable to assume of the future a continuing rise to greater levels of human complexity.

Insofar as matter cannot be extracted from phenomena, psychology would be best defined as the study of a phase of the evolutionary process, specifically at the level now perceived as human behavior. The new psychology might be characterized as evolutionary psychology, or simply termed evopsych. It would represent a phase of science—not a separate science—and so become sensitive to the philosophic needs of its study, thinking matter (Man). The tightly correlated problems of human behavior, made possible by the phenomenal extension of matter, then re-assume proper significance in the behavioral world. The existent individual, bound to the universe of matter, phenomenally free to experience and direct the profound reality of human values, goals and ideals, is psychologically threatened within life by these tenuous philosophic tenets. If, as Gordon Allport has written, "The goal of psychology is to reduce discord among our philosophies of man, and to establish a scale of probable truth, so that we may feel increasingly certain that one interpretation is truer than another,"[13] then the contribution of psychology assumes major proportions in the search for human understanding. In broad perspective, the contributions of science, well intentioned but humanistically negative, are critically appraised by Allport in these thought provoking terms: "Up to now the 'behavioral sciences', including psychology, have not provided us with a picture of man capable of creating or living in a democracy.

These sciences in large part have imitated the billiard ball model of physics, now of course outmoded. They have delivered into our hands a psychology of an 'empty organism', pushed by drivers and molded by environmental circumstance. What is small and partial, what is external and mechanical, what is early, what is peripheral and opportunistic— have received the chief attention of psychological system builders. But the theory of democracy requires also that man possess a measure of rationality, a portion of freedom, a generic conscience, propriate ideals, and unique value. We cannot defend the ballot box or liberal education, nor advocate free discussion and democratic institutions, unless man has the potential capacity to profit therefrom." The author continues: "In *The Measure of Man*, Joseph Wood Krutch points out logically the ideals of totalitarian dictatorships follow from the premises of 'today's thinking' in mental and social science. He fears that democracy is being silently sabotaged by the very scientists who have benefited most from its faith in freedom of inquiry." Allport then adds: "No paradox is more striking than that of the scientist who as citizen makes one set of psychological assumptions and in his laboratory and writings makes opposite assumptions respecting the nature of man."[14] The present insistence on the philosophic need for psychology to attain humanistic maturity is simply to insist that an appropriate balance of interest in all phases of the problem is a prerequisite in the search for truth. In a recent developmental publication, Raymond F. Gale, stressing the humanistic approach, writes: "Psychology should study the human being not just as a piece of inert clay to be helplessly molded by outside forces. Man is, or should be, an active, dynamic, autonomous, self-governing initiator, activator, and master of his own life. The stimulus-response approach of behavioristic psychology has unintentionally created a 'mechanical man'—passive, shaped, adjusted, conforming, learning the perpetuation of a culture which outlives its utility as today becomes history with yesterday. With him should be contrasted the free, responsible, creative, active man who invents, makes decisions, discovers self, relates self to others, accepts and rejects stimuli while utilizing man's freedom of choice, who in fact creates and internalizes his own stimuli for self-realization."[15] Before turning to a recent and significant trend in the biological field, which relates with extraordinary interest to the molecular level of human behavior, a final reference is given from the work of Carl Rogers, which adds a new dimension of freedom to the field: "We need no longer live in an inhibited science of psychology. The trend toward a phenomenological, existential, self-theory emphasis in the field means that we can, with fresh vigor, open our minds and our thinking, our theories and our empirical research to all the significant problems of psychology. We can utilize all channels of knowing, not simply certain prescribed channels. We can permit the full creativity of thought of the psychologist to be exercised, not simply narrowly inhibited and traditional types of thought. In this respect I believe that the psychologist will experience a new burst of creative freedom, such as has occurred in other sciences when the old bonds and boundaries have been broken. No problem, no method, no perspective will be out of bounds. Men can work freely and creatively toward discovering the significant relationships between humanly important variables in the psychological realm."[16] The range, then, of humanistic research is broad with adherents available at each level to competently state the importance of a particular sector. Each specialist finds his place on the behaviorial helix, each making his especial contribution to the overall problem. The future suggests research maturity.

Tobias Smollett, 1721-1771, observed that "Facts are stubborn things." Indeed, no one would argue seriously with the truth of the statement. Some few individuals, however, might raise the question as to *how certain* are we of the facts? It is this impish minority that tends to crimp tradition and make change possible. Thus, in a frontal assault on the commonplace, P. Fong, recently referred to, theorizes concerning the reversibility of life and death. Having established a conditional basis for his thinking, he notes that "Besides the combination and sequence the basic processes are not different from inanimate material systems in physics and chemistry and therefore it is not surprising that these lower forms sometimes behave like the inanimate material system—i.e., viruses may exist in crystal form and bacteria may exist in the dehydrated form for a long time without change and without activity. To put it symbolically, at this stage, the transformation between life and 'death' is reversible."[17] Perhaps, in narrowing the distinction between the animate and the inanimate, a closer inbreeding of the philosophic and scientific ideas will follow with the psychologist re-emphasizing the particularity of the role of existential awareness. It is theoretically possible to assume that the only real difference between non-life, life in general, and personal existence is the possession of consciousness. The hard problem for the philosopher-scientist is the acceptance of this life-matter complexity as infrangible. If, however, credible research establishes the fact that life and no-life are chronologically identical, the concept of philosophic-scientific unity will advance measurably. It seem to the present writer that one cannot assume that life was not essentially present in beginning matter: the warrant for the statement is the factual presence of life, here and now. Thus, an interesting pushing-back of the life-presence is reported in a recent general commentary relating to the work of Professors Elso S. Baghoorn, Harvard University, and Stanley A. Tyler, University of Wisconsin. It is reported: "Baghoorn, intently examining tiny sections of rock from the two-billion-year-old Gunflint rock formation in Ontario, Canada, suddenly recognized a number of tiny fossils. . . . In a single stroke, the fossil record had been pushed back an incredible 1.4 billion years. As a result of this work and a series of findings that it touched off, it now seems possible that scientists will find out when living things first evolved and when and how plants and animals started down their separate evolutionary paths." The quest continues and in 1966, "Baghoorn and J. William Schopf published data that followed the fossil trail still farther into the past and set up a new outpost almost three-quarters of the way back to the formation of Earth some five billion years ago. They reported finding fossils of bacteria and algae in the so-called Fig Tree sediments in South Africa. These rocks have been dated as being 3.1 billion or more years old." The concept of life-matter—inseparably related from the beginning—moves a notch closer to reality with this type of research finding. The intellectually irritating concept of abiogenesis (i.e., the hypothetical production of living things from inanimate matter; spontaneous generation) also seems less re-alistic or necessary in view of the recent technical advances in studies of the genetic code. In these latter studies, the implication of possible psycho-physiological developmental control is evident, and in line with a rational research expectancy with little left to chance. It is highly questionable, however, that the bio-chemical control system would 'think' for the thinker. Whatever may come out of the laboratory, ex-citing and remarkable as it may be, the synthesizing of an individual— at the test tube level—is merely drawing upon the mechanics of mat-ter: and the mechanics of matter, perceived in evolutionary terms, in-variably leads to phenomenal awareness and individual freedom. The laboratory will give us better men, more proficient individuals, highly selected persons—more intelligent, emotionally stable, and conceivably less subject to mental disorders. The trend appears to be a kind of bio-medical science which will contribute much to the humanistic capa-bility of all mankind. However, an undue public enthusiasm for the research magic of the genetic code is tempered by the observation of biologists themselves: "There is an unfortunate tendency to view solu-tion of the genetic code as a major breakthrough marking the end of the road. Solution of the complete code will be a major break-through, indeed. However, it marks a *beginning,* not an end. The problems of how a cell uses the completed protein at the proper time and place in cellular differentiation, specialization, and organization is still a very long way from being solved."[18] The philosopher has also faced this problem of organization, specialization and differentiation, wondering aloud if it does not suggest the necessity of a teleological commitment. Whatever the problems, and whatever the proposed solutions, the solitary individual does have a right to at least wonder *why* it all began. The congeries of potentials, inherent in original and universal matter, judged against the observed evolutional products are incredible in number and in variety. Certainly only a masterful and philosophic science can even foreshadow the potentials yet to be dis-played. One may wonder if scientific man is not unknowingly caught in a dynamic system which, although it remains of consuming interest to him, teases with progress inching along an infinite projection. For him, there is really no precise beginning or precise ending. The only thing he shares with the universe is existential time, and that but briefly. To be contented with the wholeness of the problem, he must join forces with all others equally competent in their technical under-standing of precisely the same problem—man and his changing universe.

PERSONALITY

PERSONALITY is the personalization of existence. It is knowing and being known. It is becoming and actualization. It is subjectivity objectifying itself. It is the human disposition expressing itself through a life style. In sum, it is a miniscule encapsulation of culture, phe-nomenologically tied in with an individual's total behavior. The central core of personality is man's humaneness. Man's personal world is the self-world phenomenologically shared with others. The environment is a co-existent necessity but not identifiable with the personal self: pe-culiarly enough, the environment is beloved by some, tolerated by others, and frequently rejected by the alienated. The normal individ-ual appears to be disposed to enjoy the attainment of higher levels of self expression, of always increasing developmental capability, and seems to desire a positive enrichment of life. The psychologist, Gordon W. Allport, Harvard University, writes in 1955 of his essentially human trait: "We maintain therefore that personality is governed not only by the impact of stimuli upon a slender endowment of drives common to the species. Its process of becoming is governed, as well, by a disposition to realize its possibilities, i.e., to become characteristic-ally human at all stages of development. And one of the capacities most urgent is individuation, the formation of an individual style of life that is self-aware, self-critical, and self-enhancing."[19] In contrast to this rather constructive and motivating view, the social scientist argues quite differently, frequently espousing the typical mechanical explana-tion of the behavioral shut-in: "Contemporary social and psychological behavorism sometimes seems to dispense with the self and deal with the human person as though he were nothing but an amalgam of social statuses and roles or a pattern of psychological responses." Although this is a 1965 comment, the principle remains true to the older and sometimes depressing views formulated by the earlier psychologists and psychiatrists. It does not seem unfair to hold that the individual was grimly condemmed to live a life of personality conflict, regardless of possibly overlooked potentialities for excellence. Thus, in a quick rundown of psychoanalytic names and concepts the following emerge: Freud—trauma is primarily sexual in nature, Adler—inferiority com-plex, Jung—collective unconscious, Rank—birth trauma, Fromm—social environment dependency, Horney—basic anxiety in a potentially hostile world, Sullivan—impact of acculturation and security need, Reik—loss of self-trust and self-confidence sets up anxieties and inhibitions in the individual. It is, perhaps, outrageously unfair to select the negative aspects of psychoanalysis and conclude that it is therefore a dehumanizing descriptive-science of man. On the other hand, it offers little hope for the inculcation of a genuine sense of psychological freedom. The over-all impression is that man is trouble bound from the beginning and, seemingly, can do little about his predictable crucifixion. Assuming that it is possible to remove one's attention from the spare hill of Golgotha, the independence and creativeness of man may then be considered in a different manner. A contemporary psychologist, A. H. Maslow, perceives man in a very different light, suggesting that he is not a psychological cripple, hemmed in by the environment and overwhelmed by society. In reflecting upon the relationship of actively normal man and the unknown, for example, he notes that "Our healthy subjects are uniformly unthreatened and unfrightened by the unknown, being therein quite different from average men. They accept it, are comfortable with it, and, often are even *more* attracted by it than by the known. They not only tolerate the ambiguous and unstructured; they like it." He continues: "Since, for healthy people, the unknown is not frightening, they do not have to spend any time laying the ghost, whistling past the cemetery, or otherwise protecting themselves against imagined dangers."[21] The new directions being established in the psychology of personality are also rather well illustrated, at least technically, by reality therapy—which demands a positive confronting of the patient with *reality*—rather than with some so-called unconscious conflict. In this same fashion, behavior therapy, based largely upon a conditioning process, also bypasses the unconscious, employing relatively routine learning procedures to modify behavior. It seems, then, that psychology has come full turn: from the esoteric and mystic doctrines of psychoanalysis to the 'let's face the facts' of reality therapy with, however, a substantial innercore of humaneness being clearly posited by contemporary social psychologists. This seems all for the good. New, fresh outlooks are badly needed in a field where expectancy is so high and productivity so minimal.

The present status of personality psychology is elemental and immature in the philosophical sense that it refuses to admit the universality of its problem. Human behavior universally penetrates every conceivable undertaking attempted by man: this, most obviously, includes science. Science is, and must always remain, a fraction less than man's potential. If man's knowledge, which generates a science, is characterized by a remarkable co-extensiveness with matter and phenomena, so also must the living-world of research contend with the same identical problem. Again, turning to the reasoned observations of Gordon W. Allport, when presenting the Terry Lectures at Yale in 1955, one reads that "Each new simplification in psychology tends to be hailed as a triumph of analysis. In recent times either the whole of our mental life or large portions thereof have been 'accounted for' by the operation of the reflex arc, by conditioning, by reinforcement; or have been viewed as an associational fusion of sensations, images and affections; or as a dynamic interplay of id, ego, superego; or in terms of some other appealing but skeleton formula. While it is surely the task of science to bring order among facts without needless proliferation of concepts, yet oversimplification brings discredit upon science, and in psychology may succeed only in caricaturing human nature." In applying the same principle to personality, he adds: "Personality is far too complex a thing to be trussed up in a conceptual straight jacket. Starting with this conviction the present essay argues for conceptual openmindedness and for reasoned eclecticism."[22] In the undue experimental reduction of personality, technically required to bring it within the framework of a given scientific method, not only does psychology remain profitless but, indirectly, society suffers. With a penetrating literary candidness, Feodor Dostoyevsky, 19th Century, has written: "Profound as psychology is, it's a knife that cuts both ways ... You can prove anything by it ... I am speaking of the abuse of psychology, gentlemen." Abuse, of course, has many forms. It is probable that to a musician the ill-playing of a master's composition is sheer abuse of a privilege—the privilege to play it correctly. Thus, Dostoyevsky's accusation is true but not particularized of psychologists. The sickness is an inherited disease of the social studies. Error and muted percepts are authoritatively accepted and continualy errorized into the present. The evil of it all is the fact that the error concerns man, a quite independent *thinking* object, who has every *right* not to accept it. It can be readily noted that the realms of active dissent have not been entirely stifled. The rediscovery of man as man and the dimensional re-positioning of phenomena on the top rung of human behavior lends a certain enchantment to the research future. In a moment of moody despair, who knows but that the psychologist may insightfully perceive man as a human being, and to his amazement, hopefully upon that good morrow, may even appreciatively and warily enter within the psychological world of Soren Kierkegaard, 1813-1855, of whom is said: "Kierkegaard discovered existentialism as Abraham discovered God. There had been many intimations but before him no full vision. The discovery was a massive push of the modern mind toward the subjectivism which has been familiar for the past decades. On the scientific side and in academic philosophy the mind was already on its way to subjectivism: Descartes' concept of man as thinking being marked a different world from the Aristotelian one in which man was a rational animal."[23] The sharp turning away from the bio-environmental credo is evident. "The biological creature vanishes in the new world and with him the external nature he inhabits and with which he interacts. In its place is consciousness or thinking, on one side, and on the other, sheer extension, occupation of space. Consciousness is of course basic, or logically prior to extension. Its existence is our first certainty, and its existence is necessary if we are to know anything else."[27] Like a final, great girder placed into the last opening, the work of the existentialist bridges the gap between living physiology and thinking physiology. Now man can be perceived as exquisitely differentiated from all other research objects: Man is thinking matter. No valid excuse remains for the researcher to maintain stubborn indifference to this fact. No material matter is like man. He is uniquely one in a universe of the many. As man, he requires unique consideration.

In a continuing concern with the developmental and dimensional concept of man, the *necessity* of the 'unique consideration' should be apparent. The human equation holds to the irreducible position that man is essentially consciousness, and lacking it, he lacks psychological existence. Asleep, he possesse phyiological life: within this realm he possesses the potential for self existence. The phenomenal insistence in no way diminishes the necessity of physiology but it does, in extensively significant terms, limit the behavioral importance of physiology when alone. Simply stated, physiology is not enough for existence: awareness is the absolute and undiminished pre-requisite. The phenomenal stance in no way denies or substitutes for personality as perceived objectively. In states of awareness, there is always the knower and the known; the subjective self and the objective world; there is always the finely interwoven web of emotion and intellection; there is the active disposition towards self-actualization.

Personality is possibly the climatic problem of psychology, involving all phases of the developmental process. It has to be perceived in its many manifestations, internal and external. The perception of personality, philosophically and historically, has frequently been colored by the impingement of ideas in extreme contrast. The appeal of the problem, and the frustration, arises when one considers some of the differing viewpoints and concludes that, within certain limits, each one is relatively true, as when Aristotle defined man as a rational animal; when Descartes emphasized the principle *Cogito, ergo sum*—I think, therefore I am; when Locke propounded the brilliant thesis of the *Tabula Rasa*, a blank slate upon which experience writes; and when Leibnitz proposed that the only true reality was that lying outside the senses. Whatever the full answer, personality is *all* that is known of man and his behavior. The practical need, then, seems to be a development of research theory in a dimensional or field format so that adequate acceptance of the contrasting views can be accommodated. The proposed helix concept appears purposeful in this regard. If, as Professor Allport says, "For Locke the organism was reactive when stimulated; for Leibnitz it was self propelled,"[24] the research technique is simply to allocate the contributions within the most appropriate areas.

In this manner, totally opposed principles, conceivably observed as specific to particular and limited aspects of the larger problem, may contribute to a solution that cannot be recognized in segmental or isolated studies. Thus, in processing the concept of personality in the suggested developmental manner, certain correlated principles evolve, all necessarily involved in the full problem. In reference to the six levels or dimensions, the following general and pragmatic rules of thumb are suggested: At the environmental level, include studies involving bio-environmental impact; at the level of physiology, involve studies which pertain to stimulus-response and conditioning principles; at the psychological level, relate those studies which tend to emphasize psycho-cultural behavior of highly deterministic nature; at the level of phenomenology, bring into focus the research which stresses the conscious and self-determining personality factors; at the level of philosophy, bring into correlated relationship all data relative to man's reflective capacity as indicated by the philosophic disciplines and not excepting existentialism; and, finally, at the level of Perfection (Contentment), a full accommodation to the diverse data relating to man's value systems and goals regardless of their extent or diversity. The extensive frame-of-reference suggested here, like the Periodic Chart of Elements in chemistry, is not an interesting theory. It is, expressed very simply, the *extent* of the problem which must be recognized in a genuine desire to understand human behavior. It is false to accept a position that is calculated to force human response into an unrealistic research gambit. Personality is the ultimate function of a myriad set of forces, relative and indecisive at times, while generally characterized by at least a fairly stable pattern of behavior typical of a given individual. The intersecting valences are, it appears, best suggested by the following observation obtained from the social psychoogists: "We may use the concept of phenomenal self to refer to each person's awareness of his own beliefs, values, attitudes, the links between them, and their implications for his behavior."[25] A concern with these subjective and humanistic factors, representing the upper levels of man when functioning in an area of self determination, are long overdue in being placed in close proximity to the so-called deterministic aspect. Essentially all levels form an integral unity.

DIMENSIONS

MAN is phenomenal matter. He represents a very special kind of matter. He is related to each of the several sciences and he is subject to none. He belongs to no science, for he is, by an act of mental creation, the father of all the sciences. Like Professor Lorenz's ducklings, the various sciences and arts are subject to imprinting and follow man dutifully if not always affectionately. A basic principle, probably shunted aside for lack of attention, is the rather flattering fact that no science advances until man's thinking has made advance possible. This same principle, applied to psychology, permits man to re-assume the central role of behavior without the slightest apology.

The term phenomena carries for man an especial connotation. It refers to the subjective, internal capabilities which define his prime sphere of activity. Thus, for example, an individual is content, happy, ambitious and well motivated *only* in terms of his internal states, certainly not so because someone in the external world has so informed him. And it is precisely in this area of continuously expanding emotional and intellectual power that man begins to exceed the logical restraints of physical data. He is at once capable of introspection, looking in upon himself, gaining nourishment and sustenance from this personalized act. It is out of this private world of reality and creative fantasy, that the greatness of the human spirit is able to manifest itself and transcend the immediate and the routine. This human self act, logically and scientifically, is impossible. Ironically enough, for the individual it is the most commonplace activity of his entire life, this crossing and re-crossing between the subjective and objective worlds. For the nettled research scientist this is the ill-fated Bridge of San Luis Rey—crossed a thousand times a day subjectively and yet impossible of being crossed a single time objectively. It is as if the bridge was there, and not there, at one and the same time. In gross terms, the range of human behavior would seem satisfactorily delimited by the terms subjective and objective. But these terms leave the problem poorly defined. In brief, where does the problem begin and where does it end? It begins with the conjunction of living cells, matter; and it ends, for the individual, in the phenomenal capacity to think and feel. Crudely speaking, this establishes a rough framework for the behavioral problem. However, there are certain intervening steps or levels to be noted in the advancing of the person from cell to phenomena. Presented in logical order, as they are observed in developmental man, the six dimensions of behavior emerge as follows:—

(I) *Physics*, specifically environment, representing the already pre-established world into which man is born. This world consists of the laws of matter and energy. It is concerned with the geology of time, the geography of space. It is concerned with all those physical factors and elements which tend to make the world substantial, predictable and manageable. It is interested in the principles of light and power, and of communication. It extends its knowledge to the depths of the sea, planning for man's preservation by desalting the water and devising techniques to farm the undersea lands. It is as concerned with the light from the stars as it is with the use of radar and the lazer beams. The physical world, in all of its ramifications, processes and possibilities, is subject to research interest. The pleas for a lack of deadening specialization, whether in physical chemistry, traditional physics or space travel, is suggested here and summed up by de Chardin in these caustic words: "Specialization paralyzes, ultra-specialization kills." A new, fresh, and exciting knowledge of the world is required. The perspective of the physical world, perceived as an artistic challenge as well as a techno-social accomplishment, is the right of a generation yet to be born. This first level, the total environment, with all its profound implications for human behavior, is coming into sharper focus as the impact of an ever increasing world population becomes sensitively evident. Contemporary recognition of the high importance of a physically controlled life-environment, in the broader sense, is interestingly demonstrated by the recent new villages of Columbia, Maryland, and Reston, Virginia, architecturally and psychologically designed for the best use of living space. Pragmatically, for the psychologist, the terms man and environment are consistently co-existent.

(II) *Physiology,* specifically nervous system, the total living mechanism which constitutes a single human being. In the comprehensive study of human behavior the second area of research relates directly to the life process. It is the point of origin for the person. It is clearly represented by the term "birth." The person is born into the environment. The essence of the problem lies in the umbilical-like relationship between the environment and the life process: the processes are not identifiably one, and yet, so long as life persists, the processes are never totally disassociated. In the universal sense, there is always present a perfect unity of function. Man and the environment are perpetually wedded. The complexity of the relationship is magnified by the various senses, the associated response systems, developmental accretions in the realm of physiology and learning, and the continued drive towards the ultimate maturation of the overall behavioral structure. The excessively sensitive *linkage* between the environment and the nervous system, representing as it does the functional activator of the total body, is the very base of original and primitive response units. Even during the fetal period there is noted the natural irritability of protoplasm acutely responding to environmental variations or so-called stimuli: subject to observation are the wonderfully useful reflex systems, structurally and functionally complete at birth. The homeostatic capability of the body, stabilizing internal temperatures despite external changes, suggest the extraordinary automatic capability of the overall nervous system. Stabilization and counter-controls are found at the glandular, emotional, and intellectual levels, all precisely interrelated but each capable of differential behavioral impact under varying bio-chemical or psycho-social variations in stress. The simply incredible correlation between environment and overall physiology, both sharing a remarkable commonness, as noted by Baker and Allen in their discussion of matter, energy and life, in that, "both inorganic and organic substances are essential for life." A further suggestion of the interdependence of the organism and the environment is also stated: "During periods of growth, for example, an organism builds complex molecules, increases the number of its cells, and shows specialization of certain tissues. The organism, indeed, becomes more highly organized. But no organism is independent of outside energy sources."[26] Thus, man, the elusive psychological quarry, is phenomenal matter, a cybernetic unit at the level of physiology, but from this level on, elusively abstracting his identity from gross matter; beyond the early chrysalis of universal matter, he emerges as conscious phenomena.

(III) *Psychology*, specifically behavior, a limited study of human behavior which places emphasis upon the dependent and controlled responses of the individaul. The individual is assumed to be dependent upon the environment and physiology. In this regard, contemporary psychology is deterministic in format. An extension of this principle forces the psychologist, correctly following his original assumption, into the interesting position that man is not responsible for his own behavior. Hence, all behavior is produced. Man is incapable of making any significant gesture in the way of modifying behavior. He is looked upon as a mechanical, non-moral, non-ethical, non-decision making, and unfree, high level animal. This is the prime, scientific basis for the laboratory psychologist, and these technicians dominate the field at the present time. The powerful and persuasive influence of the scientific method has been applied with equal success in the fields of sociology and psychiatry. The sociologist substitutes the general environment for specific laboratory equipment; the psychiatrist substitutes the individual's past experience. In any case, the individual's behavior is always relative to, and determined by, factors over which he exerts no real control. The implications of this very powerful and effective psychological movement is to isolate the individual from total reality. The dilemma is something like this: the severely limited concreteness of selected research obscures the phenomenal reality of a vastly more extensive, rewarding, and complicated world of life-experience. The individual, without knowing it, is trapped by limited methodology. In strong protest to this experimental movement, those familiar with psychology recognize the humanistic counter-movement now taking place. An unusual example of this new willingness to 'stand up and be counted' is found in T. W. Wann's report entitled *Behaviorism and Phenomenology*, concerning contrasting bases for modern psychology. Some of the most eminent men in the field report their positions, and they are not of one mind.[27] The report clearly indicates the necessity for further logical inquiry into man's total behavior: the contradictions are too many, the extensive implications too vast to be permitted to remain unchallenged.

(IV) *Phenomenology*, specifically, awareness, the individual's consciousness of his own existence. Man is peculiarly equipped to know himself in a manner unknown to others. Information is available to him from the environment, the nervous system in fact never ceasing to inform him of its contact with the external world. The quality and quanitity of information is subject to his evaluation. Additionally, the modifying internal states of the body are equally accessible for review. In this phenomenal capacity to receive information, classify it, reject it, store it, recall it, and modify it, the individual approaches the level of constructive thinking. In the qualitative area of the feelings, the individual is the final judge of his response. He may enjoy the situation, for reasons quite hidden from all others, and may even gently pretend not to be emotionally involved. He may, as a result of a long, hard decision direct his behavior in a most unexpected manner. He is, of course, both observer and participant. It is quite possible that for reasons of disinterest, fatigue, or health that he will rationally redirect his energies and his interests into new fields Transcending the material events about him, he may idealistically drive with tremendous activity against odds that would shake the confidence of a god. He may withdraw within himself, cutting off communication of a routine sort so that he may better attend to some particular problem that intrigues him. He is aware of his dependency upon physiology for life, but also of the magnificient possession of personal freedom. He is, at his superlative best, a man for all seasons. Although willing to give his life, his personal existence, for a just cause, he typically prefers the freedom of life to the determinism of death. In all of history, man has always lived with a foreknowledge of personal doom and has resolutely striven to be remembered on this earth. The type of meaningful attitude that signifies so much to the individual, and seems so distant to the psychologist, is wisely presented by Hendrik W. Van Loon, *The Arts*: "Like poor Vincent van Gogh, he may love the masses when he is off duty, or, like Ludwig van Beethoven, he may refuse to lift his hat to a mere king, but the moment he smears his paints on his canvases or fishes his little notes out of his ten-cent bottle of ink, he stands apart and recognizes no law but the law that bids him be himself."[28] In the realm of awareness, indeed, man is confidant to himself. In the words of John Dryden, 1631-1701, the fine gentleness and purposiveness of personal awareness is sketched for every human being who has known affection for another: "Our souls sit close and silently within, and their own web from their own entrails spin; and when eyes meet far off, our sense is such, that, spider like, we feel the tenderest touch."[29] Thus, man somehow transcends matter. Man's awareness is his personal signet.

(V) *Philosophy,* specifically, reflection, the art of thinking. The panoply of thoughts that fill the vast libraries of ancient and modern civilizations, attests to the insatiable desire of man to express his inner life. The ever increasing depth of man's comprehension in the present era of atomic theory, made possible by the cumulative knowledge gained from successive generations, emphasizes the tremendous power of the creative human mind. The capacity of the human being to reflect, at will, upon past events and derive new insights, tends to stimulate the intellectually articulate individual. The ability to abstract from a problem, knowing full well that the nervous system will continue to 'work upon it', frequently results in solutions not easily attained with direct attention. The complete man *is philosophically inclined,* to some degree or another, whether he is an unmatriculated student of Epicurus, Zeno, or perhaps Boccaccio; or tending towards Zen, Nietzsche and Camus; or, contemporarily enjoying the sweet reasonableness of Whitehead, Polayni and Snow. The intricate possibilities of the interests of men born and yet unborn, expressed in the works of Dante and da Vinci—Shakespeare and Moliere—Luther and Calvin—Cervantes—Dickens—and even Tom Paine—would recall to mind nothing less than the wonderful melange of human behavior reminiscent of Hogarth's 'Southwark Fair.' So, man will think his thoughts as he pleases: and his behavior will, indeed, share in those thoughts. The present insistence that the psychologist must give adequate and appropriate attention to man's philosophic inclinations, is justified in virtue of the fact that the psychologist actually shuns the term "philosophy" as if it were unclean. The experimental attention paid to the memory drum, the recall of nonsense syllables, memory span for digits, memory for stories, degree of retention, proficiency of learning, *et al,* most assuredly exhumes the depressive statement that the elephant, after much labor, gave birth to a mouse. Thus, some justified fear lurks that contemporary psychology has yet to distinguish effectively between the various connotations of the term *prestige.* Because of this, mankind has suffered a frightful inhibition of humanistic effort for the last hundred years. However, new leaders are now apparent and are injecting into the field a strong sense of human value. Among these many authorities may be mentioned Koch, Rogers, Allport, May, Maslow and de Chardin.

(VI) *Perfection,* specifically, contentment, the life state in which man is fully content. Each man determines the nature of the value system which offers him the greatest psychological return. It is undoubtedly a slowly developing process, based upon the hard laws of experience as they relate to success and failure as understood by the individual. It would seem fair to infer that the personality structure of the person plays an extremely important role, partially conditioning him to the acceptability or rejection of certain modes of behavior. It appears equally true that the intellectual and emotional factors, ranging from hard-made decisions by active individuals to passive acceptance by the poorly motivated, play their collective roles. The whole value operation reflects so much of the basic life theme that no psychologist is going to identify and tab the causes of value behavior. The overall integration of man's behavior with socio-historical forces, modified by a taste for literature and art, softened by the tragedies of life, and perhaps most importantly, the slowly dawning consciousness that life requires a meaningful philosophy, leads ultimately to full self understanding. A host of phrases, tending to collate the elements of a maturing selfhood, are presently indicated under the board principle of self-realization and self-actualization. These are all good, healthy signs that psychology itself is beginning to mature. The writings of Maslow are especially notable in this area of humanized behavior. Some few years past, Riesman referred to the inner-directed and the outer-directed individuals, proposing that man has shifted from a position of independent decision making to a stance involving the passive reception of what others are saying or doing. Further, the innocuous phrase 'peer group' falls into this same field of discussion, the stress being upon the individual as almost certainly determined by the value system of the group. For some individuals it may be so; it is not for the psychologically mature man who relishes individual decision. The leaders, of course, invariably fall into this category. As Lord Chesterfield, writing in the 18th Century, remarked to his son while speaking of the attainment of perfection: "However, those who aim carefully at the mark itself, will unquestionably come nearer it than those who, from despair, negligence, or indolence leave to chance the work of skill."[30] The quotation should not suggest or imply that perfection, or the value system which underlies it, applies only to the unusual individual. Quite the contrary, the present meaning of perfection, connoting self-content, is the prize of everyman. Thus, the rich hour of contentment, specifically fashioned in one's own image, may be as successfully possessed on the bleak shores of a foreign and desolate beach as upon the friendly, crowded, structure-studded streets of one's own town. The timeless world of personal experience, appreciatively and gracefully accepted, is probably the best measure of man's perfection. The highest level of perfection has been attained when man is content: the human equation is complete.

The implications that may be drawn from each dimension contribute to a further understanding of the behavior of the complete man. It appears, too, the common thread of *time,* weaving its way unnoticed through the emerging dimensions, ultimately brings man face to face with the changing portrait of his own life.

TIME

TIME is the root of existence. The time capsule which represents a single life for a given individual, establishes in Nature the proper boundaries for the study of the complete man. In this view, the study of a particular individual increases in merit as the individual continues to age. Just as a civilization tends to grow and change with the passing of time, becoming more complex and more sensitive to the forces generated by its own development, the individual tends to emerge from relative behavioral obscurity to an immensely intricate system of response and counter-response. Where the physical structure of the city may be dismantled, rebuilt and re-inhabited by a new generation of an entirely different political order, the human being is moderately limited by Nature to live within the confines of a fairly well defined structure, the body. Again, just as the city, through its citizens, may modify its own socio-political behavior, the individual is equally capable of extensive modification in the behaviorial areas termed phenomenological, philosophical, and perfectional. Present psychology, suggesting that man is entrapped within the limits of physics, physiology and psychology, negates the significance of the critical time factor. In view of the contemporary scientific viewpoint, *time* simply exacerbates the problem. The child, subject to early disorder, must forever suffer that disorder whether consciously or unconsciously, so preach the child specialist and social psychologist as well as the traditional psychiatrist. The sins of the father are not only visited upon the children, but in today's psychology, the sins of the children are deterministically projected upon their own adulthood. Within the present teachings lies the tragedy of a whole civilization: a civilization taught to know only personal insecurity, alienation, and fear. In absolute contradistinction, the whole panorama of history, literature, drama, music, painting, and science, attest to the correlation of time and change of a fundamental order. Every custom of man, every device brought forth from his restless mind, every technique in education from kindergarten to the university level, is characterized by change through every succeeding generation. The whole thesis, that man once committed to a given form of behavior is immutably bound by that behavior, appears clothed in child-like naivete. In brief, if indeed religion ever was the opiate of the masses, then much of psychology can be justly defined as the opiate of the gullible. Even the distinguished psychologist, Koch, was provoked to remark of conditioning: "I would be happy to say what we have been hearing could be characterized as the death rattle of behaviorism, but this would be a rather more dignified statement than I should like to sponsor, because death is, at least, a dignified process."[31] Of course, here a careful distinction is being made between the theory of behaviorism, largely inferred from a statistical-experimental study of rats, and human behavior as human beings experience it at the level of personal decision and responsibility.

One of our Presidents, Grover Cleveland, anticipated the universality of this type of problem when he observed: "It is a condition which confronts us—not a theory." Indeed, *Time* does confront us. It is not a theory. Thus, welded to psychological time is behavioral *change*. Considered as a general principle, man's behavior is continually modifying as he grows older. It cannot be said more clearly than in the well-known words of Shakespeare when relating the Seven Ages of Man:

"At first the infant,
Mewling and puking in the nurse's arms.

And then the whining school-boy, with his satchel
And shinning morning face, creeping like snail
Unwilling to school. And the lover,
Sighing like furnace, with a woful ballad
Made to his mistress' eyebrow. Then a soldier,
Full of strange oaths and bearded like the pard,
Jealous in honor, sudden and quick in quarrel,
Seeking the bubble reputation
Even in the cannon's mouth. And then the justice,
In fair round belly with good capon lin'd,
With eyes severe and beard of formal cut,
Full of wise saws and modern instances;
And so he plays his part. The sixth age shifts
Into the lean and slipper'd pantaloon,
With spectacles on nose and pouch on side,
His youthful hose, well sav'd, a world too wide
For his shrunk shank; and his big manly voice,
Turning again toward childish treble, pipes
And whistles in his sound. Last scene of all,
That ends this strange eventful history,
Is second childishness and mere oblivion,
Sans teeth, sans eyes, sans taste, sans everything."

In reading this carefully, the brutal prediction of things to come is all too real and even the most confident of men may secretly quail. Time, the taskmaster of this life, may play man fair or foul and that is part of living. Only the foolish man would add to his misery by assuming slavery to this capricious master of the material world. The wise man cautiously anchors his freedom in phenomena where it flourishes, thus guarding against the tyranny of matter.

In the developmental study of man, the richly anticipated growth activities display a remarkably coordinated time schedule. The child first lies inert, then rolls over, struggles to his knees, crawls, arises with aid, stands with aid, begins the first wonderous step in life. The child coos, laughs, sounds, imitates, initiates, says his first word, his first phrase, his first sentence, and then almost magically he is talking and the world of communication is his to exploit. At first he is utterly dependent; then relatively grateful for service; then demanding service; then independent of help; cooperative; assertive; and suddenly, so he would seem to indicate, master of his own fate. The planful unfolding of early behavior, emerging with exquisite precision, is predictably timed to days, weeks, months, and years. Even within the time-phase of dramatic infancy, the essential complications of behavior are noted or inferred. The child is, in a sense, emerging from the womb of matter. Environmentally, the child is obtaining nourishment and experience. Consciously, the child is being startled into a world of phenomenal reality where he soon learns to distinguish between pretended anger and real anger, real pain and simulated pain to gain attention. And so this intensive flowering of behavior continues into early childhood, into adolescence, into manhood, into middle age, into old age, and even into the marginal decay of senility. Interwoven into this already convoluted pattern of growth may be perceived certain vital inversions of behavior if the problem is studied over *Time*. For example, during infancy, the child is dependent; the same child, at 21 years of age, is quite independent; the child who learned to fear the dark, at 2 years of age, normally plays freely in the dark at 12 years of age; the child who is permitted the unrestrained expression of his emotions at 1 year of age, is socially expected to control his emotions at 21 years of age; the child who could not, and was not expected to solve a problem at 5 years of age, is expected to master the problem with proficiency at 18 years of age. And so the almost endless list of *inversions* of behavior are compounded with the equating of time and behavior expectancy. In general, the fundamental principle is expressed in the response inversions from non-responsibility to responsibility, from dependence to independence, and from passive receptivity to selective self-directed behavior. In brief, what may be true of the early stages of development need not at all be the proper basis for later behavior. Men change with time. And man must be measured across that full dimension.

Now, what underlies this remarkable process of behavioral change taking place with time? In a single word, it is *emergence*. Each dimension of behavior, closely tied in with the neighboring dimensions, such as physics and physiology, tend to unitively educe and produce new facets of behavior. There is much more taking place than simple growth. The changes are both qualitative and quantitative. It is more than a single directional pattern, such as to be observed in the growth of a plant. If it can be properly perceived, the emergent process is multidirectional, with the growth of the individual being externalized in terms of observed concrete behavior, and internalized by the subjective experiences of an expanding awareness. It is, coordinately multi-lateral, with the organismic changes establishing bases for yet unattained behavior, each dimension, in time, contributing a particular essence to the overall responses ultimately realized at full maturity. Thus, the intimate relationship between each of the dimensions is facilitated by a fairly well recognized type of sub-function: for convenience, the sub-functions may be termed *linkage*. Physics and physiology are, then, linked via psychophysics; physiology and psychology are linked via cybernetic processes; psychology and phenomenology, in turn, are linked by a learning activity involving a direct awareness of the self; phenomenology and philosophy are linked via the conscious decision process which, in effect, reflects the end result of creative thinking; and, finally, philosophy and perfection (self content) are linked via the meaningful selection and recognition of values which will, in the long run, determine the basic life quality of the individual. In plain terms, the growth process displays an astounding unity of procedure while presenting to the intent researcher this incredible emergent format. It is quite obvious that upon the application of a reductionistic technique—taking one minor element after another —the melded architectual grandeur of man is destroyed. The incontestable fact seems to be that man is some sort of bio-phenomenological miracle, changing from matter to man via the metronomic impact of the accretions of time. In the quality of expression found only in literature, Sir Walter Scott, in the 19th Century, gave human vitality to the measured meaning of eternal time: "Time rolls his ceaseless course."[32] Whatever the answer to this riddle of behavior may be, of which man plays his spectral part, the insistent data demands attention to the fact that man begins as an unthinking, living organism and advances steadily, so long as life persists, to the Olympian heights of self awareness. It is interesting to think of the emergent process as ranging undisturbed from a single cell structure to a complex of 26 billion cells, with the critical fact in mind that the single cell carries within itself this fantastic humanistic potentiality—to sustain itself, to give conscious life, and finally to grant the incredible gifts of emotion, social affection, and phenomenal thought. This is no ordinary problem to be subject to the pathetic limitations of the laboratory. It is a problem of years for the individual, as if in transit across a small bit of eternity, and a problem of centuries for a civilization entwined in a cocoon of timelessness.

Time is the Rosetta Stone of a man's life. It can be deciphered only with difficulty. The basic mechanisms underlying behavior are many and varied, suggested as beginning in an all enveloping environment and penetrating deeply into the substance of living matter. It is apparent that the nervous system, drawing sustenance from the world about it, clings tenaciously to physical events of remarkably different design. The eyes possess the world visually; the ears command the world auditorially; the muscle structures sense life habitually and kinaesthetically; the skin reports the world of temperature through a highly organized system of responsive sensors, each adapted to a particular and limited task. The sense receptors, then, through this intricate channelling of information into the nervous system literally makes man one with the physical world about him. The central nervous system, consisting of the brain and spinal cord, accepting the incoming data, codifies the information, initiates response, and retains in the memory bank the necessary physiological remnant for future use. The psycho-physical relationship of physical matter to living matter, between the environment and the body, is substantially automated, occurring continuously over a life time. At a higher or even more complex level, the processes are merged into meaningful units of response, characterized by the concept of cybernetics. Within the self-adjustive nervous system, the capability of external stimuli to trigger intricate internal sub-systems is evident, as for example in the seemingly simple knee reflex. Actually this form of response is neurologically intriguing, operating with definitiveness and quite without the need of any conscious directive from the subject. The whole, vast unit system underlying response is incredibly well organized, simultaneously maintaining states of equilibrium, the heart beat, breathing, glandular activity, digestion, reproduction, growth processes, the physiological substratum of awareness, the sleep cycles, hunger indices, satiation, and the numerous reflexes necessary for the maintenance of life activity. The entire nervous system has been aptly described by Norbert Wiener of the Massachusetts Institute of Technology as subject to an automatic 'steersman' or 'helmsman',[33] that is to say, the system is a cybernetic process independently capable of accepting input and responding with predictable output regardless of the complication of required response. At the level of physiology, the concept seems entirely acceptable. It accurately points up the mechanical aspects of the *sub-systems* which are necessary for total human response. It fails totally, however, to account for the phenomenological aspects of man's functioning.

The deciphering of behavior at the level of phenomenology, or awareness, is far less precise than at the level of physiology. Man lives in the routine world of awareness, accepting the capability of directing his interests and his activities with a remarkable degree of indifference. All individuals think, talk, emote, plan, and generally do what they want—so why consider this anything unusual or special? It might even be asked: what is special about the commonplace? It is this attitude, perhaps, that represents the Achilles Heel of human research. Turning the matter around a bit, note that what excites the psychologist at the level of pure physiology, i.e., controlled response, seems to be deprived of interest when perceived phenomenologically. Accordingly, what a man *does* is given more significance than what a man *thinks* about. The violation of human integrity resulting from this mean view of man, reiterated in textbook after textbook, brings to mind Donne's 17th Century barbed phrase: "Who are a little wise the best fools be."[34] It is not so much that the researcher approaches the state of foolhood but, rather, that he indirectly makes fools of those who are not well informed; he continues to curtly present his facile but limited psychology from the university podium regardless of its harmful implications. The mal-manipulation of the young mind, perhaps, is the deep injustice here. Only the science of psychology can be so damning for it speaks directly to man of man himself.

Man, in his very special way, is a creature of personal time. And in time, he writes the lyrics of his own existence. He lives as if he possesses tomorrow. He counts his passing years as a miser, weeping at the departure of each season as though it were the precious last. He calls for added zeal and added accomplishment, in vain attempting to out-pace the shadow of his own life. He raises his thoughts to the good years long past and with sweet stirrings within cries out to the ghosts of his youth. And as he approaches Land's End, he is one with courage and time, solaced by Tennyson's gentle reminder of "Twilight and evening bell, and after that the dark."[35]

NOTES

[1] T. Dobzhansky, "Changing Man: Modern Evolutionary Biology Justifies an Optimistic View of Man's Biological Future," *Science*, CLV, No. 3761, January 27, 1967, p. 409.

[2] R. May, *Man's Search for Himself* (Signet Books, New American Library, 1953), p. 138.

[3] H. Jonas, *The Phenomenon of Life: Toward a Philosophical Biology* (Delta Book, 1966), p. 58.

[4] T. Dobzhansky, p. 409.

[5] E. Shoben and F. Ruch, *Perspectives in Psychology* (Scott Foresman, 1963), p. 1.

[6] T. de Chardin, *Future of Man* (Harper and Row, 1964), p. 214.

[7] L. Eiseley, *The Mind and Nature*, John Dewey Lecture Series (Harper and Row, 1962).

[8] G. Marcel, *Philosophy of Existentialism* (Citadel Press, 1964), p. 126.

[9] P. Fong, "The Phenomenological Theory of Life," *Journal of Theoretical Biology*. 21, 133-152, 1968, p. 148.

[10] T. De Chardin, *The Phenomenon of Man* (Harper and Row, 1959).

[11] J. Donceel, "Causality and Evolution: A Survey of Some Neo-Scholastic Theories," *New Scholasticism*, XXXIX, 3, July, 1965, p. 295.

[12] *Ibid.*, p. 297.

[13] G. Allport, *Becoming* (Yale University Press, 1955), p. 17.

[14] *Ibid.*, p. 100.

[15] R. Gale, *Developmental Behavior: A Humanistic Approach* (The MacMillan Co., 1969), p. 5.

[16] C. Rogers, "Toward a Science of the Person," in *Behaviorism and Phenomenology: Contrasting Bases for Modern Psychology*, ed. T. W. Wann (University of Chicago Press, 1964), pp. 109-140.

[17] P. Fong, pp. 148-149.

[18] J. Baker and G. Allen, *Matter, Energy, and Life* (Addison-Wesley, Reading, Massachusetts, 1965).

[19] G. Allport, p. 27.

[20] W. Colville, *Abnormal Psychology: Mental Illness, Types, Causes, and Treatment* (Barnes and Noble, 1960), p. 25.

[21] A. Maslow, "Self-Actualizing People," in *The World of Psychology*, ed. G. Levitas (Braziller, 1963) Vol. 2, pp. 527-555.

[22] G. Allport, p. vii.

[23] Commentary on Existentialism, *N.Y. Times Book Week*, January 10, 1965, p. 28.

[24] G. Allport, p. 8.

[25] E. Jones and H. Gerard, *Foundations of Social Psychology* (Wiley, 1967), p. 182.

[26] J. Baker and G. Allen, p. 93.

[27] T. Wann, ed., *Behaviorism and Phenomenology: Contrasting Bases for Modern Psychology* (University of Chicago Press, 1964).

[28] H. Van Loon, *The Arts*, (Simon and Schuster, 1937).

[29] J. Bartlett, *Familiar Quotations* (Little, Brown Co., 1893), p. 274.
[30] S. A. Allibone, *Prose Quotations* (Lippincott, 1876), p. 520.
[31] S. Koch, "Psychology and Emerging Conceptions of Knowledge as Unitary," in *Behaviorism and Phenomenology*, ed. T. Wann, (University of Chicago Press, 1964).
[32] Bartlett, p. 491.
[33] N. Weiner, *Cybernetics: Or, Control and Communication in the Human Machine* (Wiley, 1948).
[34] Bartlett, p. 177.
[35] G. McClelland and A. Baugh, *Century Types of English Literature* (Century Company, 1925), p. 787.

BIBLIOGRAPHY

Allibone, S. A. *Prose Quotations*. Lippincott, 1876.
Allport, G. *Becoming*. Yale University Press, 1955.
Anastasia, A. *Differential Psychology*. The MacMillan Co., 1958.
Baker, J. and Allen, G. *Matter, Energy, and Life*. Addison-Wesley, 1965.
Bartlett, J. *Familiar Quotations*. Little, Brown Co., 1893.
Bonniwell, B. L. *Tap Roots of Psychology*. William C. Brown, 1966.
Borek, E. *The Code of Life*. Columbia University Press, 1965.
Brinton, C. *The Shaping of the Modern Mind*. Mentor Books, 1953.
Bronowski, J. "The Logic of the Mind," *Man and the Science of Man*, Coulson, W. and Rogers, C. (eds.), Merrill, 1968.
Chiang, H. and Maslow, A. *The Healthy Personality*. Van Nostrand Reinhold, 1969.
Cohen, J. *Operant Behavior and Operant Conditioning*. Rand McNally, 1969.
Coleman, J. *Psychology and Effective Behavior*. Scott Foresman, 1969.
Colville, W. *et al. Abnormal Psychology*. Barnes and Noble, 1960.
de Chardin, T. *The Phenomenon of Man*. Harper and Row, 1959.
———. *The Future of Man*. Harper and Row, 1964.
Dobzhansky, T. "Changing Man: Modern Evolutionary Biology Justifies an Optimistic View of Man's Biological Future," *Science*, Vol. 155, No. 3761, January 27, 1967. (Refer also to the Lectures entitled *Biological Basis of Freedom*, by the same author, University of Virginia, 1957.)
Donceel, J. "Causality and Evolution: A Survey of Some Neo-scholastic Theories," *The New Scholasticism*, XXXIX, 3. (July, 1965) 295-315.
Eiseley, L. *Darwin's Century: Evolution and the Men Who Discovered It*. Doubleday Anchor Books, 1958. (Refer also to *The Unexpected Universe*, by the same author, Harcourt, Brace World, 1969.)
———. *The Mind and Nature*. John Dewey Lecture Series. Harper and Row, 1962.
Farber, L. *The Ways of the Will: Essays Toward a Psychology and Psychopathology of Will*. Basic Books, 1966.
Fong, P. "The Phenomenological Theory of Life," *Journal of Theoretical Biology*, 21, 133-152, 1968.
Fox, S. "A New View of the 'Synthesis of Life,'" *Florida Academy of Sciences, Quarterly Journal*, Vol. 31, No. 1., (March, 1968) 1-15.
Frankel, V. *Man's Search for Meaning*. Washington Square Press, 1963.

Gale, R. *Developmental Behavior: A Humanistic Approach.* The Macmillan Co., 1969.

Giorgi, A. *Psychology as a Human Science: A Phenomenologically Based Approach.* Harper and Row, 1970.

Jonas, H. *The Phenomenon of Life: Toward a Philosophical Biology.* Delta Books, 1966.

Jones, E. and Gerard, H. *Foundations of Social Psychology.* Wiley, 1967.

Josephson, E. and Josephson, M. (eds.) *Man Alone: Alienation in Modern Society.* Dell, 1962.

Jourard, S. *Disclosing Man to Himself.* Van Nostrand, 1968.

Koch, S. "Psychology and Emerging Conceptions of Knowledge as Unitary," *Behaviorism and Phenomenology.* Wann, T. (ed.). University of Chicago Press, 1964.

Kuenzli, A. (ed.). *The Phenomenological Problem.* Harper and Row, 1959.

Levitas, G. (ed.). *The World of Psychology.* Volumes 1 and 2. Braziller, 1963.

Marcel, G. *Philosophy of Existentialism.* Citadel Press, 1964.

Maslow, A. *The Psychology of Science: A Reconnaisance.* Gateway Edition, Henry Regnery, Chicago, 1966.

May, R. *Man's Search for Himself.* Signet Books, New American Library, 1953.

Million, T. *Theories of Psychopathology: Essays and Critiques.* Saunders, 1967.

Penfield, W. *Excitable Cortext in Conscious Man.* Thomas Publishing Company, Springfield, Illinois, 1958.

Polanyi, M. *The Tacit Dimension.* Routledge and Paul, 1966.

Rogers, C. *On Becoming a Person.* Houghton Mifflin, 1961.

Ruitenbeek, H. (ed.). *Varieties of Personality Theory.* Dutton, 1964.

Rychlak, J. *A Philosophy of Science for Personality Theory.* Houghton Mifflin, 1968.

Schmidt, F. "Physical Basis of Life and Learning," *Science,* Vol. 148, No. 3687 (August 27, 1965) 931-936.

Shoben, E. and Ruch, F. *Perspectives in Psychology.* Scott Foresman, 1963.

Stent, G. "That Was the Molecular Biology That Was," *Science,* Vol. 160, No. 3826 (April 26, 1968) 390-395.

Vanderveldt, J. and Odenwald, R. *Psychiatry and Catholicism,* McGraw-Hill, 1951.

Van Loon, H. *The Arts.* Simon and Schuster, 1937.

Wann, T. (ed.). *Behaviorism and Phenomenology: Contrasting Bases for Modern Psychology.* University of Chicago Press, 1964.

Watson, J. "The Double Helix: A Personal Account of the Discovery of the Structure of DNA," *Atheneum,* 1968.

Weiner, N. *Cybernetics: Or, Control and Communciation in the Human Machine.* Massachusetts Institute of Technology, 1961.

Whyte, L. *The Unconscious Before Freud: A History of the Evolution of Human Awareness.* Basic Books, 1960.

Biographical Notes

Ahern, Barnabas, M., Professor, Passionist Seminary, 1943-1962; Lector in ARC program, Rome, 1970-; Asst. Professor, Gregorian Univ., Rome, 1971- ; member of Papal Commission for Anglican-Roman Catholic Dialogue; member of Biblical Commission.

Alfrink, Bernard Card., Professor, Archdiocesan Great Seminary, Rijseburg, 1933-1945; Professor, Catholic Univ., Nijmegen 1945-1951; Archbishop, Utrecht, Holland, 1955; Cardinal, 1960.

*Blake, Eugene Carson, stated clerk, United Presbyterian Church in U.S., 1951-1966; Pres., Nat. Counc. Churches, 1954-1957; member of gen. bd. & chmn., Comn. Relig. & Race, 1964-; member, cent. & exec. comts., World Counc. Churches, 1964-; Chmn. div. inter-church aid, refugee & world serv., 1964-; Gen. Secy. World Counc. Churches, 1966-.

††Bonniwell, Bernard L., Asst. Instr., Univ. of Pennsylvania, 1937-1941; Asst. Professor, Loyola Coll., 1949; Asst. Professor, St. Joseph's Coll., 1947-1952; Asst. Professor, Villanova Univ., 1953-1962; Assoc. Professor, 1964-1966, Professor, 1967-; Co-editor, *Studies in Social Mobility,* Florida Academy of Sciences, 1965; Lecturer, The Franklin Institute, 1968.

Cox, Harvey G. Jr., Protagonist of secular redemption; director of Oberlin College's religious activities, 1955-1957; program assoc. American Baptist Home Mission Society, 1957-1963; fraternal worker, East Berlin, 1962; Asst. Professor, the Andover Newton Theological School, 1963-1965; Assoc. Professor, Divinity School, Harvard Univ., 1965-1968; research assoc., Program on Technology and Society, Harvard Univ.

Curran, Charles A., Vis. Professor, Univ. of Louvain, 1953-1954; President, American Catholic Psychological Assn., 1952-1953; Consul. and Vis. Professor, Menninger Foundation, Topeka, Kansas, 1959-1963; Peritus at Vatican Council II, 1963-1966; Professor, Loyola Univ. of Chicago, 1955-.

*Diekmann, Godfrey L., Editor, *Worship,* 1938-; Vis. Professor, Manhattan College, summer, 1938, Notre Dame Univ., summer, 1945, 1948, The Catholic Univ. of America, summer, 1941, 1942, 1944, 1947, 1950, 1953, 1956, 1959; Co-founder, National Liturgical Conf., 1946; Vis. Professor, San Francisco

Univ., summer, 1960, 1971, Northwestern Lutheran Theological College, summer, 1970; Consultor of Consilium for Implementing the Constitution on the Sacred Liturgy; Co.-chmn., Ecumenical Spiritual Institute, 1965; member, Advisory Bd. International Comm. on English in the Liturgy, 1966-1971; Professor, St. John's Univ., 1946-1970; Fellow, Ecumenical Institute for Advanced Theological Studies, Jerusalem, 1971-1972.

*Fichter, Joseph H., Professor and chmn., Loyola Univ. of the South, 1947-1964; Vis. Professor, Univ. of Muenster, 1953-1954; Notre Dame Univ., 1956-1957, Universidad Catolica, Santiago, Chile, 1960-1961, Univ. of Chicago, 1964-1965; Stillman Professor, Harvard Univ., 1965-1970; President, Society for the Scientific Study of Religion, 1970-1971; Vis. Professor, State Univ. of New York at Albany, 1971-; Religious Research Assoc., Ministry Studies Board.

*Gustafson, James M., member, Yale Univ. faculty, 1955-; Professor, Christian ethics, 1963-1971; Professor, Religious Studies, 1971-; President, American Society of Christian Ethics, 1969.

*Katsh, Abraham I., chmn., Dept. of Hebrew Culture and Educ., 1937-1959; founder and curator, New York Univ. Library of Judaica and Hebraica, 1941-1967; founder and director, New York Univ. Summer Professorial Workshop, Israel, 1949-1967; Professor, New York Univ., 1959-1967; director, Institute of Hebrew Studies, New York Univ. 1962-1967; President and Professor, The Dropsie Univ., 1967-; ed.-in-chief and founder *Hebrew Abstracts;* div. ed., *Encyclopedia Judaica;* rev. ed., *Modern Language Journal.*

*Lindbeck, George A., born in China; member, Yale Univ. faculty, 1951-; Research Professor, Center of Ecumenical Studies, Copenhagen and Strasbourg, 1962-1964; Professor, Yale Univ. faculty, 1964-; Lutheran World Federation delegated observer to Vatican II, 1962-1964; Vis. Professor, Trinity Theological College, Singapore, 1968; member, Board of Theological Education of Lutheran Church in America.

*Murphy, Roland E., Professor, Catholic Univ. of America, 1948-1969; Vis. Professor, Pittsburgh Theological Seminary, 1964-1965, Yale Univ. Divinity School, 1965; member, editorial boards of *Consilium Interpretation;* President, Catholic Biblical Assoc., 1968-1969; Vis. Professor, Princeton Theological Seminary, 1970-1971; co-editor and contributor, *Jerome Biblical Commentary;* Vis. Professor, Duke University Divinity School, 1971.

*†Papin, Joseph

Schmemann, Alexander, Born in Talinn, Estonia, educated in Paris; Lecturer, St. Sergius Theological Institute, Paris, 1945-1951; Professor, St. Vladimir's Orthodox Theological Seminary, Crestwood, N.Y. 1951-; Dean, 1962-; Adjunct Professor, Graduate

Faculty, Columbia University and Lecturer, Union Theological Seminary, 1958-; Active in the work of the World Council of Churches; member, Study and Planning Committee of the Standing Conference of the Orthodox Bishops in America; member, Metropolitan Council of the Russian Orthodox Church of America.

Schoonenberg, Piet J. A. M., Professor, Theological Faculty of the Jesuits, Maastricht, The Netherlands, 1941-1953; Vis. Professor, Duquesne Univ., 1963; Professor, Catholic Univ. of Nijmegen, The Netherlands, 1964-.

EDITOR

Joseph Papin †

ASSOCIATE EDITORS

James J. Cleary †
Francis A. Eigo †
Arthur J. Ennis ††
    Prof., Augustinian International College, Rome, 1955-1959;
    Prof., Augustinian College Washington, D.C., 1959-1968;
    Prof., Washington Theological Coalition, Wash., D.C., 1968-
        1969;
    Prof., Villanova University, 1968; Chmn., Religious Studies
        1969-

ASSISTANT EDITOR

Donald R. Schultz ††
    Instr., Villanova University, 1969-
* Biographical information taken from the *Directory of American Scholars,* 1969.
† see Volume I
† † Biographical information taken from the Villanova University Bulletin

Index of Names

Large Roman numerals refer to volumes; small, to pages.